ROMAN
GAUL
AND GERMANY

ROMAN
GAUL
AND GERMANY

Anthony King

The University of California Press

FOR
CHRISTINA,
AND FOR
JUDY, DIANA AND TOM

Published by the University of California Press
in the United States, 1990

Library of Congress-in-Publication Data

King, Anthony.
Roman Gaul and Germany.
(Exploring the Roman world; 3)
Includes bibliographical references (p. 224)
1. Gaul—History—58 B.C.–511 A.D.   2. France—Antiquities, Roman.
3. Germany—Antiquities, Roman.   4. Romans—Gaul—History.
5. Excavations (Archaeology)—France.   6. Excavations
(Archaeology)—Germany.
I. Title.   II. Series.
DC63.K56   1990   936.4   89–20546
ISBN 0–520–06989–7

Half-title page Gilded silver statuette of the
goddess Tutela (protector goddess), with busts
of the deities of the week. From a hoard from
Mâcon in central Gaul, dated to the mid-third
century AD. (British Museum)

Title page Colonnaded street at Vaison-la-
Romaine (Vasio Vocontiorum).

CONTENTS

ACKNOWLEDGEMENTS

This volume came into being after numerous visits to sites and museums in Gaul and Germany during the last fifteen years. It would be impossible to name every site director and museum curator that has shown me their material, but above all I should like to thank T. Bechert, J.-L. Cadoux, H. Cüppers, I. Fauduet, P. Galliou, M. Gechter, R. Goguey, P. Halbout, M. Planson, R. Sanquer and M. Vanderhoeven for their kindness and hospitality.

British colleagues have also given me a great deal of advice, both in discussion of specific topics and in reading sections of the text. I am grateful especially to T. Blagg, A. French, C. Haselgrove, M. Henig, P. Horne, S. Keay, M. Millett, D. Nash, T. Potter, R. Reece, S. Walker and J. Wood in this respect. Bibliographic help and congenial working conditions were provided mainly by the libraries of the Institutes of Classical Studies and of Archaeology, London. Financial assistance for continental visits was very kindly made available by the British Academy, King Alfreds College, Winchester, and my parents. Steve Crummy drew all the line illustrations and Jenny Chattington of British Museum Publications did a great deal of editorial work – to both I am extremely grateful.

Lastly, I should like to thank Christina Grande, Oliver Gilkes, Diana Hale, Peter Horne, Mark Redknap, Grahame Soffe and my sister Margaret Kahan, each of whom accompanied my excursions abroad at various times, and made them more agreeable and cheerful.

ANTHONY KING

INTRODUCTION

Gaul *and* Germany? Surely an impossible task to explore the Roman past of such a large area in a single modest volume? The answer to the second question would certainly be yes, if every aspect of the subject were to be considered in full, a massive undertaking that would occupy several fat volumes. Not only are there six ancient provinces within the area under consideration (Gallia Narbonensis, Aquitania, Gallia Lugdunensis, Gallia Belgica, Germania Inferior and Germania Superior), together with the much smaller Alpine regions, but there are also several modern countries to take into account – France, West Germany, Belgium, Luxembourg, the Netherlands and Switzerland – not forgetting minor states such as Monaco and the Channel Islands. Superficially this great sweep of European territory presents a startling diversity. In physical terms it varies from the barrier of the high Alps, through rich agricultural plains, to marshy shifting swamps at river mouths. Modern human geography reflects this on many different levels: politically, as in the list of countries just given, but also linguistically, with a major frontier between Germanic and Romance languages running across our region from south-east to north. Settlement and local customs, too, are today strikingly different as one journeys within the region.

Such diversity would easily allow us to make a case for each geographical region to have its own separate study. Despite this, however, *Roman Gaul and Germany* will be laying stress on the cultural *unity* of the region in ancient times. During much of the period covered by this book, about 600 BC to AD 486, the region was regarded simply as Gaul, a Celtic part of Europe to be distinguished by ancient writers from Spain to the south-west, Italy to the south-east, Britain to the north and, most importantly, from Germany on the far (eastern) side of the Rhine. As we shall see, this is a gross oversimplification of a much more complicated ethnic mix, but nevertheless it highlights the unity of the region deriving from the dominant Celtic culture of the late first millenium BC.

Germany in many ways is a minor constituent of this volume, since the German province dreamed of by Augustus never came to fruition. His successors eventually set up the two provinces of Roman Germany, largely on the western side of the Rhine in territory carved out of existing Gallic provinces. This accounts for the book's title, since it is dealing with a part of the Empire that was essentially unified in cultural terms, despite having different Roman names for its constituent provinces.

One of the major aims of this book will be to explore how, within the framework of the pre-Roman cultures that existed in the region, firstly the Greeks and later the Romans made contact with, influenced and eventually conquered the Celtic Gauls. To a great extent we shall be trying to detect how far the Gaulish heritage survived in the Roman period – whether Romanisation suffocated local culture or allowed it to flourish as some hybrid form of the Roman ideal of provincial life. At the same time we shall also be exploring how far Roman Gaul and Germany developed as a regional unit: how was it different from other parts of the Empire, and did it have local peculiarities in, for instance, villas, religion or the economy? To counterbalance the emphasis on Romanisation in the early chapters the later part of the book goes into the way in which Roman culture changed during the later Empire, examining such themes as the impact of invasive German culture from the east, and the extent to which Gaul and Germany became more diverse in their culture. As we shall see, the monolithic provincial culture of earlier times gave way to new regional variations, which in turn laid the foundations for the post-Roman states that were to have so much influence on the map of modern Europe.

Interest in the ancient origins of modern Europe has had a major impact on the study of the Roman remains of Gaul and Germany, and on the development of ideas about each country's past. For instance, Vercingetorix was elevated to the status of a national hero in French history in the nineteenth and early twentieth centuries. He provided patriotic support to the French in times of national crisis, such as the Franco-Prussian War or the First World War, and was explicitly put in opposition to Arminius, his German counterpart. Ancient Gaul was also used more directly as a geographical basis for French claims to parts of the Rhineland after these conflicts.

Such fierce and best-undisturbed nationalistic streams have left their legacy in Europe following the Second World War. Traditions of archae-ological and historical thinking vary greatly in the different countries within our region. France in particular has often been regarded as going in its own direction intellectually, bringing forth ideas such as structuralism, which are now beginning to have an influence on the archaeology of Roman Gaul. In contrast, the German tradition has been one of the careful recording of

Excavations in progress on the site of the late Roman churches and bishop's palace at Geneva (Genava).

data, and the building up of an impressive series of meticulous excavations, fully and quickly published. In the Low Countries and, interestingly, Brittany archaeologists have sought new directions from developments in British archaeology. Currently the diverse traditions that were so strong immediately after the Second World War are increasingly breaking down, perhaps because of the cultural impact of the European Community, so that there is a refreshing and very exciting interplay of ideas. Roman archaeology, despite some gloom about resources, has never been in such vigorous good shape as it is today.

Excavations and research are being carried out at a rate that is difficult to keep up with, mainly because the region has one of the greatest concentrations of active archaeologists anywhere in the world. Sites such as Marseille, St Romain-en-Gal, Lyon and Cologne have yielded major discoveries of Roman buildings and evidence for urban life. Aerial photographic work in Picardy and elsewhere, particularly after the spectacular drought of 1976, has transformed our knowledge of rural Gaul and Germany. Finds of treasures, too, have made headlines, the Vix Tomb being particularly notable in this respect, but also including the later Kaiseraugst Treasure and many important coin hoards. It has not all been solid gain, however, since interspersed in the record of new discoveries are many stories of destruction. The very possibility of seeing villas from the air in Picardy is due to their erosion by modern agricultural methods, and several of the major urban excavations have been followed by demolition of the remains uncovered, most notoriously in the case of the baths at Metz. Luckily, public attitudes are becoming more attuned to environmental issues, and the historic environment is benefiting from the current trend to preservation rather than destruction. A large number of the sites discussed in this book are visible to the public, and are listed in the gazetteer at the end of the volume.

Accompanying the unprecedented level of fieldwork has been a constant flow of new publications coming in every week to the shelves of the major academic libraries, varying from brief reports in the popular archaeological press to multi-volume reports and papers. It has been one of the aims of this volume, and a very humbling one at that, to try to digest some of their results and present a view of recent research on Roman Gaul and Germany.

FURTHER READING

The classic work on Roman Gaul is Camille Jullian's multi-volume *Histoire de la Gaule* (1908–26). This particularly covers the historical sources in some detail, but the many recent archaeological discoveries have made some of his discussion somewhat out of date. Modern treatments of Gaul in English include J. F. Drinkwater's *Roman Gaul* (1983), and the regional surveys of *Gallia Narbonensis* by A. L. Rivet (1988) and *Gallia Belgica* by Edith Wightman (1985), the last-mentioned being one of the finest syntheses of an individual area of the Roman Empire ever written. French surveys of Gaul range from the introductory *Celtes et Gallo-Romains* by J.-J. Hatt (1970) and, more recently, *Les Gallo-Romains* by G. Coulon (1985), to detailed regional surveys in the *Aufstieg und Niedergang der Römischen Welt* series. The most thought-provoking study is by Christian Goudineau in G. Duby's *Histoire de la France urbaine* 1 (1980), mainly concentrating on towns. Still important for its archaeological detail is A. Grenier's *Manuel d'Archéologie gallo-romaine* (1931–60). The more significant historical and epigraphic sources are collected together by L. Lerat in *La Gaule romaine* (1977).

For Germany, the main text is H. Von Petrikovits, *Rheinische Geschichte I, i, Altertum* (1980), usefully supplemented by T. Bechert's *Römisches Germanien zwischen Rhein und Maas* (1982). Holland is covered by E. Van Es, *Die Romeinen in Nederland* (1972), Belgium by A Wankenne, *La Belgique à l'Epoque romaine* (1972), Luxemburg by C.-M. Ternes, *Das römische Luxemburg* (1974), and Switzerland by W. Drack and R. Fellmann, *Die Römer in der Schweiz* (1988).

— 1 —

GREEKS
AND
CELTS

T he year 600 BC has a good claim to be the most significant date in the history of Roman Gaul, even though the Romans were not to conquer the area for another five hundred years. This date marks the traditional foundation of the Greek colony of Massalia (modern Marseille), an event which was to have profound consequences for all later developments. Put at its simplest, the Greeks and later the Romans introduced the Celts to aspects of a Mediterranean way of life that appealed to them, and this fatally undermined their resistance to Roman conquest. Indeed, as we shall see, many Gaulish tribes and their leaders actively welcomed Roman intervention, and took to Roman civilisation with alacrity.

The foundation of Massalia did not mark the earliest foreign contact for the peoples of southern France at this time. Finds of seventh-century pottery with Etruscan and Punic affinities suggest that coastal trade with the other two major civilisations of the western Mediterranean was already in existence. It may be that the Greek settlers chose a southern French site for a colony because of this, realising that the sporadic trade contacts could be developed much further by establishing their own base in the area.[1]

The city from which the Massaliote colonists came was the minor eastern Greek city of Phocaea, now in Turkey and itself a colony from the Greek mainland of an unknown earlier date. Phocaea's nearest important neighbour was Smyrna (modern Izmir), and archaeological discoveries at the latter city give a possible reason why local conditions encouraged the Phocaeans to set up distant colonies. Smyrna was attacked by the powerful inland kingdom of the Lydians, and its defences were overwhelmed by Lydian use of a siege mound. The city was sacked so thoroughly that it appears to have been abandoned for a time. These events took place shortly after 600 BC, but Phocaea cannot fail to have been affected by the general hostilities

The Bourse site, Marseille, showing the defences and one of the gates of Greek Massalia, and, towards the right of the picture, part of the Greek and Roman harbour installations.

of the period, which were to result a little later in Lydian domination of the eastern Greek coast under the fabled King Croesus.[2]

Such a historical background may explain the circumstances in which the Phocaeans sent colonists out from the home city. Why they ventured to the western Mediterranean is another matter, but their reputation as navigators and sailors indicates that long-distance journeys were a feature of their city life. In the period between the eighth and sixth centuries BC many Greek cities founded far-flung colonies, and the western Mediterranean was fertile ground for the Phocaeans' colonial ambitions. They founded Elea (modern Velia) in southern Italy, Alalia (modern Aléria) in Corsica, Emporion (modern Ampurias) in north-east Spain, and other colonies in the Iberian peninsula.[3] Some were in fact founded from Massalia, the most famous and successful of them all, soon eclipsing Phocaea itself, especially after the devastation of the coastal regions of Asia Minor by the Persians from 546 BC, and the emigration of many Phocaeans to the newly founded colonies.[4]

Relatively little is known of the city of Massalia compared with other sites of the region, for which a wealth of archaeological information is available.[5] Until recently even the extent of the early city was unclear, but excavations at the Bourse site have shown that occupation extended all along the north shore of the harbour as early as the sixth century, making it easily the largest site in Gaul for several centuries. The port itself was also extensive, larger than the present harbour and partly surrounding the city on the east as well as the south side. This confirms Caesar's description of the site as being 'washed by the sea on three sides' and therefore difficult to lay siege to.[6] In the outskirts of town, on the hill of Les Carmes, an industrial area developed that included pottery- and amphorae-kilns. The pottery made there was widely distributed within the lower Rhône Valley, and the amphorae are found much further into Celtic Gaul as well, presumably because of the demand for the wine and other commodities that they contained. Masons and military engineers must also have had workshops in the city, since their products are found on many of the

Hellenised native sites. These craftsmen were also responsible for building the city wall in the second century BC, probably in response to the increasing tension between the city and the surrounding tribes. One of its gateways has been excavated on the Bourse site; it had projecting towers and a fore-wall overlooking the inner harbour. This was the wall that Caesar laid siege to in 49 BC during the Civil War.

Many aspects of city life in Massalia remain unknown, despite the recent excavations. Temples of Artemis and Apollo are mentioned in historical sources, but nothing of them has been found save an Ionic capital. The other public buildings in the city are equally obscure, except for a Greek theatre which was located during building operations before the era of systematic excavations. However, even if tangible relics of Greek Massalia are lacking, the wealth of literary evidence allows us to chronicle the history of the city and its relationship with local peoples and with Rome.

Massalia's success was due in part to its position, which interestingly is similar to that of Phocaea itself.[7] The superb natural harbour or Lacydon was the focus of settlement, overlooked by an acropolis, easily defended hills and guardian islands. Inland from the harbour was a small plain which became the initial *chora* or territory of the city and a source of food supply to the colonists. But it was not these natural features that made Massalia so important. As Strabo remarks,[8] the Massaliotes preferred the sea to the land, and he paints a picture of them leading a heroic merchant life, fighting to establish subsidiary colonies and trading posts along the coast and at the nearby mouth of the River Rhône. By these means the city dominated the zone where most trade took place between Gauls and representatives of the Mediterranean civilisations, at least for the duration of the sixth century.

Grapes and olives are mentioned by Strabo as being grown near Massalia, and it is generally believed that the Greeks were responsible for introducing these staple Mediterranean products to Gaul. Wine and the wine-drinking paraphernalia of jugs, craters, cups and amphorae certainly feature prominently in the archaeological record of Massalia's trading activity with the interior of Gaul. A revealing comment on the wine trade (albeit about a somewhat later period) is made by the Greek writer Diodorus Siculus:[9]

[The Gauls] are exceedingly fond of wine and sate themselves with the unmixed wine imported by merchants; their desire makes them drink it greedily and when they become drunk they fall into a stupor or into a maniacal disposition. Therefore many Italian merchants ... look upon the Gallic love of wine as their treasure trove. They transport the wine by boat on the navigable rivers and by wagon through the plains, and receive in return for it an incredibly high price; for one jar of wine they receive in return a slave, a servant in exchange for the drink.

Other items traded by the early Massaliotes included metalwork and pottery of Greek, usually Attic, origin, as well as locally produced versions of Phocaean pottery types. What came in the other direction is unclear, tin being favoured by many scholars, since it was an essential commodity in the manufacture of bronze; the legendary Cassiterides Islands off the British coast were known in antiquity as a source. However, this cannot have furnished all the return trade, and it was probably other primary materials such as iron, corn and slaves that forged the trading relationship between the Celts and the Greeks.[10]

Spectacular evidence for the long-distance trade in Greek luxury goods comes from two well-known sites in the centre of Gaul and southern Germany respectively. These are the burial sites of Vix and Hochdorf, where a large number of Greek and Mediterranean artefacts were placed in very high-status graves.[11] At Vix the most significant of these imports was a massive bronze crater decorated with applied bronze relief sculptures of warriors and charioteers, and elaborate handles supported by gorgons. It is the largest known Greek bronze vessel, and is widely admired as one of the most beautiful masterpieces of ancient metalworking, probably produced in Corinth early in the sixth century (although this is disputed, and it could be a south Italian product of the late sixth century). It was carefully placed in the large square burial chamber with its lid (which also served as a sieve),

The Vix crater, one of the finest and largest Greek bronze vessels known (weight 208.6 kilograms). It comes from a princely early Iron Age grave in central France. (Musée archéologique, Châtillon)

two Attic black-figure drinking cups, a wine jug and a phiale – all part of the apparatus for drinking wine in the Greek world. The crater weighed 208.6 kilograms, and its great size must obviously have posed problems in transportation, for letters of the Greek alphabet scratched into the metal indicate that it was dismantled after manufacture and reassembled, probably on arrival in the Vix area.

There has been much scholarly debate about the route taken by the Vix crater between Greece and central Gaul. At one time a route via the Adriatic, Po Valley and Alpine passes was favoured, with Etruscans acting as intermediaries and organising the trade across the Alps. Currently, however, Massalia is favoured as the entrepôt on a route that went by sea to the Golfe du Lyon and thence up the Rhône–Saône Valley to reach its destination. The distribution of various artefacts, such as Greek black- and red-figured pottery and Massaliote amphorae, seem to show that in the sixth century at least most links between west-central Europe and the Mediterranean were via Massalia.[12]

From the burial at Hochdorf comes an impressive Greek import, a large three-handled cauldron with three bronze figurines of lions seated on the rim. Meticulous scientific analysis of the cauldron has detected pollen in a deposit on the inside of the vessel, probably from honey, suggesting that it was used for making mead. This may also be the purpose of other cauldrons known from similar graves, such as the one from St Colombe, near Vix, which was also a Greek import, embellished with Orientalising gryphons' heads.[13] One of the lions on the Hochdorf cauldron is very interesting, because it is more crudely fashioned and appears to be a local copy, perhaps because one of the originals had been lost in transit. This clearly shows that the cauldron was a prized possession, and indeed many of the Mediterranean imports provide evidence of ancient repairs and restorations.

The other finds from Hochdorf were also of local manufacture, and very revealing of the nature of society at this time. Several drinking horns were found, the largest of iron and gold, the others formed of the horns of the ancient wild ox, the much-feared aurochs, which was still hunted for its horns in Caesar's time.[14] These vessels conjure up the traditional Celtic images of feasting and hunting, and it is fairly certain that the burial is that of a chieftain from the nearby hillfort of Höhenasperg. His body was laid out on furs on a unique bronze couch, which was perhaps also connected with feasting and which may have been a symbol of his status and authority within the tribe. He had gold decoration on his shoes and a gold-encased scabbard for the dagger that had been laid across him. The largest object in the burial, however, was the iron-clad four-wheeled cart that took up most of the rest of the space. Carts were a feature of high-status burials of this period (a dismantled example is known from Vix, for instance); they seem to have been the funeral carriages used during what must have been elaborate and sumptuous rituals.

Massive mounds were raised over these burials, one of which, the Magdalenenberg, is one of the largest prehistoric burial mounds in Europe. They are usually found in groups fairly close to large, well-defended hillforts, such as Mt Lassois near Vix, and Höhenasperg. The Heuneburg in southern Germany, with its burial mounds at Hohmichele and elsewhere in the vicinity, is the most famous of these hillforts, and large-scale excavations have uncovered the defences and several of the internal buildings.[15] An extraordinary feature of the defences reveals yet another facet of the links between the Mediterranean and the peoples just north of the Alps at this time. The traditional early Iron Age timber and stone defences were replaced by linked square towers made of mud-bricks resting on stone foundations. This is a Greek technique, known in the Massalia area, for instance at St Pierre-les-Martigues,[16] and such was the prestige attached to Greek artefacts and expertise that the tribal leader at the Heuneburg saw fit to have this style of fortification built for him, probably by Greek architects. It must have been somewhat unsuitable for the damp northern climate, especially if not rigorously maintained.

The links between Greeks and Celts during the sixth century BC mark a high point in such contacts, and they were due to the coincidence of the establishment of Massalia and the rise of powerful kingdoms several hundred miles to the north. It may indeed be more than a coincidence if the model of prestige-goods economies, often applied to this period, is correct.[17] This model proposes that the Celtic leaders were dependent for their position within society on the control of trade with the outside world. Having first achieved a dominant position, presumably through force of arms or dynastic succession, they monopolised the import of the much-sought-after Greek luxuries, and controlled redistribution of these items to their followers. The Greek traders dealt only with the leaders, perhaps on a quasi-diplomatic basis, and received in exchange the raw materials and goods that the tribal leaders were able to command. The Greek luxuries were prestigious precisely because they were difficult to get hold of, and because the recently founded colony at Massalia offered new possibilities of being able to obtain them. Control of these goods, and the status that went with possessing them, is reflected in the clear hierarchy of grave-goods in the burials, which range from the like of Vix and Hochdorf down to simple burials with one or two offerings placed with the body. The implication is that society was centralised, strictly hierarchical and, one suspects, autocratic.

The import of luxuries was also restricted geographically to sites such as Mt Lassois, Höhenasperg and the Heuneburg in eastern France and south-west Germany. Although the trade route ran through the Rhône–Saône Valley, few Greek objects have been found there, suggesting that the links between the tribal leaders and the Greek traders was a direct one, without middlemen. Outside this area, in the rest of Gaul, such imports are virtually unknown, probably because the type of centralised society associated with rich burials and hillforts was not so strongly developed.

Radical changes to this pattern occurred in the fifth century BC as the so-called Hallstatt D period of the Iron Age gave way to La Tène I. Mt Lassois, the Heuneburg and nearly all the other rich sites were abandoned, and the focus of power shifted further north, to the Hunsrück–Eifel area in Germany and the Marne Valley in France.[18] Trading activity also declined significantly, and the pattern altered so that Massalia no longer held absolute sway. The Etruscans, in particular, were able to establish new trade routes over the Alps, following their expansion into the Po Valley at this time. An archaeological marker of this trade is the distribution of Etruscan wine flagons in Switzerland, the Rhineland and further north.[19]

One of the features that marks out the La Tène period from its predecessor is the development of what is regarded as the characteristic curvilinear Celtic art style. This is first seen in burials in the Hunsrück–Eifel and the Marne, and at the site of Klein Aspergle, the only La Tène burial in one of the earlier rich Hallstatt D centres. The new art style was a real revolution in taste, turning away from the rectilinear geometrical motifs and very schematic human representations of the Hallstatt period, to a style that at first owed almost everything to the Greek influence flowing from the imported luxuries that had come in during the previous century. Classical palmettes, lotus motifs and swags were fairly closely copied in the earliest La Tène art style, seen in burials such as Schwarzenbach and Reinheim.[20] At Klein Aspergle, significantly, an Attic cup was mended with metal sheeting decorated in the new style. The style developed rapidly into more imaginative imitations of Greek decorative themes, and included representations of animals and humans perhaps derived from the animal art of the Steppes. The strength of expression in Celtic metalworking soon ensured that the original sources of inspiration were no longer needed as Celtic art developed its own highly characteristic style, but the Greek heritage is detectable throughout and is a good example of the cultural influence of the Mediterranean reaching out beyond the areas under their direct control.

As well as the emergence of a vigorous art style, the period sees more luxuries manufactured locally and fewer imports. Perhaps this shift in emphasis was due to unknown events connected with the demise of the rich late Hallstatt centres and of their trading links with the Mediterranean. The main consequence of this was an end to the symbiotic relationship of Massalia and the north. Henceforward, for two centuries or so, the Celtic heartland developed its own La Tène culture and grew in strength, while Massalia appears to have lost contact with the north, being thrown back on its local markets.[21] The colony proceeded to strengthen its influence along the coast and in the lower Rhône Valley by establishing subsidiary colonies or 'comptoirs', which are a feature of the fourth century BC in the area and mark a revival of Massaliote fortunes. This period also witnesses an increasing divergence in culture between the south and north of France, a difference still strong in the Roman period which saw expression in the highly Romanised Provincia (Gallia Narbonensis) in the south and the more characteristically Celtic provinces of the Three Gauls. This division is a useful one for discussing the development of Gaul in the period up to the Roman conquest.

The Hellenisation of southern Gaul

Native sites in the south were relatively unaffected by late Hallstatt and early La Tène developments, and appear to have preserved many aspects of Bronze Age culture. This particularly applied to sites along the Mediterranean coast in Languedoc, such as Pech-Maho or Cayla de Mailhac, where a fairly complete sequence spanning the period of Greek influence has been excavated.[22] Sites in this region have many Iberian traits, and one result of contact with Greek and Etruscan traders was a strengthening of their local culture, so that Hallstatt influence coming from the north was stemmed. In consequence the coastal plain sites in Languedoc were different from those inland, and they became increasingly susceptible to foreign influences in the form not only of Greek and some Etruscan imports, but also of a considerable quantity of Punic material coming via Spain.[23]

The separate cultural development of a coastal region is a common phenomenon where there is a coastal strip that can act as a 'contact zone' between sea-borne traders and inland peoples, or where the coastal population is sufficiently numerous and strong to absorb most of the trade, effectively cutting off inland regions from access to the coast. It seems that the latter was the case in Languedoc, as far east as the Hérault and the Rhône Valley.

Later developments in Languedoc are documented by the magnificently situated hilltop site of Ensérune.[24] Some La Tène I–II influence can be detected in the form of metalwork imported from the north, but Greek, Iberian and, increasingly, Italian goods are the dominant non-local products. Inscriptions appear, using a Greek script but in an unknown language; these have links with similar material from Catalonia. By about 200 BC a major phase of reconstruction shows the results of yet more intense Hellenisation, for buildings are now rectangular stone and painted plaster constructions, using local versions of classical columns, and laid out in fairly regular streets. It displays most of the characteristics of a Greek settlement. This phase (Ensérune III) lasted until the first century AD, right through the period of Roman conquest and colonisation of nearby Narbonne.

Further east in the lower Rhône Valley and on its fringes the influence of Massalia becomes more marked; this is the main area where Gallo-Greek inscriptions occur and where Hellenistic-style defences are a feature of native sites. Research in the Vaunage and nearby Nîmes, in the hillforts flanking the river valley, has revealed a sequence showing the expanding trade in Greek imports, especially pottery, from the sixth century BC.[25] Pottery styles also reveal La Tène influence at this time, showing that contacts were being made with the north and with the Alpine region as well.

The Tour Magne, Nîmes, dating largely from the early Roman period, but incorporating the remains of a massive pre-Roman monumental tower which would have overlooked the Iron Age oppidum.

These were probably trading contacts rather than any mass immigration of people into the area, as has sometimes been suggested, since there were no major changes in the society and organisation of the hillforts.

During the fourth century BC a distinctive and well-developed lower Rhône culture emerges, drawing freely but not slavishly on Greek ideas. One of its unusual features is the building of large towers in the hillforts, such as that at Mauressip, which was constructed on the highest point of the hill in Greek style, with large squared blocks. Was this a look-out tower for the inhabitants, or was it perhaps some sort of monument? In any event, it was a demonstration of their mastery of stone masonry, and it would have been a highly visible feature of the surrounding countryside. The Tour Magne at Nîmes is another such tower, and further examples are known on the other side of the Rhône Valley, for instance at Baou-des-Noirs. It is possible that the towers are a sign of insecure conditions, for at the same time there was a move to the hillforts, and virtually no undefended lowland sites were occupied after the fifth century.[26]

Soon after the middle of the third century the Vaunage area, particularly the hillfort of Nages, suffered destruction, which the excavators attribute to the arrival of the historically attested Volcae Arecomici. This was not, apparently, an invasion of peoples from outside the area, but rather a local political change, since life at the hillfort went on much as before. Nages was rebuilt with new fortifications incorporating bastions, and a strikingly regular street grid along Greek lines within. So far the apparently strict uniformity of the planning, in long thin rectangular blocks separated by comparatively wide streets, has no parallel in other south Gaulish hillforts, and indeed is unlike the known layouts of the Greek colonies in the south of France, such as Olbia. However, it is clearly of Greek inspiration, perhaps from the eastern Mediterranean or southern Italian colonies. Other hillforts, such as Entremont, also have evidence for street grids, but they are more like their local Greek prototypes in shape and proportion.

Centralised planning and authority must have been the order of the day at Nages, for subsequent alterations to the street grid were also controlled, so that encroachments on the wide streets were to a uniform depth. This resulted in new, slightly wider blocks and narrower streets. The hillfort continued until the late second century, when it was largely destroyed, an event that may well be connected with the Roman conquest of 121 BC. Revival came not long after, and in fact the hillfort expanded as never before. However, it was eventually abandoned at the time of full-scale Romanisation under the Emperor Augustus. Most of the fortified sites in the area were given up at the same time in favour of undefended settlements in the valleys: only the ancient capital of the Volcae Arecomici, Nîmes, remained occupied to become a highly important Roman city (see chapter 3).

In the lower Rhône Valley itself few sites are known because of recent sedimentation and modern settlement, but those that are form a distinct type characterised as an *emporion* or trading station serving the upland hillforts. Espeyran is typical, occupying a low headland overlooking the river from the late sixth century BC to the Gallo-Roman period. Initially the buildings were of wood and perishable materials, but soon mud-brick walls on stone foundations were being built, and there is clear evidence for a close link with Massalia in the vast number of imported pottery vessels. In fact, local handmade pottery is distinctly rare, which has led the excavators to suggest that the site was occupied by Greek colonists rather than local people. Perhaps this is the 'Rhodanousia' mentioned in ancient sources.[27] The Massaliotes are known to have set up several sites of this sort, both to promote their trading interests and to provide some protection for their merchants if need be. Arles is thought originally to have been the Greek

The oppidum of Jastres, near Aubenas in southern France. Its square bastions, of a type derived ultimately from Greek fortification practice, are a feature of many such sites.

site of Theline, and there are also Lattes (ancient Lattara) on the River Lez near Montpellier and Agde (ancient Agathe) on the River Hérault near Béziers.[28]

The east side of the Rhône estuary was even more clearly Hellenised, but in a different way because of the close proximity of Massalia itself and the apparently less-developed local culture of the region's hilly interior. The coastal hillfort of St Blaise has evidence of early regular planning, perhaps due to Greek influence in the seventh century.[29] After this there was a long period during which Massalia became more influential, culminating in the second century, when there was a radical reconstruction of the entire site. A Hellenistic-style rampart was built using large square blocks with Greek masons' marks inscribed on them. The main wall had merlons, and there was a fore-wall and projecting square towers, just like the town wall of a Greek city.[30] Inside, housing and streets in Greek style appear, which gave the impression to early excavators that St Blaise was actually taken over by Greeks from Massalia to become a sub-colony. It is more likely, though, that these developments are an extreme example of late Hellenisation of a native site rich enough to pay for such elaborate defences, probably on the proceeds from the production of salt from the adjacent lagoons.

Near St Blaise was another remarkable site that also probably owed its existence to the trade in salt and fish: the Ile de Martigues, on an island in the middle of the channel connecting the large salt-water lake of the Etang de Berre with the sea. It had ramparts and a densely occupied settlement area dating back to the fifth century BC. Unfortunately, we know nothing of the later history of this site, and so cannot be certain about the extent of Greek influence there.[31]

St Blaise may have been the capital of the small coastal tribe of the

Avatici, which was probably hostile to Massalia during the second century BC. This hostility ultimately led to a siege of the hillfort at about the time of the Roman conquest, probably by the Romans themselves, who were intervening in the area on behalf on their Massaliote allies. Shortly afterwards the site was abandoned.[32] It is paradoxical that many of the native sites close to Massalia, like St Blaise, clearly had strong commercial relations with the Greeks, but at the same time were opposed to them politically and militarily. Entremont, overlooking the town of Aix-en-Provence, is the best-known illustration of such a contradiction; this hillfort capital of the Salluvii, with its Hellenistic-style street grid and defences, was attacked by C. Sextius in 124–123 BC and the inhabitants were forcibly evacuated (see chapter 2).[33]

Inland from Massalia, and along the Côte d'Azur to the east, the Iron Age settlement pattern is somewhat different. Large numbers of very small hillforts dominate the scene, giving an impression of a decentralised society without a strong tribal hierarchy. Many of the hillforts are in inhospitable scrubland, and are consequently known primarily through aerial photography. A typical site is Mt Garou, situated on a hilltop steep enough to have needed hillside terraces for the earliest house structures. The main period of the site dates from the sixth to fifth centuries, during which appreciable numbers of amphorae and Massaliote pots were brought in. Mud-brick construction is also known, and it seems likely that Greek merchants were trading goods and expertise for agricultural produce. Many sheep and goat bones were found on the site, and since the surrounding countryside is well suited for grazing, it could be that wool, milk and mutton were the main local products. The excavators in fact suggest that over-exploitation of the hillfort's hinterland, due to the demand for produce by the merchants, led to a period of desertion in the fourth century and a reduced occupation later on.[34] If other hillforts had a similar sequence, this may account for the relatively undeveloped and conservative nature of the region's culture.

It is surprising indeed to find that some sites remained in occupation, albeit on a modest scale, up to the early Empire, more than a century after the Roman conquest. In some cases, such as the Fort at Taradeau or Roquefavour at Ventabren, the main period of occupation was in the second to first centuries BC, and this has been interpreted as a sort of 'retreat to the hills' by a society intent on preserving its traditional ways.[35] By the early Empire, though, nearly all of the hilltop sites had been abandoned, presumably for the Romanised towns and villages in the valleys, with the radical change in lifestyle that this move implies.

Small settlements were sited on the hills overlooking Massalia itself, some as close as 5 kilometres. This raises the question of the extent of the city's territory, and whether any of the hillforts were under the direct control of the Massaliotes.[36] It is known from the historical sources that Massalia had a relatively small territory, which was not fertile enough to grow a decent crop of grain. This may have been an incentive to trade with the surrounding tribes in order to obtain basic products. Gradually the economic power of the city probably led to many local sites being dependent on it for their continued existence, even if they were nominally independent in political terms. This would account for Caesar's reference to the tribe of the Albici in the hills above Massalia owing allegiance to the city from ancient times.[37] Another feature of the city's relationship with its territory was the decline of long-distance trade at the end of the sixth century, which stimulated the Massaliotes to develop their local links and expand their territory. The colony, in fact, lost influence because of this, becoming more like an ordinary Hellenistic Greek city – one dependent on its territory – than a major trading outpost. Nevertheless, Massalia continued to dominate the immediate region, much to the resentment of the surrounding tribes, who rose against the Greeks in 154 and 125 BC.

The hostilities of 154 were directed at two sub-colonies at Antibes (ancient Antipolis) and Nice (ancient Nikaia) rather than the city itself, and it may have been attempts at territorial expansion by the colonists that led to the uprising. At another of the sub-colonies along the same stretch of coast, Olbia, near Hyères, there are traces of centuriation (land allotment; see chapter 4) which are possibly of this period.[38] If so, this emphasises that the sub-colonies were more than mere trading 'comptoirs'; they were probably established to guard Massaliote interests along the coast, especially shipping, and had permanent settlement and territories of their own. The fort-like layout of the fourth- to first-century BC site at Olbia, with regimented blocks reminiscent of the interior of a Roman fort, also suggests a surveillance role.[39]

As we have seen in the previous pages, Hellenisation took place in most of the southern Gaulish native sites, and this process can be seen to have definite stages of development in those areas that were touched by it.[40] At first its main feature was the import of Greek goods, and this occurred throughout the south from the seventh century BC onwards. This need not constitute a very strong cultural influence, since artefacts may not necessarily be used for their original purposes once in the hands of new users, and native culture remained largely unaltered.

The next, much more significant stage was the adoption of Greek techniques of building, agriculture and manufacture; this was taking place from the late fifth century onwards, and earlier in some areas. Buildings altered in appearance quite radically in some instances, being much more regular and permanent. A characteristic feature was the use of mud-bricks on stone foundations. In some cases rectangular blocks of houses were laid out on the model of Greek colonial town planning, reaching a peak of regularity in the second-century scheme at Nages.[41] The spread of vine and olive cultivation can be detected in the presence of such items as the olive press weights at Entremont, apparently manufactured in Massalia and sold, presumably with the information on how to operate them, to local people.[42]

Carefully excavated mud-bricks from a building in the oppidum of Baou-Roux. This construction technique, found on many southern Gaulish Iron Age sites, is considered to have been of Greek inspiration.

New pottery-making techniques, too, were introduced, notably the potters' wheel and an improved type of kiln; the resulting pots made on native sites were often imitations of the imported types that the occupants had hitherto bought.[43]

More specialised introductions were coinage and writing. Massaliote coins had been minted since the late sixth century BC, but they tended at first to be confined to Greek sites. Early trade with the Celts, therefore, was in terms of barter and exchange, but the volume of trade grew from the fourth century onwards, when Greek coins become fairly common on Celtic sites. After this coins were used extensively in southern Gaul as a means of exchange, especially bronze issues, which were sufficiently small denominations to be useful in ordinary transactions. Local imitations appeared from the second century, for instance the silver coins of the Volcae Tectosages, which took the coins of the Greek colony of Rhode in Catalonia as their prototype.[44] Writing, or at least the use of the Greek alphabet for the Gaulish language, was broadly contemporary with the developments in coin use. The earliest inscription in Gaulish in the south is on a third-century column capital from Montagnac. Most, though, belong to the second and early first centuries, and are very simple indications of ownership scratched onto pottery, or funerary inscriptions on stone stele. Nearly all the 280 known examples are from the lower Rhône Valley, with a sparse scatter of somewhat later examples further north.[45]

New techniques and introductions of this sort would inevitably have had an effect on the environment of the native sites, making them more 'Greek' in ambience and subtly affecting attitudes and customs. This is the third stage in Hellenisation, in which more fundamental changes could occur. Art styles, for instance, especially in sculpture, began to show influence of the Greek world, although the style adopted appears markedly archaic compared with contemporary developments in Greece itself. Figures in the round appear from the third century, with a degree of accurate portrayal of human and animal forms: warriors, human heads, birds, horses and fantastic beasts.[46] Their findspots and iconography usually indicate a religious context, which brings us to another major potential area of

Hellenistic influence. Ideas of sculptural portrayal, and to a lesser degree temple architecture, certainly caused changes to the largely open-air and non-pictorial native cults (see chapter 6), so that in the material sense at least cults were Hellenised. But the gods and goddesses retained their Celtic names and, presumably, their traditional powers, so to that extent Hellenisation did not affect religious belief. The same applied to language, which remained Celtic despite the use of Greek and other scripts, and which, as far as we can tell, took very few Greek words into its vocabulary.[47]

Language and religion, therefore, were the two major aspects of Celtic society that were resistant to Hellenisation, as indeed they were in most other parts of the Mediterranean that were influenced by the Greeks, such as Asia Minor. Indeed, it is unlikely that such changes would ever have taken place in southern Gaul, since Massalia was primarily a trading station rather than an imperialistic power. Her concern was to sell Greek artefacts and expertise, very successfully to judge from the results, and it was not until the Roman conquest that the new masters were able to transform the south from a Celtic to a Graeco-Roman land.

Native society in the late Iron Age in southern Gaul has often been termed Gallo-Greek, which serves to distinguish it from later Gallo-Roman society.[48] The developments resulting from Hellenisation certainly made Gallo-Greek culture distinctive, especially in the spheres of proto-urban planning and religious art. This was partly because the Celts were philhellenes and keen to acquire the benefits of Greek civilisation, even if at times they were opposed to Massalia politically. The policy of the Massaliotes was to encourage Celtic interest whenever possible, so that although the city was politically weak on occasions during its history, Gauls still came to the city to learn Greek language and customs and to worship at Greek temples. Indeed, it did not seem 'that Greece had emigrated to Gaul, but rather that Gaul had been moved to Greece'.[49] Even after absorption by Rome Massalia continued to play an important, if diminished cultural role, and it gained a reputation as an alternative to Athens for the education of wealthy young Romans.

Iron Age towns in the interior of Gaul

The main thread linking the Hellenised south with the tribes of northern Gaul, and to a lesser extent Germany as well, is the development of some form of urban society. Generally speaking, the hillforts or oppida of the north are best regarded as proto-urban, rather than urban in the sense of a city laid out on lines familiar to Greeks and Romans. Nevertheless, the rise of the oppida was partly a result of increasing trade with the Mediterranean and the northward flow of Graeco-Roman ideas.

Oppidum is the word that Caesar generally used for describing hillforts, but he also applied it to large settlements with defences that were not on hills, and so it has entered archaeological parlance as a term to describe the pre-Roman towns of the Celtic world. Caesar's descriptions of oppida, usually while under attack by Roman forces, are very revealing.[50] Orléans (ancient Cenabum), for instance, had narrow streets and many gates, together with a bridge across the River Loire. More is known about Bourges (ancient Avaricum, capital of the Bituriges), which was 'about the fairest city in all Gaul', according to its inhabitants, so much so, in fact, that they refused to allow it to be burnt as part of Vercingetorix's scorched earth policy during the events of 52 BC (see chapter 2). Caesar besieged Bourges, which held out for a time because the defenders built towers to match the Roman siegeworks, and undermined Roman constructions by means of tunnels. The fortifications of the oppidum show considerable sophistication, and it is also clear from Caesar's account that the town commanded substantial resources: 40,000 people were within the defences, probably not all inhabitants but certainly all requiring sustenance during the siege. Caesar also refers to a forum, implying that public open spaces existed, and presumably other civic buildings as well.

Bourges and Orléans have been intensively occupied since the Iron Age, and so unfortunately little is known of the archaeology of their oppida. However, there are several other sites where excavations have revealed the extent and complexity of late Iron Age towns. The most famous of these is in southern Germany at Manching. Although this lies just outside the area covered by this volume, it is nevertheless important both as a type-site and as the most completely excavated oppidum to date.[51] It started life as an undefended settlement on low-lying ground by the River Danube, dominating a trade route along the river valley. During a gradual expansion it took on the characteristics of an organised settlement – streets lined with wooden buildings, including spacious courtyard houses, evidence for craft specialisation and the buildings in which the crafts were carried out. Long-distance trade is also attested. In the first century BC a massive defensive wall was built, enclosing 350 hectares and arranged so as to leave a substantial open area around the settlement, perhaps for markets or fairs.

Small settlements nearby appear to have been abandoned as Manching grew in size and importance, which accounts in part for the overall impression of the oppidum as an enormous version of one of the smaller settlements. No attempt was made to alleviate the inevitable problems of water supply, drainage or rubbish disposal that such a concentration of population would bring. This contrasts with Graeco-Roman towns, where civic amenities were often a major feature, and it is one of the reasons why Iron Age oppida are usually categorised as proto-towns, rather than urban centres in the generally accepted sense. Whether properly developed towns would have emerged in Gaul and Germany had the Romans not invaded is a moot point. The history of urbanisation outside the Roman Empire suggests that they probably would have done, but perhaps not so quickly without Roman encouragement.[52]

Other sites also provide evidence for the emergence of oppida. At Basel there is an undefended late La Tène settlement (the Gasfabrik) next to a defended site (the Münsterhügel). The undefended site originated in the early first century BC, continuing until the middle of the century, when the oppidum was constructed. The undefended site was consequently abandoned. The change in the type of settlement is very likely to have been due to events such as the migration of the neighbouring Helvetii and the military adventures of Ariovistus (see chapter 2), both of which could have affected this strategically important site. It is possible that Basel would have developed as an undefended riverside trading station but for the need to set up fortifications. In more peaceful areas, such as Aquitaine, oppida could develop without defences, as at Lacoste.[53]

Aulnat near Clermont-Ferrand is also undefended. It is made up of a series of small settlements positioned close to each other. These yielded evidence of industrial production of a type similar to that in Manching and the other defended oppida. Aulnat resembles a group of villages, collectively having a wide range of facilities and specialisations that justify regarding it as a form of oppidum. The chronology of the site runs from the second century BC or earlier to about 40 BC, when it was abandoned, probably in favour of the nearby defended site of Gergovie.

Gergovie (a nineteenth-century name) has been linked with Caesar's Gergovia, where he suffered a serious reverse; earlier scholars envisaged that the site had been occupied from just before the time of Caesar's conquest in 52 BC, but a date of about 40–30 BC is now favoured. Why a hillfort should be constructed after the Roman conquest is not known, unless it is to be connected with one of the sporadic later rebellions that took place. At all events, the undefended low-lying site at Aulnat appears to have been replaced by Gergovie, where an oppidum came into being in the late Iron Age and lasted into the early Roman period. This sequence is roughly the same as at Levroux, where a little earlier in the Iron Age an open site was replaced by an oppidum about 1.5 kilometres away.[54]

Plan of the interior of the oppidum of Vieux-Reims, Variscourt. A well-developed rectilinear layout of houses and streets is clearly visible, similar to those at Villeneuve-St Germain and elsewhere.

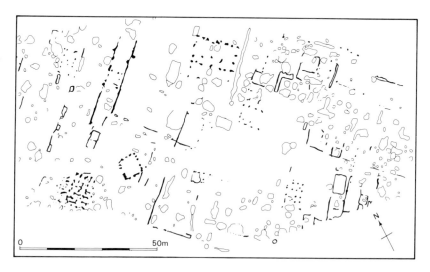

0 ⸻ 50m

The story is different further north at Villeneuve-St Germain, where an earlier hillfort at Pommiers was supplemented in the mid-first century BC by a low-lying oppidum, probably called Noviodunum ('new fortification'), enclosed by a meander of the River Aisne. Excavations at Villeneuve have revealed features similar to those found at Manching, especially courtyard buildings and street frontages on a regular street grid. There is evidence of coin production and other crafts, indicating that the site was probably a trading centre in a more convenient position than the hillfort, where occupation declined in density. Villeneuve did not, in fact, continue for very long, for in about 15 BC the Roman town of Augusta Suessionum (modern Soissons) had emerged as the regional centre.[55]

Because of variations in the histories of individual sites, due to local political and military conditions, it is difficult to generalise about oppida. Fortifications are usually considered to be late in date in northern Gaul, however, and the low-lying oppida can certainly all be placed in the first century BC. Some survived the Roman conquest and either provided the nucleus for Roman towns or, at the least, a population which could be transferred to a nearby new foundation.[56]

The production of coins at many oppida indicates that they were centres of political authority as well as trading stations. This brings us to the thorny subject of the tribes or other groups that occupied the oppida and their surrounding territories. In some cases there is a clear correspondence between known oppida and the tribes mentioned in the ancient literary sources (chiefly Caesar's *Gallic War*). Thus Bibracte (modern Mt Beuvray) can be regarded as the capital of the powerful tribe of the Aedui in central Gaul, and Vieux-Reims is almost certainly the late Iron Age capital of the Remi. Other important oppida, however, such as Levroux, are less easily attributable to particular tribes, especially if they lie on boundaries between tribal areas.[57] Levroux may have acted as an inter-tribal market-place between the Pictones and the Bituriges, and there are other oppida, too, that are more likely to have been subsidiary centres of a tribe rather than the capital.

Discussion of tribal capitals assumes, of course, that Iron Age tribes were sufficiently centralised to have a single capital. Some definitely did have a powerful single government, but others were organised more loosely, often on a federal basis. The Helvetii, for instance, had four subdivisions within their territory in western Switzerland, and the oppida known from this area could have acted as local capitals for these subdivisions.[58] In some parts of Gaul, notably Brittany, a multitude of small hillforts existed in the late Iron Age, indicating insecurity and lack of a central tribal authority strong enough to curb attacks between hillforts. The Veneti, for instance, appear to have had no single centre, which made Caesar's subjugation of the area very difficult, since he was forced to reduce each small fortification in turn.[59]

These differences in the settlement pattern in Gaul reflect the cultural and political relationships of individual tribes with the Mediterranean world.

In crude terms, those tribes in close contact with Graeco-Roman culture started to develop features which have been classified as 'archaic states', or emerging city-states based usually on a single centre.[60] This applies mainly to the Arverni, Aedui, Bituriges, Allobroges and Vocontii. The last two in this list were nominally within the Roman province from 121 BC, but this seems to have made little practical difference to their development, which is more or less the same as their neighbours conquered by Caesar.

One of the main features of the more developed tribes was the existence of an oligarchy, out of which an annual magistrate (*vergobretos*) was elected. For the Aedui, which we know best, neither the magistrate nor other members of his family could serve again once he had held office, which effectively prevented the creation of a dynasty. The tribes and their aristocracies had to be large enough to sustain this system, in other words to have enough families to provide independent annual magistrates. We do, in fact, have some figures for tribal populations which confirm this. The

Aerial photograph of a small late Iron Age settlement at Ponthoile in Picardy, typical of many throughout northern France.

most reliable are for the Helvetii, because Caesar was able to obtain written documents about them.[61] They numbered 263,000, had twelve oppida and four hundred villages.

It is also clear from Caesar's account of the Helvetii that they were organised on a clan system, whose aristocratic leaders could rely on anything up to 10,000 followers to support them. Such a system obviously helped maintain the oligarchy in power, but at the same time we know of individuals who used the strength of their following to launch bids for supremacy. Dumnorix of the Aedui and Orgetorix of the Helvetii are good examples of such figures, but the best known is Vercingetorix, who made a bid for power in his tribe of the Arverni. Clearly, the political system of the more developed tribes was vulnerable to conspiracies and *putsches*, probably because elected magistrates and large centralised tribes were fairly novel ideas for the Gauls, and they had not yet established stable administrative systems. Such instability was ideal as far as Caesar was concerned, since he could exploit the rifts that occured in tribal politics by supporting the generally pro-Roman oligarchies against the anti-Roman aristocrats making bids for individual power.

One of the ways in which the tribal aristocracy maintained its position and status within the tribe was by controlling trade. We read of men such as Dumnorix having the right to collect river tolls in the territory of the Aedui, and at same time we can gain an archaeological glimpse of this trade from the vast quantity of Roman luxury goods that was flooding into the interior of Gaul. One of the most characteristic imports was wine, and the amphorae in which it was transported are found in great numbers on many sites. We know from literary sources how fond the Gauls were of wine and how Roman merchants operating from Narbonne and other centres exploited the demand by charging large sums for each amphora (see chapter 2).[62] Wine was a prestige import, much as it had been several hundred years earlier in the late Hallstatt era, and it is thought that it was distributed as a gift by men of power within each tribe to help sustain their position in society.

This theory is supported by ancient writers on the Celts, who give a glimpse of a society that anthropologists would recognise as a 'big-man system'. Here, gift-giving to followers or clients was a vital part of the way in which leaders sustained themselves in power. To do this, a leader had to have disposable assets to give away, such as wine, or gold and silver coins (which are also an important class of artefact in the late Iron Age).[63] These assets were built up by trading with the Romans the raw materials that the latter wanted – iron, grain, hides and, most of all, slaves, for which there was an insatiable demand in the Roman world. The source of the slaves to be sold to the Roman traders was inter-tribal warfare. Thus the need for prestige Roman imports and the growth of trade had the indirect effect of promoting warfare as a means of obtaining one of the key Gaulish exports.[64] So we come full circle, returning to the oppida as one of the principal means of defence against the depredations of neighbouring tribes.

These ingredients of the late Iron Age social system – oppida, imports of Roman goods, local coinage and centralised tribes – all emerge at roughly the same time. Almost certainly this is because they were interdependent parts of an important stage in the evolution of Gaulish culture, one in which Rome had a part to play as the provider of luxuries and the recipient of exports. In this respect, the relationship between Rome and Gaul in the late

Iron Age was the same as that between Massalia and Gaul in the early Iron Age. Rome was what is known as a 'core' area, economically dominant and with cultural products that other people wanted to have or to copy. The Gauls were on the periphery of the core area, culturally vibrant, but with a need to acquire prestige Roman goods as a means of sustaining their social system. Thus they became economically dependent on the Romans. The increasing development of the tribes went hand-in-hand with the deepening influence of Rome, and 'pre-Roman Romanisation' was the result.[65]

Eventually Roman conquest came to those tribes of the interior that were the main examples of this system in action: as Caesar was to exploit to his advantage, many Gauls were happy to comply with his demands. His comments are very revealing: 'The Gauls ... through living near the Roman provinces and being familiar with goods that come in from overseas, are well supplied with both luxuries and necessities. They have gradually become accustomed to defeat, and having fought and lost so many battles do not even pretend to compete with the Germans in valour', although 'there was once a time when the Gauls were more warlike than the Germans'.[66] For Caesar, therefore, the influence of Rome was a cause of a fatal weakening in the Gaulish will to fight, and the implication is that the word 'Romans' could be happily substituted for 'Germans' in this passage.

Gauls, Belgae and Germans

The Belgae, as Caesar notes in the famous first paragraph of his *Gallic War*, were the people living in northern Gaul. These people were 'the furthest away from the culture and civilised ways of the Roman province; and the merchants, bringing those things that tend to make men soft, very seldom reach them'. Indeed, some of the Belgic tribes such as the Nervii refused to allow Roman wine and other luxuries into their territory. All this contributed, in Caesar's opinion, to the reputation of the Belgae as being the fiercest warriors in Gaul.[67]

The Belgae were different from the Gauls in other important aspects too, namely their language, customs and laws. In fact, Caesar paints a picture of three distinct groups in northern Gaul and the Rhineland, where he did much of his fighting. Celtic Gauls occupied the territory west and south of the Seine, taking up most of the vast area that the Romans regarded as Gallia. To the north of the Seine as far as the Rhine and the Channel coast were the Belgic Gauls, which on close reading of Caesar's text seem to fall into two groups: true Belgae in a zone between the Seine and Somme, and a much more loosely defined group of peoples stretching beyond to the Rhine.[68] This further group had many of the same characteristics as the Germans, who according to Caesar had the territory on the far side of the Rhine.

It is an elegant, simple scheme, further simplified in Caesar's ethnographic comparison of the Gauls and the Germans, where only these two groups figure.[69] The Germans are portrayed as fierce, nomadic, noble savages, in many ways the exact antithesis of the Gauls as they emerge from his writings. It is a black-and-white contrast, and it has to be questioned whether the images have any truth, and where the Belgae fit into this picture.

Archaeological sources on this matter give some very interesting information. The Belgae are found to fall between the two cultural groups, in such a way that the south-eastern subdivision is very Gaulish, with oppida, coinage and so on, while the northern area is comparatively impoverished, with few imports of Roman goods, virtually no oppida and a material culture that owes more to German than to Gaulish types.[70] The peoples of this northern group are very similar to those north of the Rhine in the Netherlands and north-west Germany. When the Germans themselves are examined archaeologically Caesar's simple picture becomes more complicated. From the archaeological evidence, the cultures of the North German Plain seem to correspond most readily to his portrait of a nomadic, simple life, which in fact Caesar himself confines elsewhere to the tribe of the Suebi rather than all Germans.[71] The culture of the Germans near the Rhine resembled that of the Belgae and other groups of Gauls, especially as one travels up-river towards the south. In Bavaria and Baden-Württemberg it is difficult to see much distinction between the material culture there and that of, say, Helvetia or Sequania, both definite Gaulish territories on the south-west side of the Rhine.

In contrast with Caesar's portrayal, therefore, of a Gaul separated from a Germany by the Rhine, we have a series of ethnic and archaeological groupings which divide north–south rather than east–west. They are more 'Germanic' in the north and more 'Gaulish' in the south, but are not parted by the Rhine, which seems not to have been a cultural barrier at all. It probably suited Caesar's purpose at the time to write of the Rhine as a boundary, which it did in fact become after his time. This was for two reasons, explored further in chapter 7: namely that the Roman frontier itself created a cultural boundary between the Gauls and the Germans, and that the Germans of the North German Plain appear to have been expanding and migrating to the south during the late Iron Age and early Roman period, thus restricting the area that was culturally like eastern Gaul.

As we might expect, therefore, Gaul and Germany were much more complex in social and political terms than a reading of Caesar would lead one to believe. Gaulish society had many features that made it amenable to Roman influence, and even if the Belgae and the Germans were more resistant to the lure of Mediterranean goods and lifestyle, they too were soon to feel the sharp edge of Roman military might.

FURTHER READING

Greek Marseille is the subject of a classic survey by M. Clerc in *Massalia* (1927–9), which can be usefully supplemented by more recent discussions in M. Clavel-Lévêque, *Marseille grecque* (1977), and M. Bats and H. Tréziny (eds), *Le territoire de Marseille grecque* (1986).

Morel (1983) surveys the evidence for Greek colonisation of the western Mediterranean as a whole.

The native peoples of southern Gaul are analysed from a historical viewpoint in G. Barruol, *Les Peuples préromains du Sud-Est de la Gaule* (1969). Key sites include Ensérune (Jannoray 1955), Nages (Py 1978), Nîmes (Py 1981) and St Blaise (Bouloumié 1984). F. Benoit's *Recherches sur l'Hellénisation du Midi de la Gaule* (1965) discusses relationships between Greeks and native peoples, which is also the subject of Barry Cunliffe's more wide-ranging study, *Greeks, Romans and Barbarians* (1988). P. Wells, too, discusses the Mediterranean world's links with the interior in *Culture Contact and Culture Change* (1981). Two important discoveries in this respect are the burials at Vix (Joffroy 1979) and Hochdorf (Biel 1985).

For the fast-changing archaeological developments in the rest of Gaul and Germany, works in English include J. Collis' *Oppida* (1984) and *The European Iron Age* (1984), together with Daphne Nash's influential *Settlement and Coinage in Central Gaul* (1978). French archaeology is largely drawn together in conference proceedings, such as O. Buchsenschutz (ed.), *Les Structures d'Habitat à l'Age du Fer* (1981). See also the same author's *Structures d'Habitat et Fortifications de l'Age du Fer en France septentrionale* (1984) for hillforts, together with R. Wheeler and K. Richardson's classic work, *Hill-Forts of Northern France* (1957). The best synthesis in English on the early Germans and their archaeology is by M. Todd, *The Northern Barbarians, 100 BC–AD 300* (1975), to which can be added the still useful *Völker zwischen Germanen und Kelten* by R. Hachmann *et al.* (1962).

2

THE
ROMAN
CONQUEST

Most people automatically think of Julius Caesar when the conquest of Gaul is mentioned. His military reputation was made during an eight-year campaign in Gaul, and he is generally recognised as one of the greatest commanders in Roman history. However, although Caesar's territorial gains and military achievement were immense, as we shall see, it is important to realise that the Roman conquest of Gaul and Germany was a long-drawn-out affair. It lasted for some 150 years, and was marked by long periods of little activity punctuated by bouts of intensive military campaigning. Caesar's was just one of these campaigns, and it should not be allowed to overshadow the achievement of earlier Republican commanders such as Sextius or Marius, or the Augustan campaigns that extended and consolidated Caesar's conquests.

Roman eyes were first focused on Gaul as a military theatre by Hannibal's crossing of the Alps. In 218 BC two Roman envoys arrived in southern Gaul from north-east Spain, where a defeat had been inflicted upon a Roman ally, the city of Saguntum, by Hannibal.[1] This, of course, was the event that marked the beginning of the Second Punic War, but in local terms it also represented a serious setback to Roman interests. Accordingly, the envoys not only had the task of declaring war on Hannibal, which was the reason they had been sent from Rome, but they also had to win over their allies.

Amongst these allies was the Greek city of Massalia, a long-time friend of Rome,[2] whose strategic position and influence upon the Gauls ensured that Romans were able to travel across southern Gaul to reach Spain. Massalia itself remained a steadfast ally throughout the traumatic years of the Punic War, but the envoys found that the Gauls in the region were not so true. Hannibal's envoys had arrived in the area before the Roman

Bronze statuette of a Gaulish woman prisoner, said to have been found in the River Seine. (British Museum)

embassy, winning the co-operation of many Gaulish tribes in preparation for the Carthaginian general's advance on Italy. It is not surprising to find the Gauls prepared to back Hannibal, since they realistically assessed the risk they ran if they opposed him, and also they had been given cause to dislike the Romans by recent defeats inflicted on those Gauls who lived in the Po Valley (Gallia Cisalpina).[3]

The actual events of Hannibal's crossing of the Alps are too well known to need much repetition here. He advanced from Spain with a force of some 100,000 men, making first contact with the Romans in southern Gaul – a chance meeting, since the Roman consul Publius Cornelius Scipio, with two legions (about 10,000 men) under his command, had been hoping to march into Spain to quell the problems that had arisen from the Saguntum affair. He was clearly too late to carry out this intention, and realised that he might have to face Hannibal in Gaul. Luckily for Scipio, Hannibal was keen to avoid confronting a Roman army before he reached Italy, and he retreated up the Rhône Valley.

At this point in the developing conflict the Romans apparently had no inkling of Hannibal's intention of crossing the Alps into Italy, and reportedly Scipio was 'highly astonished' when he discovered the deserted camp where Hannibal had crossed the Rhône. Finally he realised that the Carthaginian army had eluded him and was on its way to Italy, and hurriedly took himself to Rome to warn the Senate, while sending his army on to Spain.

Meanwhile Hannibal crossed the Alps, using either the Montgenèvre route or one of the passes in the Mont-Cenis area.[4] Exactly which he used has been debated long and hard by scholars since antiquity, mainly because it is one of those historical conundrums which are based on relatively detailed yet at the same time tantalisingly imprecise information. For present purposes, however, it is sufficient to know simply that the crossing was successful (despite enormous human cost), and that the Carthaginian army was never to return to Gaul. Hannibal's passage across Gaul also had considerable local impact. The fact that he had successfully crossed the Alps, and effectively humiliated a Roman general into the bargain, must have weakened the political standing of Rome in the area. In addition, the decline of Massalia's influence over the southern Gauls at this period was to store up problems for the future and eventually lead to Rome's direct intervention in the area.

The conquest of southern Gaul

Rome's domination of the western Mediterranean was assured by the outcome of the Second Punic War, and so when Massalia's interests were threatened in 154 BC it naturally turned to its old ally. Rome had good reasons for wishing to assert itself again in this area, revolving around the need to establish a land route through southern Gaul to Spain. In many ways the route to Spain was the key to Rome's interest in the region, and the reason why it was gradually drawn more and more into permanent occupation of what at this time was known as Gallia Transalpina.[5] Strategically the Romans appear to have considered south-western Gaul as an extension of their command over Spain, especially the coastal strip west of the Rhône, which was ethnically Iberian and therefore similar culturally to north-eastern Spain. They had also been fighting for a long time to gain control of the Ligurian coast on the Italian side of the Alps, and by the 150s BC had largely succeeded.

The intervening region between the Rhône and the Alps was nominally under the control of Massalia, but was in actuality occupied by two hostile groups, the Ligurian tribes in the foothills of the Alps, and the Celtic Salluvii just to the north of Massalia itself. Living in well-defended small hillforts and with an intimate knowledge of the hilly terrain, the Gaulish Ligurians proved difficult to subdue.[6] Accordingly, when Massalia needed help in 154 against those Ligurians who were harrying the sub-colonies of Nikaia (modern Nice) and Antipolis (modern Antibes), an army was sent, led by the consul Quintus Opimius. He gained two victories, and was able to hand the territory of the Oxybii and Deciatae over to Massalia. However, the Roman troops did not immediately return home; instead they were garrisoned in the area over the winter and perhaps for longer, just to make sure that the route to Spain was safe.

It was the Salluvii that caused Rome to intervene again on behalf of Massalia, and this time the army to stay. In 125 BC the consul M. Fulvius Flaccus led two legions into southern Gaul, following a request for help from the Greek colony. Because of their position just to the north of Massalia, the Salluvii posed a threat not only to the Greeks, but also to the main land route to Spain, since it cut right across their territory. Fulvius campaigned during 124, but was soon replaced by his better-known successor, C. Sextius Calvinus.[7] Sextius fought on into the following year, and his defeat of the Salluvii has been directly confirmed by the excavations at Entremont, a stronghold dominating the land route in the vicinity of Aix-en-Provence. Roman ballista balls and spearheads have been found in the upper levels of the excavation, followed by an abandonment level corresponding with the dispersal of the population attested in the historical sources.[8] Weapons of the defenders included arrows and sling-shots, and it would seem from the layout of the hillfort and other evidence that the Salluvii were a well-organised force. They had incorporated Greek defensive ideas into the layout of the ramparts, and had probably imitated other Greek military hardware as well. A curious feature of the buildings in the upper part of the hillfort (Entremont II) is their regimented layout, rather different from the houses elsewhere. Were these a form of barracks for the young warriors of the tribe?

All the archaeological and historical evidence suggests that the Salluvii were a well-ordered, Hellenised tribe with centralised political control and a high level of material culture. Paradoxically, it seems that the Massaliotes had been only too successful in their marketing of Greek culture to the

Interior of the oppidum at Entremont, the site attacked by Sextius in 124 BC. The inhabitants were subsequently evacuated to a new Roman foundation at nearby Aix-en-Provence (Aquae Sextiae).

Salluvii, for in all probability it was the tribe's Hellenisation that gave it sufficient cohesion to be able to break with Massalia and threaten the city. There were other factors, too, connected with the political alliances between the anti-Massalia faction in the tribe and other Celtic tribes in the interior, notably the Arverni of the Massif Central and the Allobroges of Savoy. Rome knew of these alliances and the threat that the Arverni in particular posed to the stability of the region. Inevitably, they were drawn into conflict with them.

In order to protect the route to Spain and watch over the Salluvii, Sextius set up a garrison at a site in the plain below Entremont, near some hot springs. This became the first permanent Roman settlement in Gaul, later to be known as Aquae Sextiae Salluviorum (modern Aix-en-Provence). Virtually nothing is known of the first occupation of the 120s BC, but it is likely that both Roman soldiers and the pro-Roman remnants of the tribe made up the population, a pattern which was to be repeated elsewhere during the conquest of Gaul.[9]

This first phase of Roman warfare in Gaul was scarcely over when a new, much more wide-ranging series of campaigns turned Rome's role from one of protector of roadways and an ally's interests to that of the fully fledged expansionist. The celebration of triumphs by Fulvius and Sextius had obviously opened the eyes of the extremely competitive Roman senatorial class to the possibility of gaining military glory in Gaul. It was to become one of the new military stamping grounds for ambitious generals during the next seventy years or so, culminating of course in Caesar's famous exploits.[10]

Cn. Domitius Ahenobarbus took over from Sextius in 122 BC, and almost at once plunged Roman forces into conflict with the Allobroges, ostensibly because they were harbouring an anti-Roman Salluvian leader, and also because they were attacking a tribe yet further north, the Aedui, that was friendly to Rome. The Allobroges and Domitius' army met in the Rhône Valley near the confluence with the River Sorgue. It was probably the first set-piece battle that the Transalpine Gauls had fought against a Roman army, and it was to be the first of many defeats for them. Our sources record 20,000 Gauls killed and 3,000 captured, figures which are probably exaggerated, as was normal in pro-Roman historical sources, but which, all the same, give some idea of the scale of the conflict.[11] Defeat in open battle was to be one of the major weaknesses of the Gauls throughout the period of the Roman conquest, and it has often been commented on. They were clearly much more successful at ambushing Roman troops while foraging or on the march, or simply at guerrilla warfare. However, for the leaders of the more centralised Gaulish tribes, maintaining their position by gaining victories was probably an important facet in the tribal political climate. So set-piece battles continued to feature in confrontations with the Romans. There were occasions when the Romans were defeated, but these were almost exclusively when Germans were pitted against them, rather than purely Gaulish armies.

The Allobrogan defeat was not a total victory for Domitius, however, as their larger neighbour, the Arverni, continued to pose a threat. More troops were needed, and in 121 BC Q. Fabius Maximus arrived with 30,000 men. He scored a notable victory against a combined army of Arverni and Allobroges, of whom some three-quarters out of a total force of up to 200,000 men were allegedly killed.

The net result of these victories was not a straightforward annexation of territory and its incorporation within the Roman Empire. The Arverni remained beyond the frontier until Caesar's conquest some seventy years later. On the other hand, the Allobroges now came under Roman juris-diction. Why this was so is difficult for us to understand without more historical sources than actually survive. Possibly the campaigning was limited by the Senate to the land on the east of the Rhône, and it was felt more appropriate to impose a treaty upon the Arverni which left them nominally independent, rather than to take on the onerous obligations of administering the territory directly. Geographically Gallia Transalpina now gained a large northerly extension into the mountainous country of the pre-Alps, probably with ill-defined and little-visited frontiers. It is very likely that the territory of the Allobroges (and the Arverni) was regarded as a buffer-zone between the developing Mediterranean coastal region and the interior tribes. Certainly there is little evidence of any rapid Romanis-ation of Allobrogan territory, and they remained more or less as Celtic as their independent neighbours. The exception is their one major settlement, the oppidum of Vienna (modern Vienne) on the middle Rhône, which became an important trading station on the lucrative route up the valley.

In the aftermath of the fighting of 125–121 BC steps were taken to establish a more permanent hold on the southerly parts of the conquered area. Domitius set up a proper road from the Rhône (and possibly from the Alps) to the Pyrenees, complete with milestones, and this was named after him, replacing the old Via Heraclea. At the same time, probably in 118 BC, the colony of Narbo (modern Narbonne) was established in the flat and marshy coastal land on the western side of the Golfe du Lion.[12]

Narbo's foundation was significant in many ways. The city was Rome's first overseas citizen colony, and initially must have had a precarious existence, since the population was probably no greater than 1,000, and it was very much a pioneering settlement. However, it was well placed to benefit from trade, being at the point where an important route from the Atlantic came down to the Mediterranean, at the same time crossing the coastal route. Not surprisingly, we find Narbo growing into a major port by the late Republic, with considerable economic development of the hinterland. In fact, south-western Gaul rapidly became as important as the area around Massalia and the lower Rhone Valley which up to this time had dominated Graeco-Roman contacts with the interior.

In Roman eyes Narbo was the equivalent of Massalia, filling a gap in the pattern of colonies around Gaul's Mediterranean coast. The area in which the city was placed was Iberian, and there seems to have been little real opposition to the arrival of the colonists. Strategically the colony provided a vital stabilising link between Roman Spain and the recently conquered regions further east, and also provided a springboard for further advances into the interior of Aquitaine. It was not long before a small Roman presence was established at Tolosa (modern Toulouse) and merchants started to gain a hold on the trade routes.

At this early date trade and the flag must have gone hand in hand, as was demonstrated by an episode that occurred in 107 BC. An expedition was sent to explore the route to the Atlantic coast, and on its return was surprisingly defeated by a group of German warriors that had migrated into the area.[13] Matters quickly deteriorated, with the imprisonment of the Roman garrison at Tolosa and the collapse of the delicately balanced diplomatic and trading network. Order had to be restored, and the experi-enced consul Q. Servilius Caepio swiftly dealt with Tolosa, sacking the native oppidum and carrying off the enormous hoard of sacred gold that had been thrown into a Celtic water sanctuary there. Caepio's impious act shocked Rome, especially when it was learned that much of the gold had subsequently disappeared on its way to the Roman treasury: Caepio's actions were later investigated by the Senate in 104 BC. Relative peace was restored in south-western Gaul after this episode, and merchants re-entered the area. Full-scale commercial development got under way, aided by the monopoly on trade that Roman citizens enjoyed. In the 70s BC a scandal about excessive duties levied on wine sold in the province caused a public furore. This episode is recorded in a speech made by Cicero in defence of the man accused of perpetrating it, M. Fonteius.[14]

Cicero's fascinating document exemplifies the gross exploitation and rapacity that could characterise late Republican provincial development. Fonteius was admittedly governing the area at a time of crisis in neighbouring Spain (see below), which required him to requisition a great many supplies from the Gauls, who were clearly badly placed to fulfil these sudden demands on their economies. Merchants were trading Italian wine to the independent Gauls of the interior via Narbo and Tolosa, and at each stage imposts were added, allegedly by Fonteius, so that an amphora of wine was far more expensive than it was in Italy. The Gauls had an insatiable appetite for wine, which they drank undiluted, and they were willing to exchange a slave for an amphora of wine – a fantastic bargain for the Roman merchants, since slaves were in heavy demand in Rome. Vast numbers of Italian amphorae have been found in south-western Gaul in native oppida such as Vieille-Toulouse and Lagaste, amply confirming the historical sources.[15] The wine scandal demonstrates that Roman officials and merchants saw the Gauls as people from whom vast profits could be made by exploiting the fact that they attached different values to commodities such as wine. (This attitude was obviously commonplace in Rome, since Fonteius was acquitted.)

In view of this and other oppressive measures, it is not surprising that there were revolts by the Gauls at fairly regular intervals during the late second and early first centuries BC. More serious in Roman eyes, though, was the threat posed by the Germans. A few decades earlier than the events just described the Germanic Cimbri and Teutones had caused consternation in Rome by crushing four Roman armies, three of them in Gaul. The catalogue of disasters reached its climax when Caepio, the man sent to sort out south-western Gaul in the wake of the previous defeat, himself lost a major battle with the Cimbri and Teutones near Arausio (modern Orange) in the Rhône Valley.[16] In all these encounters it seems that Roman generalship was more to blame than the ferocity of the Germans, particularly in the last battle, where two commanders (Caepio and Cn. Mallius Maximus) combined forces but not strategy, thus compromising the effectiveness of their troops. These defeats were a severe blow to Roman morale, and for a while it must have seemed that the very existence of the new province was threatened, given that Rome's tribal allies in the area were also wavering in their allegiance.

Luckily, the Germans were not apparently bent on conquest, but simply wanted some land on which to settle. Much of the fighting had been caused by Rome's consistent refusal to allow this, probably because of the effect it would have had on diplomatic links with the Gauls, and because Gallia Transalpina itself was heavily populated anyway. Salvation for Rome came with the appointment of the energetic reforming general C. Marius in 104 BC. He was an effective leader of the army in Gaul and chose skilled officers to serve with him, such as Sulla and Sertorius. After rallying the wavering allies with a display of military confidence and strength, he decisively defeated the Cimbri and Teutones near Aquae Sextiae in BC.[17]

It was a famous victory, for in the rumour-stricken city of Rome the German threat, possibly even to the city itself, had assumed wholly unwarranted proportions. However, it is true to say that these first direct meetings of Roman and German forces showed the impact that German migrations could have on the stability of Gaul and other provinces; this was a problem that was to be fully realised in the much more serious migrations of the later Roman Empire (see chapter 8).

Following these events Gallia Transalpina settled down again to a new wave of economic development. Immigrants came from Italy in large numbers, accelerating the process of Romanisation and at the same time creating new problems and tensions amongst the native peoples.[18] The result was a series of revolts; it was in this climate that the wine scandal erupted. Matters were made worse by developments in Spain, where a governor appointed in 83 BC, Q. Sertorius, managed to build a powerful political base for himself by cultivating the loyalty of disaffected immigrants and some of the native tribes.[19] The Roman armies sent against Sertorius used Gaul as a supply depot and staging post, particularly at the height of the fighting in 77–76 BC. Pompey (Cn. Pompeius Magnus) was the general in command at the time, using Fonteius as his agent for requisitioning supplies. He almost certainly had to campaign extensively in Gaul as well as Spain in order to deal with the growing unrest, since his victory monument placed on one of the passes over the Pyrenees cites the area from the Alps to Spain as well as Spain itself.[20]

Pompey's most important achievement in Gaul was the foundation of a town in the foothills of the Pyrenees, Lugdunum Convenarum (modern St Bertrand-de-Comminges), to serve as a settlement for men from the mountains and as a focus of Romanisation. He must also have granted Roman citizenship widely, if the frequency of Pompeius as a personal name in the area can be taken as a guide. Pompey clearly saw south-western Gaul as closely linked to Spain in strategic terms, but at the same time he is likely to have been the first to delineate the Spanish–Gallic boundary properly along the spine of the Pyrenees.[21] The other boundaries of the province are much less easy to define, and were probably not precise lines at all, especially in the Alps where hostile tribes still occupied the high mountain areas.

From the 70s BC southern Gaul emerged more and more as a proper

Defeated Gauls chained to a victory monument. Sculpted relief on the side of the triumphal arch at Carpentras (Carpentorate).

province, rather than just an area under Roman control. Previous tensions died down, except in the relatively undeveloped northern territory of the Allobroges, where there were revolts in 66 and 62 BC. By the time that Caesar arrived in 58 BC southern Gaul was able to provide a secure starting point for his thrust to the north and a valuable source of troops.

Caesar in Gaul

The campaigns of Julius Caesar from 58 to 50 BC did more than just consolidate the gains of earlier generals in Gaul. They also pushed the frontiers of the Empire forward north-east as far as the Rhineland, north to the English Channel and beyond, temporarily at least, into Britain itself. Caesar was governor of Gallia Cisalpina and Illyricum from 58 BC, but his command soon extended to Gallia Transalpina.[22]

Our best understanding of the Gallic War can be gained by Caesar's own *Commentaries on the Gallic War* in which he gave one of the clearest and most detailed accounts of an ancient military campaign known. The *Commentaries* were probably written each winter, while the troops were in winter quarters, and issued in annual parts to a highly sympathetic Roman public. There is remarkably little to be added from other historical sources, but the very completeness of Caesar's account causes a major problem. Like all autobiographies, it is self-promoting and self-censored, and since there is virtually no other independent source of evidence to check the truth of what Caesar wrote (apart from modern topographical and archaeological studies), we are forced to accept what he says. We know, though, that he played down Roman defeats and emphasised the duplicity of the Gauls in order to cast his own actions in the most favourable light.[23]

The immediate threat that drew Caesar to Gaul was the intention of the Helvetii to migrate west out of Switzerland. The Aedui, allies of Rome just to the north of the provincial frontier, sought Roman help to force the Helvetii to stay in their homeland, since the migration route lay straight across Aeduan territory. In fact, by the time Caesar arrived the Aedui had negotiated the migration around their territory to the north, but Caesar nevertheless felt it necessary to force the Helvetii back. He needed to protect Gallia Transalpina, and at the same time to bring his troops into action. There was also the matter of avenging an earlier Roman defeat at the hands of the Helvetian Tigurini in 107 BC. Thus began the long series of campaigns which Caesar makes out in his *Commentaries* to have followed naturally one from another.[24]

He marched very rapidly with one legion across the Alps to Geneva, an oppidum on the boundary between the Helvetii and Roman territory to the south. The Helvetii were surprised by Caesar's sudden arrival, and asked his permission to migrate west. This was refused, but after Caesar's withdrawal from the area 360,000 Helvetians started to move west into the territory of the Sequani on the other side of the Jura Mountains. Such defiance of Roman wishes spurred Caesar into more ruthless action. He returned to the area with a larger army and managed to surprise and defeat the Helvetii while they were crossing the River Saône. Then followed a watching action, as Caesar trailed the Helvetii, but when he stopped to give his men a rest after two weeks of marching the tribal leaders interpreted this as weakness. They moved to attack the Roman forces, but were badly defeated and their migration collapsed. The end result for the 110,000 survivors, however, was not enslavement, as would all too often have been the case, but an enforced return to their homeland in Switzerland, because Caesar wanted them to remain in a Celtic buffer-zone between Rome and the Germanic peoples further north. This relatively merciful outcome had the intended effect of neutralising the Helvetii and preventing them from wholeheartedly opposing Caesar during the great uprising of 52 BC.

Caesar's next action involved the Germans directly, for the Sequani had been employing Germanic Suebi as mercenaries in their inter-tribal fighting against the Aedui. Unfortunately for the Sequani, this scheme backfired when the Suebi demanded more payment and gave every appearance of wanting to migrate into their territory. Caesar's help was sought, and he moved north to negotiate, unsuccessfully, with King Ariovistus of the Suebi. Ariovistus must have irked Caesar considerably by casting himself as Caesar's equal, even offering to share Gaul between the two of them. Caesar also learnt that more Germans were arriving in the area, so after some manoeuvring by the two armies there was a battle some 25 kilometres from the Rhine. Ariovistus was defeated; the Suebi were forced to retreat back across the Rhine, and their hold over the Gauls was broken.

This marked the end of the first crucial year of Caesar's campaigns. He had taken on two enemies of Rome and won, unlike his predecessors half-a-century earlier. At the same time Roman influence had been decisively extended northwards, so that most of the more centralised Gaulish tribes now came within Rome's orbit.[25] That winter six legions were left in garrison in Sequanian territory. In view of this, it is not surprising that we learn of 'conspiracies' amongst the Belgic tribes a little to the north, presumably in reaction to the implied threat that the legions represented. In the spring of 57 BC Caesar advanced north, almost immediately gaining a valuable ally in the tribe of the Remi, who were to remain loyal throughout the war. Other tribes also submitted, such as the powerful Bellovaci, who were allied with the Aedui, and thus succumbed to pressure from the Aedui to surrender to Rome. Here we see the political structure of Gaul working to Caesar's advantage, allowing him to make large territorial gains without any real resistance.[26] This especially applied to Normandy and Brittany, where Caesar's legate Crassus received the surrender of many small tribes.

Fighting against the Belgae was effectively over after a single spectacular battle with the tribe of the Nervii on the banks of the River Sambre.[27] This was probably Caesar's first opportunity to witness the fighting capabilities of one of the Belgic peoples, for which he clearly developed a good deal of respect. He praises their courage in launching an attack, and when the survivors surrendered to him he took them into his protection to make sure that the now defenceless Nervii were not attacked by neighbouring tribes. This special treatment was to continue into the post-Caesarian period, when the capital of the Nervian *civitas* Bagacum (modern Bavai), became a key part of the road network of Gallia Belgica (see chapter 3).

Operations against the Belgae in 57 BC were concluded with an assault on a hillfort of the Aduatuci, further to the east. Rome must have been well satisfied with Caesar's achievements in Gaul so far, and he himself believed that 'peace had been brought to the whole of Gaul'.[28] Fifteen days of thanksgiving were voted in celebration, an unprecedented length of time. Only Aquitaine and the Massif Central remained to be conquered, so it seemed, and it was apparently felt that these areas would be easier to subdue, given that Caesar had effectively pushed north-west past them. The troops that winter were stationed along the Loire Valley, in a good central position to supervise the Gauls and prepare for next year's campaigns, which were perhaps intended to be in the central and south-western parts of Gaul. As things turned out, 56 BC was spent dealing with the first of the major rebellions, coming at a time when the northern Gauls now fully recognised Roman intentions.

The rebellion took place in Normandy and Brittany, and is chiefly associated with the tribe of the Veneti, who had control over the maritime trade of the area and were considered to be expert seafarers.[29] The seeds of the rebellion were sown when high-ranking Roman officials were seized, apparently to be used as bargaining counters for the recovery of Venetic

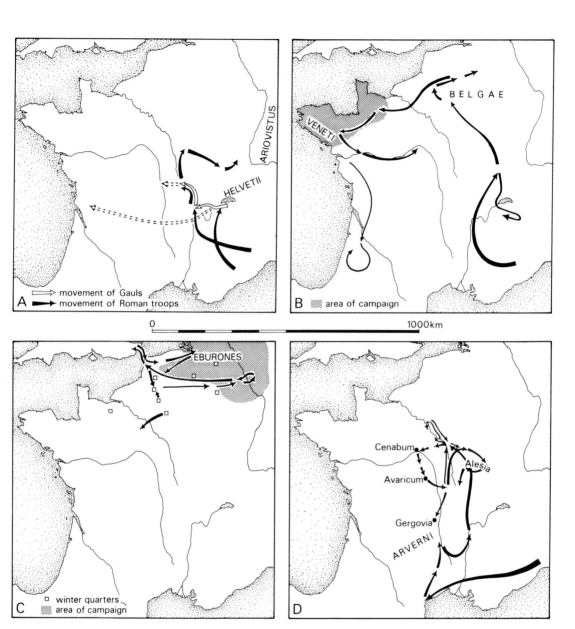

Caesar's campaigns in Gaul
and Germany. A 58 BC;
B 57–56 BC; C 55–53 BC;
D 52 BC.

hostages held by the Romans. This provoked a swift and ruthless reaction
from Caesar. Troops proceeded to take the multitude of small coastal
hillforts one by one, and a fleet was constructed to confront the Veneti at
sea as well. At first the Roman action was a failure, since the Veneti were
able to retreat from one hillfort to another by sea, and the Romans were
powerless to prevent this because their own fleet was not yet ready.
Eventually, however, there was a major sea-battle in which the Romans
virtually wiped out the Venetic fleet, using grappling hooks to pull down
their rigging. This disaster was soon to be followed by the surrender of the

Veneti's land-based forces and a terrible retribution from Caesar – the elders of the tribe were executed and the rest sold as slaves. Such an act was designed to discourage other tribes from seizing envoys or staging rebellions, but this policy failed since Armorican tribes are known to have rebelled again some two years later.

It is obvious from Caesar's narrative that the campaign against the Veneti took up much of 56 BC. But troops were fighting elsewhere at the same time, and Caesar relied heavily on his legates Crassus, Sabinus and Labienus to prevent further rebellions in the newly conquered areas. P. Licinius Crassus, in fact, had the essential task of completing what may have been the original strategic plan – an advance down the western side of Gaul into Aquitaine. In this he was highly successful, defeating a large force assembled against him and receiving the surrender of almost all the tribes of the south-west, a region which was to become the peaceful and very prosperous province of Aquitania. Crassus' achievement in subduing an enormous area with a relatively small force of Roman troops was the equal of any of Caesar's own exploits, but inevitably it was downplayed by Caesar.[30]

At the same time that Crassus was reporting his victories in the south-west, Caesar himself was failing miserably in the far north-east of Gaul. He had decided to mount an autumn campaign against two tribes that had refused to surrender to him, the Menapii and Morini. These were coastal peoples occupying the marshlands and forests of Belgium and southern Holland, and they were able to use the terrain to considerable advantage.[31] In effect, they retreated into the most inaccessible regions, and Caesar was unable to pursue them. This was one of the few successful tactics employed by the Gauls against the Romans, and it was to be used again to much greater effect by the Germans during Roman operations across the Rhine.

By the end of the year an uneasy peace had settled over Gaul, and, to judge from the events of the next two years, Caesar needed to expand his sphere of operations in order to keep up the momentum of military (and hence political) achievement. His eyes turned first to Germany, then to Britain. A migration of two German tribes into Belgic Gaul drew Caesar into his German adventure, but not before these tribes suffered the worst massacre of the whole war at his hands. The Usipetes and Tencteri had apparently crossed the Rhine because they were being harassed by the more powerful Suebi, and in doing so were probably following a well-established pattern of westward movement that had already brought the mixed peoples of the Belgae into northern Gaul. However, Caesar was determined to establish a secure boundary to Gaul along the Rhine, and rejected advances by German envoys asking for permission to settle. He goes to considerable lengths to portray the Germans as deceitful and treacherous, and therefore not to be trusted in negotiation. This is clearly to justify his own attack after having detained their envoys. With apparently no Roman losses, most of the 430,000 Germans were killed or drowned while trying to recross the Rhine.[32]

Caesar followed up his actions against the Usipetes and Tencteri by crossing the Rhine in a display of Roman military might and bridge-building skill. The Germans, however, retreated into the forests and hills, using the same tactics as the Morini and Menapii had done earlier, so that Caesar was not able to confront them. After eighteen days on the far side of the Rhine Caesar returned, breaking down the bridge behind him. This may seem to have been a less than successful venture, but nevertheless the operations can be judged a diplomatic success, since German tribes were fearful of Caesar and he was able to set up links with friendly peoples such as the Ubii. In another sense the expedition across the Rhine was to have far-reaching consequences for Roman plans for imperial expansion, since Augustus was later to follow up Caesar's initiative and launch a full-scale invasion of the region.

The two expeditions to Britain, in 55 and 54 BC, can be viewed in the same perspective. They were of little consequence militarily, although they may have succeeded in their avowed aim of putting a stop to British aid being sent to Gaulish resistance. But in diplomatic and symbolic terms they were an undoubted success, and it is very probable that Claudius was consciously following in his ancestor's footsteps when he invaded Britain in AD 43.

The second British expedition also had a more serious purpose in Caesar's eyes. The apparent success of the conquest of Gaul led Caesar to choose Britain as the next area to conquer, probably because he (rightly) judged it an easier military prospect than Germany, on the basis of his reconnaissances into both these areas in 55. South-eastern Britain had a similar tribal structure to Belgic Gaul, and the settled, fairly centralised tribes would be easier to subdue than the Germans with their shifting populations and retreating tactics. With hindsight, a more sensible alternative to Britain might have been a military campaign in the Alps, since the western Alps had for a long time formed a hostile tract between the provinces of Gallia Transalpina and Cisalpina. However, a campaign in this area did not take place, and we do not even know if Caesar considered the option, although if he did, he may have been influenced by the defeat of a Roman force there in 57 BC.

Caesar decided not to stay in Britain in the winter of 54 'because of the danger that sudden risings might break out in Gaul'.[33] This fear was fully justified by events, and his plans for the annexation of Britain had to be abandoned. The first incident was during the setting up of the winter camps in Belgic Gaul. One, at Atuatuca in the territory of the Eburones,[34] was beseiged by the local tribe. This was the prelude to the worst Roman loss of the whole war, when the troops in this camp (about a legion and a half in total) were tricked into moving out of their defences by Ambiorix, the Eburonian leader. The camp was the most easterly and therefore most exposed to attack, and Ambiorix offered safe passage to the next winter camp 80 kilometres away. After some vacillation, the Roman commanders, Sabinus and Cotta, decided to go along with this plan, and were promptly ambushed by the Eburones. Virtually every man was killed, or committed suicide the same night. This was one of the Gauls' few successful battles in the whole of the conquest period, and it gave them enthusiasm for the later, much larger rebellion of 52 BC. Ambiorix was clearly a skilful leader, able to keep a disciplined hold on his warriors.

Attention now turned to the winter camp which had been the intended destination of Sabinus and Cotta's troops. It was rapidly beseiged by hostile Belgae, who surprised the Romans by building a Roman-style siegework with rampart, ditch and moveable towers. They also managed to set fire to the Roman camp by using heated sling stones and fire-arrows. While this grim siege was going on, Caesar was busy collecting troops from the other winter camps. His arrival relieved the siege and brought an end to the immediate problem for the Romans.

Caesar was faced with a longer-term problem, however, because of this rebellion. Ambiorix's success fired the imagination of the other Gaulish leaders, and rumours of possible rebellions swept the whole region. To counteract these hostile activities, Caesar evidently decided on a major show of strength which would decisively subdue the Belgae. Much of 53 BC was devoted to this, and it is recorded that Caesar did not shave or cut his hair until the Roman defeat had been atoned for by the capture of Ambiorix and the annihilation of the Eburones. This tribe was isolated by Roman military action and its lands laid waste. Other tribes then moved into the area to plunder it, and eventually even the name of the Eburones disappeared, being replaced in Imperial times by a people known as the Tungri. But Ambiorix himself escaped the Roman dragnet.

The year ended with a legal inquiry by Caesar, designed to show that the region was now subservient to Rome. Gaul was now being treated as a conquered province, and this may have been one of the major reasons why the following winter was spent by the Gauls in concocting a last-ditch rebellion against the Roman presence. The rebels were spurred on in part by their knowledge of political developments in Rome itself, where Pompey was gradually aligning himself against Caesar. Caesar's support was not as strong as before, and there were moves afoot to bring prosecutions against him after his term of office in Gaul had expired. The rebels assumed, therefore, that Caesar would be too preoccupied with the political situation to give his full attention to Gaul.

All of Gaul was involved in the revolt except the Remi and some of the tribes in Aquitaine; even previously staunch allies of Rome, such as the Aedui, were drawn in. It was orchestrated largely by the peoples of central Gaul, an area that so far had had little direct involvement in the fighting. Caesar's campaigns from 57 BC onwards had been almost exclusively in an area north and north-east of the line of the River Loire, and he must have assumed that the more developed tribes further south were pacified and not likely to pose any further problems. This especially applied to the Arverni in the Massif Central, whom Caesar's activities had not touched at

Nineteenth-century statue of Vercingetorix erected on the site of the siege at Alesia. It is popularly said to incorporate a likeness of the Emperor Napoleon III.

all. It is all the more surprising in the light of this that the leader of the revolt came from the Arverni. He was Vercingetorix, son of an Arvernian noble who had been killed for trying to set himself up as king.[35] Caesar acknowledges the capabilities of Vercingetorix as a general who was able to sustain the morale of the Gauls when things went against them. The Gauls themselves were also happy to have Vercingetorix as their supreme leader; he must have enjoyed a considerable reputation before his elevation to power, to judge from the speed with which he was acclaimed as commander-in-chief.

The revolt started at Cenabum (modern Orléans) and rapidly spread amongst the tribes of central Gaul, thus cutting off the bulk of Caesar's legions, still in winter camps to the north, from Caesar himself, who was in Italy. The rebels clearly hoped to have wiped out the Roman presence in Gaul before Caesar could meet up with his troops and take charge of the situation. A diversion was also created by a group of rebels from tribes to the south of the Arverni, who marched on Narbonne in the hope of sacking it and forcing Caesar to deal with this problem first.

Caesar took up the challenge and hurried to Narbonne with some troops available in the area. He was too quick for the diversionary expedition, which he forced to retreat, giving him the advantage in what action to take next. He decided to attack the Arverni via the difficult mountainous terrain of the Cevennes. Complete surprise was achieved by this move, because no one expected the snow-covered passes to be crossed at that time of year, let alone by an army. This strategy turned the tables on Vercingetorix, who was forced to retire from fomenting the rebellion further north in order to protect his own homeland, exactly as Caesar had planned. As soon as Caesar learned that Vercingetorix had played into his hands, he marched day and night to the north-west to meet up with his army. The initial thrust of the revolt had been thwarted.

The war against Vercingetorix, however, was only just starting. It was largely centred on oppida, with each side attacking, occupying or destroying a series of hillforts in order to disrupt the supplies available to the other side or upset their tactical calculations. It is noticeable how prominently oppida figure in 52 BC, in contrast to the campaigning further north, and this must reflect the greater degree of urbanisation among the peoples of central Gaul.

A typical move in the war of the oppida was Vercingetorix's attack on Gorgobina, the capital of the pro-Roman Boii. This was designed to force Caesar to come to the aid of the Boii in order to protect his reputation amongst his Gaulish allies. Caesar's countermove, an attack on another oppidum, Vallaunodunum of the Senones, to obtain food supplies, followed by an advance on Cenabum, was undertaken for much the same motives. Vercingetorix was forced to end his siege of Gorgobina to protect the territory of the Bituriges.

Vercingetorix's strategy for the conduct of his campaign also involved a scorched-earth policy to cut off supplies to the Romans. In this he seems to have been quite successful, for Caesar refers several times to the difficulties of obtaining grain and other resources for his troops. However, this policy could work both ways, and Vercingetorix himself obviously encountered similar difficulties from time to time. In the territory of the Bituriges twenty oppida were burnt to prevent the Romans using their resources, all except the capital, Avaricum (modern Bourges). Vercingetorix had intended to burn Avaricum too, but the inhabitants persuaded him that it could be defended against Caesar, and so it was left in occupation.

This was a bad mistake at a crucial point in the campaign, for Caesar promptly laid siege to the oppidum, locking up 40,000 people inside and pinning down Vercingetorix, who hung back from an all-out assault to relieve the siege. The siege is described in some detail in Caesar's narrative, and was clearly difficult for both Gaul and Roman alike. The defenders had a number of ruses for harassing the Roman siegeworks, for instance by undermining the towers with tunnels, or raising their defences to force the Roman towers to be built even higher.[36] None of their tactics prevented the Romans from carrying on, however, and eventually the town succumbed to a direct assault. Only 800 managed to escape the ensuing massacre.

Vercingetorix was a strong enough leader to be able to hold his troops together after such a major set-back. The war of the oppida went on, focused now on the Arvernian hillfort of Gergovia.[37] Caesar's description of his attempts to take this site paint a graphic picture of how well defended an oppidum could be, both by nature and by Gaulish technical expertise. It proved impossible to besiege in the conventional manner with towers and earthworks, and the direct assaults that were launched against the ramparts were too costly in human lives to make any impact. Vercingetorix was content to occupy the surrounding hills with the aim of preventing Roman troops from taking them. Effectively, a stalemate had been reached, and Caesar was in an increasingly difficult position, facing the prospect of his first personal failure in an action against the Gauls.

Caesar's problems were compounded by the vacillation and then defection of the Aedui.[38] This was extremely serious, since Caesar had come to rely on the large territory of the Aedui as a vital safety-net in his overall strategy during the rebellion. His men could rest there, replenish essential supplies and retreat to it if the worst came to the worst. Now the nearest safe haven was the territory of the Allobroges, within the existing province of Gallia Transalpina to the east (which Caesar refers to as the Provincia, a name that has survived as modern Provence).

This was the low point of the entire war for Caesar, and he was faced with a choice: either a retreat to the Provincia because of lack of supplies, or a quick, risky dash north to meet up with a detachment of four legions under the command of Titus Labienus, at that time at Paris.[39] As we might expect, Caesar's nature did not let him take the easy option, and he ordered his troops on a rapid forced march to the north. Such a bold strategy was

Reconstruction of part of Caesar's siegeworks at Alesia, in the Archéodrome at Beaune. It is based upon Caesar's descriptions and the excavation work of Napoleon III in the 1860s. In the foreground are the traps and snares to deter the enemy, and behind the towers and palisade of the siegework circumvallation.

brilliantly successful, taking the Gauls completely by surprise, and he was able to reach territory where supplies were readily available. Labienus, too, successfully retreated from Paris, and the two armies met up to the south of Agedincum (modern Sens).

After a brief respite fighting resumed as the two opposing forces moved closer to each other, and Vercingetorix instigated a cavalry engagement. The Gauls were defeated, a serious blow to morale, up to this point buoyed up by the prospect of imminent victory. Use of cavalry was an important part of Vercingetorix's strategy for harassing and cutting off Roman supply lines, so to stabilise his forces and restore the cavalry strength, he decided to move the Gaulish army to the oppidum of Alesia (modern Alise-Ste Reine), where he was promptly besieged by Caesar.

Alesia marks the climax of the events of 52 BC, and the heroic defence of the oppidum by Vercingetorix's forces has long been a potent symbol in French history. As might be expected, the literature on this episode is enormous, especially following the excavations by Napoleon III in the nineteenth century, which added archaeological confirmation of Caesar's description of the siege.[40] It is a description of fascinating detail which, like the rest of Caesar's writings, opens a vital window onto the operational side of the Roman army in the late Republic.

The site of Alesia is in a commanding position at the confluence of two streams. The oppidum stands on an isolated hill, with hills of similar height all around but at some distance away. This makes it ideal for defence, but at the same time possible to surround with siegeworks. The inner ditch of the siegeworks was filled with water from the streams for part of its length, and behind it were fields of barbed iron spikes (*stimuli*) and sharpened stakes (*cippi*) set in the ground, together with half-hidden foot-traps with sharpened stakes in them (*lilia*). Behind these again were two more ditches and the rampart, further protected by entanglements of branches. The rampart had a breastwork and towers at frequent intervals, plus redoubts for detachments from the legions. These redoubts and various larger camps behind the siegeworks were placed to occupy the surrounding hills wherever practicable, and were protected by an outer rampart some 22 kilometres long which enclosed the whole of Caesar's army.

It was a massive undertaking and, if our understanding of Caesar's narrative and the results of excavation are correct, it represents an earthwork some 40 kilometres long, approximately a third of the length of Hadrian's Wall, built in under thirty days by probably ten legions (up to 50,000 men). No wonder, then, that the Gauls were intimidated by such strenuous activity. While this had been going on, though, the Gauls had not been idle. A large relieving army had been assembled – 8,000 cavalry and 240,000 infantry according to Caesar, who usefully enumerates the number of men sent from each tribe.[41]

The relieving army moved up and occupied a nearby hill, confident that their large numbers would bring about victory. Over the next few days successive assaults from the Gaulish relieving army and from Vercingetorix's own forces within the seigeworks pressed the Roman defences. The enormous numbers of casualties on both sides is dramatically represented by skeletons found at the foot of Mount Réa. Finally, the Gauls were defeated. The relieving army could do no more, and so it promptly left the area and the warriors returned to their various tribes.

Vercingetorix and his forces in the oppidum were left to their fate. Vercingetorix offered to surrender himself so as to save the lives of his men. The rebellion was over, and indeed so was the conquest of Gaul, apart from sporadic uprisings the following year. Vercingetorix was imprisoned and later executed after Caesar's triumph in Rome in 46 BC. All the men in the oppidum were allocated as slaves to the Roman soldiers, with the exception of 20,000 Arverni and Aedui who were allowed to go home because Caesar wanted to secure the loyalty of these tribes. For Caesar the outcome of the siege was naturally a great personal triumph, earning him twenty days' thanksgiving in Rome and the political might that was to carry him towards the Civil War.

Before leaving the period of Caesar's conquest of Gaul, a word must be said about the archaeological remains that are often attributed to his campaigns. Alesia has now been generally accepted as a Caesarian period siegework from such datable finds as Celtic coins of Vercingetorix. It rightly takes its place as one of the most important surviving traces of the late Republican army in action. Other sites, however, are not so clear cut, despite the widespread claims made for suggestive remains the length and breadth

Aerial photograph of a possible Caesarian military installation next to the oppidum at Liercourt-Hérondelle in Picardy. It shows up as a dark-coloured cropmark running through the fields in the photograph. The oppidum rampart is visible in the background.

of Gaul. Most of the sites called 'Caesar's Camp' have now been dismissed, usually as native Iron Age sites having no connection with the Roman army at all, but there are a handful of sites discovered by aerial photography that deserve to be taken more seriously.

One of these is just outside the hillfort of Liercourt-Hérondelle (Somme), where a ditched enclosure may have military connections. Excavations have found Iron Age pottery and coins contemporary with the Gallic War, and it has been suggested that the site represents a Roman auxiliary garrison of Gaulish mercenaries guarding the hillfort, or possibly that it was an outlying part of a larger garrison including legionaries that was occupying the hillfort after having expelled the local Gauls.[42] The archaeological evidence is not precise enough, indeed never could be precise enough, to tell us which year of campaigning this camp belonged to, and it is unfortunately too ambiguous in character to be confidently ascribed to the Roman army. Three other camps in the Somme region are much more positively military in origin, but they suffer from another problem – the dating evidence puts them in the Augustan period or later. The sites are Folleville, Breteuil and Vendeuil-Caply, all similar in shape and within sight of one another on the tops of hills. They are well defended and probably represent a military response to a threat from the local tribe (the Bellovaci). A possible historical context for these camps exists in the records of disturbances in this area in the Augustan period (see below).

Other traces of Roman military sites in Gaul are even later in date, and correspondingly more difficult to account for in what was becoming a peaceful province well behind the action on the Rhine frontier. At Aulnay-de-Saintonge in south-west Gaul there is a definite legionary camp, perhaps for a detachment from the 14th legion which is known in the area from tombstones. It dates to the first century AD, possibly from the 20s onwards, and the remains suggest that it was not just a temporary camp, but was in occupation for some years. Similarly at Arlaines near Soissons recent excavations have revealed a military site occupied from the Augustan period onwards; this by the late first century AD had been rebuilt in stone for an auxiliary cavalry unit. Nearby, at Mauchamp, the legionary temporary camp often attributed to Caesar's crossing of the River Aisne in 57 BC, is dated on typological grounds to the Flavian period. Finally, the site of Mirebeau near Dijon is the most interesting of the group. Some of the finds suggest an Augustan date, but the site that showed up so clearly from the air in the drought of 1976 is a legionary fortress, apparently for the 8th legion, and for detachments from others as well. The date is Flavian, and the site seems to have been in occupation for some time, which is curious when it is known that the local tribe of the Lingones was friendly to Rome.[43]

There are possible military contexts for most of these sites, such as the revolt of Florus and Sacrovir (AD 21), the invasion of Britain (AD 43) or the Civil War of AD 69–70. However, it is special pleading to try to attribute each of the sites to a known military event, especially when it is apparent that some of them were permanently occupied and intended to garrison an area for some time. The general conclusion must be that Gaul in the first century AD was less pacified than has been previously thought, and the need for an army presence correspondingly greater, particularly along the strategic roads to the Rhine frontier. There are many other sites in Gaul with artefacts of military origin, and so the handful mentioned may be just a selection from a large garrison. More excavation evidence is urgently needed to sort out this problem. What is clear, though, is that military activity in Gaul went on long after Caesar's departure, and even after Augustus' reign.

Augustus in Germany

After Caesar we know far less about military operations in Gaul and Germany. The detail found in Caesar's *Commentaries* is not repeated, and, in the immediate twenty years following the Gallic War, the Civil War drew the energies of the Roman forces. Only a skeleton garrison remained in the interior of Gaul, based in the old winter camps along the Loire and the Saône, in other words across central Gaul. There was virtually no actual fighting in Gaul by the protagonists in the Civil War, with one important

Map of the provinces and *civitates* of Gaul as established in the early Roman period, following Augustus' organisation of the provinces in 27 BC.

exception. The Greek colony of Massalia declared for Pompey, or to be more precise, did not declare for Caesar when he arrived in the area on his way to Spain in 49 BC. Caesar needed to have the co-operation of the city to prevent the other side from using Massalia's port or fleet, and so he resolved on an attack to force their submission. This was frustrated by the ingenuity of the defenders, and the attack degenerated into a five-month-long siege, only broken after Caesar had constructed a fleet that was able to inflict two defeats on the city's navy. Massalia submitted, and its long independence was at an end. Henceforward it became a city like any other in southern Gaul.[44]

In 39 M. Vipsanius Agrippa was appointed governor by Octavian (later Augustus), and he conducted campaigns in the south-west and the north-east: the two trouble-spots of Caesar's final year, which were continuing to prove difficult for the Roman administration. Agrippa was probably the first to set about providing an infrastructure for the province, especially the road system, which is traditionally credited to him.[45] Lugdunum (modern Lyon), already on an important road from the south, was chosen as the centre for a network which radiated also to the west, north and north-east.

The choice was made because Lugdunum was the northernmost colony in the Rhône Valley, set up a few years earlier by Plancus in 44 BC (see chapter 3). This decision played a part in the later choice of the city as the capital of what was known from 27 BC as the 'Three Gauls', the three provinces of Gallia Belgica, Gallia Lugdunensis and Aquitania, corresponding roughly with Caesar's famous tripartite division of Gaul.[46] The south was a fourth province, now known as Gallia Narbonensis.

The beginnings of a provincial administration did not mean that Gaul was pacified, however, for the Civil War was still going on elsewhere in the Empire and it was difficult to devote attention to the region. Troops had to be withdrawn for the Battle of Actium in 31 BC, with the result that there were disturbances again in the south-west and north-east. In 28 BC troops were sent back to Gaul to deal with the problems in the south-west, after which this area was more or less pacified, thanks partly to the conquest at about the same time of neighbouring northern Spain. Augustus himself visited Gaul in the following year, during which the division of Gaul into four provinces appears to have been formally set up. He realised that the Rhineland and the eastern frontier of Gaul posed the remaining problems for regional security, and were also the best areas of opportunity for new conquests. Accordingly, military attention turned increasingly towards this part of the Empire, as Augustus entertained thoughts of emulating the achievements of his illustrious predecessor.[47]

In view of the growing strategic importance of the Rhineland and the need for swift communications between Rome and the army, the first campaigns in the region were in the Alps. Up to this time the only land route controlled by the Romans between Gaul and Italy was along the Mediterranean coast, and there was a large zone of independent territory separating the two areas. This independent territory was occupied by many small tribes, who controlled the Alpine passes and made a living from exacting tolls on merchants and army units passing through. They could also harass Roman troops if they felt so inclined, and had defeated one of Caesar's legions on the Swiss side of the Great St Bernard Pass. Augustus therefore sent an army into the Val d'Aosta in 25 BC to defeat the Salassi on the Italian side of this pass. The route was now opened up and the road system was rapidly extended to take in this important short-cut to the north.[48]

These military operations were merely a preliminary to the much more ambitious campaign of 15 BC, when all the Alps east of Helvetian territory were taken and the Alpine Foreland occupied. It was a classic application of the pincer strategy. One of the commanders, Tiberius, advanced east from Gaul to the Rhine Valley in the vicinity of Lake Constance, where he fought against the tribe of the Vindelici, who had advanced from the upper Danube area to meet him. There was a Roman victory, and Tiberius moved north to explore the region where the Danube rises. Meanwhile, the other commander, Drusus, came over the newly conquered Alpine passes, annexed

Augustus' victory monument at La Turbie (Tropaeum Alpium) above Monaco. It commemorates the conquest of the peoples of the Alps in 15 BC, and dominates the main coast road from Italy to Gaul.

the lands of the Raeti in eastern Switzerland, and eventually met up with Tiberius somewhere near Lake Constance. The campaigning had been confined to the valleys, as far as we can tell from the sources, with the aim of isolating possibly hostile Alpine tribesmen, rather than engaging in a long campaign against them. These victories in the Alps fulfilled the aim of securing the Italian and Gallic frontiers and, with the peaceful annexation of Noricum in the Austrian Alps, completed the conquest of this difficult terrain with remarkable ease.[49] Augustus celebrated his success by building a massive monument at the western tip of the Alpine region, where the mountains come down to the sea at La Turbie above Monaco and meet the old coast road to Gaul. This was a powerful reminder to travellers of the Romans' military might, listing the forty-four tribes in the Alps that the emperor had defeated, and it was possibly intended to match the earlier victory monument that Pompey had placed at the other end of the same route in the Pyrenees.[50]

Augustus' attention could now be concentrated entirely on Germany. He visited Gaul in 16–15 BC to assess the situation for himself, following the defeat of a legionary force under M. Lollius at the hands of the Germanic Sugambri in north-eastern Gaul the previous year. Except for this north-eastern region, Gaul was effectively pacified, with Romanisation proceeding apace to judge from the archaeological evidence (see chapter 3). The time was now ripe for an offensive across the Rhine into Germany, partly to deal with the problem of border security in the north-east, but much more importantly to gain new provinces for the Roman Empire. There has been much debate about Augustus' exact intentions in entering Germany, the older view being that Rome needed secure frontiers in northern and eastern Europe, and the best way to achieve that was by conquering Germany, Bohemia and Illyricum. Current thinking is that Augustus had the more aggressive dream of world-wide empire, the product of a philosophy of Rome's 'manifest destiny' in world history. He considered invading Britain, but decided on Germany instead, to be followed by Illyricum, Bohemia, Dacia and who knows what other lands of the far north-east.[51] Nobody at that time knew the geographical immensity of the Eurasian landmass, and thus how impossible that dream of world domination.

The winter quarters for the legions were moved from their old, now redundant positions in the interior of Gaul to the banks of the Rhine. Sites such as Neuss, Xanten and Vechten are known from archaeological investigations, Neuss being the only one thought to have existed prior to these campaigns. To the rear, in eastern Gaul, garrisons of auxiliary troops appear to have been stationed in more sensitive areas as a precaution, an example being in the Treveran oppidum of the Titelberg.[52]

Campaigning began in earnest in 12 BC, when Drusus countered a pre-emptive strike by the Sugambri across the Rhine. He defeated them and advanced into Westphalia. Later in the same year he sent a naval expedition into the North Sea, via a canal he had ordered the troops to build between the Rhine and the Ijssel Meer (the *fossa Drusiana*). The result of this was that the local tribe, the Frisii, submitted and for a time at least was part of the Roman Empire as a client kingdom. This helped to secure the northern flank while the armies advanced to the east. In 11 BC Drusus moved across the Rhine and along the valley of the River Lippe in Westphalia, and this rapidly became the normal route for Roman advances into north German territory. He went as far as the River Weser, encountering the tribes of the Usipetes and the Sugambri on the way. Doubtless they used the tactic familiar from Caesar's day of retreating in the face of the Roman army, but we do know that on this occasion the Sugambri managed to harass the legions and almost defeat them. That winter some troops probably stayed

The Roman bridge at Trier (Augusta Treverorum) provides the footings for the modern bridge across the Moselle. Traces have been found of an earlier wooden bridge dated 18–17BC by dendrochronology. At this time the crossing would have been of strategic importance in the build-up to the invasion of Germany.

on the far side of the Rhine in the Lippe area, for a large camp has been excavated at Oberaden. This site has been dated by dendrochronological (tree-ring) analysis on several samples of wood from wells dug by the Roman troops, with the astonishingly accurate date of the summer of 11 BC for its construction.[53]

The following year Drusus set out from Mainz, further south on the Rhine, with the aim of completing another pincer movement by advancing north-east through the Wetterau area to join the territory already taken further north. It took more than one summer campaign to achieve this, for we learn that this tactic was repeated in 9 BC, when there appears to have been a double advance from both the Lippe and the Wetterau. Roman troops marched far to the east in that year, attacking the Marcomanni, Suebi and Cherusci on their way to the banks of the River Elbe. Drusus did not cross this river, possibly for fear of antagonising the German tribes there unnecessarily, and the army moved back to winter quarters nearer the Rhine soon after. It was on this journey back that a major tragedy occured: Drusus broke his leg in a riding accident and died later of an infection. This did not mean the end of the German campaign, however, since Tiberius took charge and campaigned in 8 BC against the Sugambri again. He gained a major victory, and the remnants of the tribe (some 40,000 people) were moved forcibly to the west bank of the Rhine. Tiberius celebrated a triumph at Rome in the following year.[54]

For the next few years an uneasy peace settled on Germany. Much of the region remained unoccupied by Roman troops, however, and the area they claimed by right of conquest was much larger than the area they actually held. Various forts and permanent military sites were set up, notably along the Lippe Valley and in the Wetterau, the two starting points for advance into the interior of the country. The greater number of sites are known from the former area, possibly because it was considered safe to install a permanent presence there, which of course was a major step towards consolidating the conquest. The best known of the Lippe sites is the legionary fortress at Haltern, extensively excavated at the beginning of the century, and the earliest known imperial fortress for which we have something like the complete plan. It was supplemented by stores bases and temporary camps elsewhere in the valley, of which many probably remain to be found.[55] Further west, on the Gaulish side of the Rhine, Roman occupation was much more settled, with several permanent bases and the beginnings of provincial organisation. An important indication of this was the founding of an altar (the *ara Ubiorum*) at Cologne as the provincial cult centre (see chapter 6). At this period, though, it is unlikely that there was a definite boundary between the two provinces of Gaul and Germany, and nominally at least the western side of the Rhine was part of Gallia Belgica, except for the zone controlled by the army along the bank of the river itself. The bulk of the army was garrisoned in the Rhineland, in fortresses such as Dangstetten, Mainz, Cologne, Xanten and Vechten. It was a formidable concentration of military might and a significant proportion of the entire Roman army, demonstrating the seriousness of Augustus' plans for Germany.[56]

While all this was going on in Germany, Augustus' generals had been active further south-east, in Illyricum, as well. The conquest of this area, and of Germany, together with the earlier annexation of the eastern Alpine province of Noricum, opened the way for fresh advance to the east into the territory of the Marcomanni in Bohemia (modern Czechoslovakia). Accordingly, in AD 6 a massive offensive was launched, probably the most ambitious of Augustus' reign, involving twelve legions in two forces. The familiar pincer strategy was used, with one army advancing from Germany and the other from the south. To make this possible, active troops were removed from their stations in the Rhineland, Illyricum and elsewhere, leaving a potentially dangerous vacuum which the local peoples were soon to exploit. The offensive had barely begun when it had to be abandoned because Illyricum had risen in revolt. Large numbers of troops were tied down attempting to crush the rebellion during the period AD 7–9, and it was clearly a difficult time for the army – and for Augustus, whose cherished ambitions were running into the sands. According to Pliny, he is reported as thinking of suicide at this time, as the atmosphere of confident expansion evaporated.[57]

These developments go a long way to explaining why German policy was subdued during these years. Quinctilius Varus was the governor, apparently there with a brief to bring in a more recognisable provincial administration, perhaps including taxation of the native population. He appears not to have been a military man, but of course had to lead the army when necessary. This was what he was doing when he was in summer camp in the interior of Germany in AD 9. Resistance to Rome was being stirred up by Arminius, a leader of the Cherusci who had previously served in the Roman army, probably as an officer in charge of auxiliary troops. Arminius was obviously familiar with the ways of the Roman military as a result, and he was able to lure Varus into a trap. Collaborators persuaded Varus to march out to deal with a disturbance, and he was ambushed while crossing heavily wooded country. The result was disastrous, indeed one of the worst defeats ever suffered by Roman troops: three legions were wiped out, and even the cavalry that escaped the ambush were killed later on. Varus himself committed suicide at the battle site, and all the remaining Roman forces on the eastern side of the Rhine fled. The only resistance put up to the Germans was at Aliso (possibly Haltern), from which an organised retreat to the Gaulish side of the Rhine was made. Luckily for the Romans, the victorious Germans did not attempt to cross the Rhine, and legions were brought up from further south to defend it.[58]

At a stroke the province of Germany was shattered. Although there were campaigns in the area a few years later, led by Germanicus, these had the character of punitive expeditions to recover the standards of the lost legions, rather then full-blown attempts at reconquest. For Augustus it was a bitter blow in his old age, only partly mitigated by the news received in Rome just before of success in Illyricum. Henceforward he had no offensive policy, and gave instructions before his death that Tiberius should not expand the territory of the Empire. The frontier of Gaul ran along the Rhine, and apart from a nominal territory under the control of the 'German garrison' (*exercitus Germaniae*), Roman Germany ceased to exist.

Two questions about the Varus disaster remain – the minor one of where it took place, and the much more important problem of why. The battle site is refered to in ancient sources as being in the *saltus Teutoburgensis*, and scholars have generated a vast literature suggesting possible locations. The most popular spot is the Teutoburger Wald in the vicinity of the Harz Mountains, but the name itself is modern and derived from the ancient reference. A recently proposed alternative is slightly further west, not far from Paderborn.[59] Finding the exact site is a somewhat fruitless activity and probably does not enlarge our understanding of the episode greatly, but there is general agreement that Varus was defeated in a region on the fringe of the permanently held territory. This is relevant to the larger question of why Varus was attacked and why he was defeated, in that the area was clearly not as peaceful as the Romans thought it to be. Their attempts to impose provincial administration must have stirred up resentment and resistance, with Arminius emerging as a leader in much the same way as Vercingetorix had done in Gaul. But there were important differences between Germany and Gaul which make it questionable whether the Romans would ever have succeeded in pacifying the area. In culture and tribal organisation the Germans appear to have been relatively undeveloped in comparison with the Gauls (see chapter 1). Caesar appreciated that this made the Germans more difficult to subdue in military terms, and it has also led to the convincing modern explanation that the German social and economic system was too far removed from Roman ideas of normal provincial civilisation ever to have been able to adapt to them.[60] Had the Romans been victorious against Arminius, they would probably have ended up with a province dominated by a large military zone with little civilian development, much as occured in northern Britain.

FURTHER READING

Two studies in English draw together the evidence for the Republican conquest of southern Gaul, Stephen Dyson's *The Creation of the Roman Frontier* (1985) and C. Ebel's *Transalpine Gaul* (1976). Key sites of the period include Entremont (Benoit 1981) and Narbonne (Gayraud 1981).

Caesar's exploits in Gaul have generated a vast literature. The commentary by Napoléon III, *Histoire de Jules César* (1865/6), is one of the most important because it included archaeological work, such as on the siegeworks at Alesia. Le Gall (1980) provides a more recent survey of the same site. T. Rice-Holmes, *Caesar's Conquest of Gaul* (1911) is the fullest English treatment, tempered now by the comments in A. Wiseman's translation of Caesar, *The Battle for Gaul* (1980). Recent analyses of the war include J. Harmand, *Vercingétorix* (1984) and U. Maier, *Caesars Feldzüge in Gallien* (1978).

The Augustan period is admirably surveyed in C. Wells, *The German Policy of Augustus* (1972), which can be supplemented by a summary of recent archaeological work by Von Schnurbein (1981). Formigé (1949) discusses Augustus' trophy monument at La Turbie.

3

THE
URBAN
LANDSCAPE

The Roman ideal province was one with a stable, docile population, based either in towns or in villa-type rural estates. Towns were a key element in provincial organisation, since administration, business, entertainment and many other aspects of civilisation had an urban focus, from which their influence was felt in the surrounding countryside. The towns would ideally be linked by good communications to encourage economic production and hence allow the state to recover a satisfactory level of taxes.

In the newly conquered Gaul and Germany the Romans were confronted with what could be regarded as the very antithesis of their ideal. The population was predominantly rural and potentially warlike, although impoverished and weakened by the recent fighting. The oppida were not recognised as towns by the Romans, at least not as the sort of town that any self-respecting Roman would think of as civilised. Moreover, communications in Gaul were non-existent in Roman terms, as there were no proper roads or a developed water transport system. A matter that compounded the potential difficulties faced by the Romans was that, for some thirty years after Caesar's conquest of the north, civilian Gaul and Germany had been left to their own devices while more weighty military and political affairs were running their course elsewhere.

The new provinces were not an entirely gloomy prospect for the Roman governors, however. As we have seen, many aspects of late Iron Age civilisation predisposed the local population to be favourable to the classical way of life. The oppida did in fact provide some of the functions of a typical Roman town, while many of the tribes had large centralised organisations that could serve as suitable units of Roman administration. In addition, trade between Romans and Gauls had been lively up to the time of the conquest, and continued to bring Roman material goods into appreciative Gaulish hands.

The consequence of this was that when Augustus began to focus his attention on civilian Gaul, initially through his close friend Agrippa, who was governor in 39–37 and again in 19–17 BC, the scene was set for a remarkable transformation of the new province. Within a generation Celtic civilisation became Roman (or, more precisely, Romano-Celtic) and the Gaulish way of life gave place to one that was Gallo-Roman or Gallic. French archaeologists refer to the obvious changes in material culture as 'gallo-romaine précoce', dated roughly to the Augustan–Tiberian period, and marking the transition from Iron Age La Tène III to a fully fledged Roman provincial culture. A typical feature of 'gallo-romaine précoce' was, for instance, the rapid development of new types of pottery which drew their inspiration from Mediterranean Roman types such as Arretine ware. From the Augustan period in the south and in a wide band of territory leading from there to the Rhineland (where the army was stationed) we find local craftsmen producing distinctive local versions of Roman artefacts in great quantities. Their markets lay partly in the army garrisons of the Rhineland (see chapter 7), but also, more importantly for the Romanisation of Gaul, in the new towns that were being set up, which in themselves were a manifestation of the same rapid Romanisation. As we shall see, town life developed, like the artefact types, as a distinctive local variant of its Mediterranean progenitor, and it is fair to say that 'gallo-romaine précoce' set the pattern of provincial life – urban, rural, religious and economic – up to the third century.

It becomes important in the light of these developments to establish why such rapid Romanisation came about. After all, the defeated Gauls might easily have indulged in passive resistance, which would have nipped the emergence of provincial culture in the bud, given the relatively small numbers of Roman officials in the newly occupied territories. In other provinces, notably the northern parts of Britain, and indeed that area of Germany around the Rhine mouth, it is possible to see the results of resistance to Roman rule. Forts had to be continuously manned, Romanisation of the native population was almost non-existent, and the typical Roman infrastructure of towns and roads failed to develop except where sustained by the military.[1]

The fact that this did not happen in Gaul can best be attributed to a series of political changes amongst the leaders of the tribal aristocracy. 'Political' must here be taken in its widest sense to include cultural attitudes as well as directly political concerns. The main change came about as a simple consequence of military defeat by Caesar – the old aristocracy of the Gauls was founded upon success in warfare, and its prestige had been severely dented by the defeat. Their 'warrior culture' had failed to ensure the freedom of the Gauls, and the consequent loss of status by the tribal aristocracy obviously posed problems both for themselves and, more significantly, for the Romans. The Romans were concerned, since their normal method of establishing a new province was to use existing institutions, namely the aristocracy, whenever possible. Roman provincial governors effectively relied on local men to make their provinces run efficiently, and so they had to devise means of harnessing available administrative talent, and at the same time ensure that leaders could not build up anti-Roman followings.

The means they adopted in Gaul were twofold. Initially, previously anti-Roman warrior leaders were taken into the Roman army to serve as officers of auxiliary (non-Roman citizen) units, usually of cavalry. This enabled the Romans to keep an eye on potentially unruly Gaulish leaders. For their part the Gauls were willing to be part of this political volte-face because they could retain their status and position within society. Indeed, entire units were raised and led by local Gauls, who paid their troops in local coins, and who clearly were able to prolong their warrior status by realigning their loyalty in favour of the Romans.[2] There were risks in this policy, as the Romans were to discover when one of the local troop leaders, Civilis, was able to use his position to stage a rebellion against the Roman state; but for the most part it was a successful method of political control. It was also a means of Romanising the Gaulish tribal leaders, since the army by its very organisation and nature was a source of Roman culture and values. Gaulish leaders who wished to retain their old 'warrior culture' would now have to accept the cultural attitudes of the Roman army as well. They also had another enticement to encourage them to accept Romanisation – the granting of Roman citizenship.

Citizenship was a powerful instrument in the ancient world. Because there were grades of citizenship, the idea of the in-group (citizens) and the out-group (non-citizens) could be exploited by giving non-citizens strictly limited access to promotion to the various types of citizenship. For the most part non-citizens aspired to be full Roman citizens, with privileged voting and legal rights. There was also the lesser status of Latin citizenship, which had fewer privileges and, in Gaul at least, was relatively uncommon except in the south. The non-citizens were therefore encouraged to compete with one another for the privilege and the quite definite economic advantages of being made citizens. That competition took the form of showing loyalty to the Roman state and displaying a preference for Roman culture. In Gaul there was the more obvious route of joining the army as a means of gaining citizenship, which was usually granted to officers when they joined up and to the men when they were discharged. There was also the less obvious route of helping to run municipal administration, which was the second and eventually more important means of Romanisation in Gaul.

Municipal administration, the third tier of government below the provincial administration and the imperial civil service, consisted of town councils in Roman eyes. This implies, of course, that there were towns for the councillors to administer. In northern Gaul there were none at first, so that the establishment of municipal administration had to go hand in hand with the rapid development of the towns themselves. In these circumstances showing loyalty to Rome as a means of gaining citizenship took the form of helping to set up towns, and in particular the public buildings in them. For the old Gaulish aristocracy it also offered individuals a wonderful opportunity to advance in Roman society, while at the same time retaining their status as tribal leaders. For the most part the new administrative areas (*civitates*) were the same as the old tribal areas, and the new town councillors were picked from the old tribal leadership. In the old social structure a key method of maintaining a powerful position in the tribe was by the distribution of largesse to followers, who were much the same as the *clientes* of the Roman world. After the Roman conquest expenditure on setting up towns and bringing in new Roman goods and crafts became the equivalent of distributing largesse, and had the added benefit of showing a willingness to adopt Roman culture in the eyes of those Roman authorities in a position to grant privileges to aspiring Gauls. In this way, therefore, the scene was set for what amounted to a cultural revolution in the Augustan–Tiberian period, during which new Roman ways of gaining status took over from the old Celtic social structure. The result, in archaeological terms, was the evidence we see everywhere in Gaul for urbanisation and 'gallo-romaine précoce'.

A telling example of this cultural revolution was the family of Epotsorovidos, an aristocratic Gaul living in Aquitaine just before Caesar's conquest.[3] His son was given Roman citizenship, taking Caesar's forename and name, a mark of respect traditionally paid by new citizens to their patrons. However, he retained a Gaulish surname, being called Caius Julius Gedomo; his son, Caius Julius Otuaneunos, also followed this practice. By AD 19, though, the next generation had completely Romanised names, implying that Latin may well have become their preferred language. Caius Julius Rufus identified the interests of the family much more closely with Rome, for he was a priest of the cult of Rome and Augustus at the provincial altar at Lyon – a very prestigious way of showing loyalty to the state – and he paid for the amphitheatre there, as well as for the triumphal arch in his home town of Saintes (ancient Mediolanum Santonum). He also held the army administrative position of *praefectus fabrorum*; as the man in charge of building works, he would probably have been enabled to accumulate considerable wealth. Thus in a space of four generations and a little over seventy years the family had become Roman, even in name.

Caius Julius Rufus may have been exceptional, as we know that other aristocratic Gauls retained Gaulish names much later than the Tiberian period. On the other hand, his building activity can be widely paralleled from the Augustan period onwards. Rufus, to have been able to erect an amphitheatre and triumphal arch, must have been one of the wealthiest men in Gaul. The system whereby men in his position could display their wealth by conspicuous expenditure on public works, either buildings or

Monumental arch of the early first century AD dedicated to Germanicus at Saintes (Mediolanum Santonum). Caius Julius Rufus, a wealthy Gaul, had it erected, revealing the strength of private munificence in the early Roman period.

benefactions of other sorts, is now referred to as evergetism.[4] It had the advantages for the benefactor both of boldly displaying his Romanisation and of earning him the status of patron to a grateful community, and the advantage for the community (and the state) of being a means by which privately earned wealth could be recycled for the good of all – a sort of voluntary tax on the wealthy.

Most of the towns in Gaul would have acquired their public buildings in this way, although other avenues of raising the necessary funds were also available, such as public subscription or occasionally direct imperial or senatorial patronage. Unfortunately, we do not have enough building inscriptions to be able to establish exactly the pattern of urban development in each town, or to identify who was responsible for each of the impressive surviving monuments throughout Roman Gaul.[5] But we do have the monuments themselves, which can tell us much about architectural and artistic patronage, and the sources of inspiration for building styles.

The foundation of colonies and new towns

When Caesar came to Gaul in 58 BC the only town of the highest rank, a Roman colony, then existing in the south was Narbo (modern Narbonne), founded in about 118 BC and the mainstay of Roman interests there. In Cicero's words, it was the 'watchtower and defence of the Roman people',[6] a phrase that stresses the role of the colonists, who were Roman citizens from Italy and Rome itself, in providing a stable base for military security. The whole tenor of late Republican provincial rule was generally one of dominance and exploitation rather than cultural development, and, as the wine scandal of the 70s BC shows, the local Gauls had every reason to protest against the rapacity of Roman colonists and officials. Here, therefore, Narbo functioned not only as Rome's watchtower but also as its taxation office and profitable market-place.

Although Narbo was the only Roman colony in the area, there were other Roman foundations, such as Aquae Sextiae (modern Aix-en-Provence), of uncertain civic status, and another colony of lesser standing founded by Pompey in 72 BC. Lugdunum Convenarum (modern St Bertrand-de-Comminges) in the Pyrenees near Lourdes contained colonists who had the lower-status Latin rights of citizenship rather than the full Roman citizenship of the inhabitants of Narbo. This town was created not for Romans, but for people in the Pyrenean region who had been displaced by fighting in both Spain and Gaul during the previous decades. The foundation must have helped to Romanise the local population, and was thus an early precursor of the great programme of urbanisation set up by Caesar and Augustus. Unfortunately, we know little of its late Republican history or archaeology, since most of its monuments date to the Augustan period or later.[7] However, it was eventually promoted to the honorific status of a Roman colony, the hallmark of a successful venture.

From what little is known of other towns in southern Gaul in the late Republic, there is not much evidence of strong Roman influence. Glanum, for instance, a native town in the mouth of the Rhône Valley, had a number of Hellenistic features, such as a building resembling a Greek bouleuterion (council chamber), an agora, porticoes and stone-built peristyle houses.[8] It demonstrates clearly how Massalia continued to exert a strong cultural influence in southern Gaul, especially in the region from the Rhône Valley eastwards. Although the southern Gauls were culturally Hellenised, many local traditions persisted, reflected at Glanum by the cohabitation of classical and Celtic religious ideas (see chapter 6) and by the use of a local unit of measurement for the Hellenistic houses there.[9]

It is probable that many young towns in southern Gaul came under the influence of Massalia in much the same manner as Glanum. Hellenistic

View of the excavations of ancient Glanum, a town in southern Gaul that displays many Hellenistic and early Roman features as a result of the ready acceptance of Greek and Roman culture by the native inhabitants.

culture was therefore important as the means by which the local population absorbed the values of the Mediterranean civilisations. However, Massalia and Rome had their own characteristic versions of that civilisation, and as Massalia declined in influence during the first century BC, so Roman culture came to dominate.

Southern Gaul was Romanised largely by means of the colonies planted by Caesar and Augustus. Seven full Roman colonies came into being during this period, together with a further ten or so colonies with Latin rights of citizenship. At the same time three Roman colonies and further Latin colonies were established in the newly conquered territories to the north, the whole programme giving a remarkable impetus to urbanisation. Most of the full colonies were not founded on green-field sites, but were existing settlements boosted by a new population of colonists. Generally these were discharged soldiers, of which there were vast numbers in the aftermath of the Civil War. We know of soldiers from the 2nd legion being settled at Arausio (modern Orange), and this is reflected in the colony's full title of Firma Julia Secundanorum. Other legionary veterans went to Arelate (modern Arles), Baeterrae (modern Béziers), Forum Julii (modern Fréjus), and Narbo.[10] Narbo, of course, was already a colony, but it was not uncommon for new groups of colonists to be sent out to top up the numbers, while at the same time avoiding the expense and difficulty of founding a completely new colony. From about 27 BC, following Augustus' organisation of the Gallic provinces, Narbo was elevated to become the provincial capital of Gallia Narbonensis. It was not ideally positioned for this task, being at the western end of the province – a colony at the mouth of the Rhône, such as Arles, would have been a better choice – but the honour was a reflection of its high status in the hierarchy of colonies and other towns in Gaul.

The Latin colonies were different from full colonies in that they were generally existing communities that had the privilege of colony conferred upon them. This was a reward for loyalty to Rome or for progress in Romanisation, and it had the distinct advantage of giving the inhabitants Latin citizenship. Although not as prestigious as Roman citizenship, this was nevertheless much sought after as a step on the way to becoming a Roman citizen. The magistrates of Latin colonies automatically had Roman citizenship, and the number of full citizens in a Latin colony tended to increase as time went by. Several Latin colonies were elevated to Roman status, and after the reign of Augustus all new colonies in Gaul were full Roman colonies, so that the number of Latin citizens rapidly declined.

An example of a Latin colony is Nemausus (modern Nîmes), an ancient centre of the tribe of the Volcae Arecomici. The pre-Roman site was an oppidum and an important sanctuary, both of which continued in existence after other local oppida such as Nages had gone into decline.[11] Little is known of the early town until the Augustan period, when it appears to have been settled with veterans from some of the eastern legions. These must have been an exotic addition to the town, and the presence of the new colonists was soon reflected in the names on inscriptions, by coins issued with the emblem of a crocodile chained to a palm tree, and by evidence of the Egyptian cult of Isis. Most of the town's known monuments, its defences and street grid date from this time or a little later, and there is clear evidence in the temples and gates of imperial patronage helping to establish the town as a proper reflection of Roman culture.[12]

We do not know the status of all the urban centres in southern Gaul, although it would be fair to suggest that all the large towns and most of the smaller ones had Latin and eventually full Roman status. For a small town like Glanum the evidence for the impact of Rome is mainly archaeological. A temple dedicated by Agrippa was set up in the sanctuary there, and the Hellenistic bouleuterion and agora were swept away to make room for a substantial forum and basilica. The architecture of these buildings was almost entirely Roman,[13] and the local population must have felt quite a wrench as public buildings were established or rebuilt along the new lines. It was, however, the town centre that was mainly affected, for private houses, often already in Hellenistic/Roman style, tended to remain in use with little alteration.

At Glanum new developments in urban architecture can also be traced. Metrological analysis of the buildings has shown that a Roman foot was used for the new construction work, and an Osco-Italic foot for the new temples, but in general the architecture continued with traditional (i.e. Hellenistic) volumes and proportions.[14] There is clearly an interplay of new

One of the Augustan gates of Autun (Augustodunum), built in a recognisably north Italian style following the honorific grant of a set of walls by the emperor.

and old elements, and the combination of the two would lead to new architectural traditions that were subtly different from towns in other provinces.

Study of the town walls and gates is revealing in this respect. Fréjus, Aix-en-Provence and Autun were amongst the towns to receive the privilege in the Augustan period of a set of walls, and it is in the form of the gates, particularly at Autun, that links can be established with the cities of northern Italy (Gallia Cisalpina).[15] The large late Republican and Augustan foundations in the Po Valley, such as Verona, Piacenza and Turin, had been set up in the wake of the somewhat earlier conquest of that region. Expertise in the mechanics of Roman urbanisation was already established there, and it seems very likely that their architectural, town planning and land allotment (centuriation) systems were used as a basis for the cities of Gaul. The new traditions which soon developed from the mixing of these features with pre-existing Hellenistic urbanisation in southern Gaul spread to the rest of Gaul and Germany, so that by the Claudian period town development on a largely Gallic model was well under way in all regions.[16]

Our understanding of the pattern of urban foundations in central and northern Gaul depends to a great extent on the evidence of Caesar. This is not because he himself founded any towns that we know of, but because his friendship with some of the Gaulish tribes had a lasting effect on all subsequent developments. Two tribes in particular stand out for their close alliances with the Romans during the conquest period, namely the Aedui and the Remi. The Remi were on Caesar's side even during the crisis caused by the revolt of Vercingetorix in 52 BC, while the Aedui were soon forgiven for changing sides at the height of that crisis. Both later received the privilege of federated status for their loyalty. The Aedui were granted the right to construct a walled city called Augustodunum (modern Autun) to house the inhabitants of their former tribal capital, the hillfort of Bibracte. Similarly, the Remi were encouraged to construct a large planned town on an apparently new site, Durocortorum Remorum (modern Reims). This occupied a key position in the road network, and was to become the capital of Gallia Belgica and a major administrative centre.[17]

Reims and Autun were both founded during the reign of Augustus, as Autun's ancient name implies. At about the same time some of the other tribes, including those that opposed Caesar, were granted federated or free status. Some of the tribes had in fact been opposed to Rome throughout the conquest period, but it was probably felt prudent to grant them privileges in order to encourage their loyalty. Enhanced civic status had particular advantages, for federated and free cities were nominally exempt from paying tribute to Rome (at any rate up to the reign of Tiberius), and were in a better position to receive Roman or Latin citizenship and colonial status, the final recognition of a city's worthiness in Rome's eyes. Autun, for instance, was probably promoted to a colony in Flavian times, some 120 years after the conquest.

In contrast to such generous treatment, most tribes were reduced to the status of subject peoples (*civitates stipendiariae*), liable to taxes and without true city status for their central places. By a legal fiction Augustus altered the application of the term *civitas* so that in Gaul it referred to the whole of a tribe's territory. Thus the *civitas*-capital was simply an administrative centre for the tribal area, and was often granted only the lowly status of *vicus* ('street of houses'), unless it had been conferred the title of *municipium* or colony. Legally, this would put many important Gallic towns such as Paris or Bordeaux on a par with the small towns, also known as *vici*, which were widely distributed through rural Gaul (see chapter 5). Archaeologically though this legal definition means little, since nearly all Gallic *civitates* have urban centres that are clearly distinguishable from most small towns by the presence of fora, basilicas and the other appurtenances of a Roman town.

This hierarchy amongst the cities of Gaul meant that economic and civic development tended to take place in areas with privileged status, centred particularly on the colonies – Lyon, Trier and Cologne for instance – while vast areas, such as Normandy and Brittany, became, or continued to be, backwaters. The road network was also focused on the more important towns at the expense of their lesser neighbours, and it is not surprising that as a result the privileged centres nearly all enjoyed extraordinary growth from Augustan times onward.

Townscapes of Gaul and Germany

One of the striking aspects of the siting of towns in central and northern Gaul was the relative disregard of any urban developments of the late Iron Age. At Forum Segusiavorum (modern Feurs, near Lyon), for example, Gaulish levels were covered over to make way for the new town centre; there was no continuity in the building plots. The oppida of the Celtic tribes were rarely used as major towns, and with a few notable exceptions (e.g. Besançon, Bourges, Langres) tended to survive only as lower-status rural *vici*. In Gallia Belgica, in particular, where oppida were less common and not highly developed, the Romans established many new towns.[18]

As well as being founded on new sites, most northern cities conformed closely to a distinctive pattern in their positioning. The site was usually on a shallow slope leading down to an important river crossing. The road network was the key to this, since nearly all the important towns were on major routes at points where the roads converged and crossed rivers. Military considerations may well have played an important role in the layout of the road network, especially as it has become clear through recent work that many of the towns have evidence of occupation (usually in the form of Arretine pottery) as early as the mid- to late first century BC. Such early material, and a lack of Iron Age occupation, would tend to favour the idea that many towns such as Amiens and Trier started life as military or official outposts overseeing river crossing-points.[19]

Most of these cities were planned, using what is often regarded as typically Roman square or rectangular blocks (*insulae*). Regular planning is assumed to have been so widespread that archaeologists have tended in the past to invent a gridded street pattern for many Gallic towns on rather minimal evidence, with the result that extremely regular plans were presented for nearly all the larger urban centres. More recently, however, the image of an all-pervasive provincial planning department setting up towns throughout Gaul has been dispelled by more detailed archaeological work. Some towns, notably Lyon, capital of the Three Gauls, have little evidence of a gridded layout, while those that do present such a diverse collection of grid sizes that the layout of the street pattern seems to have been undertaken at local level, not through a centralised bureaucracy. That said, however, idealised plans of towns are likely to have existed and could have been applied and adapted to local circumstances.[20]

Samarobriva (modern Amiens) is a good example of a regularly laid-out town in northern Gaul. It was founded on a new site used by Caesar as a crossing of the Somme, which is the meaning of the town's name. Early pottery, including Arretine ware, supports the notion of a bridge-head

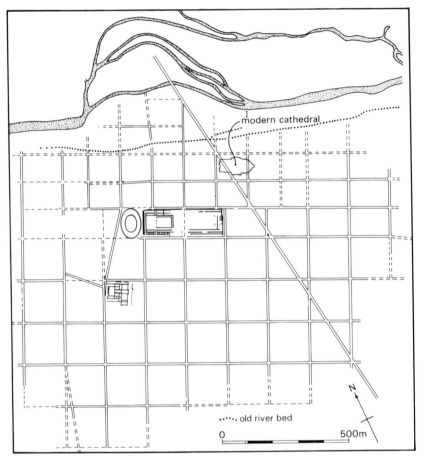

Amiens (Samarobriva Ambianorum) in the first to third centuries. Note the grid plan with the narrow forum and amphitheatre at the centre. Two phases of street grid are visible; the smaller grid size nearer the river is earlier. This plan should be compared with that of later Roman Amiens on p. 178.

settlement on the site at first, possibly a fort. This was replaced in the Augustan period by an initial street grid alongside the river, later augmented by an extended grid on a larger size of block.[21] Trier is similar, having been founded on a previously unoccupied site by the River Moselle. Its position was almost certainly due to the topography, which favours the siting of a defended bridging-point of the river there: indeed, the dendrochronological dates for the earliest bridge (18–17 BC) indicate that it was one of the first structures to be built in the town.[22] Trier too had a regular Augustan street grid, with evidence for wooden buildings soon after it was laid out. A Claudian expansion of the grid may reflect the rapid growth of the town and the need for extra capacity.

Despite the discipline imposed on a town by a gridded layout, planning in the disposition of the buildings was almost non-existent. Apart from siting the forum and basilica near the centre, there is little evidence of zoning of public buildings, or of their positioning to create vistas or close perspectives. Structures such as baths and temples were often in ordinary streets surrounded by houses, laid out without regard to their visibility or their place within an overall monumental scheme. It seems likely that once the street pattern of the town had been established, construction work was left to individual or corporate initiatives with little desire to create any sort of grand design.[23]

Early Roman towns, especially in the north of Gaul and in Germany, must have resembled to some degree modern new towns, with ambitious gridded layouts partially built up, and continual building activity. Public buildings were set up, mainly with private resources, in a piecemeal process over a period of many decades in most towns, and in the north it was not until the mid-second century that civic maturity could be said to have been reached. In the south building activity was more rapid, with most of the major monuments in place by the end of the first century, but even there towns were not instant and took a long time to develop. Some failed to live up to expectations. At Avenches, where an early set of honorifically granted walls enclosed a huge area, the grid was laid out more modestly to occupy about a fifth of the enclosure. Although there was some expansion beyond this initial grid, the whole area was never built up.[24]

In towns such as Avenches and Autun, which from an early date had very long walls, we may question what the wall circuits actually represented. Were they simply pragmatic assessments of the eventual area that a town would grow into, or was their length more a reflection of the town council's self-esteem? There are reasons for favouring the latter explanation. In many ways the larger circuits were an anomaly. They were, for instance, much longer than those of the north Italian towns, and it is notable that many of the early walls were honorific grants. Perhaps it is reasonable to suggest that the long walls, of for instance 5.5 kilometres at Avenches, represented a Gallo-Roman version of the defences of earlier Iron Age oppida. In this respect Autun can be seen as a slightly larger and, of course, highly Romanised reproduction of its Iron Age predecessor at Bibracte – it is in fact about a third larger. Indeed, it is probable that they were not intended to be intensively built up inside. Thus it has been estimated that Nîmes had approximately a fortieth of the population of Rome itself (i.e. 25,000), yet the area it covered was about a tenth, implying a much lower population and building density.[25] In this respect, too, the large areas enclosed by the early walled towns were similar to late Iron Age oppida, which also had relatively sparse population densities.

Were these long defences really needed? Although they were usually set up in the Augustan period, when part of the army was still in Gaul and when there was still the remote possibility of hostilities, most towns founded at the time had no defences. The granting of walls was more to do with municipal dignity and status than any real fear of attack.

A few of the colonies in the south, such as Fréjus and Arles, had comparatively small wall circuits. In fact, the increasing size of their population often forced them to expand beyond the walls. Fréjus has evidence for suburbs outside the walls, and at Arles public buildings were constructed over the early wall circuit as the town expanded.[26] The small wall circuits and the evidence for expansion beyond them conform more to Italian patterns of town development.

For many towns there was also another way of representing the boundaries of a city which at the same time prominently expressed both loyalty to Rome and civic pride. This was the construction of monumental archways, which could be either free-standing or built into walls. These in many ways can be regarded as symbolic gateways marking the passage into the city and representing the rest of the defences. There are some thirty arches known from Gaul, and almost certainly many more than this were built. Many of them are early in date, especially in the south, including the well-known arches at Glanum and Saintes. The latter has a dedication to Germanicus, and it was a fitting monument for the intended capital of Aquitania. Some of the arches, particularly those of more elaborate form, are later in date, usually Antonine or Severan. Examples include the large triple-arched Porte de Mars at Reims and the Porte Noire at Besançon.[27]

A case apart is the well-known arch at Orange. Its chronology is a problem: it is usually accorded a Tiberian date, possibly commemorating the defeat of Florus and Sacrovir, who staged a revolt in AD 21. However, the dating is restored from the assumed bronze lettering of the dedication, based on the fixing holes left in the stone. This is open to dispute, and it has been suggested from its sculptural style and the complicated architecture of a triple archway, attached columns and a staggered attic that the arch is much later, perhaps Severan.[28]

If walls and arches represent the external face of a town, the forum symbolises its interior. An enclosed zone, often cut off from wheeled traffic, it was the principal meeting-place for the town's population. The average Gallo-Roman forum had shops, a basilica, a curia (council chamber), often a major temple and statues honouring the town's patrons and leading citizens. The forum served many functions – commercial, legal, administrative, religious and monumental – often fulfilling these roles at the same time. It was truly a civic centre, a display and repository of a city's public wealth and status.[29] Augst and St Bertrand-de-Comminges are the classic examples of early Imperial date. Augst in particular has been well studied, and it can be seen to have reached its final form during the second century, when it had a temple facing onto the forum area, a basilica at the opposite end from the temple, and at the rear of the basilica a semicircular curia.[30] There are examples of earlier fora of Augustan date, somewhat simpler in design, such as those in the south at Glanum and Ruscino. These are made up of a plain rectangular basilica and a square or rectangular forum, not much larger than the area of the basilica itself.[31]

The fora of Gaul in their fully developed form tended to be of elongated shape. This reaches an extreme at Amiens where, to fit into the street grid, the forum is particularly long and thin. Indeed, Gallo-Roman fora were also often divided into secular and religious zones, with the large classical temple

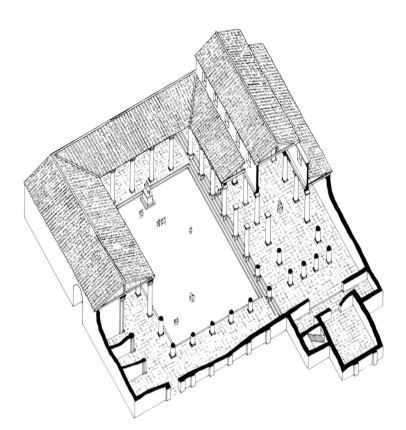

Reconstruction of the Augustan forum at Ruscino in southern Gaul. The simple layout of colonnaded basilica and small forum area can be contrasted with the larger fora incorporating temples that were typical of later urban planning in Gaul and Germany.

occupying the central part of a porticoed area separated from the rest of the forum by a subdividing arcade or set of steps. The temples usually faced the basilica; those for which the evidence exists were dedicated to the Imperial cult or the Capitoline triad (Jupiter, Juno and Minerva). As examples we may cite the well-known classical temples at Nîmes and Vienne, which are assumed to have stood in the fora of their respective cities, although as yet few remains of their precincts have been found.[32] In western Gaul classical temples were less common in fora, being replaced in some cases by large Romano-Celtic temples near the forum complex, such as the Tour de Vésone at Périgueux.[33] Inscriptions show that these temples were dedicated to both the Imperial cult and local divinities. The local cults were obviously important in the life of their communities and so were tolerated by the Roman authorities, as long as due deference was paid to the state in religious terms.

An enigmatic aspect of many classical temples in fora, and indeed classical temples in other locations (such as the temple to the Imperial cult at the Verbe Incarné site in Lyon), was the provision of a *cryptoporticus* under the portico surrounding the temple precinct.[34] There are good examples at Arles, Reims and Bavai; these are all underground arched areas, essentially serving the structural purpose of levelling the ground for the porticoes above. However, they were also subterranean open spaces, and may have been used as meeting-places, since there is some evidence to show that they were decorated with wall-plaster. They were also perhaps used for trading and for the storage of goods, but it has been pointed out that the entrance to the *cryptoporticus* at Arles is small and narrow, which would have made it difficult to bring in large goods. A related underground structure is the *horreum* (grain store) at Narbonne, which was separate from the forum and looks like a *cryptoporticus* divided up into cubicles.[35] Although it is referred to as a *horreum*, there is no certainty that this was in fact the original purpose of the building, and it may alternatively have been an *ergastulum*, or barracks for the public slaves of the town, on the analogy of the underground slave chambers recently found in excavations in the forum at Rome. The other *cryptoportici* in Gaul could conceivably have served a similar purpose as well.

Another facet of town life provided for in the cities of Gaul, as in other provinces, was bathing. Many sets of baths are known, notably the Barbarathermen at Trier, which are the largest to survive outside Rome itself.[36] They date to the late second century, and most public baths in Gaul were in fact constructed at a relatively late date after the foundation of towns, especially from the late first century onwards. The baths at Trier have a layout similar to the extensive Imperial bathing establishments in Rome, with a large *palaestra* (exercise yard) and to one side enormous symmetrically arranged halls covering the traditional sets of hot, warm and cold rooms, together with plunge baths and swimming pools. Baths in other towns were not so imposing or ordered in their arrangement, and some were rather small, being based on the simple military baths (the *Reihentyp*) found in forts on the German frontier. A good example of a medium-sized set of baths are those that now house the Musée de Cluny in Paris. The finely preserved vaulting is original and gives a good idea of the interior spaces in municipal baths. Most of the decoration has unfortunately gone, but unique carved capitals in the form of ship's prows survive at the points where the vaults spring from the walls.[37]

In order to provide an adequate supply of water to the baths, it was usually necessary to build aqueducts, if a town did not already have them for general water provision for drinking, cooking, washing and other purposes. We know of aqueducts for many towns in Gaul and Germany – Vienne alone possessed at least ten – although they were rarely of the spectacular type that marched across the surrounding countryside on arches. Usually they were in channels following the contours of the land, at ground level or dug into it.[38] The aqueduct for Cologne, for instance, has been traced for nearly 100 kilometres from the city to its source in the Eifel Mountains, double the direct distance because the channel followed the contours.

The best known aqueduct in Gaul or Germany is that at Nîmes, tapping a source 50 kilometres from the town at Uzès, and carried in a combination of a ground-level channel, a tunnel dug into the rock, a series of low arches

The Pont-du-Gard near Nîmes, which carried the aqueduct for the town across a gorge at a height of about 49 metres above river level. It is one of the most impressive surviving monuments from Gaul.

and, not least, the famous Pont-du-Gard. It is estimated to have had a flow of some 30,000 cubic metres of water per day, and was clearly a remarkable ancient surveying and engineering achievement. The fall from source to outfall in the city is calculated at 34 centimetres per kilometre; the stretch above the Pont-du-Gard being 67 centimetres per kilometre, while that downstream of the Pont was only 18.5 centimetres per kilometre. This is well below the recommended fall as given by Frontinus, and must have entailed some very accurate surveying to ensure that the aqueduct channel never sloped in the wrong direction. The reason for this small fall was the problem of taking the aqueduct across the River Gardon, and in order to minimise the height of the Pont-du-Gard the engineers were forced to make the lower stretch almost horizontal. Even so, it is the highest surviving bridge structure in the Roman world (49 metres), and its harmonious tiers of arches are justly celebrated as one of the foremost Roman remains in Gaul.[39]

It has been estimated that the construction of the Nîmes aqueduct may have cost up to 100 million sesterces (perhaps equivalent to $100 million), a cost which reflects the difficulty of its construction, and the high priority placed on water provision. Other towns must have spent similar sums, and there are engineering achievements of equal if not greater standing elsewhere in Gaul. A high-level bridge once carried the aqueduct for Metz over the Moselle at Jouy-aux-Arches. More remarkably the four aqueducts that supplied Lyon all had to use inverted siphons to cross the valleys to the south and west of the city. The longest, the Aqueduc du Gier, had no less than four such siphons along its 75-kilometre length, a unique feature in the Roman world. Inverted siphons worked by carrying the water in sealed lead pipes down one side of a valley and up the other to a point a few metres below the water level on the upstream side. They obviously circumvented the difficulties of constructing large bridges across deep valleys, but were costly to build – an estimated 35–40,000 tonnes of lead was used for the Lyon siphon pipes – and not easy to maintain. Another striking example of water provision is at Arles, where a battery of lead pipes carried water across the bed of the wide and fast-flowing River Rhône.[40]

Distribution of water within a town from the aqueduct head is best seen in the so-called *castellum divisiorum* at Nîmes. This structure was a circular settling tank at the end of the aqueduct channel, in which the water level could be controlled as it flowed into a number of large lead pipes feeding the various baths, fountains and rich private houses of the town.[41]

In the realm of entertainment, provision was generally made in Gallic and German towns for amphitheatres and theatres, but circuses were very uncommon. There was a specifically Gallo-Roman type of theatre–amphitheatre in many of the northern towns and religious rural sanctuaries as well. For example, at Paris there was a building superficially resembling an amphitheatre with central arena and seating surrounding it. It differed from a true amphitheatre, however, in that about one third of the seating is replaced by the stage and stage-set for a theatre. This hybrid type gives the air of a cost-cutting compromise, allowing less prosperous towns to have adequate entertainment facilities without the expense of building both a theatre and an amphitheatre. Some of the theatre–amphitheatres, however, are not just simple combinations of the two types, since those at rural sanctuaries in particular look strikingly like Greek theatres in their design, and may owe their origins to Greek theatres at cities like Massalia (see chapter 6).[42]

In the south both amphitheatres and theatres were generally provided in the big towns. Imposing structures survive at Arles, Nîmes, Orange, Lyon and elsewhere. Some of the early theatres may have been in wood rather than stone: an inscription from Feurs records the reconstruction in stone of a theatre originally in timber, and it is thought that the theatre at Fréjus had wooden seating resting on stone foundations. The most impressive survival amongst the theatres of Gaul, indeed of the Empire as a whole, is at Orange. Louis xiv's 'fairest wall in his kingdom' is the stage-set surviving to its full height of 37 metres, giving us a very graphic image of monumental scenery dominating the players on the stage. Sadly, most of the decoration has disappeared, but the overall scale can be appreciated, together with the size of the seating banks, since they have been largely restored. Although not the biggest theatre in Gaul – that distinction goes to Autun – it may have held up to 7,000 spectators, a massive testimony to the popularity of ancient dramatic entertainments.[43]

The amphitheatres at Arles and Nîmes both survive to be used in modern times for bull-fighting and other spectacles. They are very similar to each other, and it is suspected that they were built about the same time, perhaps by the same architects. They have links with the amphitheatres in Rome, principally the Colosseum itself (dedicated in AD 80), which would imply a late Flavian or Trajanic date of construction. Amphitheatres, too, could be constructed of timber, as at Avenches, where a probably Flavian example used earthen banks for underpinning the originally wooden seating. This may have been usual for the initial construction of many amphitheatres until stone rebuilding took place.[44] In some of the poorer towns amphitheatres may have remained in wood.

Circuses are much rarer than amphitheatres or theatres, with only five securely known in Gaul, at Arles, Vienne, Lyon, Trier and Saintes.[45] The best surviving evidence comes in the form of the Egyptian-style obelisks that were used to decorate the spine down the centre of the circus. Two are known, at Arles and Vienne, of which the latter is still in its original position. It is a rather squat obelisk on an small arch, made from local stone,

The first-century theatre at Orange (Arausio) conveys a vivid impression of the size and splendour of municipal theatres and their importance to town life.

and as such it is the poor relation of the taller and genuinely Egyptian obelisk at Arles. The list of circuses is confined to the richer cities in Gaul or, in the case of Saintes, to a city that had originally been destined to be a provincial capital. They are completely absent from northern and western areas, and although simple horse-racing tracks with wooden seating are difficult to detect by the archaeologist, and so may have existed in some of the other towns, it does seem likely that horse-racing was mainly organised in the Mediterranean towns and in those with administrative or imperial importance. It is surprising that Narbonne does not seem to have possessed a circus, given the town's status, and it would be reasonable to predict that one might be found there in the future.

If its public buildings can tell us something about the wealth and status of a Gallo-Roman town, its housing can also be very informative. Some of the best examples of houses come from towns in the south, particularly Vaison-la-Romaine and Glanum. The larger houses are typical Hellenistic- and Roman-style courtyard buildings, that would not have looked out of place in an Italian town such as Pompeii. They had a well-ordered, often axial arrangement, of atrium (covered courtyard room) and peristyle (colonnaded garden courtyard), such as in the House of the Dolphin at Vaison, where one entered from a colonnaded street via a set of steps, straight into the atrium. From there one could pass through the *tablinum* (reception room) into a small peristyle containing a garden and pool. The other rooms opened

The amphitheatre at Arles (Arelate), like the equally well-preserved example at neighbouring Nîmes, is probably of late first century AD date.

82

View into the entrance of a large early Roman house at Vaison-la-Romaine (Vasio Vocontiorum). It is of typically Roman form with a peristyle courtyard beyond the entrance hall.

off from the atrium, but mainly from the peristyle, including the *triclinium* (dining-room). There is also evidence for stairs to an upper storey which must have surrounded much of the peristyle area. To one side of the house itself was a larger open space with a portico around the garden and pool within it. This was typical of the houses both at Vaison and elsewhere in Gaul, where there was often the opportunity (and the wealth) for fairly extensive town houses.[46]

A feature of the House of the Dolphin and other large southern Gallic houses is that there were shops and smaller houses in the same block of buildings. This provides another link with Italian towns. However, in the north urban centres were by no means so intensively settled, to judge from excavations at, for instance, Amiens, or from aerial photography at Corseul. There larger houses appear to stand isolated in courtyards and the main evidence for denser occupation comes from groups of shops ranged along the main roads.[47]

There is a curious aspect to another of the houses at Vaison, the House of the Silver Bust. Behind the main house is a large set of baths, a multiple latrine and a large open space, which was either a *palaestra* for the baths or a garden.[48] The baths seem to be too large for private use, and it may be that they served a public function, perhaps being taken over by the house at a later date. Alternatively, they could have been for a *collegium* or guild that had its premises at the back part of the house. This is a reminder that large houses were not entirely private retreats, since wealthy citizens had obligations to their clients and to the population in general.

The general level of wealth indicated by the embellishments of these large houses is easily comparable with that found in the more affluent towns of Italy. Fine mosaics and decorated wall-paintings in fashionable styles appear in Gaul at the same time as in Rome itself. On occasion there is evidence for more lavish decoration in the form of marble walling and flooring, as in some of the houses at Autun. Sculpture, too, indicates a high level of sophistication, as in the copy of an archaic Greek statue of Minerva from a house in Poitiers, or in the find of a silver bust, probably of an ancestor, in the house of that name at Vaison.[49]

In some towns, notably Glanum, houses of Hellenistic type survive, which have been tentatively dated to the first century BC or earlier. Here the influence of Massalia was at work, and it is likely that most of the towns in southern Narbonensis had early stone-built houses that owed much to the example of the Greek colony (see chapter 1). Further north in the areas conquered by Caesar the first recognisably Roman-style housing dates to the Augustan period. It differs from most southern housing in being timber-framed on low stone foundations, using an infill of mud-bricks or other earth-walling techniques. Notable examples have been excavated at the Rue des Farges in Lyon, where both rich and poor houses were constructed in this manner at first (before being reconstructed in stone throughout), some adorned inside with decorated wall-plaster even at this early date. Careful excavation of the early levels of other Gallo-Roman towns is starting to reveal many more traces of such early houses, which are the structural equivalents of artefacts in the new 'gallo-romaine précoce' style, as discussed above.[50]

Although urban excavation is proceeding apace in France and Germany today, and has yielded spectacular results at Lyon, Cologne, Vienne, Aix-en-Provence, Narbonne and elsewhere, for the most part we know surprisingly little about Roman provincial housing in the region. Medieval and modern settlement on top of the Roman levels has often prevented excavation or destroyed the stratigraphy, so that when the information does survive it is all the more valuable. Glanum and Vaison are examples already discussed: their equivalent further north is at St Romain-en-Gal, a suburb of Vienne on the opposite side of the River Rhône. Here a large atrium and peristyle house has been found in a densely built-up area that included warehouses, workshops and smaller houses. Although carefully laid out, this part of the town was evidently a mixture of rich and poor, industry and housing. The general impression is one of very rapid development as an overspill from Vienne itself. There were some problems as a result of this, such as the high groundwater levels in the low-lying riverside location, which the Roman builders took pains to deal with.[51]

So far this discussion has centred on the larger town houses occupied by the wealthier classes. At the other end of the social and architectural scale, particularly in the north, were small strip houses. These were usually long, rectangular single rooms with their short sides facing onto the street, so that they occupied as little frontage as possible. They also served as a town's shops, often having counters or workshops at the front of the building, while at the back was the family's living quarters in very cramped accommodation. This type of building is likely to have occurred in most of the towns in central and northern Gaul where the Mediterranean-style blocks were not so common. Strip buildings are often found in groups together, sometimes behind a colonnaded portico like an ancient shopping arcade. As often as not, they were concentrated on the main streets into a town, or in the area around the forum, both being the most favourable zones for trading. It was not only the larger towns that had this type of building in them, for they were also common in the small towns or *vici*, whose lower civic rank meant that they contained very few large houses.[52]

Unfortunately, the information that housing can reveal about the level of wealth in Gallo-Roman towns will remain limited until more sites are excavated. Snapshots of general housing conditions are glimpsed at sites like Glanum or St Romain, which tend to show a reasonable standard of living throughout the whole range of housing within the excavated area. It remains to be seen to what extent there were poor suburbs or slums in the towns of Gaul.

Another means of assessing the wealth and self-esteem of a town's inhabitants is by looking at the grave monuments. In many parts of Gaul and Germany museums are filled with tombs and monuments, which have been published in the valuable systematic corpora of sculptured stones and inscriptions.[53] From towns like Bourges, Strasbourg or Trier there are large numbers of carved monuments, usually displaying an image of the deceased. There is often an indication of their profession, for instance wine-merchants with their barrels and amphorae, or a mason and his tools. Some of the larger tombs had sculpted scenes from the everyday life of the person commemorated. Particularly at Trier and at nearby Neumagen there are well-preserved depictions on a variety of monuments of merchants counting out money, perhaps to piece-workers in the woollen industry, and scenes of wives at their toilette and children going to school.

Besides offering an exceedingly important insight into the life-styles of those depicted and a wealth of archaeological information, these tombs show us how much it mattered in Gallo-Roman society to have a memorial that did justice to one's position. They were display monuments, designed to be seen from the roads leading into a town, the traditional position for nearly all Roman burials, since it was not permitted to inter the dead within the built-up area. As such, they are a clear indicator of the way in which a town's inhabitants viewed themselves in terms of status, and since tombs were the first things that a visitor came across on entering a town, they would be a key to appreciating how wealthy the citizens were. It has been suggested that merchants were particularly lavish in their monuments

relative to their actual status in society (which was not high), since they had ready cash to commission them and an underlying desire to leave permanent memorials behind: by contrast, the more secure land-owning élite did not need to do this. The most imposing tombs come from southern Gaul, such as the finely carved monument of the Julii at Glanum, and from the Rhône, Moselle and Rhine areas. From Cologne comes one of the largest, the tomb of Poblicius, with its statues and large columned 'portico' to cover them. The inscription records that he was merely a veteran of the 5th legion Alauda, but he must have acquired a great deal of money in civilian life to have been able to afford such a monument.[54]

The areas with the more imposing tombs were also richest parts of Gaul and Germany. This is clear from the work of Goudineau, who, using various

Large mausolea, like the early first-century tomb of the Julii at Glanum illustrated here on the far side of the contemporary monumental arch, were positioned near the gates of towns. They were potent symbols both of the status of the deceased and of the wealth of the town.

criteria of wealth and civic attainment, has devised a rank order of towns in Gaul. The criteria used include the size of the town, the number and importance of its public and private monuments, the evidence for manufacturing and other industries, the number of inscriptions, the status of the people mentioned on those inscriptions or otherwise connected with the town, and lastly its legal civic status.[55] The results are very interesting, for if Gaul alone is analysed, Lyon comes first and Narbonne second, closely followed by Nîmes, Vienne and Trier. After this there is a group of towns of lesser importance, Arles, Bordeaux, Autun and Reims, and a third group made up of Vaison, Saintes, Avenches, Béziers and Orange. Most of the towns are either concentrated along the Mediterranean coast of Gaul, or are in or close to the Rhône Valley. Trier and the Rhineland towns of Cologne and Mainz form the other main geographical grouping. The only important towns to the west or north of these core areas are Reims, the capital of Gallia Belgica; Bordeaux, the capital of Aquitania, and Saintes, the ex-capital of that province. None of the towns in the vast sweep of central and northern Gaul, and indeed in southern Aquitania as well, really figure at all. It is clear that the Mediterranean–Rhône–Rhine axis formed the richest and most important part of Gaul. Trade and the presence of the army on the Rhine had a large part to play in this, as we shall see in chapter 5.

In view of Goudineau's conclusions, it is pertinent to ask how successful were those towns that lay outside the core areas. What was their population density, for instance? Was it very low, as might be suspected from the generously spaced housing, as discussed above, and did these towns fail to be fully urbanised in the Roman sense? To take Gallia Belgica as an example, only Amiens, Reims and Trier are likely to have had a population of over 10,000, with their maximum probably being 20,000. All the other towns seem to have been rather small, with populations that averaged about 2,000 to 5,000. This can be placed in a context of an estimated overall population for the province of 1–1.5 million.[56] It was, in other words, a predominantly rural society with only a small minority based in the cities.

A pertinent case here is Limoges, where the houses are thinly represented within each block or *insula*, and were rarely renovated once they had been built.[57] Seen from this angle, urbanisation in Roman terms was not a great success. Only in the core areas, where urbanisation did take stronger hold, can we say quite clearly that there were cities on the true Roman model, exhibiting the full range of urban characteristics. The ratio of urban to rural population here was almost certainly inclined toward the cities, so that life in general was more distinctly focused on the nearest urban centre. This is best seen in the Mediterranean parts of Gallia Narbonensis, where the town-based settlement pattern was the norm. In this respect, this area could be regarded as a successful example of provincial development.

Finally, how does Gaul compare with other provinces? Even urban southern Gaul did not attain the overall level of wealth or political influence that was enjoyed by many Italian cities, or by the Mediterranean parts of Spain, North Africa or the Near East. This can be illustrated by the number of Gallic citizens who became senators, following Claudius' decree that allowed them to do so.[58] Gaul contributes just 3.1 per cent to the total number of senators in the Empire, compared with Italy's 47.5 per cent or North Africa's 14.5 per cent. The same is true for equestrians, with Gaul having only 4.2 per cent, in contrast to Italy's 44.9 per cent and North Africa's 14.3 per cent. In surface area, Gaul was one of the largest provinces, and it might be expected to have contributed more, although it does fare better than Britain, where scarcely a single native senator or equestrian is known. It is possible that Gauls did not want to enter the higher élite of Roman society, or that there was prejudice in Rome against those of Gaulish origin,[59] but even so there seem to have been few individuals in the Gallic provinces with a level of wealth which made them eligible for admission to the senatorial or equestrian ranks.

FURTHER READING

By far the best synthesis of urban life in Gaul is that by Goudineau in G. Duby's *Histoire de la France urbaine* 1 (1980). The most recent survey of the evidence is by R. Bedon *et al.*, *Architecture et Urbanisme en Gaule romaine* (1988), which gives brief descriptions and references for each town. The foundation of towns is discussed in the conference proceedings *Les Débuts de l'Urbanisation* ... (Paris 1985). Good treatments of individual towns include those of Amiens (Bayard and Massy 1983), Augst (Laur-Belart 1978), Béziers (Clavel 1970), Bordeaux (Etienne 1962), Narbonne (Gayraud 1981), Paris (Duval 1961 and the exhibition catalogue *Lutèce: Paris de César à Clovis*, 1984), Lyon (Audin 1979), and Trier (Wightman 1970, Heinen 1985, and the two exhibition catalogues by the Rheinisches Landesmuseum Trier in 1984).

For individual aspects of towns, triumphal arches are examined by Gros (1979), and the notable arches of Glanum by Rolland (1977) and Orange by Amy *et al.* (1962). Fora are most recently discussed in the conference proceedings *Los Foros Romanos de los Provincias Occidentales* (Madrid 1987). Baths are extensively analysed by Krencker and Krüger (1929) in their publication of the Barbarathermen in Trier. For aqueducts, the best surveys are of Cologne (Haberey 1972) and the Pont-du-Gard, Nîmes (Hauck 1988 – written in the style of a historical novel!). Amphitheatres are examined by Golvin (1988, 226–36) and circuses by Humphrey (1986, 388–431). Excavation reports on houses include Vaison (Goudineau 1979), Narbonne (Sabrié *et al.* 1987) and Lyon (Desbat 1984). Work on tombs is synthesised by Hatt (1986) and there is a monograph on the tomb of the Julii at Glanum by Rolland (1969).

— 4 —

RURAL
LIFE

In Gaul and Germany large towns were not only the main framework of the settlement pattern; they also formed the hubs around which the spokes of the road network radiated. Into this pattern fitted the large numbers of small towns or *vici*. These settlements, the size and equivalent of modern villages, were often sited on the main road system, and provided additional facilities of the urban sort – particularly inns, shops and markets – that were needed to make the economy and social life of the provinces run smoothly. In many ways the small towns acted as a bridge between the truly urban *civitas*-capitals and colonies, and the rural villas and farms.

A typical *vicus* is Schwarzenacker-an-der-Blies in Saarland. It covered some 25 hectares, a not inconsiderable area approaching the size of the smaller *civitas*-capitals such as Thérouanne (ancient Taruenna) in northern France, or Martigny (ancient Forum Claudii Vallensium) in Switzerland. What primarily distinguishes it from any 'real' Gallo-Roman town is the lack of forum, basilica and other appurtenances of urbanisation. Instead, virtually the whole built-up area consisted of housing. All the houses excavated are of the strip building type, as described in chapter 3, with shop counters or workshops facing onto a porticoed street and narrow rooms behind. At Schwarzenacker many of the strip buildings have cellars at the rear of the room, which may have been the back rooms of bars or taverns. In one case a large cellar is thought to have been a meeting-room: stone columns running along the centre to support the ceiling had integral circular tables to carry the plates and beakers of the people who gathered there.[1] A single main road ran through Schwarzenacker, and the emphasis there was on providing refreshment for travellers; there may well also have been an inn for official messengers.

Many other small towns offer striking evidence for industrial production.

Pottery-kilns in particular have been discovered at a large number of sites, and there are towns wholly devoted to specialised pottery production, such as Lezoux in central France or Rheinzabern on the Rhine. At Alesia we find bronzeworking; Ardres was a centre for the salt trade, and stone was quarried around Tournai. It is interesting that the small towns did not on the whole prosper conspicuously as a result of their industrial activity. Larger houses with mosaics are rare, and it is very likely that whatever profits there were flowed to the grand proprietors living in the larger towns. This has led modern commentators to assert that the large urban centres were parasitical on the small towns and the countryside. The *vici* in contrast are supposed to have been the productive centres of Roman Gaul and Germany and thus in reality more successful economically.[2] The charge is somewhat unfair, since there were large towns like Cologne where we have strong evidence for major industrial production, but clearly the inferior status of the *vici* usually did deny them the enjoyment of the fruits of their productivity.

There were several different types of small town in Gaul. Some, like Schwarzenacker, Wederath and Mâlain, were roadside settlements fulfilling a subsidiary market function. However, not all such sites were on main roads: Pommeroeul was a small town by a river, where a harbour formed an important focus of activity.[3] Other small towns had more pretentious aims, especially of becoming *civitas*-capitals in their own right, as actually happened quite frequently in Italy, North Africa and, to a lesser extent, Gallia Narbonensis. One of the most successful *vici* in the Three Gauls was at Lausanne, where early development of an important road link from Italy to Germany, together with lakeside port facilities, ensured long-term prosperity and growth for the town. Indeed, a simple forum and basilica

A cellar behind a shop of strip-building type in the *vicus* of Mâlain (Mediolanum) in central Gaul.

were set up to cater for the trade, which must have been the mainstay of the town's existence. Yet Lausanne never advanced from being a *vicus*. This seems to have been a regular pattern in Gaul and Germany, even in some of those towns that were clearly planned deliberately with the intention of future development and enhanced status. In such cases the hoped-for urbanisation probably did not materialise; at Verdes in central Gaul, for example, a forum, basilica and baths were laid out as the nucleus of a town that, judging from aerial photography, failed to develop, thus leaving the urban centre isolated in a largely unoccupied small town.[4]

Probably the best-known small town in Gaul is Alesia (modern Alise-Ste Reine). It owes its fame to Caesar's victory over Vercingetorix there (see chapter 2), but the present-day visitor is mainly impressed by the remains of a theatre, forum, basilica, temples and houses, laid out within a rudimentary street pattern. Here we can see a small town that has gone beyond being a simple market-place to having an administrative function as well, perhaps as the chief town of the local *pagus* (rural district). It is ironical to observe that Alesia, the site of a famous Gaulish defeat, became a flourishing Gallic town, but it was not the only Iron Age oppidum which developed into a small town. Quite a few, for instance Vertault and the Titelberg, continued into the Roman period in this way, rather than becoming major urban centres, for which new sites were preferred (see chapter 3).[5]

Other small towns developed for different reasons. Many were centred on religious sanctuaries, often of Iron Age origin. At Ribemont-sur-Ancre a combination of excavation and aerial photography has demonstrated that an important temple existed before the Roman period; this was later developed on a grand scale into a religious centre of regional importance. It was laid out on an axial arrangement with a Romano-Celtic temple, courtyards, a theatre, baths and inns. Many other such sites existed in central and northern Gaul, notable examples being Vendeuvre in Poitou, Sanxay and Chassenon.[6] All seem to have been planned to some extent, with most of the buildings constructed at a remarkably early date – often in the early first century AD – in one series of operations.

These religious centres have been separated by Picard from the general run of small towns in Gaul and Germany by being termed *conciliabula* rather than *vici*.[7] It is a legal term, not in fact directly attested on inscriptions from any of the sites, which tend to be called *vici* on the few pieces of evidence that we do have. However, the distinction is probably an appropriate one to make, since the *conciliabula* seem to have been established in an attempt to create rural centres with a primarily religious purpose. In addition, they also served as market and administrative centres. For a dominantly rural population that could not be happily urbanised along the Mediterranean model this may have been the best means of exerting Roman control, the *conciliabula* perhaps acting as *pagus* centres within the general structure of rural administration. This may account for their early date and planned appearance, since there may well have been official interest in setting them

Many small towns were built up round successful religious centres, such as at Grand (Aquae Granni?), whose amphitheatre was one of the largest in Gaul.

up. A measure of their importance can be seen in the fact that their architectural development in northern Gaul was in all probability earlier than in the neighbouring towns, whose embellishment with temples and public buildings took rather longer.[8]

There were other religious centres which can be termed small towns, but which were not laid out in such a planned fashion. Grand and Aix-les-Bains are examples of towns that grew up around healing sanctuaries (see chapter 6), presumably because of their success in treating supplicants. Many of the medicinal baths became centres of small towns in this way, and were every bit as important to rural society as their more secular counterparts.[9]

Villas and villages

For many readers villas are the typical feature that they would expect to find in the Roman countryside. Gaul meets this expectation, having a landscape that was thickly strewn with villas, particularly in a wide band running from Belgium south-west to Aquitaine. Two areas, Picardy and southern Aquitaine, stand out, both by virtue of recent work and by the richness of the remains. In Picardy the villas, mostly discovered by aerial photography in the 1960s and 1970s by Roger Agache, are particularly numerous.[10] Locating and mapping them has been one of the major achievements of post-war archaeology in France, opening the eyes of many to the wealth of evidence still waiting to be discovered in rural Gaul. However, Agache's photography was done just in time, since most of the traces visible

Aerial photograph of the large villa at Warfusée-Abancourt in Picardy, showing up as ploughed-up foundations in an arable field. The main house is in the field in the foreground, with the subsidiary dwellings around the courtyard beyond.

from the air are the soil marks of the very lowest foundations, and modern agriculture is rapidly ploughing these away.

The villas in Picardy were laid out in a variety of ways; but one of the most characteristic types (exemplified, for instance, by that at Warfusée-Abancourt), has the main building in a courtyard, facing onto a vast rectangular courtyard – up to 2 hectares in size – around the edges of which are other buildings. The main house is the most accomplished in its architectural elaboration, often being provided with mosaics, wall-paintings, hypocausts and colonnades. The other buildings are simpler, but in some cases they resemble miniature versions of the main villa itself.[11] This is a matter of some significance for the social structure of the people living there, and will be discussed further below.

Dating for these villas is rare, since few of them have been excavated. Those that have been dated run from the first century AD onwards, often originating in the Flavian period (AD 69–96). Interestingly, there is little evidence so far for the early Roman 'gallo-romaine précoce' period, even though the aerial photographs indicate that several of the sites had a close relationship with Iron Age sites; one, for instance, is to be found at L'Etoile, where a villa appears to lie within an Iron Age ditch system. This gap in the dating evidence is difficult to explain, for we believe that the population was almost entirely based in the countryside in the late first century BC and early first century AD, and we would expect to find many settlements of this period. A possible answer has come from the excavations at Beaurieux,

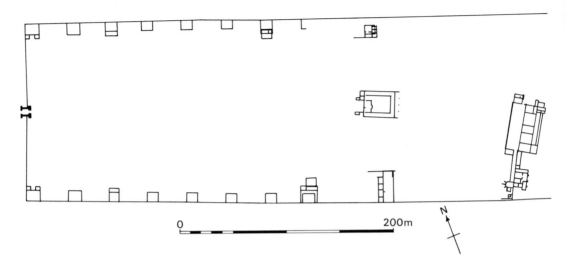

where there are simple rectangular wooden buildings using post-hole foundations, dating to precisely the time of the apparent gap. The buildings are of particular interest since they seem to be laid out around a large courtyard along the lines of the later stone-built villas, as though one developed from the other.[12] Extensive excavation of other sites is clearly needed to pursue this important question further.

Plan of the large villa at Oberentfelden in Switzerland. The building at an angle on the right-hand side was the main house, while those around the courtyard were probably for farmworkers and storage.

The characteristic layout of the larger villas of Picardy is met again in southern Aquitaine. There the classic villa sites of Montmaurin and especially Chiragan are recognisably more grandiose versions of the same type. Chiragan has the double courtyard arrangement, with one formed on three sides by the main villa itself. This lies just beside a much larger courtyard (adding up to a total of 16 hectares), which is edged by individual small buildings laid out along three ranges. Although similar to the villas further north, most of the Aquitaine villas tend to be richer. There is more evidence for pretentious architectural layouts, with ornamental pools and entrance courtyards, as at Montmaurin. Chiragan yielded some three hundred pieces of sculpture, and there are numerous villas with highly accomplished decorated mosaics. Indeed, Aquitaine has yielded more villa mosaics of high quality than most other areas of Gaul.[13] This is partly because more villas survived into the fourth century in this area, for reasons which will be explored further in chapter 8.

The double courtyard type of villa is not, however, confined to Picardy and Aquitaine, for many of the other well-known villas in Gaul and Germany conform to the general plan. These include Anthée, Echternach, Otrang, Oberentfelden, Seeb, Levet and Noyers-sur-Serein.[14] What, then, does this widespread distribution imply? The double courtyard villa may have had its roots in the social structure of the late Iron Age, as described in the writings of Caesar, Poseidonius and others, in which tribal élite families had large retinues of followers from further down the social scale. It was a system in which tribal leaders provided protection to their followers in exchange for some sort of service – their votes and support within the political system, and agricultural tribute. The suggestion, therefore, is that the Gallo-Roman large double courtyard villa perpetuated this social arrangement: the patron lived in the main villa and his clients occupied some of the smaller buildings in the outer courtyard (others obviously being for farm purposes). This would explain why some of the latter look like miniature villas in their own right. The clients would have been obliged to work the land for their patrons in exchange for housing, and political and financial protection.

This interpretation of the villas is supported by their distinctiveness when compared with other types of villa in the Roman Empire. Indeed, their distribution corresponds neatly with the Continental 'Celtic' areas of the Empire. Furthermore, epigraphic and literary evidence for the Roman period lends little support to the idea that there were many slaves in Gaul and Germany, particularly in the countryside. This may be because the patron–client system prevailed as the main means of organising agricultural labour. In fact, the Gallo-Roman villas may prefigure the forms of land tenure and social links that existed throughout the Empire by the late Roman period (and continued into the early Middle Ages): that, in effect, the late Roman *dominus* and his *coloni* (tenants) replaced the early Roman *patronus* and his *clientes*.[15]

Although the double courtyard villa is very widespread, there are also many examples which were laid out in rather more haphazard fashion. At St Ulrich in eastern Gaul, for example, the main villa has an ill-ordered straggle of subsidiary buildings leading away from it; even so, the overall arrangement here could be taken to reflect the idea of the patron and his clients.[16] In Brittany, by contrast, there are smaller units, more like those usually encountered in Britain. At La Roche Maurice there is a small block-like villa with a detached bath-building. It is designed as the well-known 'winged corridor' type, with a range of domestic rooms fronted by a veranda or corridor and flanked by two projecting rooms, which are often reconstructed as towers. In Brittany and parts of Normandy the villas are generally less extensive than those further east and south. This is not to say that they were necessarily poorer, since many of the main villa buildings in Picardy were no larger or more elaborate; but the social structure of villa life may well have been different. This would conform with what we know about the differences in tribal organisation between these areas and the rest of Gaul at the time of Caesar. However, it should be said that there are a few very large villas in this area, such as Vieux-Rouen-sur-Bresbre in Normandy, which are indeed larger than many of those found in Picardy.[17]

In the Moselle Valley a distinctive group of villas lies along the banks of the river. Most are in the Trier region, since the wealthy town provided a focus for villa development. Nennig and Welschbillig, for instance, are known to have had large and luxurious *villae urbanae* facing onto the river

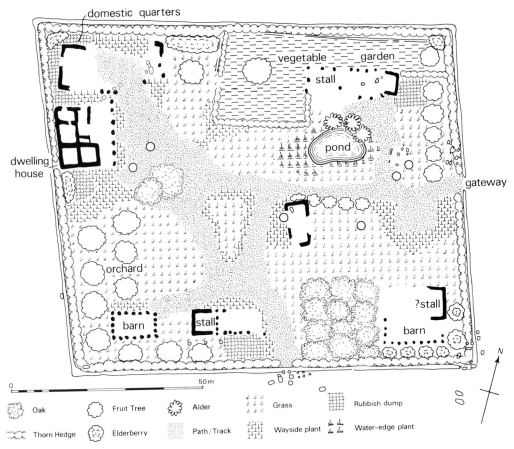

domestic quarters

vegetable garden

stall

pond

dwelling house

gateway

orchard

?stall

barn   stall   barn

0			50m

Oak   Fruit Tree   Alder   Grass   Rubbish dump

Thorn Hedge   Elderberry   Path/Track   Wayside plant   Water-edge plant

N

itself. So far there is little evidence for subsidiary buildings at these sites. If they do exist, it is likely that they would be behind the main building further up the valley slopes.[18]

There are two further areas where the villas differ from the types so far described. In the Germanic provinces, which in ethnic terms include the northerly parts of Gallia Belgica as well as the two Germanies themselves, there are distinctive types of so-called 'hall villa', with large open halls instead of groups of small rooms. Presumably they reflect a different social order (see chapter 7).[19] The other distinctive area is in the south, in Gallia Narbonensis. Here the agriculture was determined by the Mediterranean climate, with a strong emphasis on olives and vines. In much the same way that southern towns developed differently from their northern counterparts, the villas too tended to conform more to Italian types. There is evidence that villas were divided into the *pars urbana* (main residence) and the *pars rustica*, the latter often having oil and wine storage facilities. It is interesting that many of the southern villas dating from the early Empire were not particularly well appointed; this is possibly because in the south the land-owning élite was based in towns, and operated their villas through bailiffs

Hypothetical reconstruction of the vegetation and layout of a small villa enclosure in the Hambacher Först near Cologne, based largely on analysis of the preserved botanical remains. (After Knörzer).

(*vilici*). It is in the south too that the epigraphic evidence for rural slaves is strongest, and we can assume that this aspect of Italian villa life was also fairly common in the region.[20]

Estimates of how many people lived and worked in the larger villas vary, but we can conclude that they would have had a fairly large population, up to a hundred people or more in the most extensive. Such a figure would be high enough to call the villas villages, and we have to ask whether there were actual villages as well. In many areas, there is little evidence for distinctive rural settlement types besides villas, apart from the *vici* and *conciliabula*. However, in a few parts of Gaul and Germany, away from towns and roads and in the more difficult terrain, we do come across so-called 'native' settlements. Some good examples are to be found in the northern Vosges, where hill villages such as Wasserwald suggest a less Romanised style of life. Here there are irregular roads and trackways, with small buildings fronting onto them. These villages were in marginal areas, leading fairly independent existences, but even so they show some Roman features – imported Roman pottery, ashlar stone grave furniture, and occasionally even inscriptions and sculpture.[21]

Elsewhere evidence for truly 'native' settlements has proved difficult to find. Many sites in the more prosperous regions must have been like Beaurieux, eventually turning into villas after a relatively brief period of gradual Romanisation. At the more southerly site of Montagnieu, east of Lyon, recent excavations have revealed a site with progressively more Roman features in the Caesarian and Augustan periods, culminating in a very simple villa-like building in the early first century AD. It seems likely that this type of site represents the simplest and least Romanised stratum of rural life in many parts of Gaul. In the plains of northern France, where the evidence for the overall settlement pattern is best recorded, lack of dating evidence makes it difficult to estimate how many of the known Iron Age enclosures and farmsteads continued into the Roman period. It is in Brittany, Belgium and the Netherlands that we come closest to finding sites which can be regarded as more or less un-Romanised. In the Netherlands in particular excavations of sites such as Rijswijk have revealed strongly developed native culture on the very fringes of the frontier lands. This is a subject that will receive further attention in chapter 7.[22]

Farming and rural industries

The vast majority of villas had estates firmly tied to agriculture, although there were some exceptions in areas where, for instance, minerals, forestry or the sea might provide additional sources of income. Agricultural systems have long been discussed by modern historians, drawing mainly on the ancient Roman treatises on agronomy. For the most part, however, these classical sources are strictly relevant only to Italy and the Mediterranean areas where olives and vines were cultivated. This includes Gallia Narbonensis, which is precisely the area where the archaeological remains of

Part of a mosaic from St Romain-en-Gal showing farmworkers carrying manure out to the fields. (Musée nationale des Antiquités, St Germain-en-Laye)

the villas conform most closely to their Italian prototypes. For the rest of Gaul and Germany we have to rely almost exclusively on the archaeological evidence, supplemented by rare comments from writers such as Strabo, Pliny and Palladius.[23]

Evidence for fields, the most extensive feature of any present-day farm, is extremely difficult to obtain for Gallo-Roman villas. Not surprisingly, medieval and modern cultivation has swept most of the remains away, so that it is rare to be able to trace field systems. However, this has been done at Châtillon and Allain in central Gaul. Both of these sites are preserved in forested conditions, and the fields at Châtillon have boundaries made of drystone walling, and so are relatively visible.[24] These field types follow the small, square, but regulated 'Celtic' pattern known in other provinces, notably Britain. We can suspect that this type of field system was probably very widespread in central and northern Gaul, both for villas and other types of rural settlement.

In Gaul there was also what we might call a Roman type of field system, or to be more precise a land allotment system, known as centuriation. This was not related to villas directly, although villas are to be found on centuriated land, but was a feature of urban planning, particularly linked with colonies. It was a new development for many parts of Gaul, and would have marked a major change in the countryside, comparable in its impact to the urbanisation that was taking place at about the same time. Centuriation is mainly found in southern Gaul, with well-known examples around Orange, Béziers and Narbonne. Very large areas were regularly apportioned, usually on a square grid system, and for Orange we have the unique survival of the cadastral map showing the allocations of the land to the colonists and others, including the local Gaulish people. The map actually shows three different centuriation systems, all now located on the ground in the Rhône Valley and stretching as far south as the neighbouring towns of Avignon and Glanum.[25]

As far as centuriation is concerned, aerial photographs have formed the basis for some scholars to suggest that many hitherto unsuspected areas of Gaul were regularly laid out. The old Gaulish land allotments were apparently swept away in favour of a new, regulated Roman system. However, rather like the claims for urban grid plans, many of the proposed centuriations seem to owe more to faith than reality. This applies especially to those suggested for areas to the north of Gallia Narbonensis and the Lyon centuriation system. It is the technique of optical filtration with its emphasis on right angles and the rectilinear boundaries visible in an aerial photograph that is largely responsible for optimistic proposals of centuriation systems. Many land allotment areas have been assigned a Roman date but are effectively undatable, and may even be medieval or later. Another problem arising from the use of this technique is that land allotments apparently overlying one another at different angles have been inferred; at Béziers, for example, no fewer than three such grids have been proposed.[26] This seems to fly in the face of evidence of continuity from most areas through long periods of time once a system was established. Was it necessary to impose a new centuriation system at a different alignment if the existing allotments followed Roman practice and were available to be reallocated? It would seem most unlikely.

Within the centuriation systems there were villas, often, but not always, aligned onto the grid. These are presumed to be farms constructed on estates built up from a number of the colonists' individual parcels of land. Thus to a certain extent these villas represent the breakdown of the original land allotment ideal.

One of the primary purposes of all field systems, whether Celtic or Roman, was the growing of crops and the control of animals. In the north cereals, mainly wheat and barley, predominated, as today, the former grown for flour and bread, the latter also for malting and ale. The Roman period saw the promotion of a number of crops, including breadwheat, durum wheat, rye and oats. Studies of preserved seeds, particularly from Germany and Gallia Belgica, have established that these appear for the first time in the north either during the Roman period or just before. Existing strains of wheat such as emmer and spelt went into decline in the face of opposition from these new crops. Breadwheat in particular has growing and threshing advantages over the more primitive types of wheat, although the Romans were not to know that, weight for weight, it was in fact less nutritious. Other plants, fruits and nuts were also grown, in the wide-ranging variety that is available today (if introductions from the New World are discounted). Carrots, cabbages, apples, hazelnuts and many other fruits and vegetables are known from both the literary and the archaeological sources; in Gaul and Germany archaeology provides the more secure evidence for the presence of particular species.[27]

One of the most interesting aspects of farming in northern Gaul, mainly

The bank of Roman water-mills at Barbegal near Arles was established for large-scale flour milling for commercial profit. The mills were powered by water from an aqueduct, and could process up to 9 tonnes of flour per day.

in the territories of the Remi and the Treveri, is the evidence for technical innovation. A mechanical reaper or *vallus* was developed in order to cope with the grain harvest in these important cereal-growing areas. The device had tines on it rather like a giant comb, and was pushed by a horse or mule to break off the ears of wheat and collect them in a box-like hopper at the back of the comb. Evidence for its appearance comes not from archaeological sources but from relief sculptures, such as a second-century arch at Reims, and from literary descriptions in Palladius and Pliny. It seems that the *vallus* was confined to Gallia Belgica, and a debate has arisen about whether this was an early labour-saving device in use on the large villa estates of the

A sarcophagus from Arles showing olive or fruit picking. (Arles Museums)

plains of northern Gaul, and whether perhaps a lack of manpower led to the development of this type of machine. Generally speaking, the ancient world seems to have relied on the manpower of slaves or dependent labourers, rather than on machinery, so the harvesting machine is something of an exceptional development. As seen above, the villas were often large enough to accommodate a substantial number of farmworkers, which seems to argue against a shortage of manpower. Some other reason, which as yet cannot be clearly discerned, must be put forward for the use of the *vallus*.[28] In any case, we might doubt its real economic effectiveness.

Further evidence for mechanisation comes from the remarkable remains at Barbegal, near Arles. Here flour was milled by a bank of sixteen water-wheels, which, according to recent calculations, would have been capable of producing 9 tonnes of flour per twenty-four hours' operation. This was easily enough to feed the citizens of Arles, and also the surrounding country-dwellers too. Barbegal, so far, is unique in the Roman world for the concentration of mills in one establishment: it appears to have been taking advantage of a particularly favoured site where an aqueduct descended a steep slope.[29]

In the south the two main crops were grapes and olives. The Greeks were probably responsible for introducing these species, and they are attested archaeologically in the area from a relatively early date. Both were widely cultivated, and vines in particular were also grown further north fairly soon after the Roman conquest, since they are more hardy and were very much in demand because of the Gaulish predilection for wine. They were introduced along the Rhône Valley and beyond, so that by the end of the second century AD they are found in the Moselle region. Many of the areas now famed for their vintages, such as Burgundy, were already producing during the Roman period, although it is difficult to be certain about the more peripheral areas such as Champagne.[30]

Traces of vine and olive cultivation can often be recognised archaeologically in the pressing areas in the villas. At Roquebrussanne and La Garde, both in Gallia Narbonensis, we have clear evidence for olive presses, and it seems that olives were mainly raised in the warmer coastal regions of the province and in parts of the Rhône Valley. It can be difficult to tell vine from olive presses, but there is a good example of the former at Allas-les-Mines in Aquitaine. There were also storage facilities for wine, in the form of banks of large jars (dolia) from sites such as Donzère. Another facet of wine and olive oil production was the manufacture of amphorae for their transport. The kilns were often based on the farms themselves, and a number of them are known from Gallia Narbonensis. Presumably such kilns were used on an intermittent basis, producing enough amphorae to fit into the agricultural cycle each year. A related development, which according to Pliny originated in Gaul, was the production of wooden barrels. Amphorae tended to decline in popularity during the early Empire, and were rarely produced in the northern wine areas.[31]

Barrels for wine and other purposes imply that wood was an important resource in Gaul and Germany, and also that local carpentry skills were highly developed. In this respect there are some difficulties in the evidence for the extent of woodland in the region. The forest was one of the natural features mentioned by Caesar with some regularity, particularly when he was referring to northern Gaul.[32] However, pollen analysis and related environmental work paints a contrary picture: woodland was being cleared long before Roman times in many areas of Gaul, so that by the end of the Iron Age much of Gallia Belgica and Lugdunensis had as little natural forest as exists today. The image of Gaul as having vast tracts of virtually impenetrable forest is clearly a false one. In fact, the evidence for clearance implies that systematic silvicultural use was made of the woodland that could conveniently be exploited. Unfortunately, there are few archaeological traces of what must have been a large-scale industry, producing wood for building, furniture, ships, fuel and many other uses.[33]

Woodland was also used for grazing animals, principally pigs. Strabo writes of Gaulish pigs being kept in the open rather than in sties, which allowed them to grow to a larger size, developing extraordinary speed and strength, so that for anyone unused to their behaviour there was as much danger in approaching one as a wolf.[34] Animals generally were an important part of farming in Gaul and Germany. They have been well recorded in sculpture and their remains have been recovered from archaeological sites. The study of animal bones can give us an idea of regional variation in animal husbandry, and present useful pointers to such matters as diet. Although such detailed study is only just starting for Gaul (there is more evidence from Germany and the Low Countries), results so far have already provided some useful information. For instance, pigs were fairly common through much of central and south-western Gaul, and in Gallia Belgica, and finds from many sites indicate that pork was a favoured and high-status meat. Cattle were less numerous in many regions, although in parts of the north there were more cattle than most other animals. Pork and beef were the most common meats at sites such as Roman forts, but it seems that there were both regional variations and differences between rich and poor sites. There were also probably changes over time, but at present there are so few bone reports from the late Roman period that it is impossible to tell what changes and developments may have occurred in diet and animal husbandry.[35]

Sheep were relatively uncommon, and in the north mutton was viewed as a poor meat. In the very south, however, sheep bones are common on all types of site. To judge from the sculptural evidence, they were also important in the region of Trier and in neighbouring parts of Gallia Belgica.[36] It seems likely that the upland areas in the south were used for sheep pasture, mainly during the summer, in a transhumance system, probably of the sort that still existed until recently in parts of Provence (the *drailles*). Sheep-farming would be combined with the growing of olives, vines, cereals and other crops in the lowland areas in such a way that, after the harvest, the sheep would be brought down from the hills to graze the cereal stubble and manure the fields. This is the classic system described by the ancient agricultural writers, and there is good epigraphic and topographical evidence for it in Italy.[37] This is yet another link between Gallia Narbonensis and Italy, and it does not exist to anything like the same extent for the other Gallic and German provinces.

The sheep of the Treveran region were raised for their wool, and the wool textile industry figures a great deal on sculptures, such as the monument put up by the Secundinii at Igel. Here the scenes show the preparation and finishing of cloth, possibly by piece-workers who were paid to carry out different stages of the process. The families who had such monuments put up were wealthy merchants, proud to commemorate their connection with textiles. Gallic wool itself is singled out in ancient texts, and by the late Roman period there were several Imperial woollen mills (*gynaecia*) producing garments for the army.[38]

Other animals besides pigs, sheep and cattle were also raised, some figuring prominently in the surviving evidence. Gaul was famous for its horses, principally because of the Gallic cavalry in the Roman army. They

Stone relief sculpture from Grand (Aquae Granni?), showing an unknown goddess in front of wooden buckets, possibly for beer or some sort of food mixture, and a small oven (bottom left). (Musée des Beaux Arts, Nancy)

must have been an important focus of attention from well before the Roman period, since there was a Celtic goddess of horses, Epona, whose name probably derives from the same root as the English word 'pony'. Horses were raised in some numbers for transport and riding, but there is also osteological evidence that some old animals were eaten as a minor contribution to the meat diet.[39] Goats were also raised, presumably for their milk and hides, but generally they were uncommon except in the south. Domestic birds, too, mostly chickens but also geese, ducks and pigeons, were known from pre-Roman times and clearly formed a regular part of farmyard life. Dogs and cats were also present, but during the Roman period cats were fairly rare and probably did not become a familiar animal in everyday life until the Middle Ages.[40]

One of the notable features of the animal bone reports for Gaul and Germany is the low number of bones attributable to wild species. This is especially true for the late Iron Age, when it is not uncommon for more than 95 per cent of the bones to be of the usual domestic species. Hunting appears to have been a restricted activity, almost certainly a privilege enjoyed in both the late Iron Age and Roman periods by élite groups such as villa-owners and the military. The villa at Montmaurin, for instance, and some of the Roman forts in southern Germany, have much higher percentages of wild animal bones than sites of lower social status. Deer bones figure most prominently, probably because the animals were valued highly for their meat and antlers as well as for the pleasure of the chase. Wild boar, too, was hunted, and there are many lively hunting scenes on pottery and sculpture. Other animals include bears, for which the Eifel region was well known; wolves; possibly the aurochs or wild ox (especially in the Black Forest); chamois from the Alpine region; and eagles. There was also a wide variety of small game such as hares, foxes and badgers. Many of these must have been hunted or trapped for their pelts, but there was also a lively trade in animals captured for the amphitheatre, where staged hunts or *venationes* were a popular entertainment.[41] The famous white bulls of the Camargue, raised for the bullrings of Nîmes and Arles today, remind us that the practice is not yet dead.

Another source of wild food was fishing. There is little evidence for inland fishing, but around the coast, for instance in Brittany and the Mediterranean area, many fish-farms and the installations for salting fish have been found. The pools for a fish-farm attached to a villa have been uncovered at Notre-Dame-d'Amour near Les-Saintes-Maries-de-la-Mer in the region around the mouth of the Rhône, while in Brittany there is a remarkable group of sites in and near Douarnenez in Finistère. They are made up of vats on the seashore, probably for salting sardines and other fish to make the Roman savoury delicacy known as *garum*. Before these sites were recognised for what they were, *garum* had been thought of as exclusively a Mediterranean product, but it is now clear that it was manufactured in the Atlantic provinces as well.[42] Shellfish were also widely harvested, and the shells, particularly of oysters, point to a well-organised trade, transporting them, presumably in barrels of brine, to sites as far inland as Augst in Switzerland. In pre-Roman times shells are a distinctly uncommon find on archaeological sites, even those near the coast, so it seems likely that the eating of shellfish as an everyday part of the diet was a Roman fashion new to Gaul and Germany.

Salt, too, was an important product from the sea, and was made in the Mediterranean region by natural evaporation in salt-pans. In the north in many coastal regions excavation has yielded evidence for the boiling hearths used for concentrating seawater and making salt-cakes. The hearths often date back to the Iron Age, and this was tried and tested technology that continued into the Roman period.[43]

The population of Gaul and Germany

Given the enormous increase in the number of rural archaeological sites discovered in recent years, both from ground survey and aerial photography, we are now in a position to make what some may regard as the foolhardy attempt to assess the population of Gaul and Germany. Before the upsurge in the rate of discoveries surveys of various areas of Gaul gave the impression that there was approximately one site for every 1,000 hectares of land. Numbers of sites have now vastly increased, so that many modern surveys yield an average of one site for every 100 hectares, in other words ten times the number of sites than previously known. This average area now compares realistically with the only surviving description that we have of an ancient villa estate, that of Ausonius' *herediolum* or 'little inheritance'. This was a late Roman estate near Bordeaux, assessed by him as having 1,050 *iugera*, approximately 260 hectares. Given that Ausonius was in the élite of late Roman society, it is perhaps not surprising that one of his estates should exceed the average area known from the archaeological work.[44]

The distribution of rural sites is not in fact even through Gaul and Germany, so the average given above is somewhat meaningless when individual areas are considered. Fieldwork results give figures that vary from one site for 330 hectares in parts of Brittany to one site for 20 hectares in the vicinity of Massiac in central Gaul. Other representative figures are one site for 192 hectares in the Finage in eastern Gaul, one per 72 hectares in the Petite Beauce in central Gaul, and one per 92 hectares around Béziers in Gallia Narbonensis.[45] This great variation is partly explained by the fieldwork techniques used, and partly by differences in opinion as to what constitutes a site, but even so there were clearly important shifts in settlement density from one area to another.

An interesting aspect of these studies is the relationship that can be traced between villas and towns, roads and other major features in the settlement pattern. In some areas, usually the flatlands of central and northern Gaul, there is a relatively even spread of sites, with no marked peaks of settlement in any one part of the area. However, there are regions such as Picardy where the major roads appear to have attracted villas, so that their distribution is denser near them, although it is extremely rare for a villa to be positioned actually beside the roadway itself. Presumably this pattern emerged because of the possibility of easy communications with local towns and *vici*. In other areas a different settlement pattern can be discerned, with a tendency for the villas to cluster around a town. Two of the best examples are around Corseul in Brittany and Béziers in southern Gaul; both have a distinct concentration of sites in the close environs of the town, and a clear fall-off of settlement density as one moves away from the urban centre.[46] This must be linked to the trading opportunities of the towns, and it may also reflect the social importance of these towns to the surrounding countryside. Not all towns have villas focused upon them in this way though, and it is noticeable that the veteran colonies and similar important towns do not display this type of clustering. Why this is so is difficult to explain, unless the land allotment system for the colonists discouraged the growth of villa estates near the towns.

Taking the evidence from the field surveys, Alain Ferdière has attempted to calculate the population total for Gaul as a whole.[47] In present-day France the surface area is approximately 550,000 square kilometres, which would give a total of 550,000 villas if the figure of one site per 100 hectares is extrapolated over the whole country. As Ferdière points out, there are mountainous, forested and other inhospitable regions that need to be taken into account. But since ancient Gaul and Germany was rather larger than modern France, it is possible to compensate in a rough and ready way for the difference in area by accepting the total number of villas as correct for our region as a whole. This would spread the population in such a way as to allow for thinly populated zones such as the Massif Central, the Alps, the Pyrenees, the Landes and the Ardennes.

It has been suggested for pre-industrial rural societies in Europe that some 20 workers are needed to cope with 100 hectares of agricultural land. At certain times of year, such as harvest time, anything up to double that number may be required altogether. If we apply this figure, for example, to the Beauce and Eure-et-Loire region, we may assume 96,000 workers for the available agricultural land in that area. This can be correlated with a projected total of 4,800 villas at a density, known from field surveys in the region, of one site per 100 hectares, which would give us an average of 20 workers per villa. Other figures for pre-industrial societies suggest that there is one active agricultural worker for two other inhabitants, which would give a total rural population for the region of 288,000 (i.e. 60 people per villa). This is comparable with a present-day population of 335,000 in what is still largely a rural part of France, although now with a minute proportion of that population actually engaged in agriculture.

The extension of these figures throughout Gaul and Germany would allow us to propose a total of 11–12 million for the rural population. This is a very rough figure, given the amount of guesswork and assumption involved. The chief imponderables lie in the number of agricultural workers per unit of land and per villa, and also in the multiplication factor used for the number of dependants per worker. Minor adjustments in these figures would alter the total quite considerably, but even so it seems reasonable to suggest that the rural population would have been in the region of 8–15 million.[48]

This figure can be compared with Beloch's late-nineteenth century estimate of 3–4.5 million for all sectors of the population in the Three Gauls. It is a total that appears to be too low: Beloch was reluctant to give these provinces higher population densities than those he had calculated for the more developed Mediterranean provinces. He set his estimate in the context of a possible population for the Empire as a whole of 50–60 million, a figure which may also be too low in the light of recent archaeological work throughout the Empire. However, he was right to point out that the population of Gaul must have increased during the period of Roman rule because conditions were more settled. The higher density of archaeological sites for the Roman period when compared with those for the Iron Age in many regions would certainly support this suggestion, and would back his estimate that the population of the Three Gauls had risen to 10–12 million by the early fourth century. This coincides with the proposed population total based on Ferdière's figures, and indeed is a little higher, given that the area Beloch covers is smaller than that by Ferdière. Beloch's date for the Gallic population peak may be disputed to a certain extent, possibly being somewhat earlier (see chapter 8), but his overall conclusions are more in line with current thinking than Jullian's suggestion that Roman France housed as many people as it did in Louis XIV's day, some 25 million.[49]

The estimate of 8–15 million for the rural population can be seen in its proper perspective when we attempt to calculate figures for the urban and military sectors of the population, the two main groups that depended upon the imported produce of the countryside for their day-to-day needs. In order to estimate the urban population, the relative importance of towns in Gaul and Germany has been used as a rough guide to their individual population sizes, based upon the criteria devised by Christian Goudineau (see chapter 3). There were seven towns of approximately 20,000 people, four towns with 10,000, a hundred with 5,000, and some five hundred with 1,000. These figures are very rough and possibly rather conservative, but conform with ideas of settlement size and distribution as currently known. The total figure is 1,180,000. To this can be added the approximate total of 50,000 for the army units known to have stationed in the Rhineland.[50] Even if the urban and military figures are doubled, it is still abundantly clear how predominantly rural the population was as a whole. Only some 10–15 per cent of the population did not derive their living from the land.

This has implications for the economy of Gaul and Germany, since it is usually assumed that all villas were in the business of producing a surplus, sometimes a very large surplus, in order to pay for taxes, building improvements and so on. However, unless a large proportion of this surplus was exported to Rome, Italy and other provinces, Gaul would have faced the problem of an ancient version of the beef mountain or wine lake that has caused such controversy in the Europe of today. An answer may be that many villas were producing only a slim surplus, being mainly concerned to achieve self-sufficient production for the villa's inhabitants and enough extra to pay the tax revenues due. They did not need to produce much of a surplus in each villa to satisfy the feeding requirements of the urban and military populations, and it may have been the case that many villa-owners found some difficulty in disposing of their surpluses, especially in good years. This may account for the settlement pattern noted for some parts of Gaul, whereby the villas cluster near roads and towns, perhaps because of competition to get produce to market quickly in order to make a reasonable profit. Other economic and social consequences can also be deduced from the population figures suggested above, but they are best discussed in the context of the economy as a whole.[51]

FURTHER READING

The fullest and most recent synthesis of evidence for rural Gaul is by Alain Ferdière, *Les Campagnes en Gaule romaine* (1988). Accounts in English are not common, but there is a notable treatment of Gallic villas in J. Percival's *The Roman Villa* (1976). There are several regional surveys, including Agache (1978) on Picardy, Leday (1980) on Central Gaul, Galliou (1983) and Langouet (1988) on Brittany. Small towns are discussed further in the conference proceedings *Le Vicus gallo-romain* (Paris 1976); for individual sites see Kolling 1972, for Schwarzenacker; Roussel 1979, for Malain; and Le Gall 1980 for Alesia.

Villas and agriculture have also been covered in a conference proceedings, *La Villa Romaine dans les Provinces du Nord-Ouest* (Paris 1982), with notable contributions by R. Agache and J. Smith on villa plans and social structure. Further aspects of rural society and slavery are discussed in A. Daubigney (ed.), *Archéologie at Rapports sociaux en Gaule* (1984), and by E. Wightman (1978a). See also A. Pelletier, *La Femme dans la Société gallo-romaine* (1984). Two villa reports from the many available can be singled out; Montmaurin in Aquitaine (Fouet 1969) and Echternach in Gallia Belgica (Metzler *et al.* 1981). Recent work on animal husbandry is discussed by P. Méniel in *Chasse et Elevage chez les Gaulois* (1987), and olive cultivation by J.-P. Brun in *L'Oleiculture antique en Provence* (1986). Land allotments in Gaul are presented in M. Clavel-Lévêque (ed.), *Cadastres et Espace rural* (1983), and the unique Orange centuriation map in A. Piganiol, *Les Documents cadastraux de la Colonie romaine d'Orange* (1962).

— 5 —

MARKETS
AND
MERCHANDISE

Money is probably the best subject with which to start an investigation of Gaul and Germany's economy. Coins played a crucial part in ancient society, being used for army pay, tribute, bullion and commercial transactions. Much recent work has been done on the ways in which coinage was used and circulated, and the results have considerable implications for the workings of the economy as a whole.

In the pre-Roman Celtic world coinage was a well-established facet of daily life. Gold, silver and bronze coins were in circulation, issued by the powerful tribes and occasionally by their lesser allies as well. Some tribes used silver and some used gold, all struck in distinctive designs that are often miniature masterpieces of Celtic art, yet at the same time ultimately derived from various Greek and Roman prototypes.[1]

One of the immediate questions that can be asked of the Celtic coinages, especially those in gold and silver, is what exactly they were used for. Clearly the precious metal coins with a high face value were not used for everyday purposes. The answer to this question, derived from the ancient literature and modern numismatic studies, is that the coinage was produced to sustain Celtic social structure. Coins served to pay mercenary warriors, dowries, ransoms, bribes and tribute. At the same time they were used as bullion and as a means of securing loyalty from a tribal leader's followers. This is seen most spectacularly in a comment by Poseidonius that Louernios, King of the Arverni, 'in an attempt to win popular favour rode in a chariot over the plains distributing gold and silver to the thousands of Celts who followed him'. Such activity is often likened to a North American Indian potlach, and can be seen as a way in which Celtic leaders controlled wealth and its redistribution. Much economic activity must have revolved around the tribal élite, the members of which had the means to trade with the

Greeks and Romans, and the wealth to act as patrons to craftsmen and poorer dependants.[2] In the Roman period this system was to evolve into the patron–client system, as discussed above.

Celtic bronze coinage may have been used for daily trade of a sort recognisable to us today. These coins were minted in large numbers and generally came into circulation much later than gold or silver. They seem to have been issued as a response to the growth in trade that developed during the first century BC, and the increasing commercialisation and development of proto-urban communities at this time. It is clear that Celtic society was becoming more sophisticated in money matters at the time of the Roman conquest, and coins were being used increasingly widely. This is not to say, however, that the economy was remotely like that of today, with entirely cash-based transactions and all goods having an established price or value. Barter was important, even for the Roman traders, who delighted, for example, in exchanging an amphora of wine for a Celtic slave. To the Romans this was a bargain, and it is a clear indication of the quite different values that the Gauls and the Romans put on goods. Much trade must have been conducted within the confines of Gaulish customs and social structure, so that the prices paid for something may have varied according to who was dealing with whom (Gaul with Gaul or Gaul with Roman), what the goods were to be used for (e.g. a marriage feast, or weapons manufacture), or whether political favours needed to be repaid. It was only after the Roman conquest that a market economy gradually became established in Gaul and Germany.

Celtic bronze coin of the Coriosolites, a tribe in Brittany, showing the head of a deity with a human severed head on a chain attached to his forehead. (Portsmouth Museums)

The use of Celtic precious metal coinage to pay for warfare is dramatically illustrated by the great increase in the number of coins at the time of Caesar as the tribes geared themselves up to confront him. A good example is the hoard of 15,000 coins from Robache, St Dié. This site lies in the territory of the Lingones, a pro-Roman tribe, and it has been suggested that the hoard is a tribal treasure chest buried to avoid capture by an enemy.[3] Much of the gold and silver of the Gauls may have been converted into coins to pay for the war effort. Given the vast number of troops involved, this would have meant a substantial distribution of coins to the population. After the Roman victory much of this must have got into Roman hands as booty, while some remained locally and financed the process of Romanisation during the Augustan period.

At the same time that the Gauls were paying their troops, Caesar too was using silver *denarii* to pay his legions. This is clearly seen in the number of coins dropped by the soldiers at the siege of Alesia.[4] Both sides in the conflict, then, were using precious metals to pay their troops, since in this respect at least the Roman economy functioned in much the same way as the Gaulish. After the conquest, as we might expect, Gaulish gold and silver started to go out of circulation. Interestingly, there was no instant demonetisation. Gold ceased to be minted, but silver continued, almost certainly to pay for Gallic troops acting on Rome's behalf in various areas where tension threatened to flare up into rebellion. A limited number of moneyers were clearly licensed to strike coins using their own names, such as Germanus Indutillus.[5] The coins were equivalent to a Roman *quinarius*, half a *denarius*, presumably because prices in Gaul were low compared with Italy, and therefore coins of smaller value were of more use. After a couple of decades the need for these coins disappeared, as the troops were moved from Gaul up to the Rhineland, where they appear to have been paid in conventional Roman coinage.

The army played a vital role in the transition from Celtic to Roman money. Virtually all coins were produced initially for paying the army, although other expenditure included handouts to state functionaries and official contractors. Military spending therefore fuelled the economy by getting the coins into circulation, and was a major contributor to the development of a monetised trading system. As a consequence the main trading axis in Gaul developed into a corridor linking the army in the Rhine with the Mediterranean and Rome. The Rhône Valley was the main beneficiary of this, as will be seen below.

Silver coin issued by a Gaulish moneyer, Ateula Vlatos, in the period after the conquest of Gaul. It may have been used for paying Gaulish troops employed by the Roman army. (Portsmouth Museums)

Although the Roman army took over from Gaulish warriors as the main recipients of precious metal coinage, there were vast areas of Gaul in which no troops were stationed. How did these areas develop a money economy, and how did coins get into circulation there? The answer lies in part in the use of bronze coinage. In the immediate aftermath of the conquest local communities continued to issue Celtic bronze coinage, which became increasingly important as gold and silver was drained into Roman coffers. It must have been a period of considerable economic dislocation, with low prices and erratic supplies. The bronze coins were small and served the needs of local commerce, but they were at the same time valid for general provincial use, since they are found on Roman forts. This situation continued until about 10 BC, when local coinage ceased to be produced and was replaced by Roman coins issued from the newly established mint at Lyon. Both types of coin continued in circulation side by side for some time after this, but not without difficulty. Roman *asses* and other bronze coins were much larger than the Celtic ones, and must have been inconvenient to use for everyday transactions. A solution appears to have been adopted of cutting the Roman coins into halves and quarters; this must have been just for local use, since the coins would have been thus rendered worthless in Roman eyes. Many such cut coins of Augustan date are known. Gradually the Gallic economy started to prosper, and so rising prices brought the Roman coins into reasonable accord with cash needs in the market-place. Celtic coinage gradually went out of circulation, but it is known to have been used as late as the reign of Trajan (AD 97–117).[6] One reason for the continued circulation of these old coins was that the Roman authorities had difficulties in producing enough bronze to satisfy the needs of the entire western provinces from just a single mint at Lyon (supplemented, of course, by that of Rome). In the mid-first century, for instance, local copies of the

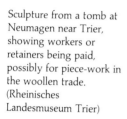

Sculpture from a tomb at Neumagen near Trier, showing workers or retainers being paid, possibly for piece-work in the woollen trade. (Rheinisches Landesmuseum Trier)

official coins started to appear. These were not intended as forgeries, since they were blatantly lighter and poorer than the real coins. They must have served as stop-gap small change for local needs.

Another means by which coins found their way into circulation in the civilian parts of Gaul and Germany was through taxation. It is generally thought that taxation was almost exclusively paid in coins. This meant that people such as villa proprietors had to sell their surpluses of produce in the market-place (i.e. the local *forum* or *conciliabulum*) for coins. As a result of this a money economy gradually evolved for dealing with agricultural and other produce. At the same time the imposition of the taxes also had the effect of stimulating the economy into surplus production. Almost certainly it was the towns that first prospered from a market economy. They housed the major market-places, and it is noticeable that coins occur mainly in urban rather than rural contexts in the early Roman period. Doubtless this is because most of the monetary transactions took place there.

It is generally thought that Roman tax levels were higher than any tribute paid in the pre-Roman period in Gaul as a whole. This, together with the more peaceful conditions, definitely stimulated economic development.[7] The result must have been a tax surplus, with a good deal of revenue going to the treasury in Rome. From there money was redistributed first of all within the city itself, to pay for the vast number of recipients of the food dole (*annona*). Secondly, it went to pay troops on the frontiers. The tax revenues were therefore redistributed in two directions, to the centre (Rome) and to the periphery where the army was stationed. Gaul was sandwiched between the two consuming zones for taxation, and thus stood to gain a great deal from the presence of the spending power of, on the one hand, the neighbouring Rhineland army and, on the other, the not-far-distant market of Rome. The money that went to pay the army circulated especially in the hinterland of the frontier zones, since here the army had to purchase many of its local material needs.

The coinage of the early Imperial period reflects the history of inflation, a matter that was fairly strongly influenced by the army.[8] As we have seen, in the first century AD the coinage in Gaul was dominated broadly speaking by smaller bronzes. Although at first they were not entirely suited to the Gallic economy (since the coinage system was essentially designed for Italian market conditions), as the province gradually became more prosperous during the century these coins became more and more useful in cash transactions. At the same time there were many *denarii* coming from the army, so that a two-metal system was effectively in operation. In the second century there was something of a change. Small bronzes and *denarii* continued in circulation, but a higher-value bronze coin, the *sestertius*, became increasingly common. The fairly high ratio of *sestertii* to *denarii* found in Gaul suggests that the military were by this time spending more in terms of the former than the latter. Meanwhile, the lower-value bronze coins started to decline in number. This pattern is compatible with the higher level of prices in the second century compared with the first, with inflation bringing the larger bronze into more general use.

By the early third century *sestertii* in turn died away almost completely, to be replaced by *denarii* and, later, *antoniniani* (double *denarii*). This can be linked almost directly with increases in army pay by Severus and Caracalla, and concurrent debasements of the silver content of the coinage in order to finance the increases. The consequence was a rapid rise in prices and the start of an inflationary spiral that lasted most of the third century. Bronze coins became effectively worthless, and silver coins of progressively poorer quality were the only important issues in circulation. The army, therefore, had an inflationary effect on the economy, particularly when its pay was raised, since it was eating more of the economic cake of the Empire as a whole.

A comparison of the coin circulation pattern in Gaul and Germany with those in Italy and Britain supports the suggestion that inflation started in militarised areas.[9] In this respect northern Gaul, Germany and Britain were fairly similar to each other, but differed from southern Gaul and Italy, where there was a more even balance in the different types of coin, and less indication that progressively higher-value coins were being used. In other words, it seems likely that there was a stronger inflationary tendency in the northern provinces during the first to third centuries. By the early third century in the north there was a distinct shortage of silver coins in circulation: too few were issued and so they tended to stay within the southern Gaulish and Italian circulation areas, getting progressively rarer further north. This led to widespread coin forgery during the first half of the century. By the middle of the third century, though, this problem was resolved by the issue of vast numbers of very debased *antoniniani*, so that the market was rapidly flooded with coins. This almost certainly had a further strong inflationary effect.

It is in the northern provinces that the pattern of scarcity, followed by sudden abundance of coins, was most marked. There was still a divergence between the north and the south, but southern and northern Gaul were in fact gradually coming together in monetary terms. By the fourth century the pattern of coin circulation in the Gallic and Germanic provinces was different from that of Italy (and Britain). Generally speaking, Gaul, Germany and Britain started to use coins more and more, while in Italy the use of coins seemed to go into decline. There were almost certainly major economic changes which favoured the use of coins, and a fully monetary economy, in the northern provinces. Large numbers of army units were of course stationed in these areas during the late Empire, and they continued to enjoy some prosperity as a result of the army's spending power. However, political and military difficulties at this time tended to offset this potential source of prosperity in many regions (see chapter 8).

Shipping and trade

The existence of military supply routes led to the development of a corridor along the Rhône, Saône, Moselle and Rhine Valleys as the main economic axis of Gaul and Germany. One of the key cities in the corridor was Lyon, the capital of the Three Gauls, situated at the confluence of the Rhône and Saône Rivers. It was a point at which goods were transhipped and traded, and we know from the abundant epigraphic evidence that there was a large community of merchants in the city. Manufacturing of pottery, glass and other goods also went on in the extensive riverside workshop areas, for distribution either by river or by the main road network that radiated from Lyon to the Rhineland, the Channel coast, Aquitaine and the south.[10]

Many of the Lyon inscriptions were put up by *negotiatores* or their families. These people were the traders of the Roman world; they organised cargoes of merchandise, struck deals with manufacturers and retailers, and generally acted as the middlemen in the market system. They often operated as businessmen dealing in a particular commodity, such as pottery, cloaks, wood and so on. Groups of *negotiatores* also formed guilds (*collegia*), which sometimes had memberships of particular trades, and sometimes particular nationalities or trading destinations. It is noticeable from the inscriptions put up by the merchants that many were foreigners, often from the eastern Mediterranean, such as Constantius Aequalis, 'decorator of parade armour and cloth of gold [*barbaricarius*], priest [*sevir Augustalis*] of Colonia Copia Claudia Augusta Lugudunum, citizen of Germanicia [a town in Syria]'.[11] Lyon, in contrast with most other towns in Gaul, must have had a very cosmopolitan atmosphere.

Other towns, too, benefited from being on the main trading axis, particularly Arles near the mouth of the Rhône, where it is thought that the large ships plying the Mediterranean were forced to tranship their cargoes onto river-going craft. North of Lyon the trade route went up the Saône to Chalon-sur-Saône, where goods were unloaded for the overland journey to the head of the Moselle Valley. The next major towns were Metz, then Trier and Cologne, or Mainz. All had significant communities of merchants, and acted as redistribution centres for trade in their respective regions. Both

Cologne and Mainz were on the Rhine, itself part of this major trade route, but it is also important to appreciate that these cities acted as gateways to trade with the barbarian world beyond the Roman frontier in Germania Libera.[12]

It seems very likely that the military supply networks for the army in the north were initially set up at the time of Caesar's conquest. Food, equipment and raw materials were obtained first of all from the south of Gaul and Italy. As the army moved further north and east during the reign of Augustus these supply routes became ever more extended, but they still existed for some time to come. For instance, metal ingots were shipped from south-western Gaul through the city of Narbonne and up the Rhône on the main trade route. A number of industries developed by taking advantage of this supply network, such as the south Gaulish samian potteries, which valued the army as an important element of their market, and used the Narbonne–Rhône route as the means of transporting their products northwards.[13]

In the early Roman period the main economic stimulation by the army was in the south, where the necessary means of production already existed and where the population could respond to demands for military supplies. However, with the gradual development of the interior of Gaul army supplies could be obtained from sources closer to where the troops were stationed. This reduced the problems of long-distance transport of bulk goods. Central Gaul started to benefit, and the production areas gradually moved north and east, roughly following the main trade corridor itself.

Roman bridge at St Chamas on the road from Arles to Marseille, embellished with a pair of monumental arches. It was built following instructions in the will of L. Donnius Flavos, probably in the second century AD, and demonstrates the importance of roads for Roman commerce and communications.

Thus we see the centre of gravity of samian ware production shifting towards the Rhineland. Vines were planted further and further to the north, so that Trier became a major wine producer by the late second century (and remains so down to this day).

Although the army was important for this trade route, it was by no means the only agent for the development of commerce within Gaul. Extensive trading networks survived from the days of pre-Roman contact, and it was not simply the Roman conquest that opened the way for long-distance trade. Strabo mentions how the geography of Gaul made it easy for goods to be transported from sea to sea, specifically referring to routes from the Saône to the Seine and the English Channel; from southern Gaul overland via the territory of the Arverni to the Loire and thence the Atlantic coast; and from the Aude in the vicinity of Narbonne overland to the Garonne and the Bay of Biscay. Archaeological evidence confirms that the Rhône–Saône–Seine and the Aude–Garonne routes were the most important in the late Iron Age. Both served to channel raw materials from the interior of Gaul to the Mediterranean, and finished, usually luxury goods in the other direction. The development of the Rhône Valley route during the Roman period has already been discussed, but the other route, linking Narbonne, Toulouse and Bordeaux, was also of considerable importance. The wine export trade along this route in the pre-Roman period, when large quantities of amphorae were shipped to Britain and Brittany, paved the way for general trade during the Roman period. Wine amphorae are in fact less in evidence, but there are inscriptions from Bordeaux and eastern Britain mentioning traders between the two provinces, and also wrecks from such places as Guernsey and Ploumanac'h-Malban along the Atlantic coastal route.[14]

These two major routes meshed in with the third major trading axis in Gaul, which ran along the Mediterranean coast, linking Italy with Spain, via the mouth of the Rhône. The most striking evidence for this trade route comes in the form of the many wrecks excavated in southern Gaulish waters. By dating the wrecks and analysing their numbers it can be shown that there was a gradual build-up in shipping activity during the late Republic, reaching a peak in the first century BC and the first century AD. Numbers then appear to diminish again, which may be a reflection of the rise and fall of trading activity in southern Gaul and the western Mediterranean generally.[15]

Individual wrecks have revealed a great deal of evidence for the nature of sea-borne trade, not only off the coast of Gaul, but in the Mediterranean as a whole. For instance, one of the early wrecks (about 100 BC) in the Baie de Cavalière appears to have been a coaster.[16] It started from Africa, voyaging via Sicily and Italy to Liguria, finally stopping at Antibes before reaching a premature and unforeseen end a little further round the coast. The journey should possibly have ended up in Spain. The cargo included North African amphorae, a large number of Dressel 1A type amphorae

Part of the cargo of amphorae from the first-century BC wreck at the Madrague de Giens, off the south coast of Gaul.

from Italy and cuts of pork which probably originated in Gallia Cisalpina and were loaded in a Ligurian port.

One of the most famous wreck sites is that of the Grand Congloué, now fairly convincingly shown to be two vessels almost on top of one another, not one as originally thought.[17] The earlier dates to 210–180 BC and the later, with a large cargo of amphorae, to 110–70 BC. Many of the amphorae carry the stamp of Sestius, and were containers for wine from southern Etruria in Italy. The overall distribution of amphorae of this type has been plotted, and they have been found along the coast from western Italy to Gallia Narbonensis, up the Rhône Valley and into the interior of Gaul.[18] The wreck predates Caesar's conquest, and thus is valuable direct evidence for the trade in wine with the Celtic Gauls, and for the way in which Italian producers took advantage of these new markets.

Another wreck, at the Madrague de Giens, gives an important insight into the scale of shipping activity.[19] This also dates to the first century BC, and contains Dressel 1B type wine amphorae originating from the Terracina area to the south of Rome in the 60s and 50s BC. The excavators of the wreck have estimated that the number of amphorae loaded onto the vessel may have been about 6,000, stacked in three levels in the hold. Such a number would give the ship a total displacement weight of 290 tonnes, very large in comparison with the tonnage calculated from the literary references to ancient ships.

The Mediterranean wrecks show that trade was not just going from east to west, but that ships were also picking up cargoes in Spain for transport via southern Gaul to Italy. The Port Vendres II wreck, near the Spanish border, is interesting in this respect since it was carrying a cargo of tin ingots, dated AD 41–2, plus copper and lead, pottery, wine, olive oil and almonds.[20] It is very likely that the olive oil was destined to be off-loaded at a port in the mouth of the Rhône, since amphorae of the type on the wreck have been found along the Rhône Valley, in Switzerland, the Rhineland and southern Britain, but only a few examples are known from Italy. The trading arrangements for this brand of oil seem therefore to have been mainly with Gaul. Other shipwrecks carrying Spanish products are also fairly common off the coast of Gaul. There is a group dating to the first century AD, including La Chrêtienne H, carrying large pottery vessels (dolia), for northern Spanish wine. The containers were probably permanently mounted in the ships for the purpose of bulk transport of wine to Rome and elsewhere.[21]

Generally speaking, the evidence from the wrecks suggests that cargoes were mixed, although often dominated by one type of product. Amphora wrecks, with their cargoes of wine, olive oil or fish sauce, are the most easily detected, because the pottery survives well for modern divers to locate. However, other merchandise was carried, such as metal ingots from Spain or, in the case of the recently discovered wreck in the English Channel off Guernsey, pitch.[22]

Study of amphorae has proved a fertile field of research into ancient trade. A combination of the wreck evidence and distribution maps of particular types can give us a valuable insight into the trading patterns within Gaul and in the Mediterranean basin generally. Recent work on the amphorae from Lyon and Vienne shows that Italy clearly dominated the wine trade in the late first century BC, but that Italian wine gradually declined in popularity, to be replaced by Spanish wine during the early first century AD. Perhaps the latter was cheaper, better, or easier to transport than Italian wine. Whatever the reason, the inflow of Spanish wine in great quantity was relatively short-lived, for by the later first century both it and Italian wine had fallen out of favour, being replaced by the home-grown product from southern Gaul itself. This seems to confirm the literary references to protective measures being taken by emperors such as Domitian to safeguard Italian wine production in the face of growing provincial competition.[23]

The rise of Gallic wine production is also witnessed by the kiln sites for the manufacture of amphorae in Gallia Narbonensis. Vineyard estates had their local kilns, and there was large-scale production of distinctive types of amphora, based ultimately on Greek Massalian types.[24]

Minerals and their extraction

The indications of an increase in trade and prosperity during the late Republic and early Empire are borne out not only by the evidence of the amphorae. Archaeology has revealed that other areas of production, like mining, quarrying and pottery manufacture, also benefited.

Ancient authors, such as Strabo and Pliny, make several references to the mineral wealth of Gaul. For instance, the territories of the Tarbelli, Ruteni and Gabali in south-western Gaul are all mentioned as having deposits of gold, silver and other minerals. There were also the famed islands of the Cassiterides (Cornwall and the Isles of Scilly) with their tin resources, served by a trade route running up the Atlantic coast of Gaul from Bordeaux. Brittany was on this route, and it too produced tin and copper, making it an important centre for the raw materials of bronze production. This part of Gaul was one of the mineral-rich regions during the Roman period, producing lead and silver ores and iron as well. Also important were the area around Limoges, where gold was mined; the southern part of the Massif Central, particularly the Montagne Noire, where there was iron, lead and silver; and the foothills of the Pyrenees, for reserves of lead, silver and iron.[25]

Archaeological evidence for mining and ore-processing comes from many of these areas. One of the most interesting recently studied areas is the territory around Limoges.[26] It is fairly certain that the gold-bearing deposits there were exploited from the late Iron Age onwards. The Lemovices gained considerable wealth from this source, producing large numbers of gold coins, and they were able to provide a substantial body of troops to Vercingetorix at the time of the siege of Alesia. Many of these men were probably involved in the goldworking, but there is as yet little direct evidence of the actual workings themselves. By the Roman period Limoges had emerged as a centre for the mining industry in the region, together with three *vici* a short distance from the city – Praetorium (modern St Goussaud) and Carovicus (modern Château-Chervix) for the gold deposits, and Blotomagus (modern Blond) for the tin ores. The last site has been studied in some detail, showing that just to the north of the *vicus* lay some 50 hectares of workings.[27]

Further south, in the Pyrenees, particularly the region of the Séronais, there has been exploration of various mines that still survive from antiquity with little subsequent disturbance. Le Goutil is a good example of a galleried mine which has not collapsed or been destroyed by later workings, so often the fate of ancient mining activity. It has an interconnecting warren of galleries in the zone where the veins of copper ore were present; as much of the ore as possible was quarried out, leaving columns of unworked stone to support the roof. The technique used was to open up horizontal unshored galleries into the hillside, employing wooden shoring only where there was the threat of a collapse, as at Massiac. Mines also had vertical shafts, sometimes in wood, to connect galleries at different levels.[28] The technology for mines such as this was probably introduced during the immediate pre-Roman period or soon after the conquest, in the late second century BC.

Work in the mines must have been arduous and difficult, yet most were probably run on the labour of nominally free citizens in Gaul and Germany, since there is little evidence for slaves. A lot of the workings were fairly small, and it seems that many deposits were exploited early and worked out fairly quickly. Gaul, in fact, was not as rich in minerals as Spain and Britain. Consequently, it may be that the more difficult Gaulish deposits ceased to be worked after it was known that easier profits could be made in other parts of the Empire. Le Goutil and the other southern Gaulish mines appear to have been active in the first century BC and early first century AD, but not much later. It is interesting that the mines in the Séronais can be dated mainly by amphorae found in the mines themselves, conjuring up a picture of the miners exchanging copper ingots for amphorae of wine as recompense for their labour. The ingots, as we have seen, are found along trade routes from the interior of Gaul and on wrecks along the Mediterranean coast, clearly indicating the value of the trade in metals to Rome and Italy.[29]

While the mines were in operation, there was a well-organised industry for smelting the ore and producing the ingots. Evidence for this industry exists in various forms. The remains of ore-mills have been discovered, and lead seals sometimes depict ore-furnaces. Tools can provide valuable information about technology, and ingots of lead, silver and copper survive, apparently made in traditional shapes. Lead ingots are common, and although the intensive exploitation of the province's mineral resources was relatively short-lived, trade in lead from other provinces continued longer; ingots of British origin are known from various locations in northern Gaul.[30]

Although in Gaul much of the impetus to develop mines, especially deep mines, appears to have come during the Roman period, there was already considerable expertise in mineral- and metalworking before the conquest. Many of the skills, especially in metalworking, may have been developed locally by the native pre-Roman population and numerous fine examples of work in bronze and precious metals testify to the virtuosity of Celtic craftsmen. To some extent metalworking skills declined during the Roman period, for although iron and other metals became more widespread and were used for everyday purposes (such as tools), the artistry and manu-facturing skill was often of a lower order than during the Iron Age. It was mainly the bronze-casters, producing jewellery, statuettes and other small ornaments, who perpetuated the high accomplishments of the pre-Roman metalsmiths.[31]

In contrast to mining for precious metals, exploitation of iron ores was fairly widespread in Gaul. Many areas have evidence for workings, usually open-cast pits. Unfortunately, these have often been destroyed by medieval and modern exploitation of the deposits. The same is true of Roman slag-heaps. These were once of enormous size, since Roman methods were relatively inefficient and left a great deal of usable debris: many were dug up for road metalling in the nineteenth century. Occasionally, however, galleried mines do survive, as in the Montagne Noire, where alongside the copper and lead mines, are some mines for iron ore as well.[32] It is relatively rare to find galleried iron mines, which must have been dug to retrieve high-quality ore.

Some of the iron furnaces that have been investigated could produce on a very large scale indeed. It has been estimated that the shaft furnaces at Les Martys (Aude) used a total of 8–10 million tonnes of ore during the three centuries in which they were operating, from about 50 BC to AD 280. This would have produced from 400,000 to 1,000,000 tonnes of iron, which, as the excavators point out, means that at least 4 tonnes of iron were being made per working day.[33] The iron was mostly converted into ingots, which would then have been transported to places where secondary working took place. Many *vici*, for instance, have yielded plentiful evidence for secondary working. This has been best studied at Alesia, where a small quarter of the town near the forum contained forges and other installations for working metals, including bronze. Primary working of iron and other ores is also attested here, and there was clearly a well-developed industry which may have been the town's speciality.[34]

Some of the iron production was imperially controlled. We know this mainly from the *procurator ferriarium galliarum* based at Lyon, who may have overseen the acquisition of iron, either ingots or finished items, for the army. There is also archaeological evidence for the early manufacture of Roman weapons in Gaul for the army on the Rhine. The types of dagger indicate that in the early first century AD southern Gaul was the main source for the weapons in Germania Superior, while northern Gaul produced those used in Germania Inferior. By the later first century military areas were establishing weapons workshops for themselves. As a result there was a decline in trade with the interior of Gaul, in weapons and presumably in other goods as well. However, we do know that by the later Roman period there were weapons factories in several Gallic and German cities: Strasbourg, Mâcon, Autun, Soissons, Reims, Amiens and Trier.[35]

Study of the iron works suggests that their organisation varied from one region to another. For instance, in the territory of the Namnetes to the north-west of the town of Nantes there appear to have been a large number of iron workings in a more-or-less deserted area, with no villas and little trace of other occupation. A similar situation is encountered in parts of Britain, for instance the Weald, where it has been suggested that some of the workings may have been officially controlled. In contrast, the Entre-Sambre-et-Meuse area of Gallia Belgica had many villas in reasonably close association with iron workings. This area was not particularly suited to traditional agricultural production, and so this may be a case of private enterprise exploiting a known natural resource.[36]

Many of the iron-working sites seem also to have been involved with quarrying. Quite often there was suitable stone for building in roughly the same locations as the iron ore deposits, as at Minot in central Gaul, and in the Pyrenees.[37] It seems likely that the networks for transporting the iron

Bronze statuette of the Celtic god Sucellus, from Vienne (Vienna), a fine example of Gallic metalworking craft. (British Museum)

Tomb of a pottery or bronze-vessel seller from Bourges (Avaricum). Only the traders in pottery and metalware could afford tombstones such as this. The craftsmen making the vessels were generally much poorer. (Bourges Museum)

and other metal ingots were linked in some way with those for the transport of blocks of stone for building and sculpture.

One of the most widely distributed stones was marble from the quarries at St Béat, near St Bertrand-de-Comminges. This generally white marble has been found in many towns in Gaul, principally western towns such as Bordeaux, Limoges, Rennes and Rouen. It is also found in the major towns of the south and east such as Marseille, Arles and Lyon, and further afield in other provinces of the western Mediterranean.[38] It is rare, however, for a stone to be distributed this widely, and it must be a measure of the high quality of St Béat marble. Most quarries tended to serve only their local areas, unless the stone was of exceptional quality or a specialised product, such as lava millstones from Niedermendig in the Rhineland and Volvic in the Auvergne. Many towns had quarries closely associated with them in order to reduce as far as possible the obviously high transport costs. Indeed, for some countryside monuments, such as the Pont-du-Gard or La Turbie, the quarries are very close to the building site itself.[39]

Transport of building stones was by river wherever possible, since it was much slower and more costly to use teams of oxen to pull large blocks along the road system. Quarries near rivers were thus at a considerable advantage; this is seen most dramatically at Seyssel, where the quarries were organised so that the blocks could be lowered directly into barges waiting in the River Rhône below. Harbour-works have also been found at the foot of the quarries into the Drachenfels Mountain on the free German side of the Rhine, not far from Bonn. Also from the Rhineland is the wreck of a river-boat discovered just outside Strasbourg, which was carrying about a tonne of new Niedermendig millstones. Sea-going vessels, too, have been found with cargoes of stone, such as the wreck off St Tropez: this contained columns and other pieces which were, in all probability, destined for a temple at Narbonne.[40]

Most of the stone quarries were open-cast pits, and remains of them can still be seen in many parts of Gaul and Germany. One of the most impressive is at Glanum, where stone was removed to a depth of 23 metres for construction work in the town. This depth is marked by the deliberate preservation of a slender pillar of living rock showing the working faces upon it, a witness to the enormous activity of the quarriers. In its way this memorial has the same purpose as Trajan's Column in Rome, whose height marked the depth of earth removed in the construction of Trajan's Forum.[41]

Rarer than open-casts were the drift and galleried mines. The best studied is at Kruft, near Mayen in the Rhineland, where underground volcanic tufa beds were exploited. There are well-preserved remains of entrances and galleries; marks within the mines indicate that various legions were involved in winning the stone.[42] In both types of quarry traces often survive of the techniques used in the removal of blocks of stone. In one method iron wedges were used to split stone along the bedding planes, leaving the wedge marks in the quarry face and, occasionally, the tools themselves as evidence for this practice.

In some quarries there is evidence for on-the-spot production of architectural ornament and sculpture, usually in the form of unfinished columns, capitals, altars and other elements. For instance, at another legionary quarry at Norroy near Metz there are altars with blank spaces where the inscription was to have been carved, waiting to be transported from the quarry site. At St Boil near Autun many pieces of unfinished sculpture have been found, giving a fascinating insight into the sculptors' techniques.[43] It is especially interesting that sculpture was being produced at source, rather than in workshops in town, as one might expect.

The general impression from the overall dating and distribution of quarries is that the most highly developed stone sources tended to be in the economically successful parts of Gaul and Germany. Particularly in the south-west of Gaul, the fringes of the Massif Central and the Rhineland well-known quarries supplied stone and stone artefacts over a wide region. By contrast, in parts of Gaul away from the economic axes, such as the north-west, good-quality stone was available but hardly exploited except for local purposes. By the later Empire even the more highly organised quarries were starting to run down. Many towns appear to have resorted to reusing stones from monuments of earlier centuries, especially during the great surge in town-wall construction from the late third century onwards. Dismantling existing monuments was often seen as an easier way of obtaining building stone than transporting blocks from a quarry, particularly if the nearest source was some distance away.[44]

An industry related to stone-quarrying was the production of lime. Evidence for this comes generally in the form of the kilns in which limestone was burnt to make lime for building mortar and other purposes. Various kilns have been discovered – usually single kilns built for particular building projects, such as at Treteau near Vichy, but sometimes banks of kilns for large scale production. The best-known multiple kilns are to be found at Iversheim, where they were set up by the military for the building of the nearby legionary fortress at Bonn and other army works along the Rhine. It has been estimated that the kilns produced 2 million kilograms of lime per month.[45]

Kilns and potters

Clay was also exploited as a natural resource. The building trade used fired-clay products such as tiles, bricks and architectural terracottas on an enormous scale, especially in areas where stone was not readily available and consequently where brick, both fired and unfired, was a common feature in walling. Brick- and tile-kilns are known from most regions of Gaul and Germany. It has been established that the earlier kilns of the first century AD or so in the south – Gallia Narbonensis and Aquitania – tend to be circular in form, of a type used in Italy, but they also incorporated some distinctive Gallic characteristics which were probably derived from local pottery-kiln developments; Greek influence can be detected here. From about the end of the first century AD, however, the kilns tended to be rectangular, and became more common in the north. This type is virtually the only one found in the Three Gauls and Germany, and probably had military associations. It was also easy to load because the bricks and tiles themselves were rectangular in form, even though the shape made the kiln rather less efficient in its firing characteristics.[46]

It is interesting to note that several of the early circular kilns are known to have been used for mixed purposes. The group of kilns at Sallèles-d'Aude, for instance, was used for bricks, amphorae and pottery, without the specialisation usually seen elsewhere in ceramic production.[47]

A great deal of research and publication has been devoted to the subject of pottery in recent years. In Gaul and Germany much of this has concentrated on samian pottery (terra sigillata), although recently there has been an upsurge of interest in the so-called coarse wares, for which regional characteristics and dating schemes have been worked out for several areas.[48]

Circular amphora-kiln, and a square kiln for pottery and tiles (foreground), at Sallèles-d'Aude, near Narbonne.

However, it is still the manufacture of samian ware that is understood best, and it gives a valuable insight into the production and distribution systems of an important ancient industry.

Samian ware was one of the luxury pottery types of the Roman world, in its early days vying even with metal vessels as an item of status to grace the dining table. The styles in Gaul were derived essentially from Italian production centred on Arezzo from the mid-first century BC onwards. There had, of course, been earlier home-produced fine wares in Gaul of both La Tène and Hellenistic inspiration, but the taste of the Roman army favoured the red-gloss, relief-moulded, metal-imitation samian ware. By the end of the first century BC samian ware was easily the dominant fine pottery available in Gaul, and indeed in most other provinces of the Empire.[49]

Arezzo itself exported what is now known as Arretine ware widely throughout the Roman world and even beyond. In Gaul the distinctive Arretine vessels have been found on many sites, but most commonly in southern Gaul, the Rhône Valley and the Rhineland – the familiar economic corridor of the region. A recent and very important discovery has established that Arezzo itself was not the only centre of production of this ware. Not only were there kilns at other towns in Italy, but a branch factory also existed in Lyon.[50] Arretine potters had decided, perhaps for reasons of cost, to set up workshops by the banks of the Saône, and sent potters, vessel moulds and other equipment out to Lyon. They produced drinking-vessels and other tableware in the Augustan period and early first century AD that were visually identical to pots from the mother kiln centre. The products can only be distinguished today through the use of chemical analytic techniques. It is clear that the Lyon branch distributed its pottery widely, but especially to military sites on the Rhine frontier, such as Haltern or Neuss. Arretine and its Lyon version were expensive items even for the military to purchase, for their artistic and technical quality was unsurpassed. Yet in Italy itself the pottery went into decline, possibly because its status dropped in the face of the wider availability of gold, silver and glass vessels. Arretine became a more humble product, and an opening was made for provincial samian ware producers to expand and take advantage of its eclipse.

Production at Lyon went into decline at roughly the same time as at Arezzo itself, reinforcing the hypothesis that it did not have an independent existence. The workshops that came to the fore instead were La Graufesenque near Millau in southern Gaul, and Lezoux near Clermont-Ferrand in central Gaul.[51] Both are situated in valleys in the Massif Central, with good clay deposits and the other resources needed for pottery-making on a large scale. Of the two, it was La Graufesenque that was to achieve the greater success. Early Lezoux production had various technical problems, and went into decline about the middle of the first century, although it revived strongly after the collapse of south Gaulish production in the early second century.

La Graufesenque is a massive kiln site and *vicus*, covering many hectares. Recent excavations have revealed a dense pattern of workshops, kilns and vast scatters of waster pottery. One pit alone contained 30,000 vessels. From these remains and from the pottery itself we can get a fairly good idea of the organisation of the industry. Moulds were used to produce relief decoration, and the vessels incorporated name-stamps of the potters involved, often making it possible to identify the styles of individual factories. There was large-scale production of a range of decorated and undecorated vessel types, apparently in communal workshops. However, potters in the workshops made vessels in very similar styles, obviously sharing decorative motifs, so that it can be difficult to distinguish one individual from another. There must have been a primitive sort of mass-

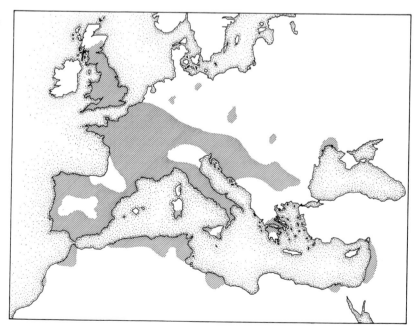

The distribution of south Gaulish samian ware, one of the most successful pottery products in the ancient world.

production system, with some potters making the punches used for design elements in the moulds, some making the moulds themselves, some turning out the vessels from the moulds and some producing the special red-gloss samian slip that coated the finished pots.

It also seems very likely that the pots were fired communally as well. Large kilns holding up to a 100 cubic metres of pottery have been excavated, and there is also a remarkable series of graffiti scratched into samian plates that were probably put into the kilns as tallies of the work of individual potters. Most of the graffiti record kiln firings, often using the word *tuθos*, probably the Celtic word for a kiln, together with a record of the number of vessels made by each potter, often adding up to 30,000 or more.[52] It may be that the kilns were operated by specialists as well, who perhaps fired the kilns on a contract basis with the potters involved.

The southern Gaulish samian from La Graufesenque and its numerous related sites was extraordinarily successful. The pottery is known throughout the Mediterranean, from the east to Spain and Morocco, and also north to Britain, where it was much used by the army on the northern frontier. It started to replace Arretine ware in Italy itself, as is graphically shown by an unopened crate of south Gaulish ware from Pompeii, buried in the volcanic explosion of AD 79, approximately the date at which production at La Graufesenque reached its apogee.[53] Many millions of vessels must have been made at the main kiln centre during its lifetime, and samian ware was one of the most ubiquitous Roman products, vying with wine and oil amphorae in the wide-scale distribution that it achieved. One of the reasons for its success was that the pottery was not just a slavish imitation of Arretine. The pedestal-footed classical vessels of Arezzo and Lyon were replaced by forms and decoration that reflected provincial and military tastes much more closely. In artistic terms, south Gaulish ware marks a decline from the standards set by Arretine production, but the technical quality was just as good and it may well be that the potters consciously decided to appeal to lower-status tastes. The change in style proved to be a great commercial success, and was combined with changes in the form of many of the vessels, which made them easier to transport. These factors set the pattern for all subsequent samian production.

After the Flavian period La Graufesenque started to go into decline. The reasons for this are not entirely obvious, but there does seem to have been a change in the market conditions in the Mediterranean area. Demand for red-gloss decorated pottery was not so widespread, and long-distance export of south Gaulish ware became difficult in the face of local production in Spain and North Africa. The kiln centre could not maintain the dominant position it had enjoyed up to that point, and so by the beginning of the second century the dormant central Gaulish kilns started to revive and challenge La Graufesenque's hold on the northern market. The centre of gravity of samian ware production now moved north, and the traditional types of samian ware became confined more and more to the north-western provinces, particularly the Three Gauls (excluding Aquitania), Britain, Germany, and along the Danube as well.[54] It is very interesting to see that Gallia Narbonensis and Aquitania effectively ceased to purchase traditional samian ware, especially the decorated types, relying instead on locally produced, somewhat simpler variants on the samian theme.

Lezoux and other central Gaulish sites, such as Les-Martres-de-Veyre, started to develop strongly from the early second century. At the same time workshops were established in eastern Gaul by potters migrating from central and, to a lesser extent, southern Gaul. The earliest of these dates from the mid-first century, at Boucheporn, and an area defined by Trier, Mainz and Strasbourg became the main focus of activity in the east.[55] It is noteworthy that the location of samian ware centres lay along the fringes of the main north–south economic axis, with a gradual move north which reflects the shift of emphasis northwards in other areas of the economy during the early Empire. There were, in fact, many other suitable clay deposits in Gaul that could have produced samian ware, but it seems that the marketing conditions had to be favourable for the establishment of a new kiln centre: hence the concentration of kilns in the area of the main trade route.

During the first half of the second century Lezoux and related sites rose to prominence as the main samian production centre. The distribution network was on a smaller scale than that of La Graufesenque, but the area of distribution was still extraordinarily wide. Britain was dominated in the fine pottery market by Lezoux samian, as was most of Gaul, and there was also an important distant market in the Danube area. The two major areas that central Gaulish ware was not able to penetrate to any extent were the Rhineland, where the burgeoning east Gaulish industries managed to establish themselves relatively early on, and the south, where substitutes came into fashion.

The organisation of the workshops at Lezoux was somewhat different from that of La Graufesenque. They were less communally organised, so

Decorated samian ware bowl by Cinnamus, one of the principal potters at Lezoux (Ledosus) in central Gaul during the later second century. (British Museum)

that it is possible to identify the work of individual potters more easily. Cinnamus, Paternus and Doeccus, for instance, had relatively distinctive styles, although they are known to have produced vast numbers of pots: indeed, it is conceivable that they were not individuals but workshops with a house style, run perhaps by a master with apprentices. Workshops also appear to have had their own kilns and production facilities, so that they were more self-contained than the potters at La Graufesenque.[56]

This trend towards individual workshops operating from a single centre continued in the later east Gaulish potteries. For instance, at Rheinzabern, where there has been considerable excavation in recent years, there were groups of workshops which appear to have been fairly independent of one another, but which were nevertheless grouped together for mutual benefit in a potting town. The interesting thing about many of the east Gaulish centres is that their wares tended to be more locally distributed, and some were producing on a fairly small scale by comparison with the gigantic volumes of earlier years. Only Rheinzabern and Trier were exporting samian on a scale approaching Lezoux.[57]

By the late second century the market for samian ware was starting to decline in a slow process that continued well into the third century. There were economic problems during the third century (see chapter 8), and increasing difficulties in the movement of goods over long distances started to restrict the export market for the pottery. There was also a gradual decline in the quality of the product, and the high status that the pottery once enjoyed was effectively lost. Samian ware had gone down-market, while at the same time coarse-ware producers were raising the quality of their products, so that the gap between red-gloss tableware and the general run of crockery in use in a Gallic or German household decreased. Samian ware, and other fine and coarse wares, were often being produced in the same kiln centres by this time, and eventually production of traditional samian ware ceased altogether. Moulded decorated ware, in fact, totally disappeared by the late third century. There were successors, such as the Argonne kilns, which produced imitations of the glossy finish and forms of true samian ware, but by then tastes had swung away from the highly decorated bowls and cups that characterised samian ware production in its heyday.[58]

One important area in which samian ware can give us information concerns the social status of the potters.[59] Because many of the potters signed their names on their vessels we can get some idea of their citizenship status. For the Arretine wares of Italy it is fairly clear that most of the actual potters were slaves or freedmen, while the proprietors were Roman citizens who owned the land and the workshops in which they worked. However, the proprietors themselves were neither particularly wealthy nor of high rank within the Roman hierarchy. Even such high-quality pottery as Arretine and Gaulish samian did not apparently occupy a place within the higher economic spheres of the Empire as a whole.

Slaves figure very rarely in the records for the Gaulish samian industry, in contrast to that of Arezzo, and it seems likely that the potters were free men, although not Roman citizens, since there are very few instances of potters with the three names (*tria nomina*) that indicated the status of citizenship. The social organisation of the Gaulish and German pottery workshops was thus radically different from those of Arezzo, and reflects the generally lower slave population that is assumed for the north-west provinces. We can here return to the concepts of the patron and his clients discussed in chapter 4, and suggest that patrons were the proprietors of workshops who set up facilities for their skilled clients. The patron would have looked after the sale of the pottery and tried to ensure the livelihood of his clients, while the clients provided him with income and enhanced his social standing by acting in his employ. The social status of the potters, of course, remained fairly low, and it was the proprietors and particularly the *negotiatores artis cretariae*, the businessmen who dealt in the wholesale market for the pottery, who held the key to the prosperity of the industry. They usually operated from nearby large towns, and they were the only people involved who were likely to become wealthy themselves as a result – able, for instance, to afford commemorative inscriptions. Nevertheless, these traders too were often freedmen, or Roman citizens of fairly low rank. The pottery industry was clearly not of the standing, even in Gaul and Germany, that traditional occupations like landholding and agriculture enjoyed.

FURTHER READING

There has been no general survey of the economy of Gaul since A. Grenier's *An Economic Survey of Ancient Rome III, la Gaule romaine* (1937), 379–644. However, many individual aspects have been investigated, and current thinking is now rather different from that of Grenier's day. Coins and the economy are covered best by R. Reece in *Coinage in Roman Britain* (1987), which has much of relevance for Gaul and Germany. Celtic coinage is discussed by D. Nash in *Coinage in the Celtic World* (1987). Transport and shipping are analysed in various publications, notably J. Taylor and H. Cleere (eds), *Roman Shipping and Trade: Britain and the Rhine provinces* (1978), and Y. Roman, *De Narbonne à Bordeaux* (1983). Notable shipwrecks include the Grand Congloué (Benoit 1961) and the Madrague de Giens (Tchernia *et al.* 1978). River-boats from Zwammerdam in the Rhineland are published by Weerd (1988). See also A. Tchernia, *Le Vin de l'Italie romaine* (1986) for a wide-ranging discussion of the wine trade and the evidence from amphoras.

Nearly all the recent work on metal-working and mining is brought together in three conference proceedings, *Les Mines et la Métallurgie en Gaule et dans les Provinces voisines* (1987), *Mines et Fonderies antiques de la Gaule* (Paris 1982) and F. Braemer (ed.), *Les Ressources minérales et l'Histoire de leur Exploitation* (1986). Stone quarrying is discussed in R. Bedon's excellent monograph, *Les Carrières et le Carriers de la Gaule romaine* (1984).

Work on pottery, especially samian ware, is notoriously scattered through a large number of different publications, but fortunately has been recently surveyed in C. Bémont and J.-P. Jacob, *La Terre sigillée gallo-romaine* (1986), *Les Potiers gaulois* (DossHA 6, 1974) and *Céramique en Gaule romaine* (DossHA 9, 1975). D. Peacock has a very good general survey of the subject in *Pottery in the Roman World* (1982). Amphora- and tile-kilns are discussed by Laubenheimer (1985) and Le Ny (1988) respectively.

6

ROMANO-CELTIC
AND OTHER
RELIGIONS

Of all the provinces in the western part of the Roman Empire, the Three Gauls, Britain and, to a lesser extent, Germany are distinguished by their adherence to an indigenous, Celtic religion. Many impressive temples and religious sculptures are known, particularly in Gaul, all displaying the characteristic style that is usually referred to as Romano-Celtic. To judge from the surviving remains, the vast majority of the inhabitants of Gaul and Germany followed this religion or its Romano-German equivalent (see chapter 7), leaving little opportunity for the other major religious groupings – official classical cults, and eastern mystery cults – to become well established. Indeed, it was not until the advance of Christianity in the late fourth century that the Romano-Celtic cults lost their predominant position.

Since Romano-Celtic religion was indigenous, we can only hope to understand it by going back to the Iron Age, before Roman influence made itself felt very strongly. An episode in Lucan's *Pharsalia*, describing a shrine near Marseille which was destroyed during the siege of 49 BC, gives a glimpse of this early period:[1]

A grove there was, untouched by men's hands from ancient times, whose interlacing boughs enclosed a space of darkness and cold shade, and banished the sunlight far above. No rural Pan dwelt there, no Silvanus, ruler of the woods, no Nymphs; but gods were worshipped there with savage rites, the altars were heaped with hideous offerings, and every tree was sprinkled with human gore. Water, also, fell there in abundance from dark springs. The images of the gods, grim and rude, were uncouth blocks formed of felled tree-trunks. Their mere antiquity and the ghastly hue of their rotten timber struck terror. Legend told that often the subterranean hollows quaked and bellowed, that yew trees fell down and rose again, that the glare of conflagration came from trees that were not on fire, and that serpents twined and glided around

Stairway leading from the water shrine to the hilltop sanctuary in the town of Glanum in southern Gaul.

the stems. The people never resorted thither to worship at close quarters, but left the place to the gods ... The grove was sentenced by Caesar to fall before the stroke of the axe.

In this splendid passage we are introduced to most of the well-known features of Celtic religious practice. The idea of the open-air sacred grove is particularly strong, and a number of the Greek and Latin authors refer to them.[2] The other aspects given here, such as human sacrifice, sacred piles of votive offerings, crude cult-images and the primitive power of the religion, are also recurrent themes in the ancient sources, so much so that there is a suspicion that these descriptions are more of a literary convention than factual reporting.

This suspicion is strengthened by two considerations. The more important is the widespread anti-Gallic feeling amongst the Romans, which dated back to the sack of Rome by the Gauls in about 390 BC and which was still significant at the time of Claudius' speech in the Senate about the admission of Gauls as senators.[3] Literary references tend to emphasise the bloodthirsty nature of the Gauls, together with other undesirable traits, such as their quarrelsomeness, vanity and dishonesty. Moreover, it is clear that many of the ancient writers derived their information from earlier literary descriptions, which were thus hearsay, without dependable authority. Nevertheless, there is no need merely to dismiss Lucan's sacred grove as a figment of his imagination. It almost certainly bears some resemblance to shrines that existed in southern Gaul during the late Iron Age, and in fact there is archaeological evidence to back up what Lucan wrote.

As we have seen above (chapter 1), a strong Greek influence in southern Gaul was absorbed by inhabitants of towns such as Glanum, and we can talk of Gallo-Greek culture. But there were other places such as Taradeau, which remained virtually untouched by this influence right up to the end of the Republic. A similar contrast is also evident in religious matters. Temples at Glanum, Roquepertuse and Entremont owed much to Greek (and Etruscan) influence in aspects of their architecture and sculptural technique.[4] They had stone lintels, tall stele, free-standing painted stone sculptures and occasionally such details as columns with distinctively styled capitals. Yet all these temples also had features which compare remarkably well with Lucan's flamboyant description. Severed human heads abound, either in stone, or in the form of skulls with iron spikes for fixing them to the temple. The lintels and pillars of the shrines had niches for these trophies, and there were statues of gods sitting cross-legged and holding severed heads in their hands. The gods were seated on pedestals and wore the armour of the warriors of the tribe.

Such temples seem to imply a warrior cult which depicted the god as a military hero, and which can be related to the references to head-hunting and trophies provided by Poseidonius and others.[5] In many ways the most significant of these sites is at La Cloche at Pennes-Mirabeau, a small hillfort only a few kilometres from Marseille. It appears to have been destroyed at the time of Caesar's siege of the city. Finds from the recent excavations include a cross-legged statue and human skulls with nails and metal fittings for their display.[6] The skulls were probably placed on the rampart and the gate. Lucan's sacred grove, if it really existed, would have been in the same general area as this hillfort, perhaps on lower-lying ground to the northeast of the city, and it is easy to see the correspondences between the archaeological and the historical evidence. It may even be the case that the apparently deliberate mutilation and destruction of the statue was connected with the capture of the hillfort by the Romans, suggesting a link with the destruction of the sacred grove on Caesar's orders.

Worshippers at the shrines on these sites also venerated water and sky gods. This is best seen at Glanum, where a stone stairway runs up from a sacred pool to a cave via series of terraces cut into the hillside. Soil erosion has made it impossible for us to know exactly what was set on the terraces, but it is likely to have been some sort of open-air temple. The god's name was Glanis, and he had female counterparts, the Glanicae, who are usually thought to be mother goddesses. These were Celtic deities, but it is significant that an inscription mentioning them also has a dedication to a Roman goddess, Fortuna Redux.[7] It was made by a retired soldier from one of the legions on his return home some time in the first century AD. Clearly the cult at Glanum had been altered from its purely Celtic state by this time, and had acquired some Roman characteristics.

The sacred pool of Glanis at Glanum, with a shrine to Hercules beyond.

Glanum, in fact, provides a good illustration of the way in which Celtic deities were transformed by Graeco-Roman culture. Almost certainly the original cult on this spot was one without monumental temples, sculpture or inscriptions: it was 'atectonic and aniconic', to quote one of the commentators on Celtic religion.[8] However, under Greek influence, derived mainly from Marseille, new ideas about portraying the gods made themselves felt. The cross-legged gods typify this period, probably to be dated at Glanum to the third to second century BC. This is the start of a process that fundamentally transformed Celtic religion – the process of 'reification', in which religious feelings and ideas were expressed increasingly in specific material form, so that deities previously conceived on an abstract level were given human shape as gods and goddesses. Set iconographic poses were also introduced as part of this process, to make individual deities easily recognisable. This was common in the Greek and Roman worlds, so much so that abstract concepts, such as good fortune (Fortuna), could be portrayed in human guise.

The next stage at Glanum, probably in the second century BC, saw the introduction of Greek architectural ideas. The stone stairway was constructed at this time, and the sacred pool made into a regularly shaped stone-built monument. Just to the south of the sanctuary there was a portico with columns and decorated column capitals. These are of particular interest, since a variety of gods are depicted amongst the volutes and foliage of the capitals. Each capital has four heads; on one, for instance, are shown Mercury, a bearded man, a woman, a Celtic water-god with a torc round his neck, and two fish. It is a remarkable combination of the Graeco-Roman and Celtic religious worlds, carved in a local style so that the heads have typically Celtic almond-shaped staring eyes. Yet the capitals themselves are undoubtedly a product of artistic ideas emanating from the civilisations of the Mediterranean.

These capitals show both the developing trend for depicting Celtic gods in human form, and the tendency to add classical gods to those already being worshipped. This second feature can be explained by the tolerance of both religions towards new gods and goddesses, with the result that traditional and introduced cults were worshipped alongside one another. The important question, of course, is who introduced the classical gods to Glanum, and why. The excavator of the site, Henri Rolland, favoured the idea that Greeks from Marseille were living in the town, following their own religion; but it is equally possible that the very strong Hellenisation of the native population led them to adopt not only Greek (and Roman) material values, but some of their spiritual ones too.[9] It could also have become a status symbol to be a follower of the relatively novel classical cults.

Despite the Hellenistic influence, there was no toning down of the Celtic cults themselves. This is indicated at Glanum by a lintel carved with bead-and-reel details; it also has small niches cut into it for severed human heads, showing that the warrior cult clearly continued, possibly right up to the mid-first century BC and the establishment of proper Roman rule in the area. We do not find any evidence at this stage for what was to happen later further north, namely the identification of native gods with their better-known Graeco-Roman counterparts. For a time cults coexisted, but gradually Celtic religion dwindled at Glanum in the face of an upsurge of Romanisation at the beginning of the Imperial period. This meant that the sacred pool became dominated by a temple to the Roman god of health, Valetudo. Marcus Agrippa himself dedicated this temple,[10] perhaps at the time that the town received the privilege of *ius Italicum*. It was a temple in the standard Roman style, with a porch of columns facing the road of the sanctuary. Celtic influence was not entirely absent, but was restricted to a roof ornament with a human bust wearing a torc. By the first century AD the cult of Hercules had also established itself on the other side of the pool, and if we include Fortuna Redux, it would seem that the once all-important Celtic gods, Glanis and the Glanicae, now formed a minority amongst the deities within the sacred area. Hercules and Fortuna are mentioned on inscriptions put up by people with military connections, and it may have been through the army that further influence on the Roman religion of the town made itself felt.

The conclusion to be drawn from looking at religious life at Glanum is that the Celtic cults were open to Graeco-Roman ideas and customs, but probably retained their individuality, not being absorbed by their classical counterparts. Instead, classical religion was established alongside traditional beliefs, which had the effect, probably unforeseen at the time, of diminishing the status of the Celtic cults. Eventually they almost completely disappeared throughout the south of Gaul as the local population took more and more to fully developed Roman culture. The demise of Celtic religion may have coincided with the disappearance of Gaulish language in the south, since the 'Gallo-Greek' inscriptions die out at about the same time.

Native religion developed very differently further north. Iron Age cults and rituals untouched by direct Mediterranean influence continued for much longer, as shown by the dramatic recent findings at two sites in Picardy, Gournay-sur-Aronde and Ribemont-sur-Ancre.[11] At Gournay an area within an Iron Age hillfort was marked off by a square enclosure. In the centre the excavators found a sequence of structures dating from the third century BC to the fourth century AD. This was the shrine, which at first was probably an open-air sanctuary, surrounded by large pits into which offerings were put. Later a wooden temple was constructed, and the offerings continued to be placed in the boundary ditch of the enclosure. These offerings give us spectacular confirmation of Lucan's 'savage rites': human bones were found, together with weaponry and other artefacts. Close examination of the bones reveals that axes were used to behead the humans and to sever the heads of animals (oxen, horses, sheep). It seems fairly clear that these are the remains of sacrifices, including the human sacrifices that the Romans

Human limb bones, probably the remains of sacrifices, piled up in the pre-Roman sanctuary at Ribemont-sur-Ancre in Picardy. After the conquest the bones were covered over to make way for a Roman-style rural sanctuary.

deplored so much. Similarly, at Ribemont, a site best known for its imposing Roman period rural sanctuary, an extraordinary find of an ossuary of human bones has brought the literary references to Celtic religion into sharp archaeological focus.

The human bones were not individual skeletons, but the dismembered remains of 200 to 250 people, for the most part young males. There were no skulls, ribs or backbones, and the bones had been very carefully placed around a central post in a square pattern. Thigh and arm bones were positioned in rows, with alternate rows on top of one another at right angles. Many of these bones had cut marks caused by weapons. This gruesome monument probably belongs to the third century BC, to judge from the associated weaponry, but it may have continued in use up to the time of the Roman conquest or possibly just after. Evidence of burning over the pile of bones suggests that the ossuary was destroyed at this point and partially dismantled – not surprisingly, in view of the Romans' detestation of human sacrifice, and their objection to the burial of human remains within sanctuaries. To explain this unique find the excavators propose three hypotheses: that it represents the remains of human sacrifices, a victory trophy, or a special type of burial rite.[12] One of the first two explanations seems, however, preferable, in view of what we know from other sources about Celtic religion. Human sacrifice was definitely part of the ritual, including, for instance, the dismemberment of human victims who were suspended from a tree in a ritual to appease Esus (equated with Mars).[13] War trophies, made up of piles of weapons and the sacrificed remains of prisoners and animals, are also mentioned by Caesar and others.[14] These trophies were placed in sacred areas where no one could touch them, on pain of death. This would seem to conform well with the nature of the Ribemont find. Presumably the heads of the sacrificed prisoners were displayed elsewhere, as we have already seen at the southern Gaulish sanctuaries. This, then, is the equivalent of the warrior cult of the south, and is probably linked with the Celtic Mars.

Reconstruction of a small Romano-Celtic temple of typical square plan, at the Archéodrome at Beaune.

Roman intervention in northern Gaul led to great changes in the character of Celtic religion there. Decrees were passed against human sacrifice and its practitioners, the Druids.[15] From the Augustan period onwards temples were built using Roman construction techniques and with classical embellishments, such as Corinthian columns and painted wall-plaster. This can be seen at Ribemont, where the destruction of the ossuary was followed firstly by the construction of a wall enclosing the sacred area and then by a large square temple with a portico around it.[16] This architectural form, with its double square plan, was distinctive to Gaul, Britain and parts of Germany, and is usually termed Romano-Celtic, since it is by far the most common temple type in the region – over four hundred are known.[17] Well-preserved examples at Autun, Fréteval and elsewhere indicate that the central part of the temple was a tower, with an east-facing entrance and a position for the cult-image within it. Generally the central tower was small, being designed primarily as a house for the god rather than a place for congregational worship. The portico around was more variable, sometimes being a colonnade, sometimes a solid wall with windows. It was not, in fact, present at every temple. It is also not known how these porticos were used; explanations of their suggested function range from their use as ambulatories for processions around the central shrine, to their being shelters for worshippers and offerings. In support of the latter viewpoint are finds of altars in the portico at Pesch, near Bonn, and a series of life-size statues at Avallon.[18]

The square temple plan was not the only one linked with Romano-Celtic religion, for there were polygonal and circular shrines as well, also equipped with porticos. In western Gaul, from Aquitaine to Armorica, the dominant temple type was a large circular tower, several of which survive, notably at Périgueux and La Rigale.[19] The Tour de Vésone at Périgueux still stands to a height of 24 metres, a gaunt, windowless cylinder today, but originally provided with a colonnaded portico and an embellishment of plaster and marble facings inside and out. It stood within a large square courtyard which formed the sacred area of the temple; here most of the public rituals would have taken place, particularly at the altar just to the east of the east-facing doorway into the temple.

Most Romano-Celtic temples had surrounding courtyards, and excavations in them have revealed that the remains of sacrifices and votive offerings were commonly deposited there. The usual offerings were joints of meat, pots with food in them, and trinkets such as rings or bracelets. Specifically religious items tend to be rarer, but include pottery figurines, miniature tools and weapons, and Stone Age axes.[20] Many of these objects must have possessed symbolic significance. For instance, the axes were probably regarded as Jupiter's thunderbolts, and the miniature wheels as sun-symbols associated with Taranis, a Celtic god equated with Jupiter. All these items were dedicated to the gods by worshippers, either on festival days or as private supplications. It is interesting to see that the types of offerings vary a great deal from temple to temple, which must be a reflection of the different deities venerated.[21] This is an area of research that is only just beginning as temples start to be excavated under modern scientific conditions, and doubtless it will eventually be possible to determine which deity was worshipped at a temple, even if direct indications, from sculpture and inscriptions, are lacking.

As far as religious sculpture and inscriptions are concerned, it is fortunate that Gaul and Germany have a large number of very interesting examples.[22] It is from these that we get our main understanding of the way in which Roman ideas were introduced into Celtic religion. Most striking is the development of Roman 'interpretation' of the native gods (interpretatio romana). Romans such as Caesar and Tacitus wrote, mainly for the benefit of their Latin readership, of the equivalences that could be made between Roman and Celtic or Germanic gods.[23] It is clear from these that they believed the religions to be essentially the same, so that Taranis could be equated with Jupiter, for instance, or Esus with Mars.

In reality matters were not quite so simple, as the varied and complex Romano-Celtic depictions and inscriptions clearly show. A sculptured stone from the large temple site of Les Bolards in Burgundy showing three divinities brings us firmly into the realm of syncretism, or the combination of attributes of different gods.[24] On the left side is a mother goddess holding a cornucopia (horn of plenty) and a patera (dish for making offerings at an altar). She is a Celtic goddess attired here in Roman fashion and holding Roman-style attributes. The same deity often appears elsewhere as three goddesses seated side by side: the practice of multiplying images by three to strengthen their religious power was very widespread in the Celtic world. On the sculpture from Les Bolards she is probably the consort of one of the other two male gods. On the right of the stone is a man with a triple

Three deities on a sculpted relief from the important temple at Les Bolards near Dijon. On the left is a mother goddess, in the centre probably Apollo, and on the right the powerful Celtic god Cernunnos, with antlers growing from his triple head. (Nuits-St Georges Museum)

face, carved with three mouths and three noses, but only four eyes. Antlers grow out of his head, and there is a torc round his neck. He is dressed in tunic and cloak as a hunter, but has in his lap a bag which probably has coins in it, and another lies at his feet. This god is Cernunnos, one of the most powerful of Celtic deities. He appears to have ruled over life and death, but he had no obvious equivalent in Roman religion, although attempts have been made by modern scholars to equate him with Apollo or Dis Pater. The third figure presents, in many ways, the greatest problems of interpretation, since he is seated in the typical nearly naked, rather effeminate pose of Apollo, and is accompanied by a snake at his feet; he does not, however, have Apollo's lyre. Instead, there is a cornucopia, and he wears a head-dress in the form of a town wall – a 'mural crown'. This person is a type of genius, or protective spirit, perhaps in this case to be linked with Apollo, who, as we know from other sculptures, is often depicted with Cernunnos. However, it seems odd that he occupies such a prominent position in the centre of the stone while Cernunnos, the more powerful god, is placed to one side. There is much that cannot be explained easily on this stone, and it is typical of many from Roman Gaul and Germany in having a bewildering combination of the Roman and the Celtic in its religious attributes.

The most interesting manifestation of the combining of Roman and Celtic religious ideas can be seen in the so-called 'Jupiter-Giant' columns.[25] These are found in Germany and the eastern parts of Gaul, often in the courtyards of Romano-Celtic temples. At the top of a column up to 15 metres high a god, sometimes in armour and carrying thunderbolts, rides down another god, who is usually depicted as a giant with serpentine legs. In artistic terms it is a classical gigantomachy or giant-slaying scene, but here it is adapted to fit the Celtic idea of the sky-god. The sky-god may be Taranis, and equivalent to Jupiter, as in fact dedications at the foot of some of the columns indicate. The columns themselves are carved in Graeco-Roman style, and there are often gods and goddesses adorning the shaft and base. No evidence survives for 'Jupiter-Giant' columns before the Roman conquest, and indeed most date to the second or third centuries. However, few would deny that they are a distinctive product of Celtic religion in its Romanised form.

This brings us to the crux of the problem of characterising Romano-Celtic religion: was it a diluted overlay of conquering Roman culture on true Celtic religion, as pro-Celticists maintain, or was it more the culmination of Celtic religious expression, taking advantage of new artistic and archi-tectural opportunities offered by the advent of the Romans? The evidence from Gaul and Germany suggests the latter, since the tower-like temples and the religious iconography have their roots in the pre-Roman world, yet this world was strongly influenced by Graeco-Roman civilisation. Ideas came into Gaul that brought about a change in religious outlook, manifested in temples and cult-images from the first century BC onwards.[26] This marks a stage in the development of Celtic religion, in that its 'atectonic and aniconic' nature was no longer of central importance. Worshippers now came to prefer the paraphernalia of buildings and statues, and this preference can be connected with other aspects of 'pre-Roman Romanisation', par-ticularly among the aristocracy of the Gaulish tribes. What is of great interest in this development is that Graeco-Roman temples and iconography were not adopted wholesale by the Gauls, but were tailored to their specific religious needs: thus the tower-temple came into being for their shrines, and the cross-legged god as one of their deities. Both of these features are virtually unknown outside the Celtic sphere of influence, yet their expression in Celtic (and Romano-Celtic) religion employed the art and architecture of the Mediterranean world.

After Caesar's conquest of the north, particularly from the Augustan period, Romanisation of religion became much more intense, with craftsmen arriving from the south to build stone temples and carve sculptures. It is noticeable, in fact, that the earliest stone Romano-Celtic temples were either in the south (which was already Romanised), or in the vicinity of the Rhône–Rhine route, along which influences from the south could easily pass.[27] Some temples, such as Elst near Nijmegen in the Netherlands, were early enough to be the first stone structures in their areas. Elst was built only a few years after the pacification of the north, and may well have been the result of official encouragement. Most, however, were purely local expressions of religious devotion, and we consequently get a fascinating insight into the importance attached to religious sanctuaries by people keen to enter into provincial Roman culture and life. This burst of temple-building coincided with new iconographic ideas which, for the first time at many shrines, gave two- or three-dimensional form to divinities such as

Cernunnos, Epona, Sucellus and Nantosuelta. Purely classical representations of gods were also made, such as Zenodorus' statue of Mercury for a shrine in the territory of the Arverni, and the life-size bronze statue of Mars from Coligny in eastern Gaul, dated to about AD 50–100, which was almost certainly from a Romano-Celtic temple, perhaps at nearby Villards-d'Héria. The Coligny Mars was found with a famous bronze calendar of Celtic festivals, which is in itself evidence of the Romanisation of Celtic religion, for the pre-Roman tradition had been wholly oral. Here we see the relaxation of this tradition, and the production of a classical-style calendar for display in a temple precinct.[28]

The number and variety of religious representations of the first and second centuries is such that it is possible to obtain a clear idea of the distribution of cults, for instance the tricephalic god in Champagne and Burgundy, or Sucellus in the Rhône Valley.[29] Some cults, such as that of the goddess Epona, spread from their original centres, in her case the territory of the Aedui, and it is possible to see how the movement of peoples caused Celtic cults to become less localised and more diversified. For Epona the recruitment of Aeduans into the Roman army may have played a considerable part in the spread of the cult, which is found as far afield as Rome itself.

Another type of cult centre that became particularly popular after the Roman conquest was the healing shrine. Most of such shrines were associated with water and had pre-Roman origins, but it was not until the establishment of the provincial road system and the building of large bath complexes that pilgrims came in great numbers. Sites such as Mont-Dore, Vichy, Fontaines-Salées, Badenweiler, Luxeuil-les-Bains and Aachen had large bath complexes associated with temples. Some, such as Mont-Dore and Fontaines-Salées, were rural centres, providing hostels and other facilities for the pilgrims, while others, such as Aachen and Vichy, were successful enough to grow into towns around the sacred springs.

One of the most evocative of the rural healing shrines lay at the Sources de la Seine, where a set of baths and a temple stood by a spring in a small enclosed valley, just over a kilometre from the main source itself.[30] A small hoard of objects found in one of the rooms of the baths encapsulates the significance of the site as a place to obtain a cure: a pot inscribed with the name of the goddess Dea Sequana contained 120 gilded or silvered bronzes of eyes, breasts and sexual organs, and about 800 coins. The bronze parts of the body are ex-votos, dedicated by worshippers wishing to draw the attention of the goddess to their afflictions, and to thank her for cures. This practice still continues today at efficacious healing shrines in parts of Europe, and can be regarded as a form of sympathetic magic, in which the waters symbolically wash away the affliction from the ex-voto, and thus cure the person who presented it.

Many of the ex-votos at the Sources de la Seine are of eyes, and it seems that poor sight was a particular preoccupation of the Gauls, for there are many finds throughout the region of the curious square stone objects known as oculists' stamps. These are makers' marks for pressing into cakes of ointment (*collyria*) to treat eye diseases, and occur commonly in the Celtic provinces but rarely elsewhere in the Empire: they are probably to be linked with Romano-Celtic religion.[31] How effective the ointments were is not known, but finds of eye-cataract needles, notably an extremely well-preserved set from the River Saône at Montbellet, together with a sculpture from Moutiers-sur-Saulx depicting an eye operation, show that direct methods of attempting a cure were also available. Surgical instruments are relatively common finds in Gaul and Germany, and are witness to the influence of medical practices that were ultimately Greek in origin.[32]

The Sources de la Seine shrine is also remarkable for another group of ex-votos made of wood. They were found preserved in waterlogged conditions near the baths. A whole series of different carvings of parts of the body, such as arms, legs and torsos, as well as of men and women dressed in cloaks, illuminates an aspect of ancient art and religion that is rarely encountered because wood is usually not preserved. The human figures are probably depictions of worshippers, carved for similar therapeutic reasons that those of parts of the body were. About 350 were found in all, and it is likely that originally there were many more, lining the stream bank and the paths to the baths. The Sources de la Seine is not the only site to yield wooden sculptures; notably there is a much larger and very similar group recently excavated at Chamalières, near Clermont-Ferrand. The wooden representations at both sites are like the stone carvings of worshippers and anatomical details known from several central Gaulish sites, and we may presume that wooden carvings were a common and relatively cheap form of dedication at many healing shrines. More wealthy patrons would have had stone carvings, or ex-votos and statuettes in metal, such as a bronze boat with the goddess Sequana standing in it, from the Seine sanctuary.[33]

A different form of healing is to be found at Grand in eastern Gaul, where an inscription has the phrase *somno iussus*. This refers to the rite of 'incubation', or sleeping in sacred chambers, during which the god, in this case Apollo Grannus, would appear in a dream to announce the cure or a prophecy. Grand had an important temple to this god, to judge from the very fine sculpture from its presumed site, and it appears to have been accorded the honour of a visit by Constantine in AD 309. He is recorded as having a vision in 'the most beautiful temple in the world'. Apollo and Victoria promised him thirty years of power, and he recognised his own features in those of the god. Our source for this is probably exaggerating, since it is a poem in praise of the future Emperor, but the circumstances of the visit place it in eastern Gaul, and Grand (or, less possibly, Aachen) is the most fitting place.[34] Apollo Grannus was indeed a Romano-Celtic god favoured by the emperors, since Caracalla visited another shrine to him at Faimingen in Raetia, when the Emperor was ill in AD 213.[35]

Grand is what is known as a rural sanctuary, having a temple, amphi-theatre and various other facilities, all apparently devoted to religious use. The location of the sanctuary is curious, being isolated on a high forested plateau away from the main roads. No one had any reason to go there except for religious purposes, although this appears to have been no deterrent, if the impressive remains are anything to go by: the unfinished amphitheatre is one of the largest in Gaul. Other rural sanctuaries, such as Sanxay, Champlieu or Ribemont, all had features similar to those at Grand, namely a major temple, a theatre or amphitheatre, baths and hostels. It has been suggested that many of them may have been deliberate foundations, to encourage the development of urban centres in the early Roman period (see chapter 3).[36] The regular planning of some of them supports this notion, and also shows the official interest in religion in early Roman Gaul.

The theatres in the rural sanctuaries are of considerable interest, as they are not of the standard Roman form, but represent a regional Romano-Celtic type, just as the temples do. They are curiously like classical Greek theatres, and it would be of great interest to establish whether the Greek colony of Marseille may have provided some sort of architectural inspi-ration. The seating banks in Romano-Celtic theatres are often greater than a semicircle, the stage is very small, and much of the action probably took place in the orchestra. Some theatres may have doubled as amphitheatres, with the orchestra forming the arena. The earliest known examples in northern Gaul date from the Julio-Claudian period (27 BC–AD 68), at Argenton and Trier.[37] These are simple affairs with stone benches, located in or near known late Iron Age oppida. They are also contemporary with the earliest Romano-Celtic temples there. It seems very likely that the theatres fulfilled a primarily religious function, and there may be pre-Roman predecessors yet to be found at one or other of the rural sanctuaries.

Although the Celtic cults in the first century came to adopt Roman forms

An early Roman ritual theatre in the Celtic sanctuary at the Altbachtal in Trier (Augusta Treverorum). The stone benches (1) encircle a small stage area (4).

of expression, they still retained their own names for the deities, and occasionally traditional worship also continued, as represented for instance by the bronze cross-legged statuette from Bouray, or the wooden sculptures from the Sources de la Seine.[38] It was not until the second century that Roman names for gods started to predominate, and there was possibly a decline in the Celtic side of Romano-Celtic religion. This may be linked with a decline in the use of the Celtic language, particularly amongst those classes rich enough to have inscriptions carved, although it is impossible to be certain about the general extent of language change.[39] By the fourth century most references to deities in Gaul were exclusively to those with Roman names, and it seems that Romano-Celtic religion had effectively become a regional variant of the Empire-wide classical cults. Indeed, this may have helped clear the path for the advance of Christianity from the mid-fourth century onwards, leaving only the more remote rural shrines to maintain the traditions of Romano-Celtic religion into the fifth century.

Classical religion

In contrast to Romano-Celtic monuments, temples of classical form are distinctly rare in Gaul and Germany, but they are of the greatest interest. Gaul has two of the best preserved Roman temples anywhere in the Roman Empire, the Maison Carrée at Nîmes and the Temple of Livia and Augustus at Vienne. The Maison Carrée, in particular, has been the subject of detailed

The Maison Carrée at Nîmes (Nemausus), dated about 2 BC–AD 4, one of the finest surviving classical temples in the Roman world. It was dedicated to the Imperial cult and probably stood at one end of the town's forum.

architectural studies which group it with the temples of Rome in style and quality.[40] It has six columns at the front and engaged columns at the sides and back, and is similar in plan to the temple of Apollo in Circo in Rome, which was completed some twenty-five years before the date that has been suggested for the building of the Maison Carrée, 2 BC–AD 4. This date depends on another temple in Rome, that of Mars Ultor in Augustus' forum, dedicated in 2 BC. Stylistically the Maison Carrée follows Mars Ultor in details of moulding and carving, but not slavishly, since local craftsmen almost certainly did all the work, perhaps under guidance from Italian masons, or using drawings supplied from Rome. The carving of the Corinthian column capitals betrays the existence of three teams of workmen, one apparently more competent than the others. They seem to have begun work at the back of the temple and worked towards the porch, since the acanthus leaves of the capitals are carved in a looser, more naturalistic style towards the porch end, suggesting that by then the sculptors had got into the rhythm of their work.

The attached and free-standing columns of the Maison Carrée also give it a superficial similarity to temples of classical Greece, despite the distinctively Roman podium and frontal stairway. This is no accident, for the period during which it was built coincided with a Greek, neo-Attic revival in Rome, fostered by Augustus as a way of setting an artistic seal on the new constitution. Several Gallic temples were built in this style, all in colonies and with imperial patronage: those at Nîmes and Vienne are still standing, while the foundations of another, somewhat larger example can be seen beside the theatre at Orange, and there are the remnants of the most splendid of the group at Narbonne.[41]

The podium at Narbonne suggests a temple approximately twice the size of the Maison Carrée, with a front elevation rising more than 30 metres above podium level. It was built of Carrara marble from Luna in Italy, but was possibly not finished, since some of the column capitals are incomplete. Indeed, a most interesting shipwreck discovered off St Tropez contained columns and other architectural pieces, also of Carrara stone; these are strikingly similar to those discovered on the site of the temple, and may well have been intended for it. Perhaps the citizens of the chief Roman city in Gaul had rightly wanted to erect what would have been one of the most splendid temples anywhere in the Empire. Italian materials and craftsmen were used, but setbacks, probably including the shipwreck, prolonged the construction beyond the dedication day, after which enthusiasm to complete it waned. It was left unfinished until the early second century, when Hadrian encouraged renewed building activity. Almost certainly this temple was the city's Capitolium, dedicated to Jupiter, Juno and Minerva. However, it cannot have been the only large classical temple in Narbonne, since long inscriptions commemorate the dedication of a temple to the Imperial cult in AD 11, and the sacrifices that were performed annually thereafter.[42]

Most towns, particularly the colonies, would have had temples to the

Imperial cult or to the Capitoline triad, or indeed to both. They were expressly set up as a focus of loyalty to the state, and as such represented the most political aspect of ancient religion. That is not to say that worshippers at these temples were merely paying lip-service to religion. It is clear that temples such as the Maison Carrée were built, in part, because of the personal relationship that Augustus, Agrippa and the Imperial family had with Gaul. There was probably a genuine heroisation and affection for them, which found an outlet in ruler worship.

It is very significant in this light that the Maison Carrée was dedicated to Gaius and Lucius Caesar, the two sons of Agrippa for whom Augustus had great hopes as his heirs. First Agrippa and then Gaius were patrons of the colony of Nîmes, and the best explanation for the dedication of the temple is that it was built originally for the Imperial cult in general, i.e. to Rome and Augustus, but following the deaths of the two brothers was dedicated to them as a specific manifestation of the Imperial cult, and also as a funerary memorial. This was not the only temple where a dedication was changed, for at Vienne an original inscription to Rome and Augustus was altered to include Livia following her divinisation by Claudius in AD 41.[43]

Classical temples were not the only sanctuaries in which the Imperial cult was practised. In Celtic Gaul especially the ubiquitous Romano-Celtic temples often included dedications to Rome and Augustus, or to the Imperial family (*domus divinae*), or the health and safety of the Emperor. A good example comes from Rennes (ancient Condate) and is worth quoting in full:[44]

IN HONOREM
DOMVS DIVINAE
ET PAGI SEXTANMANDVI
MARTI MVLLONI
L CAMPANIVS PRISCVS ET VIRI
LIS FIL SACERDOTES ROMAE
ET AVG STATVAM CVM SVIS
ORNAMENTIS DE SVO POSV
ERVNT
L D EX D S

In honour of the Imperial household and the *pagus* of the Sextanmandui, L. Campanius Priscus and his son Virilis, priests of Rome and Augustus, set up this statue and its ornaments to Mars Mullo, from their own resources; the position having been given by decree of the senate [of Rennes].

The Imperial household takes prime position, then the local area (*pagus*), then the name of the god, which itself has the Latin name first and the Celtic equivalent following. The priorities in this inscription are very clear, even though the deity being invoked is Mars Mullo, and it demonstrates the way in which ruler worship was practised in northern Gaul. It seems likely that this is more of a political gesture than an exhibition of religious piety towards the *domus divinae*, particularly in view of the fact that Priscus and Virilis were priests of Rome and Augustus. Their priesthoods were not, in fact, held in Rennes itself, but in Lyon, where there was a major provincial cult centre, the altar (*ara*) of Rome and Augustus.

This had been set up by Drusus in 12 BC, and was situated between the Rhône and the Saône just opposite the Roman colony. Lyon, of course, was the provincial capital of Lugdunensis, but the Imperial cult had a wider scope, including both Aquitania and Belgica as well. The cult centre was set up to hold an annual gathering of delegates (perhaps in continuation of a pre-Roman assembly, mentioned by Caesar), drawn from all parts of the Three Gauls, who would meet to elect a priest. To judge from the large number of inscriptions that record individual priesthoods, this was a highly prestigious and sought-after honour; but the cult was much more impersonal than the municipal Imperial cults of southern Gaul, and was manipulated by successive emperors, who wanted changes in the form of homage that was paid to them. This process culminated in the changes imposed by Severus, who instituted a more personal form of worship of himself and his family, a move which anticipated the quasi-divine status of the later emperors. His reasons for doing this were almost entirely political, since Gaul had been loyal to his defeated rival, Clodius Albinus, and Severus needed to refocus that loyalty onto his own dynasty. Not surprisingly, the cult fell into decline soon after this.[45]

Germany had a provincial cult centre too, at Cologne, called the *ara Ubiorum*. It had been set up in the Augustan period before the Varus disaster, and was presumably intended to serve the anticipated new province of Germany. This, of course, was not to be, and consequently we know little of the Imperial cult there, except for the position of the altar in the centre of the town. However, there may have been a revival of the notion of a German regional cult centre in the Flavian period, for in the newly conquered *agri decumates* of Germania Superior modern Rottweil was known as Arae Flaviae.

The Imperial cult offers a clear-cut example of a branch of classical religion that was introduced to Gaul. It is much more difficult to be certain of the extent to which the classical pantheon was worshipped in its purely Graeco-Roman form, especially in the northern areas dominated by Romano-Celtic cults. Representations of gods such as Jupiter, and the foundation of classical temples in cities such as Xanten, Augst and Paris show that worship of the major Graeco-Roman gods, the Capitoline triad of Jupiter, Juno and Minerva, did occur in the more Romanised centres. Indeed, at Augst a Romano-Celtic temple was replaced by a classical one. Very occasionally there is evidence for a rural classical shrine, such as in central Gaul at Antigny or at Masamas, where two small temples in a courtyard appear to have replaced one of the Romano-Celtic type.[46]

At the domestic level, houses in Gaul, as elsewhere, have yielded a wide range of everyday objects decorated with representations of the classical deities. How far these indicate religious piety is very much open to question, but more definite evidence of worship comes from the remains of household shrines that are occasionally found. These are usually connected with the deities of the household, the Lares, and there is little doubt that they were worshipped more or less in their classical form, to judge from the statuettes of Lares found in Gaul and Germany. However, the two domestic shrines that have been excavated with their figurines still in place, at Rezé and Argenton, both have Romano-Celtic religious associations, showing that in the domestic sphere, too, local forms of worship had a strong influence, especially in the Three Gauls.[47] In southern Gaul, on the other hand, remains of classical temples and altars, as for example at Glanum, attest a fairly widespread interest in the Graeco-Roman gods: this is further confirmed by finds such as votive mirrors, which are evidence for a popular following for some of the cults.[48]

Cybele, Mithras and other eastern gods

It was also in the south that eastern cults made the most headway. Their popularity, which gradually gathered pace during the second and third centuries, was mainly due to the new ideas of worship that they put forward, including beliefs in personal salvation and betterment. Inscriptions, sculptures and the rare discovery of temple sites indicate that Mithras, Cybele, Sarapis and their associated deities were worshipped in Gallia Narbonensis, the Rhône Valley and along the Rhine frontier. Elsewhere in Gaul there is, however, little evidence for them. This is because the names on the dedications indicate that the worshippers were largely soldiers or people of eastern or Greek origin who, for the most part, were involved in trading activity along the Rhône–Rhine axis.[49]

The most impressive surviving sanctuary of an eastern cult is that of Cybele next to the theatre at Lyon. It is not surprising that this goddess had a sanctuary in such a central area of the city, for her cult had been accepted by Rome since the second century BC, and it enjoyed a degree of official recognition. A massive rectangular basement, 50 by 84 metres, survives today, and would have supported an open courtyard with an altar in the centre and gallery around. The courtyard was the area where many of the rituals took place, including perhaps the notorious rite of the *taurobolium*, or baptism in the blood of a sacrificed bull. The *taurobolium* is mentioned on several inscriptions from Lyon, including one dated AD 160 found in or near the site of the temple; this appears to correspond with the foundation date of the temple itself.[50] This particular inscription is remarkable in a number of ways, for it shows that official sanction was granted for the rite to be performed for the health of the Emperor Antoninus Pius, and for the city of Lyon. It also appears to indicate that the *taurobolium* in question was actually carried out in Rome at the chief temple of Cybele, and that the genitals and skull of the bull were then transported to Lyon. This probably marks the inauguration of a new priest and shrine of Cybele at Lyon, since the bull's genitals were a substitute for the castration of the priest, which used to be the initiation ritual of the cult. Worship of Cybele was certainly strong in Lyon, and conflicts were to arise between followers of the cult and the early Christian community, which was largely drawn from the same ethnic groups (see chapter 9).

Other less certain sanctuaries of Cybele have been identified at Vienne, where there is a possible cult 'theatre' or 'stairway', and at Neuss, where a cellar has been identified as the *fossa sanguinis*, or pit in which the priest was drenched in the blood from the sacrificed bull.[51] Inscriptions and sculptures from towns such as Nîmes, Die and Mainz show that others also existed.

If evidence for the worship of Cybele is to be found mainly in cities and in semi-official locations, Mithraic sanctuaries more commonly took the form of small shrines set mainly near forts, although they occasionally occur in rural settlements. Mithras was a relative latecomer to Gaul and Germany, and most of the evidence dates to the third century, although a few earlier shrines are known. The main group worshipping Mithras was the army, probably those units that were transferred from the east to the Rhineland.

Mithras slaying the bull, a scene that was common to all Mithraic temples. (Musée d'Art et d'Histoire de Metz)

A great many of the forts along the frontier had mithraea, especially in the vicinity of Mainz. Notable among them is the fort and *vicus* of Heddernheim, where there were at least four Mithraic shrines and a large series of sculptures.

The most interesting of the sculptures, now in Wiesbaden Museum, shows on one side the conventional scene of Mithras slaying the bull in a cave, together with other depictions of the legends surrounding the cult. It is not known exactly what significance each part of the myth cycle had for worshippers, since it was a mystery cult, revealed only to initiates and thus not well understood today. However, the bull-slaying scene is crucial; it was part of a creation myth representing death and rebirth, since vegetation springs from the dying bull's flesh and blood, which the forces of evil, shown as a scorpion, try in vain to prevent. All mithraea appear to have had such a depiction, following the same pictorial convention, with Mithras kneeling on the bull and pulling its head back, while plunging a dagger into its neck. What is interesting about the Heddernheim sculpture is that this panel has a reverse side, showing the dead bull in the foreground with Mithras, the sun-god and two companion deities, Cautes and Cautopates, behind it, taking a meal in celebration of the sacrifice of the bull. This scene is hardly ever depicted, but the Heddernheim stone apparently could be made to turn, so that during a ceremony the bull-slaying scene was replaced by the subsequent celebration. Mithraic temples were, in part, laid out to represent the cave where the bull was slain, and indeed two of the known sites in our area, Bourg-Saint-Andéol in the Rhône Valley and Saarbrücken in Gallia Belgica, are arranged so that the sculpture was carved or stood in a niche cut into the living rock.[52]

Since so many of the mithraea in Gaul and Germany were attached to military sites, the upheavals of the mid-third century in the Rhineland dealt the cult a blow from which it appears not to have recovered. This was followed in the fourth century by opposition from Christians, who regarded Mithraism as a blasphemous parody of their own beliefs. In this way, the rising popularity of Christianity finally brought Mithraic worship to an end.

The cult of another eastern deity, Jupiter Dolichenus, appealed even more than Mithraism to the military, and was in vogue for a short period from the mid-second to the early third century. Its end can be dated fairly precisely, to the reign of Maximinus Thrax (AD 235–8), when all known temples of Dolichenus in the Rhine and Danube areas seem to have been violently destroyed. This is a rare example, apart of course from Christian persecutions, of a religious purge. The reasons are not fully understood, but are perhaps to be connected with a reaction against the fallen Severan dynasty and its eastern religious associations. Easterners in the army, who formed the majority of adherents to the cult, may well have been discriminated against, and with their fall from favour the cult fell too and never recovered, especially after the capture of the original shrine at Doliche in Syria by the Persian King Shapur.[53]

Temple 'leaf' or votive plaque depicting the eastern god Jupiter Dolichenus, who was worshipped almost exclusively by army personnel. From Heddernheim (Nida), Germany. (British Museum)

Of the other eastern cults little can be said, since they are represented by objects and inscriptions rather than by temple sites. These casual finds are sparsely scattered in Gallia Narbonensis and the Rhine area, and occasionally elsewhere. Inscriptions record a temple to Isis and Sarapis at Nîmes, in this instance probably to be linked with the presence of an Egyptian population amongst the colonists; Sabazios is represented by several finds of his very characteristic votive bronze hands, covered in cult symbols; and there are also the very rare finds of lamps and other objects with Jewish associations. The evidence for Judaism, apart from the political exile of two Jewish leaders to Gaul in the early first century AD, is virtually all of late Imperial date, and the expansion of Jewish communities in Gaul may be linked with the rise of Christianity, which will be considered separately later (chapter 9).[54]

FURTHER READING

The world of Celtic religion has been the subject of many studies, in English notably by M. Green in *The Gods of the Celts* (1986) and S. Piggott in *The Druids* (1976), and in French by J.-L. Brunaux, *Les Gaulois: sanctuaires et rites* (1986), now translated into English, P.-M. Duval, *Les Dieux de la Gaule* (1976) and E. Thevenot, *Divinités et Sanctuaires de la Gaule* (1968). Brunaux's book is mainly archaeological in orientation, as is his report on the important Gournay sanctuary site (Brunaux *et al.* 1985). Other Romano-Celtic sacred sites are discussed in W. Rodwell (ed.), *Temples, Churches and Religion* (1980), which includes a gazetteer of temples. See also Gose (1972) for the large and important Altbachtal site in Trier. Southern Gaul, separate in religious terms, is discussed by F. Benoit in *Art et Dieux de la Gaule* (1969), and the sanctuary at Glanum by Rolland (1968). Healing shrines are examined in Green's, Brunaux's and Thevenot's books above, and also in A. Pelletier (ed.) *La Médecine en Gaule* (1985). The remarkable wooden statues from the healing shrines at Sources de la Seine and Chamalières are discussed by Deyts (1983) and Romeuf (1986) respectively.

Classical temples in Gaul are not the subject of any single volume, but J. Ward-Perkins in *Roman Imperial Architecture* (1981) has a useful discussion. The Maison Carrée at Nîmes is examined in detail by Amy and Gros (1979). D. Fishwick is the main authority for the Imperial cult, especially in his *The Imperial Cult in the Latin West* (1987). Eastern cults, in contrast, have been the focus of a number of regional studies, notably R. Turcan, *Les Religions de l'Asie dans la Vallée du Rhône* (1972), E. Schwertheim, *Die Denkmäler orientalischer Gottheiten in römischen Deutschland* (1974) and V. Walters, *The Cult of Mithras in the Roman Provinces of Gaul* (1974). Audin (1985) and Pelletier (1980) discuss the two Cybele sanctuaries at Lyon and Vienne.

7

THE
FRONTIER
LAND

W as Germany different from Gaul? The simple answer to this
question is yes, but the differences are not clear cut because
there was a high degree of interdependence between the two regions. One
of the best ways of showing that Gallo-Roman and Romano-German
-societies almost certainly did not have the same structural form is in the
plans of villas.

The characteristic type of villa in the German region had a large room
as a dominant feature, usually behind the familiar façade of a veranda and
projecting side rooms (probably towers). The large room is often regarded
as an open hall; it had a hearth and perhaps steps down into a cellar. Many
of the other rooms opened off the central hall, so that it must have formed
the focus of life within the villa unit. It was very different from the common
arrangement in Gallic villas, with their small groups of rooms opening onto
the veranda, and this villa type seems to indicate a different social structure
from that of Gaul.[1]

In all probability this social structure had its origins in the pre-Roman
period. The classic site of Mayen, as well as more recently excavated villas
at Kaalheide-Krichelberg and elsewhere, have wooden hall-type buildings
underlying the stone halls. These early buildings do not have the façade
with veranda, but simply the hall itself, which is the dominant central
feature. The hall obviously holds the key to understanding the way in
which this type of villa operated. Direct evidence for its use is not really
forthcoming, except that a hearth and a very simple earth or cobble floor
were usual. Interpretations tend to paint a picture of a communal life along
the lines of a medieval manorial hall, with extended family and retainers
under the same roof. It is clear that the hall continued to hold significance
even when the owners were rich enough to build villas with private wings,

bath-suites and mosaics, since it usually remained the focus even when surrounded by a mass of other rooms. Both Otrang and Köln-Mungersdorf are examples of this kind of development.[2]

As in Gaul, hall-type villas seem to reflect the patron–client system. The hall itself served as the focus for a family group, either for the patron, as at Otrang, or for the clients, as at Echternach. At the latter site the subsidiary dwellings were of hall type, but the main villa was a luxurious example of a Gallic villa with smaller rooms and peristyle courtyards. If the hall-type villas reflect a Germanic strand in the population, as has often been suggested, then it is clear that quite wealthy villa-owners at Otrang and elsewhere were happy to show their ethnic origins in this way.

Hall-type villas are common both in the Eifel and Mosel areas and in a wide band that extends to the north-east, on the left bank of the Rhine, down as far as Nijmegen; it thus includes much of eastern and northern Belgium. Examples are found to the south of the Eifel as well, in the zone to the rear of the frontier (*limes*) in Upper Germany, and as far south as Switzerland. This distribution corresponds roughly with the area indicated by Caesar and other writers to have had a Germanic element in the population: the territory of the eastern Belgae, and that on the left bank of the lower Rhine into which Germans migrated or were settled by the Romans. If this correspondence is more than just a coincidence, it is reasonable to suppose that the villas can be used to identify groups of Germanic origin.[3]

Interestingly, the distribution of the hall-villa does not reflect provincial boundaries established by the Romans in the late first century AD. For example, the Treveri, whose *civitas* remained in Gallia Belgica, claimed German ancestry and their traces in the archaeological record show some German traits. German culture is, in fact, most clearly manifest in the northern German province (Germania Inferior); in Germania Superior, in the southern reaches along the middle Rhine Valley and in Switzerland, numerous Gallic or mixed features can be recognised, and indeed many of these are also found in eastern Gallia Belgica. By contrast, Germania Inferior stood apart culturally,[4] and it was this region that by the later Roman period first became a German (i.e. barbarian) stronghold within the north-western provinces.

Religion also plays a part in the search for cultural indicators in the frontier region. Deities like the Matres and Matronae were often linked with native gods of Germanic origin, such as the Matronae Vacillinehae, or Hercules Magusanus. Evidence for these gods is concentrated in the Rhineland, where they were worshipped by troops on the frontier, as well as by local people.[5] The frontier temples in the military *vici* tend to be simple affairs, though at some, such as Osterburken, there are startlingly well-preserved remains of altars and other dedications surrounding a temple. In the civilian hinterland temples were usually of classic Romano-Celtic form, even if the gods worshipped there were in the Germanic tradition.

Altar to the Germanic goddess Nehalennia, dredged from the eastern River Scheldt near Colijnsplaat, Netherlands, c. AD 200. (Rijksmuseum van Oudheden, Leiden)

This may be because the Germans are recorded as having no indigenous temple architecture, and so borrowed the form of religious building that was *de rigueur* for Gallo-Roman deities.[6]

This evidence of religious practices and villa plans is not, however, entirely clear cut in demonstrating the presence of Germanic as opposed to Gallic customs. There must have been considerable mixing of populations along the frontier region, as Caesar recorded when he described the Belgae as claiming Germanic descent. Tribes like the Treveri were, to judge from the archaeological record, Gaulish to a large degree, although historically they claimed German ancestry. The villas within Treveran territory quite frequently display mixed traits, and the distribution of hall-type villas overlapped with those of more Gallic type.

Mixing of Germans and Gauls was a process that continued after the Roman conquest, and indeed was manipulated for political ends by the Romans. Tribes such as the Ubii were moved by Augustus from the far side of the Rhine into Roman territory. The Tungri are also thought to have been invited to settle in the area laid waste by Caesar in his quest to punish the Eburones.[7] Such actions would have strengthened the ethnic German element in what was to become Germania Inferior. In Upper Germany after the conquest the reverse process occurred on a lesser scale. Gaulish settlers appear to have moved to the east across the Rhine into the Black Forest area. It was a sort of pioneering movement into an area that at one time had been ethnically Celtic but had suffered from German inroads not long before the conquest. Interestingly, these settlers may have been moving in before Roman troops had set a clear frontier line, perhaps because the native population was very small. At all events, the region became known as the *agri Decumates*, possibly a Gaulish term meaning the ten cantons.[8]

Although ancient writers regarded the Rhine as the boundary between the Germans and the Gauls, movements of people in the frontier zone meant that reality was rather different. The Rhine was not so much a barrier as a means of communication, and even after it became the limit of the Roman Empire (from Bonn downstream), the political frontier was no obstacle to cultural and economic links across the river. In very general terms, the lower Rhine was largely Germanic on either side of the river; the middle Rhine mixed, with strong elements of both cultures; and the upper Rhine largely Gallic.[9]

One of the most interesting aspects of the Germanic land around the mouth of the Rhine is the nature of so-called native settlements. Here villas are extremely rare, but evidence meticulously gathered by Dutch archaeologists has shown a wealth of un-Romanised sites, and a large local population during the period.[10] After about AD 40 the frontier ran along the Old Rhine, emerging in the North Sea at Katwijk north of The Hague. As a result the region to the south saw the development of civilian communities under the eye of the Roman garrisons. The Canninefates and the Batavi occupied these lands just behind the frontier, and were organised as Roman *civitates*, despite what right-thinking Romans must have regarded as their primitive state of culture.[11]

An important excavation at Rijswijk near The Hague, in the territory of the Canninefates, has given us a very clear idea of the nature of one of the native settlements.[12] It was a farming community, perhaps producing a surplus in crops and cattle for supply to the army, and was in existence from the first century. The small village-like group of rectangular wooden buildings grew in number and elaboration as time went on, until occupation came to an end in the third century. The buildings were of hall type, although not of the same form as the hall-villas, since they were more elongated: this was a Frisian and north German tradition, which nevertheless suggests that the social origins of these people were close to those of the inhabitants of the hall-villas. An interesting development is that by the early third century one of the houses had been replaced by a stone-built structure. This is best termed a villa, but it clearly followed the native tradition in that it had a long hall, perhaps a longhouse for animals, crops and humans. While this reflects some Romanisation in the frontier area, the general impact was very low, despite the presence of the Roman garrisons. Here, obviously, were people fairly resistant to the Roman way of life, perhaps, as Groenman-van Waateringe persuasively suggests, because the native Germanic culture was too alien to be easily assimilated into Roman provincial life. Above all, the seeds of urbanisation had no socio-economic base on which to flourish.[13]

One of the positive aspects of Roman conquest of this region was the establishment of a long period of peace, the famous *pax romana*. This must be one of the reasons for an expansion of the population that is attested on both sides of the frontier. But such expansion also had disadvantages, since overpopulation presented dangers for the inhabitants; indeed, it can be argued that the land became exhausted as a result, bringing about a rapid decline in population in the political, economic and climatic instability that prevailed during the third century.[14]

Attempts were made by the Roman authorities to create an urban centre for the Canninefates. Left to its own devices the tribe would almost certainly not have wished for such a centre, but for Roman administrative and legal convenience Forum Hadriani (modern Voorburg-Arentsburg, near The Hague) was set up in the early second century over an existing settlement.[15] Excavations have not given us a clear picture of how it operated, but archaeologically it presents a fairly Romanised group of buildings and artefacts, at any rate by comparison with the surrounding settlements.

Other deliberately founded urban centres were set up for the tribes upstream as well. At Nijmegen, for instance, which was to become the capital of the Batavi, an early military base soon attracted a civilian community. Many of these were immigrant Gauls trading with the Romans, and were perhaps deliberately encouraged to settle in order to encourage the growth of urban life in what was later to become the Oppidum Batavorum, and then Noviomagus Batavorum.[16] It has been suggested that a number of the towns in Germania Inferior, such as Xanten, Cologne and Tongeren were all founded by similar influxes of traders. Xanten went on to become a colony from the time of Trajan (Colonia Ulpia Traiana); Tongeren became the *civitas*-capital of the Tungri (Atuatuca Tungrorum); and Cologne, most importantly of all, became the capital city of the province.[17]

Cologne's development was based on an Oppidum Ubiorum, set up for a German tribe transplanted from the east bank of the Rhine, either in 38/37 or in 19/18 BC. Because of the later and continuous development of the city there is considerable doubt about the form of the early settlement. Epigraphic and literary evidence shows that a double-legionary fortress existed at Cologne, as well as the oppidum and a major religious centre, the *ara Ubiorum*, which was to function as a provincial cult centre for Lower Germany. It seems likely that part of the area of the later Roman colonial foundation was taken up by the legionary fortress, and the rest of the area by the fortress's *canabae* or civilian settlement. The latter formed the oppidum and contained the *ara*, almost certainly to be identified with a later large semicircular structure at the heart of Roman Cologne. Both fortress and oppidum could comfortably be accommodated within the area of the later city walls.[18]

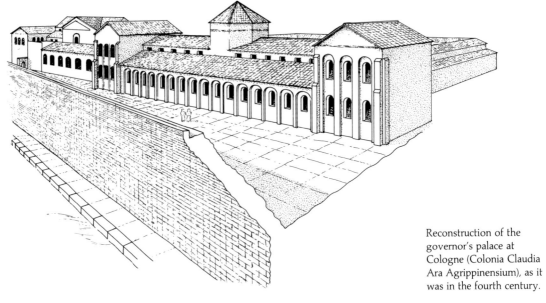

Reconstruction of the governor's palace at Cologne (Colonia Claudia Ara Agrippinensium), as it was in the fourth century.

In the thirties AD the legions moved out, and in AD 50 Colonia Claudia Ara Agrippinensium was established. The rapid elevation in civic status was partly due to the fact that Claudius wished to honour his wife Agrippina, who had been born there. The Ubii, though, lost their tribal name as a result, being called the Agrippinenses, and were taunted for this by other Germans during the rebellion of Civilis in 69–70 (see below). Cologne also became a veteran colony for retired soldiers, and a very strong bastion of Romanisation.

Cologne was to emerge as the major town of Germania Inferior, and one of the most important urban centres in Gaul as a whole. It had the privilege of walls from an early date, not surprisingly in view of its position right on the frontier itself. It was also the seat of the governor, whose palace (*praetorium*) has been uncovered, providing us with a valuable insight into the arrangement of the lavish accommodation allocated to him and his staff. In addition to the religious centre of the *ara*, it must have had other large temples, specifically a Capitolium, which was usual in Roman colonies. Rich town houses have been excavated near the cathedral: Cologne was clearly a wealthy city, and the various industries established in the suburbs must have contributed to its prosperity. Pottery-kilns, glasshouses, leather- and bone-working shops all helped to make Cologne into the prime manu-facturing centre in northern Gaul and Germany from the second century onwards. The products were widely distributed along the frontier lands, and to Britain, the Danube and elsewhere. We also know that the rural hinterland of Cologne was rich and densely settled, with a large number of villas.[19]

Two other frontier towns merit consideration, Mainz and Xanten. Mogontiacum, modern Mainz, was the capital of Germania Superior from

The reconstructed town wall of Xanten (Colonia Ulpia Traiana), second century AD, viewed from the interior of the town.

the 80s AD, but differed from Cologne in that it retained its military garrison. Built on higher ground away from the river, a double-legionary fortress provided the key defensive manpower for the region, while the civilian settlement grew up in the space between the fortress and the river, where a bridge crossed into the Wetterau. The civilian area expanded, acquiring a set of walls in the third century, and eventually covering a larger area than Cologne. By the fourth century the fortress had been abandoned, but although the civilian settlement declined, it did continue after the troops had left, no doubt because of the town's dual role as the seat of the governor and a major trading centre. It is to this period that can be attributed the spectacular recent discoveries of waterlogged military or official river-boats in a backwater of the Rhine.[20]

Colonia Ulpia Traiana (modern Xanten), established by Trajan in Lower Germany, acted as another bastion of Romanisation on the frontier. It came into existence about AD 100 over an earlier civilian settlement. The latter may have been a deliberate appendage to the nearby legionary fortress for the provision of goods and services. Xanten's legionary fortresses were vital for the protection of this part of the frontier during the first century. Originally a double fortress, it was replaced by a single fortress (Vetera II) after AD 70. The later fortress continued into the second century, overlapping in time with the colony, but it was eventually given up. In this context the colony plainly took over the role of guardian of the frontier, using the veteran colonists as a reserve force. Xanten as a city, however, could claim to be one of the most isolated of Roman colonies in cultural terms, with a surrounding population of largely German extraction, few villas, and the nearest neighbouring Roman establishments being forts rather than towns. As we shall see, the local people had shown how hostile they could be

The fort and *vicus* of Zugmantel on the German frontier, as they may have appeared in the early third century.

when the first legionary fortress was besieged in AD 69, and it perhaps not surprising that town life developed relatively late in this area and went into decline relatively early. In its heyday Xanten had the full range of urban features: walls, amphitheatre, classical temples, forum and so on. But if any town in Gaul and Germany can be said to be an artificial creation without support from a Romanised hinterland, Xanten has a good claim to the title. In the second century a major fire occurred and Imperial help was required for the subsequent rebuilding. Little more than a century later there was a marked decline in the density of occupation and by the early fourth century a fort appears to have been established in the centre of the old town. Civilian life did continue on a reduced basis outside the walls of the colony around a Christian shrine to local martyrs. It was this settlement, known as Ad Sanctos, that became the medieval and modern town of Xanten (see chapter 9).[21]

The significance of the army in the sustenance of town life along much of the frontier is clear. It is one of the features that marks out Germany from Gaul, since the economic and cultural influence of the permanent garrison was probably out of all proportion to its size. We have already seen (chapter 5) that long-distance routes ran back to the Mediterranean for conveying supplies to the army. The economic axis that developed as a result was vital for the towns of Germany, since they depended on traded and manufactured goods as their principal means of absorbing the cash made available to the troops. When army pay was raised in the early third century great benefits flowed to the German towns as the money boosted the local economy. This tipped the economic balance in favour of the northern towns at the expense of places in the interior of Gaul such as Lyon.

One of the direct consequences of the huge military presence was the development of civilian *vici* around many of the forts along the frontier. A prime example is Zugmantel on the Upper German *limes*, where an extensive settlement came into existence during the later second and early third centuries. It was to become larger than the fort itself, and it contained shops and workshops of the strip building type usually associated with *vici*. Many of these buildings had cellars, the excavation of which has provided a wealth of evidence about the fairly basic, but nevertheless comfortable standard of living of a frontier community.[22] The people living there probably had very diverse origins, some being Gallic traders, some retired soldiers with their wives, and some even from the eastern part of the Empire. Troops from the east stationed in the Rhineland often remained in the locality after being paid off, so it is not surprising to see strong evidence for the worship of eastern cults such as Mithras and Jupiter Dolichenus in the military *vici*.[23]

It was perhaps inevitable that most of the *vici* were parasitical on the forts, rising and declining with the fortunes of the fort itself. Some, however, were able to break out of this pattern and establish an independent existence. This mainly applied to settlements around the forts behind the frontier line; many of these military posts were evacuated at a relatively early date because the troops were moved forward, but the *vici* remained in occupation. Nida (modern Heddernheim near Frankfurt) shows this well. This large *vicus* lay in a key position on the the road network of the Wetterau, and it grew into a substantial town, eventually with its own circuit of walls and civic status as the capital of the *civitas Taunensium*.[24] But like all the Roman settlements in the Wetterau and the *agri Decumates*, Nida ultimately relied on the army for its existence, and life there collapsed when the frontier itself gave way in the mid-third century.

The stress laid on the army as the motor and protector of the region's economy tends to obscure a minor but important aspect of the frontier. The trade routes to Cologne and the other cities did not stop at the frontier line. They went through it, into Germania Libera. Extensive research has been carried out on finds of Roman imports in the interior of Germany, mainly to establish the chronology of the Germanic peoples there, but more recently to illuminate the trading relationship between Romans and Germans.[25] The most obvious impact of this trade, and of the existence of a fixed frontier line as well, was the growth of Germanic settlement on the far bank of the Rhine in Lower Germany. In the relatively peaceful conditions of the second century sites such as the village at Wijster in the Netherlands were common.

In form Wijster was remarkably like some of the native settlements on the Roman side of the Rhine, and received Roman goods such as samian ware, albeit on a smaller scale than sites within Roman territory. Statistics show that there was a distinct rise in the number of settlements through the first and second centuries, when they reached a peak. Then followed a decline, sometimes quite rapid, during the third century and the late Roman period.[26] It has been suggested that this was due to changes in the pattern of Roman trade through the frontier, perhaps officially induced, perhaps for economic reasons explored further in chapter 10. Yet the decline in the Germanic settlements coincides with the increase in attacks on the frontier, and it may be that raiding had replaced trading as the means by which German warriors of the interior tribes obtained the luxury goods that they wanted from the Romans. The settled communities along the frontier itself would have fared very badly if this was indeed the case, and it may be the principal reason for their decline.[27]

The army on the frontier

Frontier relations with the barbarian Germans involved much more than commerce and occasional warfare. Complex political considerations also came into play whenever the Romans had dealings with peoples beyond their borders. Augustus, at the end of his life, expressed a wish that the limits of the Empire should not be extended, and in general his immediate successors followed this advice. For the next fifty years or so the Rhine was maintained as the frontier of Gaul and Germany, although this did not inhibit Roman armies from crossing the river, nor did it prevent diplomatic intervention beyond the frontier. Indeed, there was some fighting almost at the start of Tiberius' reign in AD 14–16, during which Germanicus led campaigns to avenge the defeat of Varus in AD 9 (see chapter 2).[28]

Eight legions were normally stationed along the frontier, divided into two armies, the *exercitus Germania Inferior* in Lower Germany, and the *exercitus Germania Superior* in Upper Germany. Both were technically speaking within the province of Gallia Belgica, but it is clear that from an early date these armies were sufficiently important to operate largely independently of the constraints of provincial civil administration, and were able to create what were effectively military zones along the frontier.[29]

Silvered horse trapping from Xanten with an inscription referring to Plinius *praefectus*, possibly the writer Pliny the Elder, who served in Germany in the mid-first century AD. (British Museum)

Cologne was the administrative centre for the Lower German frontier region, and Mainz its equivalent in Upper Germany. We know of various legionary fortresses and other installations of the Julio-Claudian period: a large fortress for a legion and auxiliary troops at Batavodurum (modern Nijmegen) up to AD 30; another for two legions at Vetera I (modern Birten near Xanten); a single-legion fortress at Novaesium (modern Neuss) from AD 30; two legions at Mainz; one legion at Argentorate (modern Strasbourg); and one at Vindonissa (modern Windisch) in Switzerland. There may also have been two legions at Cologne for a period, but at this early date no other bases are known for specific units, except the fort for the fleet at Alteburg near Cologne.[30] There must of course have been considerable numbers of auxiliary troops stationed in the Rhineland and in the immediate hinterland, but it is uncertain exactly where.

Auxiliary troops were probably also stationed within the interior of Gaul as well, since trouble continued to flare up on occasion until AD 21, the date of the short-lived rebellion led by aristocratic Gauls Florus and Sacrovir from tribes in the centre. This was the last attempt by Gauls to restore their pre-Roman freedoms, but even so a military presence continued for some time at forts such as Arlaines, Mirebeau and Aulnay.[31]

From the time of Claudius the Rhine itself emerged as the defined frontier line. Many troops were settled in garrisons along the river, with a marked reduction in military occupation behind. It was a system of defence that maintained concentrations of troops in vulnerable areas, and used client kingdoms (friendly independent tribes) to act as barriers in more stable areas. An illustration of the use of a client kingdom can be seen in the case of the Frisii, a tribe to the north of the Rhine in the Netherlands. Up to the time of Claudius this tribe was a client kingdom, with Roman territory nominally extending as a result throughout the Netherlands. Roman installations, such as Velsen near Amsterdam, are evidence for imperial interest in this area. The Roman garrison in this region was very small, since it was felt that the Frisii themselves and other client kingdoms in the area provided sufficient protection.[32] However, in AD 28 there was a revolt by the Frisii, partly in reaction to overbearing exactions imposed by the Romans. Not long after this the decision was apparently taken to exclude the Frisii from Roman territory by running the frontier along the Rhine itself. Accordingly, Claudius extended the system of auxiliary forts to the Rhine mouth, including the well-known fort of the Valkenburg, an almost completely excavated waterlogged site, which has yielded valuable insights into the internal arrangement of first-century forts.[33]

In the southern part of the frontier region, in the area of the Black Forest, the frontier was not very well defined. It certainly ran forward of the Rhine, so that the river itself did not really mark a clear-cut boundary between unconquered Germania Libera and Gaul. In fact, the Black Forest started to house pioneering settlements of Gauls migrating across the river to form the territory known as the *agri Decumates*. Eventually the area was incorporated within the Empire, and we see the establishment of a frontier further east by the Flavian period.[34]

In the Julio-Claudian period the only offensive moves were some rather desultory skirmishes by Caligula in the central Rhine area. More important was the conquest of Britain under Claudius, which had implications for the disposition of troops in the Rhineland. There had been ten legions in the region at the time of Caligula, but this was reduced to seven by the transfer of legions to Britain. At other times up to the Civil War of AD 69 events were relatively peaceful along the frontier, despite actions against the Chauci (and possibly the Frisii) in AD 47, and defensive measures against the Chatti, a powerful tribe based in the Wetterau opposite Mainz, in AD 50. The Romans at this time could take some comfort from the evident desire of the Germans to fight more amongst themselves than against the Romans: the Cherusci were fighting the Marcomanni, for instance, and the Chatti were in conflict with the Hermunduri in AD 58 over the use of some salt springs.[35]

The relative inactivity along the frontier at this time created problems for the Rhineland armies which resulted from their sheer strength. This particularly affected the central sector, since after the abandonment of Nijmegen in AD 30 six legions were concentrated in the strip from Xanten to Mainz, all within easy reach of one another. Idle troops were always a problem for the emperor, and it may have been partly in appreciation of this fact that Claudius decided to invade Britain. Indeed, it was the lack of forethought by Nero that helped to create the major crisis of the Civil War of the years 68–70. Nero compounded the innate hostility of his Rhineland garrison by executing or forcing the suicide of Corbulo, a very respected general, and two of the commanders of the Upper and Lower German armies. The resulting resentment was fuelled by the knowledge that the aristocracy in Rome had grievances of their own against the emperor.[36]

In AD 68 Nero committed suicide, and the triumphant aristocracy welcomed Galba as the new emperor. This event was the prelude to the Civil War, which was to involve the Rhineland armies to a very significant extent. Exact details of the crisis need not concern us here, but in bare outline we can say that Galba made a series of bad policy decisions affecting the Rhine armies, with the result that on the 1 January 69 the two legions at Mainz overthrew Galba's statue and asked the Senate and People of Rome to choose a successor. Events moved swiftly, with Galba being murdered in Rome and replaced by Otho shortly afterwards, but Otho, too, found that the Rhineland legions were not willing to follow his command. The defiance expressed at Mainz soon spread to the garrison in Lower Germany, who proclaimed their commander Aulus Vitellius as emperor. This was accepted by the Mainz legions and the British garrison, and gained the support of the governors of adjacent provinces. Thus the scene was set for armed confrontation.[37]

In the savage fighting in the Po Valley, which followed Vitellius' advance

Bronze statuette of Mars wearing the armour of a Roman commander, said to have been found near the Rhine. (British Museum)

into Italy and confrontation with Otho's forces, the Rhineland legions were triumphant, and Vitellius, now declared emperor, advanced to Rome. Back in Germany the frontier was reinforced by a levy and by troops brought from Britain. However, Vitellius apparently took no steps to secure the loyalty of the powerful group of legions along the Danube, or the smaller garrison in the east. The Danubian legions had supported Otho, and so by the summer of 69, they were casting about for a successor to Vitellius, encouraged by the bad reputation that he was forging for himself in Rome. Vespasian, a well-respected general and governor of Judaea, emerged as a candidate willing to bid for supreme power.

The Danubian legions now advanced on Italy, and the end result of a bloody clash near Cremona was defeat for Vitellius, effectively securing the emperorship for Vespasian.[38] Vitellius himself might have been able to continue fighting, had he been able to draw on troops remaining in the Rhineland. However, a wily move by supporters of Vespasian ensured that they could not stir. This was the rebellion by one of the client kings in the lower Rhine area, Julius Civilis of the Batavi, who had been asked to take steps to pin down the remaining Roman garrison.

Vespasian was now undisputed victor, and was to rule for a decade as the first of the Flavian emperors. He almost immediately had to turn his attention to the Rhineland, where Civilis, now bent on his own designs, was keen to expand the revolt into a widespread native rebellion, with the aim of weakening and excluding Roman rule in the area.[39]

Civilis had started the revolt by attacking the legionary fortress of Vetera, which was at this time manned only by half its usual garrison, some 5,000 men. When news came of Vespasian's success, the Lower German legions at first reluctantly swore allegiance to the new emperor, but discipline soon lapsed and troops started to express open disloyalty. Rebellion then spread to Upper Germany, where Mainz was besieged. At this point Civilis was able to bring some of the tribes of north-eastern Gaul into his revolt. The Gaulish leaders, notably Julius Classicus and Julius Tutor, were enthusiastic about declaring an Empire of the Gauls (*imperium Galliarum*), an idea that Civilis went along with as a means to further his own ends, but which was vigorously rejected by some tribes, such as the Sequani and Mediomatrici, who remained loyal to Rome.[40]

The loyal Roman commanders were in a perilous position, since they could no longer trust their troops. Vocula, for instance, while on his way to relieve the siege of Vetera, was murdered by his own troops. They subsequently joined Civilis and swore allegiance to the Empire of the Gauls. Vetera was forced to surrender; despite guarantees for their safety, all the men in the fortress were slaughtered and the legionary legate, Lupercus, was sent as a sacrifice to the priestess of the rebels, a certain Veleda. After this matters deteriorated rapidly. All the legionary quarters north of Mainz were set on fire and were in the hands of the rebels. The colony at Cologne fell too, but was spared from burning.

Meanwhile Vespasian sent Petilius Cerialis, a distinguished general, and Annius Gallus with a massive army to the Rhineland. The rebels were defeated first near Mainz, then at Trier, which Cerialis occupied. Here he received the remnants of Vocula's old force of troops that had ignominiously sworn allegiance to the rebels at Neuss. Though the rebels continued to pose a threat for a while, reinforcements from Britain finally helped to quash the revolt and the Empire of the Gauls collapsed.

The various Gaulish tribes backing the revolt returned to the Roman fold. Only the Batavi and their close allies held out. Civilis himself made a stand at Xanten, probably opposing Cerialis' forces on deliberately flooded ground, which hampered the Roman attack. Civilis in fact was winning this final confrontation until a deserter enabled Cerialis to send his cavalry into the rear of Civilis' force. Civilis retreated to his own territory, and thence east to the mouth of the Rhine, where he eventually agreed to meet with Cerialis to make terms. Unfortunately, we do not know what happened next, since the narrative provided by Tacitus is lost. However, it is probable that Civilis was treated fairly leniently, and certainly the Batavi retained their previous privileges until the end of the century, apparently providing troops in lieu of money taxes. A legion was also stationed at Nijmegen as a garrison watching over the Oppidum Batavorum nearby.[41]

The terrible events of 68–70 obviously required Vespasian to reorganise the frontier garrisons. Legions were redeployed, some being disbanded and others created to take their place. Auxiliary troops, too, were dispatched to other sectors of the frontier to prevent them from serving in their region of origin, thus removing a potential focus of revolt. The ill-starred double-legionary fortress at Xanten was given up in favour of one on a nearby site for a single legion only. There were now four legions in Lower Germany, each in single-legion fortresses, Nijmegen, Xanten, Neuss and Bonn. This almost entirely changed the pattern of garrisoning the frontier: the legions were now much more spread out, none in Lower Germany being in the double fortresses which may have harboured such disaffection. A strong river frontier was thus created, supplemented by auxiliary troops placed in forts at intervals along the bank. In addition, stronger auxiliary units were placed in the more vulnerable sectors, such as the stretch between Xanten and Bonn.[42]

Further south change on the frontier was less radical, since it had been less affected by the revolt. Four legions were based in Upper Germany, two at Mainz, one at Strasbourg and one at Windisch. Pre-Flavian dispositions of legionary strength thus continued, especially at Mainz, where the double legionary fortress remained as a strong point against the potential threat of the Chatti. Indeed, the army built a number of forts on the eastern bank of the Rhine in the Wetterau region precisely in order to exercise control over this tribe. To their south in the Black Forest there was also forward movement of troops in 73–4 as part of a strategy designed to fill the awkward tongue of barbarian territory between the Rhine and the Upper

Danube, and to ease communications in the region. Roads, forts and regular patrols were set up, and as the frontier moved east the legionary fortresses at Strasbourg and Windisch were left some distance behind. Eventually Windisch became an anachronism, and the legion was moved away, although Strasbourg remained a base.[43]

The next series of military developments also occurred in this part of the frontier. In 83–5 Domitian launched a war against the Chatti, the last offensive to be initiated by the Romans in Germany. Mainz was the springboard for an advance that was perhaps intended to conquer Germany, a final attempt to achieve what Augustus had so nearly succeeded in accomplishing. Five legions and many auxiliaries were involved; but even so it was a failure, and there was no real advance beyond the Wetterau. Although Domitian celebrated a premature triumph in 83, it is clear that the Chatti were not defeated, and by 84 they were even strong enough to attack the neighbouring German tribe, the Cherusci.[44]

The one positive result of Domitian's Chattan war was the creation of the first *limes*, or continuous land frontier. Frontinus tells us that 120 Roman miles of lines were laid out, 'to alter the military situation and bring the enemy into subjection, and drive them from their hiding places'. What he seems to be referring to is a cleared trackway running through what was essentially a hilly and forested region. From about AD 85 onwards watch-towers were provided along the trackway, together with some small fortlets. It was not, therefore, a very strong frontier, since the auxiliary forts and legionary fortresses lay further back. However, it marked out the limit of advance in the Chattan war, running close to the east bank of the Rhine, and then down to the Wetterau region; from here it swept north-eastwards in a horn-like shape to take in the higher ground, before turning south towards the River Main. Roman territory was thus clearly defined.[45]

Once these changes had been set in motion, Domitian's attention switched to the Danube. Troops were withdrawn, including a legion that was moved from Mainz to serve there. By 88–9 inactivity on the frontier fed dissatisfaction against Domitian, and the commander Antonius Saturninus was raised as emperor. It was a short-lived but dangerous rebellion, bloodily put down. Further troop reductions followed, so that after 92–3 there were only three legions in each part of Germany: at Nijmegen, Neuss and Bonn, and Mainz, Strasbourg and Windisch.[46]

It was also at this time that the provinces of Germania Inferior and Superior were created. Hitherto the armies had been operating from the province of Belgica, but the increasing civilian development of the Rhineland and the realisation that the armies were there to stay brought pressure for provincial reorganisation. The boundary changes meant that Gallia Belgica lost a large part of its territory. The Tungri and the frontier zone behind the Rhine went to Germania Inferior, while to Germania Superior went the middle Rhine Valley, the *agri Decumates*, Helvetia and, more surprisingly in view of their westerly position, the Sequani and the Lingones in the Vosges.

Belgica retained the all-important town of Trier and its territory, despite the importance of this region for the frontier. This may have been a political decision, in view of the recent rebellion, so that the German provinces were divided by the land of the Treveri.[47]

The frontier itself gradually settled down and became stabilised. After about AD 90 many of the forts in Lower Germany were rebuilt in stone,

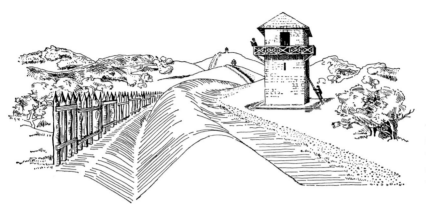

The *limes* as it appeared in the later second century, with wooden palisade, earthen bank and watchtowers. (After Baatz)

and others were also being constructed in Upper Germany along the *limes*; these were first built in wood and earth, but were reconstructed a few decades later in stone. Many have been excavated, as at Zugmantel and, most notably, at the Saalburg, a site subsequently rebuilt in the early twentieth century to give an image of what a frontier fort may have looked like.[48]

Also after AD 90 the Black Forest area was formally incorporated as a part of the Empire, so that civilian administration started to operate in the area. The frontier itself was now extended south of the River Main as a land *limes* as far as the River Neckar. It is known as the Odenwald *limes*, and was similar in form to the frontier in the Wetterau, but not so strongly fortified, presumably because the threat was less intense in this area. There were small guard fortlets housing fairly low-grade troops (*numeri*), interspersed with a watch-tower system.[49] It is, however, difficult to establish what happened at this date to the south-east of the Neckar, where the frontier presumably ran to meet with the Raetian *limes*, which was being developed at roughly the same time. It seems likely that the threat diminished the further one travelled south along the frontier, so that the angle between the two provinces had a low priority in the construction work.

By Hadrian's reign the frontier was effectively keeping the region pacified and preventing incursions by the Germans. As a result legionary strength was further reduced to just two in each province, being placed at Vetera II near Xanten, Bonn, Mainz and Strasbourg. Auxiliary strength, however, was probably maintained, because of the need for frontier fort garrisons. Increasingly, therefore, the auxiliaries took on any problems posed by the

German tribes, which in turn led to a gradually diminishing role for the legions.

Hadrian was also responsible for setting up a wooden palisade along the land frontier in Upper Germany, probably in AD 121–2. This made it much more of a barrier and, as such, the immediate predecessor of his wall in Britain, which was made considerably more imposing because of the greater threat there from beyond the frontier. The palisade *limes* was intended to be a static frontier, the culmination of a process of continuous experimentation and development of the frontier since the end of Domitian's Chattan war.[50]

The frontier was further developed under Antoninus Pius. Wooden watch-towers were replaced in stone during the 140s, and inscriptions of 145–6 on watch-towers in the Odenwald *limes* record the manning of this part of the frontier by 'numeri Brittonum', probably from northern Britain. Antoninus, though, soon authorised a major move of the frontier in this region. By about 161 the line moved eastwards approximately 25 kilometres to the so-called Forward *limes*. Its central section was a masterpiece of the surveyor's art, since it ran in a quite straight line without deviation for 81 kilometres, the longest straight frontier in the Empire. It linked the Main with the Raetian *limes*, which had itself been pushed forward (i.e. northwards) at the same time. This reduced the length of the frontier in this area, and at the same time minimised the angle between the German and Raetian *limites*. The new forts and frontier system corresponded almost directly with old forts on the Odenwald *limes*, and there were roads connecting the two systems which were presumably built as the frontier was moved forward. One difference, though, was that the Forward *limes* had more closely spaced watch-towers than its predecessor, 400–600 metres apart as opposed to 700–1000 metres. It was also more carefully constructed as a barrier. Possibly the Germans were starting to pose more of a problem in this part of the frontier, and it is notable that the powerful confederation of the Alamanni first appeared here a few decades later.[51]

It was, in fact, in the second half of the second century that problems of frontier security began to affect many different parts of the Empire. The German frontier was attacked by the Chatti, who caused some destruction in the Wetterau in 162 and 170, while the Chauci raided the coast of Gallia Belgica by sailing round from the North Sea area in 172. Much more severe than these minor episodes, though, were the wars of the 160s against the Marcomanni in the Danube frontier area. Marcus Aurelius took strenuous steps to relieve the turmoil of Germanic pressure on the frontier, a first sign of the much more serious attacks which were to follow.[52]

For a while after this peace returned to the frontier. Under Commodus there was little to report except for some disturbances around Strasbourg in 182, perhaps connected with a revolt led by Maternus. Construction continued along the *limes*, with the addition of new forts such as Niederbieber and Holzhausen. In many ways this period was the high point in the development of the frontier. Most forts and their internal buildings were by now in stone, with extensive *vici* surrounding them. Inscriptions occur commonly, and the material evidence points to a high standard of military culture. Some of this development may have been due to the presence of Caracalla in Upper Germany. He fought a campaign in 213 against the Alamanni, who were just starting to make their presence felt, and who were later to cause major problems. Mainz was probably one of his bases, and it is also known that he crossed the frontier at the western end of the Raetian *limes*, where an honorific gateway has been discovered at Dalkingen. Building activity is recorded at many forts at this time by large commemorative inscriptions to the Severan house in gilded bronze lettering. The *limes* also reached its final form, with a bank and ditch now backing up the palisade along the frontier line itself. In places along the Forward *limes* there were stretches of stone walling, perhaps an indication of the intention to rebuild the system with a stone wall throughout, as already existed along the Raetian *limes*.[53]

Caracalla's campaigns were not simply a matter of fighting: by buying off the Alamanni he was able to claim a victory and ensure peace in Upper Germany for some two decades. However, this action may ultimately have made matters worse, since it set a precedent for emperors to use money to buy their way out of difficult situations, thereby encouraging inflation at home and demands for more from the barbarians. In 233 problems flared up again. The Alamanni crossed the frontier in Upper Germany and caused severe damage – forts were destroyed and several of them had only reduced garrisons thereafter. This was the first time that the frontier had suffered a major breach, and the Emperor Severus Alexander launched a counter-attack in 234–5, using reinforcements from the eastern legions. Although the campaign was a bold move, Alexander's efforts were not deemed a success by the troops in Germany. Both he and his mother were murdered at Mainz in 235.[54]

A self-proclaimed strongman, Maximinus Thrax, succeeded him, and he was able to repel the German threat. Some of the forts were rebuilt, such as those at the Saalburg and Zugmantel, in what was probably the last restructuring of the defences before the end of this part of the *limes*. After this the frontier became the focus of repeated attacks. The crisis was deepened by further withdrawals of troops by the short-lived emperors of this era, who needed military resources to pursue their own claims and counter-claims to supreme power.[55]

Despite this reduction in effectiveness, which can be detected archaeologically in the signs of reduced occupation in many forts, the frontier as a whole continued to 259/60. It was at about this date that the difficult strategic decision was taken to evacuate the *agri Decumates* and the associated frontier installations in favour of the Rhine. This was in the aftermath of a major attack in 254 upon Upper Germany and north-western Raetia, following some troop withdrawals. It is just possible that some sections were given up before 259/60, but there is no definite evidence for the date of the abandonment, except for a somewhat oblique statement in a later document of 293 blaming the Emperor Gallienus for the loss of Raetia and other provinces.[56]

While these major upheavals were taking place in the south, in the northern region of Lower Germany the problems only started in earnest after 257, when another new group of Germans, the Franks, invaded. Skeletons found scattered in the ruined remains of a mithraeum in one of the Rhineland forts at Krefeld-Gellep have been interpreted as victims of this attack.[57] Such was the turmoil caused along the whole length of the frontier, both north and south, and such was the low morale and low opinion of the emperor's response to the threat, that the army and people of Germany and Gaul took matters into their own hands. This resulted in the political confederation known as the Gallic Empire, and it marked a turning point in the history of these provinces.

FURTHER READING

Roman Germany has a considerable literature, ranging from J. Von Elbe's introductory text in English, *Roman Germany: a guide to sites and museums* (2nd edition, 1973), and T. Bechert's highly illustrated *Römisches Germanien zwischen Rhein und Maas* (1982), to more academic analyses by H. Von Petrikovits, *Rheinische Geschichte I, i, Altertum* (1980) and C. Rüger, *Germania Inferior* (1968). Other general works worthy of mention are the East German publication by R. Günther and H. Köpstein, *Die Römer an Rhein und Donau* (1975) and W. Van Es, *Die Romeinen in Nederland* (1972). The most important recent discussion of military–civilian interaction in the frontier area is R. Brandt and J. Slofstra (eds), *Roman and Native in the Low Countries* (1983). Individual sites are listed and discussed for Westphalia (Horn 1987), Hesse (Baatz and Herrmann 1982), Baden-Württemberg (Filtzinger *et al.* 1986) and Switzerland (Drack and Fellmann 1988). Sites that can be singled out are Neuss fortress (Chantraine *et al.* 1984), Cologne (La Baume 1967, in English, and 1980, German), Nijmegen (Bogaers *et al.* 1980), Rottweil (Rüsch 1981), Valkenburg fort (Glasbergen and Groenman-van Waateringe 1974), Rijswijk settlement (Bloemers 1978), Köln-Mungersdorf villa (Fremersdorf 1933) and Lauffen villa (Spitzing 1988).

The frontier itself is analysed by D. Baatz, *Der Römische Limes* (1975), with an update on recent work given by Schönberger (1985) and in recent proceedings of the Roman Frontiers Studies congresses. The *limes* in the Black Forest is described by E. Schallmeyer in *Der Odenwald Limes* (1984) and W. Beck and D. Planck in *Der Limes in Südwestdeutschland* (1980). E. Luttwak's *The Grand Strategy of the Roman Empire* (1976) is a thought-provoking study of the strategy that led to the establishment of the frontier. Civilian settlement next to forts is given detailed treatment by Sommer (1988), and the episode of Civilis is analysed by Urban (1983).

8

BREAKDOWN
AND
REVIVAL

I f the second century is regarded as a time of peace, the third century, by contrast, is usually characterised as a time of crisis. Gaul is thought to have been particularly affected by this, although, as we shall see, the idea of crisis throughout the century is a gross oversimplification. Problems were effectively brought to a head in the two or three decades from the late 250s onwards, precipitated by the loss of part of the frontier at this time, combined with a slowly developing economic deterioration that hit hard during the middle years of the century.

We must, however, start by going back to the end of the second century. Signs of internal problems surfaced with the revolt led by a certain Maternus in about 182, when a band of disaffected soldiers and brigands reputedly wrought considerable damage to villas and towns; these probably lay in southern Gaul, since the sources also refer to Spain and to the escape of the brigands to Italy.[1] Convincing archaeological evidence for this event is, however, lacking, but whatever its actual effects, the episode is the first sign of popular revolt, and suggests that resentment was gradually building up against the wealth and power concentrated in the hands of villa-owners, merchants and others. Similar revolts were to flare again during the next two centuries.

The other event of major importance for Gaul at the end of the second century was the defeat of Clodius Albinus, governor of Britain in the 190s. Albinus was a contender for imperial power after the assassination of Commodus, but he reached an agreement with Severus, who actually became Emperor, that he would be Severus' successor. However, it became increasingly clear that Severus wanted to create a family dynasty instead. The result was a short civil war, and the battleground was Gaul. Albinus removed troops from Britain, and raised more from both the Rhineland and

Gaul itself. He met with Septimius Severus' forces in the vicinity of Lyon in 197. There were 150,000 troops on each side, according to the historian Cassius Dio, and the outcome, after a bloody and costly battle for both sides, was victory for Severus and the suicide of Albinus. In the aftermath of the battle Severus attempted to ensure the loyalty of the Gallic provinces, using force where necessary, confiscating lands, depriving officials of their positions and executing known opponents.[2] Lyon was apparently sacked, although little evidence of this survives in the archaeological record. It also used to be thought that the central Gaulish samian ware industry was destroyed or closed down as a result of Severus' proscriptions. This, too, now seems unlikely, and there is no indication from the kilns themselves, or in the chronology of the pottery, that production came to an abrupt end at this time.[3]

Although direct evidence is lacking for Severus' sack and destruction of the fabric of the central part of Gaul, a case can be made for severe economic effects on the Lyon region. The town and the surrounding countryside suffered an economic decline during the early third century which was much worse than in neighbouring regions.[4] Lyon may well have been in official disfavour in the Severan era, so that its long-time rival, Vienne, could gain at Lyon's expense. These changes could also have affected the economic climate of the southern part of Gallia Lugdunensis, of which Lyon was, of course, the capital, and thereby sowed the seeds of decline in the samian ware and other industries.

It is fair to say, however, that economic decline was not merely confined to this region. There was a widespread coin shortage in the civilian parts of Gaul and Germany, worse in the north than in the south. On the frontier itself coin circulation remained healthy, but it was nevertheless the army that was both the cause of the problem and its beneficiary.[5] Army pay had been increased, particularly by Caracalla, with the result that bullion resources became scarce. Official coin issues started to be debased in an effort to cope with this, leading to economic dislocation and, apparently, the beginning of the inflation that was to hit trade hard a few decades later. Since the army was the beneficiary of these changes, it might be thought that its additional spending power would actually have improved the position of the Gallic hinterland of the frontier. This was not in fact the case, because of the static or declining number of soldiers in the Rhineland, and a shift in imperial favour to the middle Danube area, as far as defence was concerned. Provinces such as Pannonia became prosperous at exactly the same time that problems were coming to the surface in Gaul.

One of the consequences of the coin shortage was widespread forging. Moulds for casting coins are known from many sites, even from regional capitals such as Mainz and Lyon, which might be expected to have attracted enough cash to service their merchants' needs.[6] This, though, was not enough to ensure that coin-based trade could continue as before, and the period saw a gradual decline in economic activity, particularly in sectors such as long-distance trade, which relied on coins to fulfil contracts. It is also apparent that the centres from which the trade was being conducted, namely the towns, were also going into a gentle decline at the same time. New buildings are less common than before, and by the 230s commemorative inscriptions, which can be used as a rough index of civic pride, are but a small percentage of their second-century numbers.[7]

Despite these problems, life in the Empire in the period up to the late 250s continued, generally speaking, much as before, and there was no abrupt rupture with the world of the second century. The frontier, and its economy, were being sustained, so that the illusion of security and the *pax romana* could continue in Gaul, for the time being at least. Military problems that did occur, such as the incursion by the Alamanni in the 230s, were probably considered as far-off, irrelevant events by the majority of citizens not living close to the frontier. But the decade of the 250s, with its chain of political upheavals and military disasters, can be seen as the onset of crisis. In Gaul the raids by Alamanni and then Franks, followed by the loss of the *agri Decumates* and a stream of refugees into Gaul (eventually to be settled in all probability in the *Decem Pagi* in Alsace), appear to have sent a shock-wave of apprehension through Gaul. For the first time, too, Germanic raiders appeared deep inside the heartland of Gaul, and Franks are recorded as having sacked the Spanish city of Tarraco in 262 after crossing the length of Gaul. Even if the vast majority of the population did not actually see or suffer from the German raiders, the sense of panic must have been profound, and there are hints in the literary sources of this period of a feeling of impending doom.[8]

One of the immediate reactions to these events may well have been the burying of coin hoards and other treasure. There is considerable disagreement amongst specialists about the exact significance of the great increase in the number of coin hoards from about 259/60 onwards, since this date coincided with the release of a great number of debased coins into the economy, but there is broad agreement that two things happened. More coin hoards were buried in the 260s and 270s than ever before and, perhaps more significantly, fewer hoards were recovered.[9] This may imply dislocation and movement which prevented owners from returning to dig up their hoards, but there is also a possible economic motive for leaving them in the ground, since rapid changes in inflation and the debasement of the coinage meant that old coins may not have been worth recovering from their hiding-places. The balance of the evidence inclines towards the first explanation, which is supported by the telling deposition of a number of valuable fine silver treasures, such as those from Chaourse, Rethel or Graincourt-lès-Havrincourt. Temple treasures, too, such as that from Berthouville, were also buried and never recovered, and it must surely have been the case that the buriers of these hoards would have returned to collect them had they been able to.[10]

It used to be thought that the deposition of hoards could be directly

Silver bowl from the large and fine treasure from Chaourse in northern Gaul. It was probably deposited during the troubled mid-third century. (British Museum)

linked with the passage of Germans through the locality, so that their depredations could be mapped by the distribution of hoards in Gaul. This notion has now fallen out of favour, and the current view is that there was more generalised panic and dislocation. Strong backing for this comes from the fact that Britain, too, has many hoards of this period, but as far as we know did not suffer direct German raids as did Gaul. In Gaul itself a notable feature of the archaeological evidence is that large numbers of villas and other sites, such as temples and *vici*, appear to come to an end at this time. This is particularly marked in Gallia Belgica, and it was once automatically attributed to German destructiveness, especially if any traces of burning were found in the debris. Such a direct chain of cause and effect is now regarded as unlikely, and it has been pointed out that the extent of abandonment and destruction seems far greater than the capabilities of the fairly small raiding parties involved.[11] An alternative explanation is that a lot of the destruction was caused by internal forces at work in the provinces, either through direct action by brigands (as seen, for example, earlier at the time of Maternus), or through more generalised economic decline which was brought to a rapid crisis point in reaction to the barbarian threat. If the economic system was in any way vulnerable to the dislocation of trade, the events of the mid-third century may easily have tipped the balance so that villas were no longer viable. Any upset to the fragile pattern of agriculture that had grown up over the previous two centuries would have made it difficult to sustain the largely rural population, and if many people lost their agricultural livelihood, brigandage and looting was probably their only means of survival.

Other changes in the period include the eclipse of some of the productive industries, notably samian ware and stone-quarrying. The disruption to the long-distance trading networks was probably a major factor, with the economy becoming increasingly localised. Communities were thrown back on their own resources, and it was difficult, if not impossible, to obtain supplies from overseas, other provinces or indeed anywhere outside the local region.

Regionalisation and change were not confined simply to the economy. Just as significant, and probably a cause of some of the problems, was the response of the military to the events of the 250s. M. Postumus, probably the governor of Germania Inferior, with a base in Cologne and later in Trier, declared himself Emperor in 260. His claim was not for the whole Empire, but for Gaul, Germany, Britain and Spain, which he managed to control without, apparently, any desire to extend his power over Italy and other lands held by the legitimate Emperor, Gallienus.[12]

This separatist movement has come to be known as the Gallic Empire (AD 260–74), and in both political and military terms it marks a major turning-point in the history of Gaul. Postumus and his successors obtained the grudging recognition of the central Empire, largely because the latter was not powerful enough to do much about it, despite various attempts. As the first Gallic Emperor, Postumus was an effective ruler and general, maintaining a good state of defence along the frontier. There is, for instance, no evidence that town walls were being built in the interior of Gaul at this time, which would indicate that he was able to prevent further serious Germanic incursions, at least until 268. Much of the evidence for destruction in the countryside is also thought to date to the 270s, after the power of the Gallic Empire had waned and finally collapsed. In the realm of the economy, Postumus at first managed to maintain the standard of the coinage and increase the rate of issue, so that there were a few years of respite from the monetary problems of the mid-century.

Postumus' successors were not such effective rulers and all, except the last, Tetricus, fell victim to the military feuding that pervaded the later Gallic Empire. Victorinus was the most able, but he was faced with the loss of the southern part of his territory to the central Empire, and the need to attack the rebellious city of Autun, which fell only after a long seven-month siege. At the same time the central emperors were gaining in strength, and eventually Aurelian was able to advance into northern Gaul and secure the surrender of Tetricus.

Following hard upon these disruptive military actions in Gaul came another, very serious invasion of the frontier: Vandals, Franks, Burgundians, Alamanni and others probably took deliberate advantage of the confusion to cross in large numbers into Gaul in 274/5, sacking Trier and many other towns. It is this series of raids that is most likely to have caused the destruction seen on archaeological sites, if the burning levels are to be attributed to the barbarians. Many hilltop refuges are thought to date from this period. In Germany and Gallia Belgica, and particularly in the Ardennes and the Eifel, many old Iron Age hillforts and other remote rural positions were provided with defences and used by the civilian population as a means of escape from the raids. Excavated examples, such as Furfooz (Belgium) or the Wittnauer Horn (Switzerland), show the erection of defences on simple

Third-century town wall of Le Mans (Subdinum Vindinum), constructed in decorative stone and tile-work with projecting bastions at intervals.

military lines and temporary buildings within; finds from these sites indicate a fairly basic standard of living. The evidence tends to suggest that these refuges were an effective means of avoiding attack by Germanic raiders, since the latter were lightly armed and not equipped for sieges, and so preferred to set their sights on undefended villas and settlements.[13]

Towns at this time also remained undefended in the vast majority of cases, and so presented an equally easy target for the raiders. The lesson was quickly learnt that walls were a necessity for deterring future attacks, and so there began a massive programme of wall-building in Gaul and Germany.[14] During the next century and a half virtually all the surviving towns in Gaul acquired defences, many of which are still in existence, such as those at Le Mans, and they serve as a vivid reminder of the insecurities of the age. It has often been assumed that many of the walls were rapidly erected in the 270s, but recent work has shown how little direct dating evidence exists. Some walls, such as those at Tours, Orléans and Poitiers, are now known to be late fourth century in date, and so it is considered that the provision of defences took a long time, and was perhaps done on regional initiative, since groups of towns show marked similarities in their wall design.[15]

The most notable feature of the late Roman town walls is the small size of the circuit. Many enclosed remarkably small areas, such as those at Amiens and Bavai, which included just the forum and immediate surrounding structures. At Paris the whole town was left undefended except for the Ile de la Cité, and at Périgueux only the amphitheatre and a single block were inside the wall, leaving the rest of the town outside.[16] Indeed, in nearly

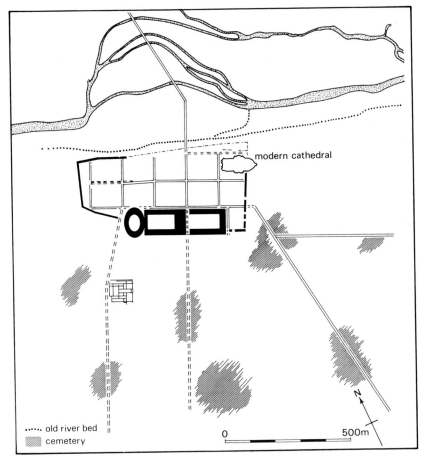

Amiens (Samarobriva Ambianorum) in the later third and fourth centuries. The defensive wall enclosed a much shrunken town compared with that of the second century (p. 74). The cathedral possibly occupies the site of an early Christian church.

..... old river bed

cemetery

modern cathedral

0   500m

every town areas of housing, baths and other civic amenities were left outside the defences, and it has to be asked why this was so. Had they declined so much by the late third century that only a small circuit was necessary to house the population, or was a decision taken only to defend one important area within the town, to act as a refuge in times of need? Unfortunately, little evidence is available to show what was happening in the extramural areas, but in Poitiers archaeological work seems to indicate that houses *inside* the later wall continued to the third century, but were effectively abandoned by the fourth. If this is typical of other towns, then there may have been a process of contraction at work, so that many towns, even if once larger than their wall circuits, shrank to fit inside, and eventually became even smaller than the circuit. In other words, many towns were in decline as population centres, with perhaps only the *civitas* administration, the forum and basilica maintaining a semblance of town life.[17]

This has major implications for a change in the manner and tenor of life in the late Roman period. Gone is the idea of life being centred around the town, the Roman ideal painstakingly built up over the previous two centuries. Gone, too, is the notion of evergetism, the spirit of competition that had existed amongst Gallic notables to erect public buildings. In their place we see a radical change in outlook, which can be taken as far as a psychological change in attitude to the Roman Empire as it had existed in the now far-off golden age of the second and early third centuries. This is most dramatically seen in the demolition of many early Roman monuments to provide masonry for the new town walls, such as at Arlon. Some of them had been put up only a few decades earlier, and must include tombstones to people whose descendants were still living in the town. This rejection of such a link with the past represents a remarkable change from the earlier reverence for these monuments. Other aspects of the early Roman Empire seen in the archaeological record, such as samian ware and styles of glass and metalware, underwent major changes in taste at this time. In the case of samian ware, figured decoration and scenes of classical mythology and hunting in the design repertoire went out of fashion; vessels were now either undecorated or used simple geometric designs. In general pottery took on much more local characteristics, and no longer looked to the Mediterranean for inspiration, in the northern parts of Gaul at least. In the south changes of this sort were less marked, and pottery fashions continued with less interruption during the third century. Even here, however, styles had decisively moved in a characteristic late Roman direction by the end of the century.[18]

Some scholars have characterised these and other changes of the period as a Celtic Renaissance. Evidence for this comes from the use of words such as the Celtic *leuga* or league in place of the Roman *milia* on third-century milestones, and the emergence of more localised production of goods in local styles.[19] 'Celtic Renaissance', though, is probably a misleading term, for there was no harping back to the Iron Age in artistic or other terms. Reoccupation of hillforts and local pottery production in new styles were more a reaction to the economic and social conditions of the times than a conscious revival of the old ways. What emerged in the late Roman period was essentially a Gallo-Roman culture that owed much more to the interaction of Roman and native than to dim folk memories of a Celtic past. The other feature of the late Roman change was that pan-imperial early Roman culture ceased to be dominant, which allowed local cultures to express themselves more strongly. To this extent at least, there was a cultural renewal.

Recovery and imperial patronage

After the major incursions of the 270s the strong Emperor Probus came to Gaul to sort out the problems. He was able to defeat the barbarians and impose on them a treaty that allowed the Germans back across the Rhine to their own lands, provided that they surrendered their prisoners and booty. Although this treaty was violated, requiring further fighting, the late third century was generally much calmer. Probus started to build new forts, including some on the right bank of the Rhine, such as Kastell-bei-Mainz, in zones that were once part of Roman territory but had been lost since 259. New garrisons were installed, and policies altered so that the frontier eventually changed out of all recognition from its early Roman predecessor. For instance, it is thought that this period saw the settlement of Germanic groups within the boundary of the Empire. The Batavian area received increasing numbers of Franks, probably allowed in under a treaty which obliged them to provide the Romans with military assistance against further German raids. It was a policy of using German against German, and this became much more important during the fourth century.[20]

Probus and his contemporaries can also take the credit for changes in the defensive network itself. Fort-building programmes along the Rhine, in Switzerland and on the Gallic coast reflect new styles of defensive architecture, and a new overall strategy that has been termed 'defence in depth'.[21] The army, instead of holding a thin frontier line at all costs, now provided a much more flexible response to threats within a deeper frontier zone. One of the problems of the earlier strategy had been that once barbarians had breached the frontier there was nothing to stop them advancing hundreds of miles inland and threatening distant civilian communities. The new policy operated more on the basis that raiders would be detected crossing the frontier by the garrisons there, but after entering Roman territory they would be apprehended by mobile forces, largely of cavalry.

The consequence of this strategy was that the area behind the frontier became a war zone, liable to devastation without much warning, and thus needing strong defences. Apart from towns, with their new walls, road stations also acquired fort-like defences. Neumagen and Bitburg in the territory of Trier are good examples, having small circuits and strong, bastioned wall curtains. For the civilian population in the countryside there were either the hilltop refuges or, in the flatter countryside, strongly defended towers, often referred to as *burgi*, such as those excavated at Froitzheim and Moers-Asberg. They must have looked like large versions of military watch-towers of the sort found on the early Roman *limes*, and the indications are that they were in use from the late third century onwards.[22]

As for the forts themselves, they underwent a radical change in design, coming to resemble medieval castles. They had high, strong walls with projecting bastions used for *ballistae*, bowmen and other defenders. Although this is not by any means certain, it is thought that the new ideas came from the east of the Empire, where strongly defended town defences incorporating similar features are known to be earlier than those found in the west. Defensive techniques used in forts were also similar to those used in towns and other defended sites, which clearly reduced the differences that had once been so obvious between civilian and military sites. Because of this, it is sometimes difficult to tell whether a fortification in, for instance, a *vicus* was built for military purposes to defend the road, or as a civilian

The seaward defences of Boulogne (Bononia), largely medieval, but constructed on Roman foundations. The walls enclosed the fleet base for the protection of the coasts on either side of the English Channel.

place of safety. It is known that the major roads were officially defended, so that on the road from Cologne to Boulogne, for example, we find forts constructed in roadside *vici*, such as Liberchies.[23]

Accompanying such alterations to the design of forts were major changes to the complexion of the army itself. We have already seen in chapter 7 that the legions were declining in status by the third century. This process continued and intensified, so that by the end of the century the élite troops in the army were now cavalry field armies that often accompanied the Emperor and important military commanders on campaign. The legions were increasingly confined to a role of frontier defence, along with other infantry auxiliary regiments. They no longer played any significant role in attacking raiding parties and actually engaging barbarians in battle.[24]

Apart from the developing military defence network, there were other factors which characterise the history of the later third century, not least the activities of rural brigands, or *bagaudae*. Under the leadership of Aelian and Amandus one group was able to wage a form of guerilla warfare, harassing rich landowners who had fortified themselves against attack in their large villa estates. Although these events are not securely located in any one part of Gaul, it is clear that the *bagaudae* were a phenomenon of regions such as Brittany and the area between the Loire and the Seine, rather than the frontier. It is just possible that some of the fortifications in central-western Gaul, such as at Jublains (defending some sort of official installation), Le Rubricaire and Larçay, were constructed to take account of this internal unrest, as much as the rather more distant threat of a Germanic attack.[25]

Problems of this sort in northern Gaul were compounded in the 280–90s by another attempt at a secessionist empire, this time based in Britain. Carausius, a Batavian by birth, was in command of the fleet charged with defending the English Channel against Saxon and other raiders. His headquarters was Boulogne, and he was able to take advantage of this crucial military post to declare himself emperor, with control over Britain, northern Gaul and parts of Germania Inferior. His was but a pale reflection of the Gallic Empire, however, and Rome was able to confine Carausius' power and eventually invade Britain to defeat his sucessor, Allectus. The military leader who carried out this operation was Constantius Chlorus, father of Constantine, and he commemorated his victory by issuing gold medallions showing him entering London. One of them survives in the spectacular gold hoard from Beaurains near Arras, together with other medallions and gold coins indicating that Constantius was using Trier as a mint and his capital city.[26] This is one of the first indications of the growing power and importance of Trier (see below). Another consequence of the defeat of the British Empire was that more bands of Franks were settled in Batavian territory as a means of securing the loyalty of the *civitas* to Rome, and we also see *laeti* or groups of Germans settled in various Gallic *civitates* in 294–5.

Carausius' bid for power coincided with the accession of Diocletian to the emperorship, and it was during his reign that important administrative changes were made in Gaul and elsewhere. By far the most important of these was the subdivision of imperial responsibility, and one of the four Tetrarchs was allocated Gaul, Germany, Britain and Spain. Within this area new provinces were created by subdividing the existing ones, and they were grouped into *dioceses*: the *diocesis Galliarum* covered the old Gallia Belgica, Gallia Lugdunensis, Germania Inferior and Superior; and the *diocesis Viennensis* covered the old Aquitania, Narbonensis and the Alpes Maritimae.[27] In addition, there were many changes in the civil service and the taxation system, so that the reforms give the distinct impression of an increasingly bureaucratic and overbearing administration.

The capital for the northern and western corner of the Empire was Trier. Lyon, the old capital of the Three Gauls, was not chosen, probably because it had gone into decline after Severan disfavour in the early third century, but also because Trier was near the frontier, making a convenient base for the emperors. Constantius Chlorus was the person most responsible for the creation of Trier as the capital, while his son Constantine and subsequent members of the dynasty embellished it with fine buildings, many of which survive today.[28]

Of these the most spectacular is part of the imperial palace known as the *aula palatina* or basilica. Although much restored, it still gives the best impression anywhere in the Empire of an imperial reception hall, with its large church-like open space, 67 metres long, 27.5 metres wide and 30 metres high, with an apse at the end where the emperor would receive supplicants. Its architecture is unique in Gaul and it has been suggested that it was a new development at the time, perhaps drawing on eastern expertise. Today it gives an austere appearance, but originally both the walls and floor were covered with marble and with gold mosaics, and the exterior almost certainly had other buildings attached.[29]

Other parts of the palace have not survived so well, but there is enough to indicate that a large zone in the eastern part of the town was given over for imperial use. The palace may have extended from the basilica to

The imperial reception hall (*aula*) in the palace at Trier (Augusta Treverorum). Although partially restored, this fine building conveys the magnificence of the building work in the town when it was an imperial capital in the fourth century.

the cathedral, a remarkable early Christian church built by Constantine, apparently over the foundations of some of the palace buildings. This church is described further in chapter 9, where its full significance for the development of Christianity in Gaul and Germany is considered. To the south-east of the cathedral and the basilica was an open space, used by the emperors for entertainment purposes: a circus is thought to have been built there, not far from the well-preserved remains of the amphitheatre. In this part of town, too, was a large set of baths, the Kaiserthermen. These were the second large baths in the town and, like the Barbarathermen, were based on the design of massive imperial baths in Rome itself. It is possible that the Kaiserthermen were reserved for imperial use, but there is some doubt as to whether they were ever used before being converted into a public building for some other, as yet unknown purpose towards the end of the century.[30]

Trier's importance can not be understated. It was the one large city in the north-western provinces with a significant number of new buildings. There was some construction work in other towns at this time, such as the Constantinian baths at Arles or the small version of Trier's basilica at St Pierre-aux-Nonnains in Metz; but generally speaking secular public buildings after the early Imperial period are distinctly rare.[31] Nothing approached the imperial patronage lavished on Trier, which extended not only to buildings in the city, but showed its influence in magnificent villas in the countryside as well, such as Welschbillig, with its pool surrounded by herms; Konz, possibly an imperial property; and the remarkable fortified villa at Pfalzel.[32] The imperial presence also attracted writers and other intellectuals, so that literary evidence survives to give us some indication of life at court, and its influence on the town and region as a whole. Ausonius, notably in his *Mosella* and other writings of the late fourth century, sings the praises of both the emperor and the Treveran region.

The 'Baths of Constantine' at Arles (Arelate), one of the few late Roman baths to be constructed in Gaul, and testimony to the importance of the town in the fourth century.

Other pagans at court included Symmachus, the famous senator and man of letters, as well as various leading churchmen, such as Lactantius and Jerome.[33]

Amongst the literary works produced for the emperor were the Panegyrics, which praised his deeds; these are a valuable source for the historical narrative of the Constantinian period in particular. One of the best known takes the form of a petition from Autun for the restoration of some of its famous buildings, including a university, which had been destroyed as a result of Victorinus' siege several decades earlier.[34] Autun was seeking imperial patronage, apparently the only way of restoring a town's fortunes by this date.

Other towns which were prominent in this period include Vienne, which became the capital of the southern Gallic *diocesis* and which had risen as Lyon declined. Although no imperial palace has been found there, it had a number of churches and clearly functioned as an important centre for its region. Further south down the Rhône Valley, Arles also became important. It did not have any special status in the Constantinian period, but by the end of the fourth century, when conditions became too difficult to maintain the capital at Trier, the mint was transferred to Arles, and the town became a major Christian centre, well known for its sculpture.[35]

Elsewhere in Gaul a very different picture can be painted. Apart from the construction of churches, towns such as Amiens, Poitiers and Orléans saw the continued abandonment of buildings and contraction of the built-up area. Cemeteries started to be laid out in areas that formerly contained housing, while in Arras huts of Germanic type appear within the town. By the mid-fourth century town life was in serious decline in northern Gaul, especially where there was no direct imperial or official interest. Patronage was of overriding importance, and may for instance be relevant to the late Roman history of Paris, which was favoured by the Emperor Julian and may thus owe some of its later prominence to this fact.[36]

Many of the same considerations also applied to the countryside. Areas not too badly affected by brigandage, panic or direct German raids continued to prosper. Aquitaine was luckiest in this respect, and both from literary references by Ausonius, Salvian and others, and from the archaeological evidence of fine villas and mosaics it is clear that wealthy landowners were able to continue a privileged existence and sophisticated lifestyle well into the fifth century.[37] The evidence relates almost exclusively to the rural élite, however, and it is difficult to establish how far Aquitaine sustained a reasonable living for poor tenants (*coloni*) as well.

In northern Gaul, and much of the centre and east as well, the picture is one of decline. In the north-east in particular – in Picardy and northern Gallia Belgica – large numbers of villas came to an end in the late third century and were never rebuilt. It is widely accepted that climatic changes and flooding may also have contributed, over and above the destruction wrought by human factors, and as a result the countryside there must have presented something of a devastated image to the traveller, as indeed did the towns. Even in areas relatively unaffected by Germanic incursions, such as southern Burgundy, many sites on marginal land were given up. We might well ask where the population went. Was there an actual drop in the total, or were there new, less easily investigated sites that now housed the population? Recent excavations at sites like Dambron in central Gaul may hold the key. Meticulous recording has shown that a sunken-floored rectangular hut, 7 by 3.5 metres, was built in the early fourth century on the fringes of a small, largely deserted *vicus*. Its feeble wooden walls and low standard of accommodation represent perhaps the norm for the majority of the population at this time.[38]

Many more such sites need to be found before we can be sure of the fate of the late Roman population, but the evidence is starting to point to a major shift in site types and settlement patterns. One of the possibilities, especially in southern Gaul, is that the sites now underlie medieval and modern villages. Hilltop villages such as Lunel-Viel show evidence of late Roman occupation, and in southern Burgundy, too, it is thought that the medieval settlement pattern was coming into existence by this time. We also see the use of hilltop refuges starting in the south, such as Lombren, and the occupation of rock-shelters, like the Grotte de l'Hortus, as a variant on the refuge type of site.[39]

It is, however, known is that even in the more devastated areas of the north some large villas survived, presumably acting as estate centres for the surrounding countryside. Not far from Dambron, for instance, is the well-appointed site of Mienne-Marboué with its fine mosaics. Elsewhere, for example at the Marais-de-Famechon in the Somme, subsidiary villa buildings continued in occupation after the main house itself was abandoned; this may well be a satellite within a large estate, whose main centre lay at a villa like Mienne-Marboué. Here the archaeological evidence gives us a hint of the lifestyle enjoyed by the rich landowners known from late Roman literature, and also allows us to gauge the enormous social distance between this small but powerful élite and the rest of the population. This social inequality was much more marked than in the early Roman period, and contributed to brigandage during the third to fifth centuries, a point underlined by the complaints of authors such as Salvian.[40]

An important conclusion can be drawn from these rather tenuously understood trends in late Roman settlement. For northern Gaul, and to a lesser extent for the south as well, it was the mid- to late third century that appears to be the real break-point. Villas, *vici* and towns all started to change radically in their nature, with a few notable, mainly aristocratic or imperial exceptions. Ideas of Romanity which had been the ideal to which most Gauls aspired in the early Roman period disappeared, so that late Roman sites had few of the appurtenances of the traditional Roman way of life. Many people were displaced and forced to live in more temporary buildings, and there is little evidence of a revival in material culture even when stability returned in the early fourth century. Overall there was much more of a break in the third century than at the end of Roman rule in the fifth century. We see the gradual emergence throughout the late Roman period of patterns of life and settlement that were to crystallise into medieval civilisation. That this was so was due in large part to two factors: the Church and the way in which the German invaders were absorbed by the existing population of Gaul (see chapters 9 and 10).

The frontier from Constantine to Valentinian

The recapture of Britain by Constantius Chlorus in 296 was not the only military success of the late third century. Vigorous campaigning against the Germans in the 290s, especially the Alamanni in 298, saw imperial control being reasserted strongly in the frontier area. It was a period of revival in military terms, and the army showed its loyalty to Constantius by elevating his son Constantine to the emperorship after the former's death in Britain in 306. Constantine returned to Gaul, where he was faced with groups of Franks that had crossed the Rhine, and was able to defeat them in 310. Two Frankish kings, Ascarius and Merogaisus, are recorded as being imprisoned and made to fight against wild beasts in Trier amphitheatre at this time. Constantine went on to reinforce the frontier with new fortifications, such as Köln-Deutz, on the far side of the bridge crossing the Rhine from Cologne.[41]

From 313 to 316, and again in 328, Constantine was relatively frequently in Germany and Gaul. It was the need to maintain a strong army in the Rhineland that, more than anything else, contributed to the rise and prosperity of Trier as capital. The presence of the emperor and his field army, together with a strong system of defences, meant that Germanic raids remained insignificant until the 350s.

In about 355 the Alamanni and the Franks yet again took advantage of imperial weakness, brought about by the civil war after the death of Constans, to cross the Rhine. As before, the Germans clearly knew what was going on within the Empire, and were able to exploit their intelligence to best advantage. These attacks were only contained when the future Emperor Julian was put in command to restore order. He scored a notable victory over the Alamanni near Strasbourg in 357, recorded in some detail by Ammianus Marcellinus, the last historian to give anything more than a bare outline of events in Roman Gaul. He tells us that 35,000 Alamanni were opposed by 13,000 Romans, and that 6,000 Alamanni and only 250 Romans were lost by the end of the battle. This is a typical example of the sort of picture given by Roman historians, and it is very difficult to tell how far the numbers have been exaggerated in the Romans' favour.[42] However, Julian's victory gave Gaul and Germany a welcome respite before renewed mass movements overwhelmed the frontier in the fifth century.

Julian may also have been responsible for starting the second major phase of late Roman fort-building, which was to culminate under Valentinian.

Alzey, Boppard and Koblenz forts were amongst those constructed at this time, while permission was also granted for further Germanic settlements within Roman territory near the frontier. This bolstered the strategy of defence in depth by using Germans as a buffer in the areas most liable to attack. It was possibly the Franks who benefited most from these moves, and we find Germanic settlements in the frontier region of Germania Inferior during the second half of the fourth century, as well as cemeteries with characteristic Germanic grave-goods.[43]

These measures, however, failed to ensure peace, so that Julian was forced to campaign against the Franks in 360 near Xanten. The active presence of the emperor continued under Valentinian (364–75), with fighting against the Alamanni, especially in 368 when he crossed the Rhine to campaign against them in their own territory. Valentinian, too, built forts in order to consolidate the frontier, and was the last emperor to do so on any scale. Building activity is particularly marked in southern Germany, where we see the creation of what is known as the Rhine–Iller–Danube *limes*. This was a system of highly fortified river crossing-points, combined with watch-towers and other installations, designed to form a continuous frontier around the southern boundary of the Alamanni and prevent them from expanding south into Switzerland and Italy. In the Rhine Valley Valentinian set up further fortifications, such as the extraordinary fort of Altrip with its trapezoidal defences.[44]

These measures appear to have set the frontier on a strong footing, provided, of course, the forts were manned by adequate garrisons. Unfortunately, within a few years of their construction this ceased to be the case, and after Valentinian the history of the frontier is one of breakdown and eventual collapse.

FURTHER READING

At present there is not an extensive literature on later Roman Gaul and Germany, but the situation is likely to change as recent research is published. For the third century, there are several important papers in A. King and M. Henig, *The Roman West in the Third Century* (1981), and J. Drinkwater's *The Gallic Empire* (1987) is the best treatment of the episode of Postumus' separatist state in the middle of the century. Fortifications during the late Empire have received exemplary attention in S. Johnson's *Late Roman Fortifications* (1983), which can be supplemented by his discussion of the coastal defences (1976), by Von Petrikovits on the Rhineland forts (1971) and by Wood on the town wall of Tours (1983). The key site of this period, Trier, is the subject of monographs by Wightman (1970) and Heinen (1985), also having a splendidly illustrated exhibition catalogue by the Rheinisches Landesmuseum Trier, *Trier: Kaiserresidenz und Bischofssitz* (1984). Two other exhibition catalogues deserve mention: *Gallien in der Spätantike* (1980) for its good general survey of the period, and F. Baratte and K. Painter (eds), *Trésors d'Orfèvrerie gallo-romains* (1989) for its fine illustrations of many late Roman silver hoards.

9

CHURCHES
AND THE
CHURCH

O ur knowledge of the Christian Church in Gaul can be said to begin properly with an episode that occurred in about AD 177. This was the persecution and death of a small group of Christians in Lyon. One of them was Blandina, a slave woman, whose fortitude in the face of torture and exposure to wild beasts in the amphitheatre has ensured canonisation and a place in the annals of the early Church.[1]

The exact events are given in some detail by Eusebius, who quotes a letter sent by the Christian communities of Lyon and Vienne to colleagues in the east. It appears that the Christians were first of all excluded from public places, then subjected to abuses by angry locals, investigated by officials, imprisoned, tortured and eventually brought before the provincial governor. He sought to have them recant or else confess to the antisocial nature of their faith, popularly held at that time to include incest and cannibalism. In the end they were condemned to the beasts (*condamnati ad bestias*) and sent to the amphitheatre, where Blandina, although tied to a post, was not touched by the animals. At this stage the Emperor Marcus Aurelius intervened through his provincial governor by releasing those who repudiated Christianity and returning the others to the amphitheatre, except for one Roman citizen who was ordered to be beheaded.

The time of year was summer, when Lyon was filled with crowds from all over Gaul for the festival at the provincial altar which took place on 1 August. There were games and gladiatorial combats in the arena, which included the killing of condemned prisoners.[2] The authorities seem to have bowed to the demands of the crowd, keeping Blandina until last in the spectacle, since she was the most resistant of the Christians. This time the animals were not cowed by her presence, and she was killed. The bodies of the martyrs went on display before the crowds, then were burnt and the

ashes scattered in the river. As a further popular gesture Attalus, the Roman citizen ordered to be beheaded, was burnt alive in the amphitheatre instead.

The nasty events of 177 throw a spot-light on the nature of Gallic society at this time. Christianity was a small, misunderstood cult, whose membership in Lyon may not have numbered much more than the forty-eight reputed to have been martyred. For the population at large Christians were deviants, following antisocial rituals and refusing to comply with accepted norms of worship. In addition, and perhaps crucially, a large number of the Lyon Christians were foreigners, as many as half having Greek or eastern names. Lyon, in fact, was probably exceptional amongst central and northern Gallic towns in having a substantial foreign population, mainly engaged in trade along the Rhône.[3] Despite the town's cosmopolitan nature, it is clear from the events of 177 that considerable social tensions existed, perhaps as a result of a local downturn in trade due to the Marcomannic wars.[4] These tensions found a convenient outlet in persecution. Matters were exacerbated by the presence of the provincials for the festival, many of whom were undoubtedly ignorant of Christianity, probably never having come across practising Christians before. From the description of events in the amphitheatre, they were fascinated more by the display of religious fanaticism by the martyrs than any desire to eliminate Christian belief within the city.

The subsequent history of the church in Lyon shows how resilient, in fact, the Christian community was. Irenaeus became the bishop and proceeded to become involved in internal controversy within the Church concerning the Gnostic heresy, against which he wrote a tract.[5] The local anger towards the Christians appears to have died down, since we find Irenaeus preaching in local dialect in order to spread the religion outside the confines of the existing Christian community.

For the next stage in the history of the Church in Gaul we must leap forward more than a century, since events during the intervening period are not of any great significance. The focus of attention now shifts to Trier, by this time an imperial capital, and by far the most important centre for the Gallic Church after the Edict of Toleration for Christian worship of AD 313. The reason for this is not far to seek, since the presence of the Emperor Constantine and his family ensured that church-building was officially encouraged and generously funded. In 321 or a little later the cathedral was started, and this building is almost certainly the first manifestation of church architecture in Gaul or Germany.

In plan the cathedral resembled the large congregational basilicas constructed by Constantine in Rome, such as St John Lateran, and was part of an imperial church-building programme that also encompassed Constantinople, Bethlehem and Jerusalem. At Trier there were, in fact, two churches side by side, occupying one and a half blocks within the street grid, each one approximately twice the size of the present-day cathedral on the same site.[6] They were of basilical shape, with a long nave and aisles, ending in a

above The amphitheatre of the Three Gauls at Lyon (Condate), scene of the martyrdom of Blandina in AD 177.

right The massive double cathedral at Trier (Augusta Treverorum), started in AD 321. The southern church was perhaps for initiates (catechumens) and the northern one for baptised Christians.

chancel at the eastern end, and an open portico or atrium at the western end. The northern church was probably begun later than the southern. Underneath it the excavators found the demolished remains of a building that had once been decorated with fine fresco portraits. They are of early fourth-century date and may well have been of the female members of Constantine's household. This would fit with the tradition that Helena, Constantine's mother, gave part of the imperial palace as a site for the cathedral.

The setting up of two enormous churches side by side is not easy to explain, although it is paralleled elsewhere in Gaul and in northern Italy, for instance at Aquileia. However, there was a baptistery between the two churches and this may give a clue about the answer to the problem: the southern church may have been for catechumens (newly converted Christians preparing for baptism), who passed through the baptistery into the northern church for fully baptised believers.[7] An alternative explanation, put forward to explain the similar arrangement at Geneva (see below), is that one of the churches, perhaps the southern one, was mainly for preaching, while the other was more for ceremonial use, with the large space used for a 'liturgy of movement'.[8] A fascinating detail in the southern church is the presence of numerous graffiti on the altar screen, scratched into the plaster by worshippers. A typical text is *Maxima vivas in Deo* (Maxima, may you live in God).

Athanasius of Alexandria visited Trier in 336–7 and 346, and wrote that he saw crowds of worshippers in the still-unfinished cathedral.[9] The northern church, in fact, appears to have undergone considerable alteration not long

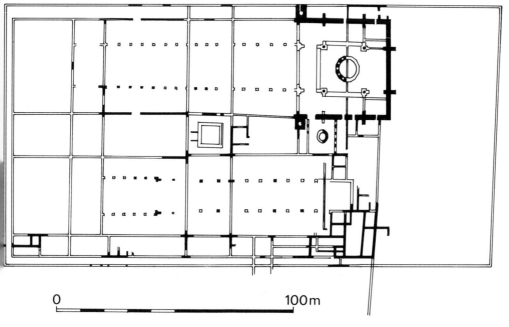

0   100m

after the original construction, which is probably what Athanasius was referring to. During the 330–40s the chancel was rebuilt with large windows, and thick walls which still survive in the modern cathedral to a height of 25 metres. Its interior was decorated with marble facings and mosaics on the upper parts of the walls. In the centre of the chancel was a twelve-sided construction, the exact purpose of which is not entirely clear. It may have contained a relic, possibly the tunic of Christ presently held in the cathedral, or, since there are no early references to the tunic (which therefore may have been acquired in the Middle Ages), was possibly destined as a tomb for one of the imperial family. Alternatively, it may have been based on the similar arrangement at the church of the Holy Apostles at Constantinople, where Constantine prepared his tomb. The twelve sides in the Trier construction would correspond with the twelve apostles.[10] Whatever its original purpose, the east end of the cathedral now had a massive appearance, probably with corner towers similar to those of churches in Milan and elsewhere in north Italy, an area which had a powerful influence on Gallic church architecture.[11] It would also have had close architectural links with the basilica of the imperial palace in Trier itself.

Trier cathedral reached its peak of development in the late fourth century; there are indications of destruction during the fifth century, and the northern church was possibly abandoned for a time. Revival did not come until the sixth century, when rather smaller churches existed on the same sites. However, we know from the bishops' lists that Church organisation remained intact throughout, and that the Church in Trier, as in so many other towns in Gaul, provided a vital bridge between Roman and post-Roman times.[12]

The double cathedral was exceptional amongst the churches of Gaul and Germany by virtue of its large size, regular layout and early date. Apart from the remarkable oval church of St Gereon, Cologne, which may have drawn on imperial mausoleum architecture for inspiration, little if any influence flowed from the imperial building programme to the numerous small churches that were erected in Gaul from the second half of the fourth century onwards. This is true even of Trier, where several other ecclesiastical buildings are known. One of these is St Mathias, situated in the cemetery area just to the south of the city walls.[13] Here a suburban villa was overlain by a cemetery in the third century, and there are also a large number of graves, many with Christian inscriptions, which date from the fourth and early fifth centuries. The more elaborate tombs of the third century were used as the foundations for chapels from the fifth century onwards. For instance, the one under the chapel of St Quirinus contained a fine sculpted and painted sarcophagus dated AD 260/80, and it has been suggested by archaeologists in Trier that this was the tomb of Albana, who was held to have given land in this area to the first bishop of Trier, Eucharius, as a construction site for a church. Eucharius and his successor Valerius were later buried in the same spot. The chapel of St Quirinius would appear to be typical of many churches in Gaul founded in cemetery areas; although the cemeteries predated the churches, they became the focus of worship in their own right because they were used as specifically Christian burial areas. The tombs and *memoria* of early bishops and other holy persons attracted veneration from subsequent generations, and as the cults of the saint-bishops grew in importance during the fifth century churches were founded over their tombs. The cult that grew up around the burial place of St Martin of Tours is the most conspicuous example of this.

What was the relationship then between Christianity and paganism in such a place as Trier? The city had several large pagan temple areas, mostly devoted to Romano-Celtic cults, of which the best known is at the Altbachtal. This site was past its peak of development by the third century, but it certainly continued in use until about 380, when many of the shrines were desecrated and the cult-images broken. Subsequently domestic houses spread over the site, perhaps in a deliberate bid to obscure the original nature of the area. It is during this period, in the late fourth century, that Christianity finally gained a strong hold in Gaul, and the episode at the Altbachtal may also be connected with the presence of the devout Emperor Gratian in the city. Another act of desecration probably occurred a little later, when a statue of Venus, whose battered remains may still be seen in St Mathias, was set up to be used as a target for the stones thrown by Christian passers-by. Paganism did not entirely disappear, however, since in the centre of Trier was a meeting-room containing an elaborate late-fourth-century floor mosaic. This shows participants engaged in a ritual in which eggs played an important part. It was probably a mystery cult, the exact meaning of which we shall never know, but it testifies to the survival of quite sophisticated pagan beliefs in the midst of one of the most strongly Christianised towns in Gaul. In other areas, especially in the countryside, paganism maintained a strong hold well into the fifth century.[14]

In the next phase in the history of Christian Gaul the spot-light returns to Lyon. For here we have a wealth of literary evidence contained in the letters of Sidonius Apollinaris (Bishop of Clermont, 470–c. 483), and the information given in them can be compared with the results of recent excavations in Lyon. In the area of the cathedral, situated in the lower, late Roman town by the banks of the Saône, there were the three churches of St Jean, St Etienne and St Croix. Excavations under the medieval buildings have revealed structures from the late fourth century onwards. St Etienne seems to have been the earliest, taking the form of an apsidal baptistery with a font in the centre. St Croix, to the north, probably originated in one of a group of rooms attached to St Etienne, while St Jean, the present cathedral, seems to have been a much larger building to the south. The date of St Jean is difficult to determine archaeologically, since only a small part of the original apse has been found, probably to be placed in the fifth to sixth century, but perhaps the gaps in our information can be filled by Sidonius, who wrote in AD 469/70 of a new church recently completed. His description clearly refers to the cathedral, and he lets it be known that he was commissioned to write some verses to be inscribed on the wall of the church. Charmingly, he dismisses his versifying as 'doggerel', but this does not prevent him from publishing the poem for posterity! The content of these verses is extremely valuable for our knowledge of Gallic churches, for he describes the interior:[15]

Geneva cathedral under excavation. The earliest levels revealed a late Roman double church and the bishop's palace.

The building shines, and neither leans to right nor left, but from the summit of its front [i.e. the apse] looks towards the rising sun at the equinox. Inside the light sparkles and the sun is drawn to the gilded ceiling as it passes over the warm-hued metal, matching its colour. Marble in different shades gleams across the vaults, floor and windows; and below the multi-coloured figures a green lawn of sapphire stones is tinged with emerald glass. Set against the building is a triple portico, proud in its Aquitaine marble. To mirror it, a second portico further away encloses an atrium, and there is a stone forest in the middle area [i.e. the nave] with its columns placed further apart.

This evokes the richly decorated churches at Ravenna, some of which were being built at about the same time, and we must imagine that many of the larger churches in Gaul would have been similarly adorned. The fact that Sidonius refers to the church as new is interesting, since it accords with the evidence from Gaul as a whole for a burst of building activity from the mid-fifth century onwards, after the half-century gap caused by the Germanic invasions (see chapter 10). By this time Gaul was gradually coming under German political control, and indeed Lyon itself had only just been taken by the Burgundians when Sidonius wrote his poem. However, it is clear from both literary and archaeological evidence that the Church was remarkably unaffected by the traumas of secular change.

The arrangement of the cathedral at Lyon, with its two churches flanking the baptistery, is similar to the layout at Trier, although smaller and less formal. Elsewhere we have further evidence that this was a regular practice in Gaul, and must reflect liturgical ideas in the province, as outlined above. At Geneva, for instance, a notable recent excavation has revealed two mid- to late-fourth-century churches flanking what must have been a richly decorated baptistery. A bishop's residence lay nearby, incorporating dec- orated fifth-century mosaics, an unusual feature north of the Alps. The buildings were altered quite rapidly after their first construction, but the essential format continued into the Burgundian period and later.[16]

The existence of early baptisteries in separate buildings reflects the practice at that time of complete immersion, conducted, at least initially, only at cathedrals. Later there were changes in liturgical thinking which resulted in the use of small fonts incorporated within most churches. Geneva is interesting in this respect, since the excavations have shown that the dimensions of the font were gradually reduced until it was too small in the sixth century for complete immersion. Soon after this date, in fact, the baptistery was demolished to make way for another church (the predecessor of the present cathedral). Elsewhere, too, many baptisteries became redun-

dant from the Carolingian period, and were either converted into chapels or passed out of religious use. As a result several have been preserved in other structures, or as small, unaltered chapels. Those at Aix, Riez and – the best preserved – Fréjus are good examples, all in the south of France. However, there are also some further north, most notably at Poitiers, where it is now known that the baptistery dates to the fourth century, not the seventh as traditionally thought.[17] Baptisteries generally took a common form, with a square or rectangular exterior enclosing a round or octagonal interior. There was often a colonnade in the internal space around a central font, also usually octagonal in shape, and occasionally there was an altar on the east side. At Valence a mosaic showing animals and streams of water surrounded the font, an indication of what may have existed at most of them.[18] Because of the need for water, several of the baptisteries were equipped with lead pipes, probably linked to cisterns or the aqueduct system. Sometimes, as at Cimiez, an old bath-building was used, since there was a readily available water supply.[19]

In Germany separate baptisteries do not appear to have been built, and from the evidence fonts usually seem to have been located within churches from an early date. Boppard is the best example, where a seven-sided font one metre in diameter lay at the western end of the small early fifth-century church, partitioned off from the rest of the nave. It is clear from the excavation that the building was not simply a large baptistery, since an ambo or pulpit had been placed in its usual central position and formed the focus of the church.[20]

All the early Christian churches with baptisteries that we know of in Gaul and Germany were probably cathedrals – the seats of bishoprics and the centres of ecclesiastical life. It was natural for preaching and instruction to be linked with the admission of new believers into the church. Cathedrals almost certainly existed in all the *civitas*-capitals and other large towns by the fifth century, if we can take the medieval bishopric boundaries as an accurate guide. Their bishops were prominent members of society, and often played key roles in leading and organising local communities when secular authority broke down, as it so often did during the fifth century. Ecclesiastics like Hilarus of Poitiers, Martin of Tours, Germanus of Auxerre and Sidonius Apollinaris of Clermont emerge as leaders of men, both on the spiritual and practical planes.[21]

Germanus, who left a career in the civil service to become a bishop after popular demands that he should do so, combined both military and religious duties during his many missions to outlying regions such as Armorica or Britain. In Britain he is recorded on one occasion as having fought the pagan Saxons, while on another he disputed the Pelagian heresy with the Christian community in Verulamium (modern St Albans). Sidonius, too, energetically strove to preserve his see against the Goths, whom he regarded as public enemies. His writings make it clear that he saw his position within the Church as an opportunity to fight for the preservation of Roman culture.

The baptistery at Aix-en-Provence (Aquae Sextiae), fourth century.

Viewed in this light, it is not surprising that so many churches in Gaul can be shown to have early Christian origins and more or less continuous occupation on the same sites. Other types of buildings, meanwhile, were almost without exception being given up and abandoned. Even where there have not been excavations, we can often surmise from the bishops' lists and existing churches that there was an early Christian church on the same site. At Autun, for instance, the splendid Romanesque cathedral is situated on the edge of the town, not far from the walls, in just the position of so many early cathedrals in Gaul. The bishops' list goes back to the fourth century, and the earliest documentary mention of the predecessor of the present cathedral dates to AD 675/6. It is thus almost certain that an early church existed here.[22]

Cathedrals were not the only types of churches, as we have already seen at Trier. Cemetery churches were common, indeed probably more common in central Gaul and Germany than cathedrals. The veneration of saints became an important part of church life from an early date, but particularly from the late fourth to early fifth century in Gaul, when local holy men became known for their miracle-working, both in person during their lifetimes, and via their tombs after death.[23] The saints tended to be local, partly because of the physical difficulty of getting relics from further afield (although this certainly did happen, for instance at Rouen), but also due to the more immediate appeal of a cult based on a person who had served the local Christian community.

We find a lively account of the worship of just such a local saint in the writing of Sidonius. The popularity of the cult of St Just made his shrine at Lyon into a centre for pilgrims. Iustus (St Just) had been a Bishop of Lyon in about 381, and had died while in retreat in the Egyptian desert. His body had in due course been brought back to Lyon and buried in a cemetery that had grown up in one of the abandoned parts of the upper town. The tomb became a shrine, and by 469, when Sidonius visted it for the saint's birthday, a vast church had been constructed over the site. Sidonius found the crowd of worshippers too large to fit into the church, and he was nearly suffocated in the press of people during the night-long service. The large number of lamps and the hot night air of early autumn contributed to his discomfort, which he managed to relieve after the ceremony by playing a ball game with some of the other leading citizens of the city who had been present![24] The site has recently been excavated, and Sidonius' church is probably the lowest of the three found superimposed on one another. It appears to have been an aisled apsidal building up to 38 metres long, which would well justify Sidonius' description that it was a *capacissima basilica*.[25]

Such ceremonies were not the only manner in which people could venerate holy men. Many desired to be buried near the tomb of the saint, *ad sanctos*, so that its sanctity pervaded their graves. The closer the burials could be to the holy tomb, the better, and consequently 'privileged inhumations' came to be positioned around such tombs (or, alternatively, close

Sarcophagus carved by sculptors of the Arles school of sculpture, showing Christ and St Peter. (Arles Museums)

to the altar of a church). Often it was the rich and powerful who were accorded privileged burial, as well as those who had led a saintly life.[26] Burial within the church was the most prestigious, and failing that, along the nave and apse walls outside. At St Just nine bishops were buried near the saint's tomb, together with a large number of other people – there were also coins that the faithful had left as offerings.

There are several other notable cemetery churches where excavations have revealed something of the original arrangements. In the centre of the present church of St Seurin, Bordeaux, but some 5.5 metres below floor level, is a small nave and apse filled with stone sarcophagi. This is thought to be the burial place of Severinus, and therefore to be dated to the early fifth century, although no direct indication of this is given on any of the coffins themselves. It is a very fine example of the way in which burials crowded up to a holy coffin. The sarcophagi both within the shrine and throughout the rest of the cemetery are of good quality and, in several cases, elaborately carved in the distinctive Aquitaine style.[27] Clearly, the cemetery as a whole was for the élite of Bordeaux, which was under Visigothic control at this time.

Similar central shrines have been located in the German churches, for instance at St Severin, Cologne, and St Viktor, Xanten. Careful excavation at the latter has revealed the original building erected over the burial of St Viktor soon after AD 383. This was probably a wooden memorial chapel (*cella memoria*) within the cemetery, with a *mensa* or altar table for offerings. The chapel had been rebuilt in stone by 450, and formed the nucleus of subsequent developments. A notable feature of Xanten is the placename itself, which is derived from the Latin *ad sanctos*, 'at the place of the saints'.[28] At Bonn, too, there was a *cella memoria* under the present minster, with a solid altar table into which samian ware dishes had been set to receive offerings. Partly on account of these dishes, and partly from the tradition that Cassius and Florentius were martyred there in the 250s, this structure has been dated to about 260, and it must therefore be one of the earliest known Christian buildings in Gaul or Germany.[29] It was not a church in the true sense, and may possibly have been an open-air enclosure set up in the middle of the cemetery.

Lastly, as far as cemetery churches are concerned, there are the elaborate arrangements under the church of St Victor at Marseille. Two chapels were set up, the main one being the 'confession', which was focused on a double burial cut into the rock. This burial is thought to have contained two local saints, whose names are not known, since the more famous St Victor was eventually substituted for them. The shrine, however, continued to be venerated, and burials were placed all around it, as well as in an underground gallery resembling a small catacomb. Burial in catacombs was an Italian custom, and this demonstrates the links between Provence and Rome at this period. The other chapel is smaller, and may originally have been a mausoleum or simple cemetery chapel. In and around it, too, are numerous sarcophagi, at least one having carved scenes in the style of the Marseille school of sculpture. There were also simpler graves made out of tiles arranged like a roof over the body (known usually as *tombe a cappucina*): the tiles must have come from the numerous abandoned Roman buildings in the town. Some of the finer sarcophagi show definite signs of having been reused later in the Middle Ages. This appears to have been a common practice, and causes archaeologists considerable dating problems.[30]

Marseille and the south of France also saw the strongest development of another aspect of early Christianity – monasticism. In the city itself were two early-fifth-century monasteries founded by John Cassian, who had been a monk in Bethlehem and Egypt, and who played a important role in bringing an eastern style of monasticism to Gaul. One of his monasteries was for men and the other for women, but generally speaking such urban foundations were rare, since the Syrian and Egyptian model was one of retreating to the 'desert' and seeking out uninhabited places.[31] Along the coast from Marseille was the most famous of these isolated monasteries, on the island of Lérins. Founded in the early fifth century by Honoratus, the monastery soon established a reputation throughout Gaul as a spiritual centre, and was visited by many ecclesiastics from further north, some of them refugees from the fighting and destruction there. The monks from Lérins also ventured out from their island to found monasteries elsewhere, or, as in the case of Honoratus himself, who became Bishop of Arles, to take on other religious duties.[32] Monasteries in Gaul were widely influential in maintaining the strength of belief and the sense of mission of the early Church.

One of the earliest monasteries in the Western Roman Empire is associated with the most renowned Gallic monk, Martin of Tours. He set up a monastic community in 361–70 at Ligugé near Poitiers. It was founded on the site of a Roman villa which had been given to him, and excavations have shown how the rooms of the Roman building were adapted for use as a church. There was a simple nave and apse some 18 metres in length, to which a cruciform *martyrium* was added in the early fifth century.[33] Although it is now difficult to disentangle the archaeology of the site, mainly because of later developments at the monastery, Ligugé is virtually the only early Gallic monastery to have been excavated, and therefore is of considerable interest.

Martin himself did not stay long at Ligugé, for in 370 he became Bishop of Tours, and spent many years travelling through Gaul on missionary work. He remained faithful to the monastic ideal, however, for not long after arriving at Tours he set up a new monastic community at Marmoutier, four kilometres from the city. This was partly to avoid the crowds in the city, yet was close enough for him to fulfil his role as bishop.[34]

Our main interest in Martin, though, at this stage of his life is his travels. He converted pagans, sometimes destroyed their shrines, and set up a rudimentary parish system so that the hitherto city-orientated Church organisation had more influence in the countryside. This was especially important in central and northern Gaul, where towns were not a dominant feature of the landscape, and where Romano-Celtic religion was still very strong. The word *paganus* means country-dweller; therefore the link between the countryside and paganism was generally recognised at the time. A pagan temple whose destruction is traditionally associated with Martin's activities is at the one-time oppidum of Bibracte (modern Mont Beuvray). Here a Romano-Celtic temple underlies a chapel to St Martin, and excavations have shown that a fire destroyed the temple in the late fourth century. Martin is credited in local legend with this destruction, carried out in the face of popular opposition.[35]

Despite the evangelism of Martin and others, many country areas remained obstinately pagan. Northern Gaul, for instance, required missionary work in the post-Roman period because of the low level of belief there.[36] The barbarian invasions also hampered the progress of Christianisation in these areas, at least until the conversion of the Franks in the late fifth century.

A country church set up by a Germanic community is to be found at St

Julien-en-Genevois, near Geneva. This was Burgundian territory during the fifth century, and excavations in the nearby cemetery of Sézegnin have shown that they were following Christian burial rites from early in the century. At St Julien traces of a Burgundian domestic settlement with sunken-floored buildings were found under the church, which was set up at the end of the fifth century. It was a simple building, with a nave and apse probably of wood resting on stone footings, and it contained a number of burials, resembling the 'privileged inhumations' seen in other early churches. The architecture and general arrangement are, in fact, very similar to urban churches serving the Gallo-Roman community and, significantly, it was dedicated to St Martin, like so many early churches in Gaul.[37]

The importance of the Church in Roman Gaul and Germany is centred upon the relationship between the Romans and the various Germanic peoples that occupied the area. The main framework of Church organisation – bishoprics, churches, monasteries, perhaps also parishes – had come into being before the period of major Germanic settlement. This meant that as secular authority crumbled during the fifth century the Church was able to assume a more and more important role as standard-bearer of Roman values and culture. By contrast, the old religions lost their influence, even, gradually, in the countryside. Perhaps this was because Christianity offered a more powerful hope of salvation in the Hereafter, and certainly some Christians' faith was based on this, as an escape from the tribulations of their lives. Mostly, however, we see Christians taking on the responsibility of leadership in fifth-century Gaul, rather than escaping from it. Men like Martin, Germanus and Sidonius took an active part in worldly affairs, and if they had not acted as they did it is almost certain that the level of Christian belief in late and post-Roman Gaul would have been lower and, consequently, the legacy of Roman culture in the early Germanic kingdoms would have been significantly less.

FURTHER READING

Christianity in Gaul can best be seen in its Empire-wide context in W. Frend's massive *The Rise of Christianity* (1984). The historical background and the role of church leaders has been carefully reviewed by R. Van Dam in *Leadership and Community in Late Antique Gaul* (1985). Individuals and episodes in early Christian Gaul are the focus of various studies: Lyon in AD 177 (Rougé and Turcan 1978), St Martin (Stancliffe 1983, Bulliot and Thiollier 1892), St Germanus (Thompson 1984) and Sidonius Apollinaris (Stevens 1933).

Regional surveys of Christian antiquities include the exhibition catalogue *Premiers Temps chrétiens en Gaule méridionale* (Lyon 1986), and the very detailed multi-volume *Topographie Chrêtienne des Cités de la Gaule* (ed. Gauthier and Picard, 1986). N. Gauthier in *L'Evangelisation des Pays de la Moselle* (1980) considers the role of Trier as the most important ecclesiastical centre north of the Alps, as does the exhibition catalogue by the Rheinisches Landesmuseum Trier, *Trier: Kaiserresidenz und Bischofssitz* (1984). Other important church sites are discussed, by Bonnet (1987), for Geneva, by Reynaud (1986) for Lyon, and by Février (1981) for Fréjus. Monks and monastic sites are the object of Prinz's authoritative study *Frühes Möncktum in Frankenreich* (1965).

10

FROM GAUL TO FRANCE

On the last day of December 406 a large number of Alans, Vandals and Sueves crossed the frozen Rhine into Roman territory. If any date can be taken to mark the end of Roman Gaul, this one has the best claim, for after this the region was never really the same again. Despite the continuation of some form of Roman rule up to 486, the fifth century, for northern Gaul at least, was a period of political and, to a rather lesser extent, cultural turmoil. There is little trace of Romanised life continuing after the first decade of the century, with the major exception of the Church. The decline in town and countryside continued; at the same time coin use came to an effective end, pottery production virtually ceased, and there were hardly any new secular Roman building projects. In fact, the trend for buildings to be abandoned, already seen in the fourth century, now accelerated.

In the fifth century, therefore, the fabric of Roman civilisation broke down as decisively in northern Gaul as it did in Britain, which is known to have been given up politically by 410. Despite the seventy-six year gap between the official end of Roman Gaul and that of Roman Britain, the changes in these two regions during the fifth century are surprisingly similar in archaeological terms. Both areas witnessed the Germanisation of their cultures as a result of direct migration of peoples from northern and central Europe, but at the same time both saw the substantial survival of local life and the intermixing of migrant and indigenous populations. Where northern Gaul diverges from Britain is in the extent of the survival of Roman culture, which was much more marked in certain key areas such as language than in Britain.

A specific archaeological example of the interaction between local and incoming groups of people can be seen in the cemetery of Frénouville, near

Caen. Its beginnings lie in the late Roman period, during the fourth century, and it continued, apparently without a break, into the Frankish period, up to the seventh century. Anthropological study of the skeletons of the late Roman phase suggests a relatively self-contained community, probably of local origin (i.e. not Germanic in type), but there is a certain amount of evidence even at this stage of mixing with incoming, probably Frankish elements. During the early fifth century the orientation changed from north–south to east–west, and there was a decline in the number of grave-goods being deposited, but essentially the cemetery continued as before. The skeletal remains still suggest that the population was largely local in origin, so that although Frankish grave-goods started to become common in the cemetery during the latter half of the fifth century, the people they were buried with were not markedly Germanic. Much intermarriage of the population must have taken place, and indeed the skeletons also show that the community was becoming more exogamous, and genetically less self-contained.[1]

The pattern seen at Frénouville is by no means unique. Cemeteries as far

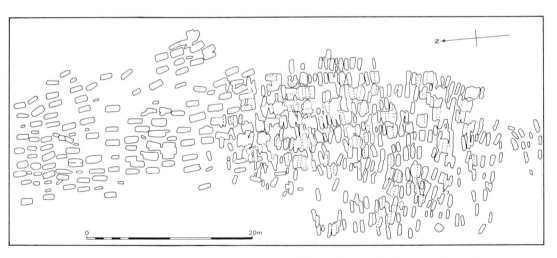

The late and post-Roman cemetery at Frénouville, Normandy. The graves aligned north–south are late Roman in date, while those orientated east–west are Frankish, of the early fifth to seventh centuries.

apart as Vron in Picardy, Krefeld-Gellep in the Rhineland and Sézegnin near Geneva show similar traits.[2] All are marked by a relatively high degree of continuity between the late Roman and early Frankish or Burgundian periods. Although it is difficult to use the cemetery evidence to draw clear ethnic conclusions, it does however suggest that elements within the Gallo-Roman population of the fifth century took up Germanic customs and burial rites. A possible explanation of this lies in the increasing political and cultural dominance of the Franks and other Germanic groups, even if they remained a minority of the population as a whole. In areas such as northern Gaul, where Romanised culture was fading, and perhaps among people such as the *bagaudae*, for whom it was already a dead ideal, the ground was prepared for cultural change. The Church remained a strong bastion of

Roman culture, but otherwise Germanic customs appear to have been adopted by the local population. Cultural influences flowed in the other direction too, so that by the end of the fifth century the Franks were no longer truly Germanic, nor were the Gauls still Roman.

Further information from the anthropological study of the Frénouville skeletons indicates that life expectancy fell from 31 years in late Roman times to 29 in the Frankish period. Although the drop is a small one, it is probably a reflection of the worsening conditions of daily life in the fifth century. Such very low figures can largely be explained by the high infant mortality thought to have existed at the time; adults who reached the age of 20 could in both periods expect to live into their 40s.[3]

The settlement evidence for the period is more difficult to interpret, mainly because it is so very sparse. Most Frankish settlements, such as Brebières or Juvincourt-et-Damary, date from after the fifth century, as in fact do the great majority of the cemeteries. Three important exceptions, however, are at St Martin-de-Mondeville in Normandy, Neerharen-Rekem in Belgium and Sézegnin. Their sequences of occupation are remarkably similar; each lay in amongst the ruins of a Roman structure, probably a villa, and each consisted of a village of Germanic sunken-floored buildings and post-built houses which started life in the fourth century. They all, in other words, present striking evidence for the change from a villa site into a village.[4]

Evidence from towns is equally poor, with very little archaeological indication of occupation, except for churches and associated buildings. There is indirect evidence for continuity of life in some of the urban centres,

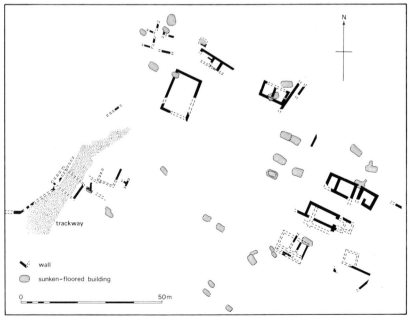

Plan of the settlement at St Martin-de-Mondeville, Normandy, where a small Roman villa or *vicus* was replaced by a village of Germanic sunken-floored huts during the fourth century, lasting until the seventh century. Some of the Roman foundations were subsequently reused for buildings during the medieval period.

N

trackway

wall

sunken-floored building

0   50 m

however, as in the case of Cologne, which was taken by the Franks in 459. It appears to have persisted as a manufacturing centre during the fifth century and later, producing glass and other materials. Pottery-making too, in the area just to the south around Mayen, also shows a good measure of survival, for late Roman Mayen wares closely resemble succeeding forms of early medieval ware. This sort of evidence, when added together, demonstrates an astonishing level of continuity in specific areas of everyday life, given the political upheavals of the times.[5]

One of the most important questions concerning the Germanic invasions of the fifth century is why the Germans crossed the Rhine and entered Gaul in such numbers. In part, this question has already been discussed in chapter 8, where we saw that as early as the late second century Germanic raids may have been stimulated by the breakdown in the trading relationships with the Romans, as a result of which there seems to have been an upsurge in direct attacks: raids replacing trade. There is also the possibility that the tribes in the interior of Germany away from the frontier may have depended upon luxury goods imported from the Roman world (known from burials in the region) to help sustain their tribal social structure, much like the Celts of the middle to late Iron Age. A breakdown in this trading relationship may have provoked internal instability in the tribal organisation, and therefore a much increased propensity for raiding both their neighbours and the Roman frontier zone.[6]

These theories may well account for the small raiding parties which attacked the Empire up to the fourth century and carried off loot back to their homelands. Mass movements of peoples, for which we have clear evidence from the late fourth century onwards, cannot however be explained in the same way. The best-attested early example concerns the Goths, who in 376 asked to be allowed to cross the Danube into the eastern part of the Empire. The reason in their case was the arrival from the east of the Huns, who would have posed a very real threat to the Goths had they stayed where they were. This powerful movement from the east into the fringes of the more settled Germanic tribes may have had a destabilising effect, sparking off several mass migrations as tribes encroached on one another's territory.[7]

It was probably well known amongst the Germans beyond the frontier that the Goths had succeeded in persuading the Romans to allow them to cross into the Empire. Although there was resistance to further migrations, it was not long before the defences of the Empire crumbled in the west. After the reign of Valentinian I (364–75) no further frontier constructions are known in the Rhineland. The existing defences might have proved adequate, however, but for developments elsewhere in the Empire. In the east the Goths, having crossed the Danube, defeated Roman forces at the Battle of Adrianople in 378. In the aftermath of the battle, in which the Eastern Roman Emperor Valens was killed, troops were required from the west to protect the Eastern Empire. The garrisons in the Rhineland were

Silver dish (*missorium*) depicting Valentinian I (AD 364–75) surrounded by troops, who at this date were largely of barbarian extraction. (Musée d'Art et d'Histoire, Geneva)

now gradually reduced and even the presence of the western Emperor Gratian in Germany to campaign against the Alamanni in 378 did not prevent further invasions. The Alamanni themselves attacked southern Germany and Switzerland in 383.[8]

Under Gratian, the last emperor to be present personally in the Rhineland, there was some building work on the cathedral in Trier and it is known that court life continued much as before. With the ending of the imperial presence, however, Trier ceased to be capital of the Gallic prefecture in 395, and thenceforward Arles housed the mint, and Milan and Ravenna became the imperial seats for the west. Gratian's successors were more interested in protecting themselves and the central provinces such as Italy than in attempting to keep a grip on the frontiers.[9]

In 395 troops were removed from the Rhineland by the *magister militum*, Stilicho, to campaign in the Balkans, and there is evidence that forts began to be abandoned in southern Germany and Raetia. More troops were removed from 401 onwards to cope with Alaric's invasion of Italy, which culminated in 410 in the sack of Rome, a massive psychological blow to imperial prestige and morale. Although field armies were deployed in Gaul during this period, they did not apparently stay for very long, and few other high-quality troops remained to defend the frontiers. This was the situation in 406 when the frontier was breached, probably in the vicinity of Mainz, by Alans, Vandals and Sueves; at the same time the Alamanni crossed into eastern Gaul and Switzerland.

Surprisingly, the Franks, the main Germanic group in the northern frontier region, did not take advantage of the confusion to invade, and indeed are recorded as being employed to defend Roman interests. This is an important reflection of a policy that was of mutual benefit to both the Romans and the Franks, since the latter stood to gain settlement rights in recognition of their service to the emperor. From an initial foothold within the Empire in Batavia, they were able to expand south and east during the late fourth and fifth centuries, gradually building up a strong power base in an unspectacular way, unlike some of the other Germanic peoples with their far-flung migrations. They also appear to have been used by the Romans for policing duties deep within Lugdunensis and Belgica, being amongst the groups of Germans known as *laeti* and *gentiles* deployed in *civitates* as far west as the Riedones in Brittany for the purpose of forestalling uprisings by the *bagaudae*, known to have been active in the early fifth century in the Loire Valley and Brittany. Archaeological evidence that Germans had a military role in the interior of Gaul comes from cemeteries; some late Roman male burials have fairly certain Germanic associations (see above) and, tellingly, include weapons, which were not permitted to civilians in the Roman Empire. The distribution of such graves with weapons has in fact been used to demonstrate the spread of Frankish influence across northern Gaul.[10]

One of the consequences of Frankish loyalty to Rome in 406 was that some of the forts and towns in Lower Germany continued to be held under Roman control. Amongst these was Cologne, with its fort on the far side of the Rhine at Köln-Deutz. The garrisons of forts such as this were almost certainly raised and trained locally, so that even if they had official Roman titles they acted as local militias. After the coin supply had dried up in the early fifth century it must have been difficult to retain the loyalty of these garrisons, except for the defence of their immediate localities.[11]

The first military reaction to the incursions of 406 came not from Gaul itself, but from Britain, Consternation was such that the army there put up a series of usurpers, of which the third, Constantine III, took a large portion of the British garrison into Gaul to deal with the deteriorating military situation. He was successful in restoring some form of order, so that by 408 he had nominal control of Britain, Gaul, Germany and Spain. The barbarians had been pushed south-west; the Vandals, for instance, moved into Spain and from there on to North Africa. Constantine might have been able to bring effective Roman government back to Gaul but for his own ambition to be emperor of the west. In 409 the legitimate emperor, Honorius, recognised Constantine's jurisdiction over the provinces he held, but his desire to extend his power into Italy proved his undoing. In 411 he was forced to surrender to the emperor and was executed.[12]

One of the legacies of the usurpation of Constantine III was the loss of Britain to the Empire. Indeed, in 409 it is recorded that the Britons took up arms themselves to repel Saxon raiders, as apparently did Armoricans and other peoples in Gaul. It is quite possible that communities on both sides of the English Channel were forced to fall back on their own resources from this time onwards. In northern Gaul this may have meant increasing reliance on Germanic *laeti* and other mercenaries to protect local interests. It is for this reason that the year 406 takes on its significance, since direct Roman authority in the region had evaporated, and Gallo-Roman (and Romano-British) peoples now looked to independent leaders to take care of their defence.[13]

In the political anarchy of these years the Franks were able to benefit

considerably in their slow expansion of power over the region. In 420–1 they plundered Trier and took control of that area. Archaeological evidence for the Trier region suggests that in some respects there was continuity, such as at the villa of Pfalzel, which emerged by the sixth century as a Frankish manor. However, in the town itself the cathedral and cemeteries declined for some fifty years in the middle of the fifth century, perhaps as a consequence of the sack.[14]

Fortified villa or *mansio* at Thésée (Tasciaca) near Tours. This enigmatic structure of late Roman date was probably erected to deter *bagaudae* (rural brigands) or Germanic raiders.

While these events, which were of such significance in the transition from Gaul to France, were taking place in the north, in the south changes came about in a different and rather more orderly manner. In 412 the Visigoths, one of the groups of Goths which had come into Roman territory in the late fourth century, entered Gaul, having been persuaded to leave Italy following the sack of Rome in 410. They crossed Provence and siezed Narbonne, Toulouse and Bordeaux but, meeting resistance to their presence, they went on into Spain. The passage of the Visigoths is not easily detected archaeologically, unless refuges such as Marduel and the fort guarding the pass between Gaul and Spain at Le Perthus represent Roman reaction to their arrival. Sites like Marseille and Narbonne show signs of continued occupation and trading activity, with no evidence of a hiatus that might have followed a Gothic assault. Wrecks, such as Port-Vendres I with its cargo of Spanish sardines, indicate that sea-borne trade was also continuing much as before.[15]

More significant than the initial arrival of the Visigoths in Gaul was their settlement in Aquitaine in 418. After much fighting in Spain, they agreed to return to south-west Gaul and be settled there on a formal basis. Local Roman landowners appear to have been the hosts for Visigothic settlers, who were allocated a portion of lands and other benefits such as slaves, all within the framework of a treaty between the Romans and the Visigoths. It may seem extraordinary that the rich villa-owners of the region should go along with these arrangements, and it has to be asked why they apparently did so, and why Aquitaine emerged as one of the few rich and stable areas of Gaul during the fifth century. The answer may be that the settlement of the Visigoths was a deliberate move by the Romans to protect their interests in the south-west from the problems further north. The Visigoths would act as a stabilising military presence, capable of deterring uprisings by *bagaudae*, who had caused so much trouble in the Loire and Brittany from 407 to 417, and they would also have been a means of preventing further damaging incursions by German migrants.[16]

This policy must be judged a success, since towns like Bordeaux show evidence of trading and other activity right through this period, and in the country many wealthy villas are known, such as Palat, near St Emilion, and Loupian, where distinctive mosaics were laid. A notable feature of the villa sites in the region is that a number have chapels built over them, as at Plassac and Herblain. These chapels may originally have been founded by Christian communities living in the villas. The Christian writer Salvian refers to the region in glowing terms as 'the best part of all Gaul' and the 'image of Paradise'. The archaeological record shows that this was a period of prosperity and cultural sophistication for Aquitaine, especially compared with the north.[17]

The idea of settling Germanic peoples deep within Gaul was taken a stage further by the general Flavius Aëtius, who defeated the Burgundians in 436 and settled them in Savoy in 443. He also reaffirmed the treaty with the Visigoths, perhaps giving them a greater share of power and jurisdiction over Aquitaine. The settlement of the Burgundians, like that of the Visigoths, can be seen as a means of stabilising a strategically important area in order to forestall rural unrest, and to create a new buffer-zone between the Romans of southern Gaul and the Alamanni, who were attempting to expand into Switzerland at this time. An interesting possibility arises from the creation of the buffer-zones, in that they may have encouraged the development of a cultural frontier between the north and south of Gaul. This had always existed between Narbonensis and the rest of Gaul, but now it appears to have been extended northwards in a line running roughly from the Saintonge on the west coast, around the north of the Massif Central, across the Rhône Valley and into the Jura Mountains. This coincides remarkably with the later line between *langue d'oc* to the south and *langue d'oïl* to the north, and it has been suggested that the origins of this division lie in the period under discussion, and in the difference between the relatively Romanised south and the increasingly Germanic north.[18]

Aëtius was successful in other areas too. In 437 he campaigned in Armorica against the *bagaudae*, and he drove a Frankish army back across the Rhine following a victory in 446. The efforts of Aëtius and his military contemporaries and successors mark a revival of Roman control in Gaul, but it was only to be a temporary respite. The arrival of the Huns in Gaul in 451, hitherto a distant threat, now presented a very real challenge to both Roman and German authority. From 435 the Huns under Attila had been building up a powerful realm to the north of the Roman Empire, and Attila entered Gaul in a further bid to expand his territory. Apparently he saw the Visigoths as his main adversary in Gaul, since he considered them to be the most powerful group in the region. Trier was burnt by the Huns, but thereafter resistance to the threat was swift, with Franks and Visigoths both assisting the Roman force under the command of Aëtius. Attila was defeated at the Battle of the Catalaunian Fields near Troyes in 451, after which he retreated; he died soon after.[19] The Hunnic threat had passed, but so too had any illusion that Roman armies could maintain the security of Gaul on their own. The various groups of Germans in the province had to be treated as equals, and they were able to expand their power bases to take in much of what had been Roman territory.

After 451 Gaul was quiet for a while. The Franks took Cologne in 459, and began to exercise independent control over most of north-east Gaul. To the west of this Aegidius apparently held a large area north of the Loire in the name of Rome, while further west still, in Armorica, considerable turmoil was caused from the 440s onwards by its colonisation by Britons. This migration from south-western Britain was to result in the eventual establishment of the Celtic-speaking, largely independent territory of Brittany. To the south-west of Aegidius was the Visigothic kingdom, and to the south-east were Burgundian lands. Effectively, Roman-held territory was becoming increasingly confined to an area in northern-central Gaul, together with Provence in the south. Soissons was Aegidius' main base, and his son Syagrius appears to have been in control of the same area in the late 460s. He is termed 'king of the Romans' by the later historian of the Franks, Gregory of Tours, although there is some dispute as to exactly what power Syagrius actually had.[20]

Aegidius and Syagrius were not governors of Roman provinces in any sense that would have been recognisable to an early Roman, or possibly even to one of Diocletian's or Constantine's day. They were war-lords, probably sustained largely by local supporters keen to have a leader capable of defending their interests. As such, they were probably not very different from the so-called 'tyrants' in Britain in the early fifth century, who were busy mobilising local defence against the Saxons. They were also probably little different from the German kings, such as Childeric of the Franks, in that they must have exercised fairly autocratic control over the area held in the name of Rome, and while they paid lip-service to the emperor, in reality imperial control was so weak that Aegidius and Syagrius could act much as they liked.

By 469 the link between Aegidius' territory and the Mediterranean had been effectively severed by the expansion of King Euric of the Visigoths into the Auvergne. Local resistance had been offered to this expansion, organised by Sidonius Apollinaris, Bishop of Clermont-Ferrand, but by 475 most of the Massif Central had been ceded to the Visigoths by the Emperor Julius Nepos. This was probably an attempt to protect Provence, by now the one remaining part of Gaul in direct contact with the shrinking remnants of the Western Empire. Nepos' strategy, however, failed, since he was powerless to prevent Visigothic expansion into Provence itself not long after this, mainly because of the collapse of Roman rule in Italy in 476.[21]

Roman territory was now nominally confined to the area to the north of the Loire. Childeric was able to expand Frankish rule into Belgica as a whole in 475, and Syagrius' lands must gradually have contracted more and more. Childeric died in 482; his rich and exceptional tomb at Tournai was discovered in the seventeenth century, and more recently associated horse sacrifices immediately around the burial place have been excavated. He was succeeded by Clovis, who brought Syagrius' rule to an end at the Battle of Soissons in 486.[22]

The year 486 is usually taken to be the point at which Roman Gaul finally came to an end. In reality it marks no more than the death of a pro-Roman war-lord whose territory was a mere fraction of what Roman Gaul and Germany once had been. For the history of the Franks, though, it is a much more significant date, since the victory allowed them to expand over most of Gaul north of the Loire, with the important exception of Brittany, and to establish a strong kingdom under Clovis. After this there are much clearer signs of the Germanisation of the population; Frankish grave-goods became more common, and the area under Frankish cultural influence expanded. The subsequent history and rise of the Franks is effectively another story. However, their defeat of the Visigoths, Burgundians and Alamanni in the sixth century, and the beginnings of a Frankish 'nation' under single Merovingian control owed almost everything to their fifth-century heritage, a century during which Gaul gave way to early France.[23]

FURTHER READING

There has been a burgeoning literature on the end of Roman Gaul and the establishment of the Franks in recent years. The best syntheses are by E. James in *The Franks* (1988) and *The Origins of France* (1982), the latter covering a slightly later period than the former – the centuries following the point at which ⸱⸱s book leaves off. Full treatment of the Franks in French is given in P. Périn and L.-C. Feffer, *Les Francs* (1987), and the Germanic invasions generally are fully discussed in E. Demougeot, *La Formation de l'Europe et les Invasions barbares* (1979). Also useful are P. Geary, *Before France and Germany* (1988), E. Thompson, *Romans and Barbarians: the decline of the western empire* (1982), J. Matthews, *Western Aristocracies and the Imperial Court AD 364–425* (1975) and the exhibition catalogue *Gallien in der Spätantike* (1980). There have also been several regional surveys, including Pirling (1986) on the lower Rhine area, Berry (1987) on Burgundy, Landes (1988) on Aquitaine and Septimania, and the exhibition catalogue *La Picardie: berceau de la France* (Amiens 1986). The end of town life in much of Gaul is examined by Février (1980) and the Germanic graves by Böhme (1974). Two important cemeteries spanning the late Roman/early German period are Frénouville (Pilet 1980) and Sézegnin (Privati 1986a).

Gazetteer of sites to visit

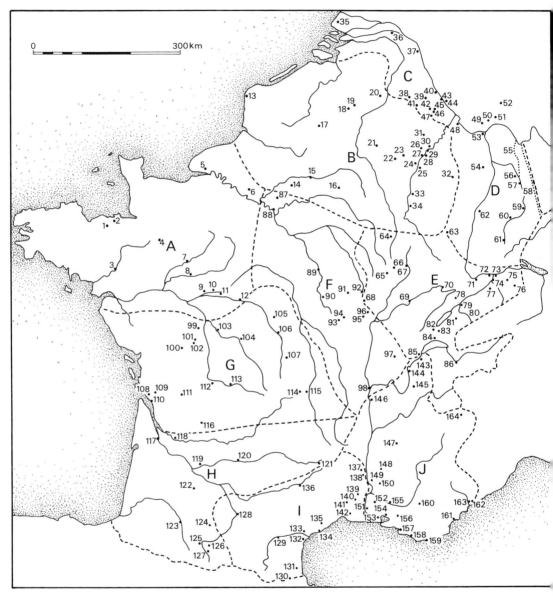

KEY

1 Corseul	12 Thésée	23 Arlon	34 Jouy-aux-Arches/
2 Alet	13 Boulogne	24 Dalheim	Ars-sur-Moselle
3 Langon	14 Champlieu	25 Nennig	35 Rijswijk
4 Jublains	15 Soissons	26 Echternach	36 Nijmegen
5 Lillebonne	16 Reims	27 Igel	37 Xanten
6 Genainville	17 Bavai	28 Konz	38 Heerlen
7 Le Mans	18 Liberchies	29 Trier	39 Hambacher Först
8 Aubigné-Racan	19 Cortil-Noirmont	30 Pfalzel	40 Cologne
9 Cinq-Mars	20 Tongeren	31 Otrang	41 Aachen
10 Luynes	21 Bertrix	32 Schwarzenacker	42 Vussem
11 Tours	22 Montauban-Buzenol	33 Metz	43 Bonn

44 Drachenfels
45 Iversheim
46 Pesch
47 Nettersheim-Zingsheim
48 Boppard
49 Zugmantel
50 Feldburg
51 Saalburg
52 Butzbach
53 Mainz
54 Kriemhildenstuhl
55 Odenwald Limes
56 Bad Rappenau
57 Lauffen
58 Vorderer (Forward) Limes
59 Köngen
60 Rottenburg
61 Rottweil
62 Baden-Baden
63 Donon
64 Grand
65 Langres
66 Andilly-en-Bassigny
67 Jonvelle
68 Mâlain
69 Besançon
70 Mandeure
71 Augst
72 Laufenburg
73 Zurzach
74 Windisch
75 Winkel-Seeb
76 Irgenhausen
77 Lenzburg
78 Pierre Pertuis
79 Studen
80 Berne-Enge
81 Avenches
82 Orbe
83 Ursins
84 Lausanne
85 Nyon
86 Martigny
87 Senlis
88 Paris
89 Escolives-St Camille
90 Fontaines-Salées
91 Alise-St Reine
92 Sources-de-la-Seine
93 Mont Beuvray
94 Autun
95 Cussy-la-Colonne
96 Nuits-St Georges
97 Izernore
98 Lyon
99 Naintré-Vieux-Poitiers
100 Sanxay
101 Poitiers
102 Ligugé
103 Yzeures-sur-Creuse
104 Argenton-sur-Creuse

105 Bourges
106 Drevant
107 Néris-les-Bains
108 Tour-de-Pirelonge
109 Saintes
110 Talmont
111 St Cybardeaux
112 Chassenon
113 Limoges
114 Puy-de-Dôme
115 Clermont-Ferrand
116 Périgueux
117 Bordeaux
118 Montcaret
119 Villeneuve-sur-Lot
120 Cahors
121 Lanuéjols
122 Montréal
123 Maubourguet
124 Montmaurin
125 St Bertrand-de-Comminges
126 Valentine
127 St Béat
128 Toulouse
129 Carcassonne
130 Le Perthus
131 Château-Roussillon
132 Narbonne
133 Ensérune
134 Agde
135 Loupian
136 Millau
137 Alba
138 Bourg-St Andéol
139 Pont-du-Gard
140 Nîmes
141 Nages
142 Lunel
143 Geneva
144 Seyssel
145 Aix-les-Bains
146 Vienne
147 Die
148 Vaison-la-Romaine
149 Orange
150 Carpentras
151 Arles
152 St Remy
153 St Blaise
154 St Chamas
155 Cavaillon
156 Aix-en-Provence
157 Marseille
158 St Cyr-sur-Mer
159 Almanarre
160 Riez
161 Fréjus
162 La Turbie
163 Cimiez
164 Susa

Only the main visible sites are included here, since a full list of monuments that are possible to visit would run to several hundred entries. The gazetteer has been arranged on the basis of the boundaries of the Roman provinces of the early Empire, insofar as they are known. This means that for some of the provinces (e.g. Germania Superior), more than one modern country is covered, and it should be noted that the modern boundaries are not shown on the map. An additional point of importance is that museums are not included in the gazetteer, with the consequence that many ancient sites with no significant visible remains are not listed, even if they have a museum. Most towns in Gaul and Germany, in fact, have museums in them, and listings of museums can be found in the various international Museums Yearbooks that are regularly published.

The gazetteer is intended to be a simple list of sites. As such, it does not contain details of access and opening times, which will need to be checked before visits are made, especially to some of the rural sites, which can be difficult to find. Maps such as the 1:200,000 Michelin series, and their equivalents for Switzerland, Germany and the Low Countries, are particularly useful, especially if they are in atlas form with a place-name index. There is also the Princeton *Encyclopaedia of Classical Sites* (1976), which has most of the sites included here, together with further information about them and a bibliography after each entry. Some countries have good specialist guidebooks, such as J. H. Farnum, *Guide romain de la Suisse* (1975), and J. von Elbe, *Roman Germany: a guide to sites and museums* (1973), and further information can also be obtained from the general works listed at the end of the Introduction and chapter 7. Finally, tourist handbooks such as the Michelin and Blue Guides have details of the more important sites, including opening times.

Note: the number against each site in the gazetteer refers to the map. Ancient names are added in parentheses where they are known.

A. WESTERN GALLIA LUGDUNENSIS

2 Alet (*Aleto*): fort
8 Aubigné-Racan: theatre
9 Cinq-Mars: funerary monument
1 Corseul (*Fanum Martis Coriosolitum*): temple
6 Genainville (*Petromantalum*): rural sanctuary
4 Jublains (*Noviodunum Diablintum*): fort, baths, theatre
3 Langon: mausoleum
7 Le Mans (*Subdinum Vindinum*): walls
5 Lillebonne (*Juliobona Caletorum*): amphitheatre
10 Luynes: aqueduct
12 Thésée (*Tasciaca*): fortified villa or mansio
11 Tours (*Caesarodunum Turonum*): walls

B. Gallia Belgica

23 Arlon (*Orolaunum*): walls, baths
17 Bavai (*Bagacum Nerviorum*): forum, cryptoporticus, walls
21 Bertrix: refuge
13 Boulogne (*Gesoriacum/Bononia*): walls
14 Champlieu: rural sanctuary
19 Cortil-Noirmont: tumulus
24 Dalheim (*Ricciacus*): *vicus*
26 Echternach: villa, refuge
27 Igel: funerary monument
34 Jouy-aux-Arches and Ars-sur-Moselle: aqueduct
18 Liberchies (*Geminiacum?*): *vicus*, fort
28 Konz: villa
33 Metz (*Divodurum Mediomatricorum*): baths, basilica
22 Montauban-Buzenol: refuge
25 Nennig: villa, tumulus
31 Otrang: villa
30 Pfalzel: villa
16 Reims (*Durocortorum Remorum*): arch, cryptoporticus
32 Schwarzenacker: *vicus*
15 Soissons (*Augusta Suessionum*): walls
20 Tongeren (*Atuatuca Tungrorum*): walls
29 Trier (*Augusta Treverorum*): gate, walls, amphitheatre, basilica, baths, cathedral, bridge, granaries

C. Germania Inferior

41 Aachen (*Aquae Granni?*): baths, walls
43 Bonn (*Bonna*): fortress
40 Cologne (*Colonia Claudia Ara Agrippinensium*): governor's palace, houses, walls, temples, churches; fort (Köln-Deutz); tomb (Weiden)
44 Drachenfels: quarry, harbour
39 Hambacher Först: villa
38 Heerlen (*Coriovallum*): baths
45 Iversheim: lime kilns
47 Nettersheim-Zingsheim: temples
36 Nijmegen (*Noviomagus Batavorum*): fortress; temple (Elst)
46 Pesch: temples
35 Rijswijk: rural settlement
42 Vussem: aqueduct
37 Xanten (*Vetera/Colonia Ulpia Traiana/Ad Sanctos*): walls, amphitheatre, temple, church; fortress, amphitheatre (Birten)

D. Northern Germania Superior

62 Baden-Baden (*Aquae*): baths
56 Bad Rappenau: villa
48 Boppard (*Bodobriga*): walls, church
52 Butzbach: watchtower
63 Donon: refuge, temple
50 Feldburg: fort

59: Köngen (*Grinario*): fort
54 Kriemhildenstuhl: quarry
57 Lauffen: villa
53 Mainz (*Mogontiacum*): walls, funerary and triumphal monuments
55 Odenwald Limes: watchtowers and frontier works
60 Rottenburg (*Sumelocenna*): baths
61 Rottweil (*Arae Flaviae*): baths
51 Saalburg: fort, *vicus*, frontier works
58 Vorderer (Forward) Limes: various forts, watchtowers and frontier works
49 Zugmantel: fort, watchtower, frontier works

E. Southern Germania Superior, Alpes Poeninae. Alpes Graiae

66 Andilly-en-Bassigny: villa
71 Augst (*Augusta Raurica*): theatre, amphitheatre, temples, forum/basilica/curia, houses, walls; aqueduct (Liestal); fort, baths (Kaiseraugst); bridgehead (Wyhlen)
81 Avenches (*Aventicum Helvetiorum*): amphitheatre, theatre, temples, baths, walls, gate
80 Berne-Enge: amphitheatre, oppidum
69 Besançon (*Vesontio Sequanorum*): gate, aqueduct, nymphaeum, amphitheatre
64 Grand (*Aquae Granni?/Andesina?*): amphitheatre, basilica
76 Irgenhausen (*Cambiodunum*): fort
67 Jonvelle: villa
65 Langres (*Andematunnum Lingonum*): gate
72 Laufenburg: villa
84 Lausanne (*Lousonna*): *vicus*, temple
77 Lenzburg (*Lentia*): theatre
68 Mâlain (*Mediolanum*): *vicus*
70 Mandeure (*Epamanduodurum*): theatre
86 Martigny (*Octodurus/Forum Claudii Vallensium*): amphitheatre, temple, houses
85 Nyon (*Noviodunum/Colonia Julia Equestris*): forum/basilica
82 Orbe (*Urba*): villa
78 Pierre Pertuis: road tunnel and cutting
79 Studen (*Petinesca*): *vicus*, temples
83 Ursins: temple
75 Winkel-Seeb: villa
74 Windisch (*Vindonissa*): fortress, amphitheatre
73 Zurzach (*Tenedo*): fort

F. Eastern Gallia Lugdunensis

91 Alise-St Reine (*Alesia*): oppidum, *vicus*, theatre, forum, houses
94 Autun (*Augustodunum Aeduorum*): walls, gates, theatre, temple
95 Cussy-la-Colonne: votive column

89 Escolives-St Camille (*Scoliva*): baths

90 Fontaines-Salées: rural sanctuary

97 Izernore (*Isarnodurum*): temple

98 Lyon (*Lugdunum/Condate*): theatre, odeon, amphitheatre, temples, houses, churches; aqueducts (Chaponost, Beaunant, Craponne)

93 Mont Beuvray (*Bibracte*): oppidum, temple

96 Nuits-St Georges: temple, *vicus*

88 Paris (*Lutetia Parisiorum*): baths, amphitheatre, walls

87 Senlis (*Augustomagus Silvanectum*): walls

92 Sources-de-la-Seine: rural sanctuary

G. NORTHERN AQUITANIA

104 Argenton-sur-Creuse (*Argentomagus*): temples, amphitheatre

105 Bourges (*Avaricum Biturigum*): walls, arcade

112 Chassenon (*Cassinomagus*): baths, rural sanctuary

115 Clermont-Ferrand (*Augustonemetum Arvernorum*): temple; baths (Royat)

106 Drevant (*Derventum*): rural sanctuary

102 Ligugé: monastery

113 Limoges (*Augustoritum Lemovicum*): baths, amphitheatre, church

99 Naintré-Vieux-Poitiers (*Vetus Pictavis*): theatre, votive stone, *vicus*

107 Néris-les-Bains (*Aquae Neri*): baths, amphitheatre

116 Périgueux (*Vesunna Petrucoriorum*): temple, amphitheatre, walls, houses

101 Poitiers (*Limonum Pictonum*): baptistery

114 Puy-de-Dôme: temple

111 St Cybardeaux (*Germanicomagus?*): theatre, rural sanctuary

109 Saintes (*Mediolanum Santonum*): arch, amphitheatre, baths

100 Sanxay: rural sanctuary

110 Talmont-Moulin-du-Fâ (*Novioregum?*): rural sanctuary

108 Tour-de-Pirelonge: funerary monument

103 Yzeures-sur-Creuse: votive column, temple

H. SOUTHERN AQUITANIA

117 Bordeaux (*Burdigala Biturigum Viviscorum*): amphitheatre, church

120 Cahors (*Divona Cadurcorum*): baths

121 Lanuéjols: mausoleum

123 Maubourguet: villa

118 Montcaret: villa

124 Montmaurin: villa

122 Montréal-Séviac: villa

127 St Béat: quarry

125 St Bertrand-de-Comminges (*Lugdunum Convenarum*): forum, temple

126 Valentine: villa, mausoleum

119 Villeneuve-sur-Lot (*Excisum*): temple, *vicus*

I. WESTERN GALLIA NARBONENSIS

134 Agde (*Agatha*): walls

137 Alba (*Alba Helviorum*): theatre, church

138 Bourg-St Andéol: mithraeum

129 Carcassonne (*Carcaso*): walls

131 Château-Roussillon (*Ruscino*): forum/basilica

133 Ensérune: oppidum

130 Le Perthus-L'Ecluse (*Summum Pyrenaeum*): forts

135 Loupian: villa

142 Lunel (*Ambrussum*): bridge: oppidum, *vicus*

136 Millau-La Graufesenque (*Condatomagus*): *vicus*, kilns

141 Nages: oppidum

132 Narbonne (*Narbo Martius*): underground granaries

140 Nîmes (*Nemausus*): amphitheatre, temple, water, sanctuary, walls, gates, 'watchtower' (Tour Magne), acqueduct head

139 Pont-du-Gard: acqueduct bridge

128 Toulouse (*Tolosa*): amphitheatre, walls; temple (Vieille-Toulouse)

J. EASTERN AND NORTHERN GALLIA NARBONENSIS, ALPES MARITIMAE, ALPES COTTIAE

156 Aix-en-Provence (*Aquae Sextiae Salluviorum*): baptistery; oppidum (Entremont)

145 Aix-les-Bains (*Aquae*): arch, temple, baths

159 Almanarre (*Olbia*): Greek town, walls

151 Arles (*Arelate*): amphitheatre, theatre, cryptoporticus, forum, baths, walls, church; water-mills, aqueducts (Barbegal)

150 Carpentras (*Carpentorate Meminorum*): arch

155 Cavaillon (*Cabellio*): arch

163 Cimiez (*Cemenelum*): baths, amphitheatre, houses

147 Die (*Dea Augusta Vocontiorum*): walls, arch

161 Fréjus (*Forum Julii*): theatre, amphitheatre, houses, walls, baths, harbour, lighthouse, baptistery

143 Geneva (*Genava*): cathedral, walls

162 La Turbie (*Tropaeum Alpium*): victory monument, quarry

157 Marseille (*Massalia*): harbour installations, walls, church

149 Orange (*Arausio*): theatre, arch, temples, walls

160 Riez (*Alebaece Reiorum Apollinarum*): temple, baptistery

153 St Blaise: oppidum

154 St Chamas: bridge, arches

158 St Cyr-sur-Mer: villa

152 St Remy (*Glanum*): houses, forum/basilica, temples, sanctuary, baths, arch, mausoleum, quarry

144 Seyssel: quarry

164 Susa (*Segusio*): arch, walls, gate, amphitheatre

148 Vaison-la-Romaine (*Vasio Vocontiorum*): houses, theatre, church, bridge

146 Vienne (*Vienna*): temples, theatres, circus, churches, walls; houses, baths (St Romain-en-Gal)

Notes

1 Greeks and Celts

1. Clavel-Lévêque 1977, 9; Bouloumié 1979; Py 1969, 55–8.
2. Boardman 1980, 95–7; J.-P. Morel 1983. See Kimmig 1983a for a general survey of colonisation in the western Mediterranean and its effects north of the Alps.
3. See J.-P. Morel 1982, and other papers in the same conference proceedings.
4. Strabo 6, 1, 1.
5. For discoveries and discussion of Massalia see Clerc 1927–9; Clavel-Lévêque 1977; Euzennat 1980; Goudineau 1983; G 44, 1986, 413–25.
6. BC 2, 1.
7. Clerc 1927–9, I, 78.
8. 4, 1, 5. See also Justinus 43, 3, 5.
9. 5, 26, 3.
10. Villard 1960; J.-P. Morel 1975, 878–83 for a recent review.
11. Vix: Joffroy 1979. Vix crater dating: Gjødesen 1963, 335ff.
12. Kimmig 1983a; Gjødesen 1963 for the Etruscan route.
13. Hochdorf: Biel 1985; Ste Colombe: Joffroy 1960.
14. BG 6, 28.
15. Kimmig 1983b.
16. Kimmig 1983b, 74. Also G 44, 1986, 430–1, where it is pointed out that mud-brick construction at St Pierre does not occur as early as the sixth century. However, the general link is clear.
17. See Collis 1984a, 82–99. For a more 'entrepreneurial' point of view see P. S. Wells 1981.
18. Collis 1984a, 81ff.; Nash 1985.
19. Bouloumié 1973; Boucher 1973.
20. For Celtic art see Megaw and Megaw 1988.
21. Villard 1960; Clavel-Lévêque 1977, 28–35. The recent excavations in Marseille (see note 5) have undermined Villard's hypothesis of a severe recession in the fifth century, but a major change is still evident.
22. Pech-Maho: Solier in Salviat and Barruol 1976, 253–62; Cayla: Hodson and Rowlett 1974, 159–78; Cunliffe 1988, 40–1.
23. Solier 1968.
24. Jannoray 1955; Gallet de Santerre 1980; Hodson and Rowlett 1974, 188–9.
25. Py 1969; 1971; 1978; 1981 for various aspects of the Vaunage and Nîmes.
26. Towers: Février 1983. Tour Magne: Py 1981; Varène 1987. Baou-des-Noirs: Latour 1985. Undefended sites: Michelozzi and Py 1980, 134–5.
27. Barruol and Py 1978, esp. pp. 94–100.
28. Arles: Rouquette in Salviat and Barruol 1976, 101. Lattes: Arnal et al. 1974. Agde: Nickels 1982.
29. Bouloumié 1982; 1984.
30. Bessac 1980; Bouloumié et al. 1981; Tréziny 1986, 197 ff. (and article by Bouloumié and Fincker in the same volume).
31. Chausserie-Laprée et al. 1988.
32. Arcelin and Cayot 1984; Bouloumié 1984, 59–64. For tribal names and areas see Barruol 1969.
33. F. Benoit 1968; 1981. G 44, 1986, 375–9 for recent excavations on the site.
34. Arcelin et al. 1982.
35. Taradeau: Goudineau 1976. Ventabren: Musso 1985. For La Cloche, occupied until mid-first century BC, see Chabot 1983. See also Février 1975.
36. This is discussed in Bats and Tréziny 1986, especially Arcelin's article therein. See also Goudineau 1983.
37. BC 1, 34.
38. J. Benoit 1985.
39. Coupry 1968; 1986; Bats 1982; G 44, 1986, 473–5.
40. Py 1978, 338–9; Clavel-Lévêque 1977, 169ff. See also van der Leeuw in Brandt and Slofstra 1983, 24–5.
41. Earliest Greek-style mud bricks are at Bessan, late sixth century: Nickels 1976. The best preserved examples are at Baou-Roux: Boissinot 1984. See also Dedet 1987, 176–200 for general

discussion of architectural changes on native sites. For Nages see Py 1978.
42. Goudineau 1984. See Justinus 43, 4.
43. Clavel-Lévêque 1977, 171–2; Rancoule 1984; Duhamel 1979. For a fifth-century kiln see Ugolini and Olive 1988.
44. Colbert de Beaulieu and Richard 1969; Clavel-Lévêque 1977, 172–8.
45. Lejeune 1985. The Montagnac inscription is G-224 in Lejeune's catalogue.
46. F. Benoit 1969.
47. Clavel-Lévêque 1977, 197–8.
48. Charmasson 1968; 1971; Barruol et al. 1979.
49. Justinus 43, 4; see also Strabo 4, 1, 5. For Gauls worshipping at the temple of Aristea on the Iles d'Hyères, see Coupry and Giffault 1982.
50. Rivet 1971. For oppida generally see Collis 1984b. Orléans: Caesar, BG 7, 11. Bourges: ibid. 7, 13–18, 29–32.
51. Collis 1984a, 147; 1984b.
52. Collis 1984a, 149ff., 175–6.
53. Basel: Furger-Gunti 1979; Berger and Furger-Gunti in Buchsenschutz 1981, 172–86. Lacoste: Sireix and Sireix 1984.
54. Aulnat: Collis et al. 1982, 30ff. Gergovie: Brogan and Desforges 1940. Levroux: Buchsenschutz 1982; Bruyer and Buchsenschutz in Collis et al. 1982, 72–89.
55. Debord 1982; 1984; Ilett et al. in Buchsenschutz 1981, 201–6. Most people refer to Pommiers as Noviodunum, rather than to Villeneuve, but the name is more logically applied to the latter. Villeneuve was probably occupied at the time Caesar refered to Noviodunum, but exact dating is not possible.
56. Buchsenschutz 1984; Cahen-Delhaye et al. 1984, esp. the articles by Boucly, Cahen-Delhaye and Metzler. See also Guilane 1976, 789ff.
57. Bibracte: Bertin and Guillaumet 1987. Levroux: Buchsenschutz 1977; see note 54.
58. Caesar, BG 1, 12.
59. Giot 1973; Wheeler and Richardson 1957.
60. Nash 1978a; 1978b; Haselgrove 1987. For cultural groupings in Gaul see Duval in Collis et al. 1982, 298–335.
61. BG 1, 29 and 1, 5.
62. River tolls: Caesar, BG 1, 18. Amphorae: Fitzpatrick 1985; Cunliffe 1988, 71ff. and ch. 5.
63. Cf. Strabo 4, 2, 3. Iron Age coins and their usage: Allen 1976; Cunliffe 1981; Nash 1978b.
64. Slavery in Gaul: Daubigny 1979. Slave-chain from Glanon: Daubigny and Guillaumet 1985.
65. See Haselgrove 1987 for the best description of the core–periphery system in action in Gaul. See also Cunliffe 1988, ch. 1 and Haselgrove in Blagg and King 1984, 5–63. A. Duval in Collis et al. 1982, 298–335 gives a different model, which places the Gaulish aristocracy as opposing Roman influence.
66. BG 6, 24.
67. BG 1, 1; 2, 21.
68. Hachmann 1976.
69. BG 6, 11–28. For commentary see Walser 1956 and Thompson 1965.
70. Hachmann et al. 1962; Hachmann 1976; Roymans in Brandt and Slofstra 1983, 43–69.
71. BG 4, 1–3. For summaries of the archaeological evidence see C. M. Wells 1972, ch. 2; Todd 1987, ch. 1; Rowlett 1968.

2 The Roman Conquest

1. Keay 1988, 27.
2. Ebel 1976, ch. 2.
3. Livy 21, 19; Potter 1987, 49–50; Picard 1967, ch. 8.
4. Polybius 3, 50–6; Livy 21, 35–8. Melvin 1980 is a good recent review of the alternative routes. See also Connolly 1981, 153ff. and Prieur 1986 for two other recent views on the route.

5. This is Ebel's thesis (1976). His is the main discussion of the conquest of southern Gaul, but see also Dyson 1985, ch. 4.

6. Strabo wrote that it took eighty years to make a safe route through the area (4, 6, 3).

7. Possibly because Fulvius wanted to return to Rome to play a part in the dramatic political developments of the Gracchan era; cf. Ebel 1976, 68.

8. F. Benoit 1968; 1981. It is generally accepted that the finds correspond with Sextius' assault in 124–123 BC, but there is some confusion in the stratigraphy which opens the possibility of other sequences and interpretations.

9. Ambard 1985. There is much confusion in the ancient sources about the exact status of Aix, cf. Ebel 1976, 69, n. 24; Dyson 1985, 150–1.

10. See Harris 1985, 248–9, who suggests that this was the main motive for Roman involvement from their very earliest days in the province.

11. Ebel 1976, 71ff.; Dyson 1985, 152ff.

12. Milestone of Domitius: P.-M. Duval 1968. Narbo: Vell. Pat. 1, 15, 5 for the date of foundation. The date has been disputed – see Ebel 1976, 90ff., and Gayraud 1981, ch. 3.

13. Dyson 1985, 158ff.

14. *Pro Font.*, especially 11, where the monopoly on trade is refered to, and *ibid.* 19–20 for the wine scandal itself. See also Tchernia 1983 and Rancoule 1985.

15. Diod. Sic. 5, 26, 3. Daubigny 1979 discusses the effect of the slave trade on Gaulish society. Vieille-Toulouse: Labrousse 1968. Lagaste: Rancoule 1980.

16. Dyson 1985, 158ff. *CAH* IX (1932), chap. 3, 139–50 remains the best discussion of the episode of the Cimbri and Teutones.

17. Plutarch, *Vit. Mar.* 18–21.

18. Dyson 1985, 164. Speeches made in Rome at this time advocated Gaul as a good area for new settlers.

19. Keay 1988, 42–4.

20. Dyson 1985, 166; Ebel 1976, 96ff.; Greenhalgh 1980, 43–4.

21. Ebel 1976, 100.

22. Gelzer 1968 has commentary on Caesar's political career. Meier 1982 is the fullest recent biography. See also Maier 1982 for Caesar and the Illyricum command, and for his relationship to general political developments during the period of the Gallic War.

23. The nature of Caesar's writing is discussed further in A. and P. Wiseman's introduction to their excellent translation of Caesar's *de Bello Gallico* (Julius Caesar, *The Battle for Gaul*, London, 1980).

24. Rice-Holmes 1911 is still the main topographical commentary, which relies heavily on Napoléon III 1866. Rambaud 1953 and Stevens 1952 are forthright in condemning Caesar's veracity, writing as they were in the light of the propaganda of the Second World War. Jullian 1908–26, III, 201, and Rice-Holmes 1911, 211–56 are more conciliatory. See Keppie 1984, ch. 3 for Caesar's army in Gaul.

25. Stevens 1952, 169ff. suggests that Caesar deliberately broke the Helvetian migration because they were intending to help defend the Gauls against the Germans. This left the Gauls exposed to Ariovistus, thus allowing Caesar to intervene on their behalf and consolidate his hold on the area. See Christ 1974 and especially Walser 1956, ch. 1–3, for critical commentary on Caesar's handling of the German threat.

26. See Szidat 1970 for analysis of Caesar's diplomacy in Gaul.

27. *BG* 2, 18–28.

28. *BG* 2, 35.

29. See Merlat 1982 for a study of the Veneti. Venetic ships: Weatherhill 1985. Maritime trade and the Veneti in the late Iron Age: Cunliffe 1988. Hillforts in the region: Wheeler and Richardson 1957.

30. Bost 1986.

31. See Delmaire 1976 for discussion of the Morini, and Wightman 1985, chap. 2.

32. See Plutarch, *Cato Minor* 51, 1–5. Also Gelzer 1968, 129–32. The political impact of this in Rome was dramatic, since his opponents pressed for him to be handed over to the Germans because of his dishonourable conduct.

33. *BG* 5, 22. For the events in the winter camps see Wightman 1985, 40ff.

34. Possibly the modern town of Tongres. In Imperial times this site was called Atuatuca, but it may not have been the site Caesar refers to (cf. Wankenne 1972, 75–8).

35. Harmand 1984 gives the most recent discussion of Vercingetorix and the events of 52 BC. Thevenot 1960 discusses the localisation of many of the places mentioned by Caesar during the year's fighting. Dyson (1971 and 1975) places the rebellion in the context of other similar uprisings in the western provinces.

36. *BG* 7, 14–28. The siege is discussed by Wimmel 1974.

37. For the problem of the modern location of Gergovia see Rambaud 1974. Gergovie, the traditional site, is now known to be post-Caesarian in date (see chapter 1). The name Gergovie is nineteenth century, created on the basis of the presumed association with Caesar's oppidum.

38. As the title of Thevenot's book implies (*Les Eduens n'ont pas trahi*, 1960), he makes a spirited case to explain the difficulties of the Aedui's position at this critical time.

39. For the military operations by Labienus at Paris see D. Morel in *Lutèce . . .* 1984, 75–8.

40. Napoléon III 1866. For more recent excavations and aerial photos of the siegeworks see Bénard 1987; also Le Gall 1980. For the oppidum defences see Mangin in Cahen-Delhaye et al. 1984, 241–54. The best recent discussion of the episode as a whole is Harmand 1967, supplemented by articles by Le Gall, Bénard, Mangin and others in *Rev. Hist. des Armées* 167, 1987, 1–76. See also Harmand 1984 and, of course, Caesar, *BG* 7, 68–90.

41. *BG* 7, 75–6. For the number of Roman legions in Gaul at this time see Keppie 1984, 92, 97.

42. Agache 1978, ch. 4 for Liercourt and the other Somme sites.

43. Aulnay: Tassaux and Tassaux 1983–4. Arlaines: Reddé 1984. Mauchamp: Peyre 1978, who points out that the presence of *claviculae* would normally date the camp to the Flavian period, not the Caesarian, as Napoléon III 1866 has it. Mirebeau: Goguey 1978; Wightman 1977c, 211–3.

44. Caesar *Bell. Civ.* 1, 34–6; 56–8; 2, 1–16; Lucan *Pharsalia* 3, 298–762. See also Clerc 1927–9.

45. Strabo 4, 6, 11. Drinkwater 1983, ch. 6. See also Wightman 1974, 1977a and 1977b.

46. *BG* 1, 1. For the provincial divisions and administration see Drinkwater 1983, ch. 5.

47. C. M. Wells 1972, ch. 1 discusses the policy behind Augustus' campaigns in Germany. His book is also the best discussion of the course of events.

48. Walser 1984; Gabba 1988.

49. Schön 1986. This area is not part of Gaul or Germany, strictly speaking, but is made up of the small provinces of Alpes Maritimae, Alpes Cottiae, Alpes Graiae, Alpes Poeninae, and part of the larger province of Raetia.

50. Formigé 1949; C. M. Wells 1972, ch. 3–4.

51. C. M. Wells 1972, ch. 1. See *CAH* X (1934), ch. 12, for the older view.

52. Neuss: Chantraine et al. 1984, especially the chapters by Rüger and Müller. Other recent archaeological work along the Rhine is discussed by Schönberger 1985 and Gechter 1979. For the Titelberg and the occupation of oppida by the army, see Todd 1985; Metzler in Rheinisches Landesmuseum Trier 1984a, 68–78.

53. Hollstein 1980, 102–3; Kühlborn 1981. For the Frisii as a client kingdom see W. Will 1987.

54. C. M. Wells 1972, ch. 6.

55. Von Schnurbein 1981 reviews current knowledge of Haltern and the other Lippe sites. See also C. M. Wells 1972, ch. 6. For the other Augustan sites on the far side of the Rhine see Schönberger 1985 and recent volumes of *Ausgrab. u. Funde Westfalen–Lippe*.

56. Gechter 1979; Schönberger 1985. For the altar at Cologne see Fishwick 1987, and for the early provincial organisation, Rüger 1968. For the rather poorly known events of this period see C. M. Wells 1972, 158–9.

57. *NH* 7, 147–50. See also C. M. Wells 1972, 159–61, 237–8; *CAH* X (1934), ch. 12.

58. Böcking 1974; C. M. Wells 1972, ch. 7. Dyson 1971 discusses the episode in relation to other revolts of the early Empire.

59. Liese 1986. Böcking 1974 reviews the earlier literature.
60. Groenman-van Waateringe in Hanson and Keppie 1980, 1037–44. See also Dyson 1971, and chapter 1 above for Caesar's comments on the Germans.

3   The Urban Landscape

1. Groenman-van Waateringe in Hanson and Keppie 1980, 1037–44 suggests that this is due to the lack of a pre-Roman social organisation that included towns or other central places. The Romans needed to build upon existing structures, and found it difficult to Romanise areas that did not already approximate to their ideas of an ordered society. See chapter 7 for further discussion of Germany.
2. Nash 1978c, 21. See Wightman 1977a and 1977b for general discussion. For the link between army recruitment and Roman colonies see Kraft 1957.
3. Goudineau 1980, 234; *CIL* XIII, 1036; Wuilleumier 1963, no. 217.
4. For evergetism see Veyne 1976, esp. 20ff.; Frézouls 1984.
5. See Duncan-Jones 1985.
6. *Pro Font.* 5, 13; Gayraud 1981.
7. May 1985. See also *DossHA* 120, 1987, 45ff.
8. Rivet 1988, 198–200 for summary of site and bibliography. See also notes 9 and 31 in this chapter, chapter 6, note 4.
9. Roth-Congès 1985.
10. Goudineau 1980, 88–93; Rivet 1988, ch. 5 and entries for individual colonies. See also for Béziers: Clavel 1970, 161–7; Fréjus: Février 1973, 1977; Narbonne: Gayraud 1981, 175–86. For Roman and Latin colonies in Gaul and Germany in general see Wolff 1976.
11. Py 1981. Water sanctuary: Gros 1984. For the foundation of the colony see Christol and Goudineau 1988.
12. Rivet 1988, 162–82; Lasselle 1976. For the Maison Carrée see chapter 6, note 40.
13. Temple: see chapter 6, note 10. Forum: Roth-Congès in *Los Foros Romanos ...* 1987, 191–201. General phase plans, now somewhat out of date, are in Salviat and Barruol 1976, 55–85.
14. Roth-Congès 1985.
15. Ward-Perkins 1970; 1981, 222. Hassall (1983, 1) in contrast emphasises the Hellenistic antecedents of the gateway ground-plans at Arles, Fréjus and Aix-en-Provence.
16. E. Will 1962; De Laet 1966; Bedon and Mertens in *Les Débuts de l'Urbanisation ...* 1985, 83–102, 261–80; Drinkwater 1985; Goudineau 1980; Février 1980, 101ff.
17. Autun: Grenier 1958, 234ff.; Drinkwater 1983, 131. Reims: Neiss 1984; Wightman 1985, 78. For the status of cities and Caesar's conquest see Goudineau 1980, 314–15; Drinkwater 1983, ch. 5; Mertens 1983, 42.
18. Wightman 1985, ch. 4. Feurs: Vaginay and Guichard 1988, 24. Besançon: Passard and Urlacher 1983.
19. Wightman 1974. Amiens: Bayard and Massy 1983. Trier: Heinen in Rheinisches Landesmuseum Trier 1984a, 32–47; Ternes 1978.
20. Goudineau 1980, 261–7; Frere 1979. For a conspectus of town plans see Bedon *et al.* 1988, vol. 2. For the idea of an idealised 'programmatic plan' see Pinon in *Les Débuts de l'Urbanisation ...* 1985, 187–201.
21. Bayard and Massy 1983.
22. Hollstein 1980, 135; Cüppers in Rheinisches Landesmuseum Trier 1984a, 48–51; Wightman 1985, 49.
23. Drinkwater 1985, 51.
24. Bögli 1984, 4–7.
25. Autun: Guillaumet and Rebourg in *Les Enceintes augustéennes dans l'Occident romain* (1987). See also the other contributions in the same volume. Drinkwater's suggestion (1983, 131) that Autun's wall was originally constructed for Roman military purposes is unconvincing. For the comparison of Rome and Nîmes population densities see Goudineau 1980, 259–60.
26. See note 10 for references; also Février in *Les Enceintes augustéennes ...* 1987 (above note 25), for Fréjus.
27. Ward-Perkins 1981, 236–7; Gros 1979; Wightman 1985, 87. Glanum: Rolland 1977. Saintes: P. Audin 1985; Maurin 1978.
28. Anderson 1987. Amy *et al.* 1962 and Gros 1979 propose the now traditional date of AD 21.

29. Goudineau 1980, 272–9; Ward-Perkins 1981, 220–1.
30. Augst: Laur-Belart 1978, 32–48. St Bertrand-de-Comminges: see note 7.
31. Glanum: Roth-Congès in *Los Foros Romanos ...* 1987, 191–201, who dates the earliest forum to the 30s BC. This structure underlies the better-known existing remains, which she puts a few decades later, while Gros and Varène (1984) put them in the Augustan period. Ruscino: Barruol and Marichal in *Los Foros Romanos ...* 1987, 45–54.
32. Amiens: Bayard and Massy 1983. Other similar fora include Paris (Périn in *Lutèce ...* 1984, 154–60), Feurs (Vaginay and Valette 1983), Bavai (Cüppers and Biévelet 1965; Hanoune and Muller 1988) and Trier (Wightman 1970 76–8). For Nîmes and Vienne, see chapter 6, note 43.
33. Tour de Vésone: Horne and King 1980, 446. Doreau *et al.* 1985 hypothesise a forum temple, but there is no direct evidence and it seems likely that the Tour de Vésone was the major religious sanctuary instead.
34. The general problem of *cryptoportici* and the Gallic examples are discussed in *Les Cryptoportiques dans l'Architecture romaine* (Rome 1973). Lyon: Mandy 1983; *ibid.* in *Los Foros Romanos ...* 1987, 179–83.
35. Wall-paintings: Allag 1985. Arles: Goudineau 1980, 277. Narbonne: Solier 1986, 35–9.
36. Krencker and Krüger 1929, 241–6; Wightman 1970, 82–5. For general discussion of baths see Grenier 1960, 231–384, and Krencker and Krüger 1929.
37. P.-M. Duval 1961, 141–61; Caillet in *Lutèce ...* 1984, 386–96.
38. Grenier 1960, 23–227 is the main survey of the subject.
39. Cologne: Haberey 1972; Grewe 1986. Nîmes and Pont-du-Gard: Ward-Perkins 1981, 223–5; Hauck 1988 (a useful recent account, but written in the style of a historical novel).
40. Metz: Grenier 1960, 199–213. Lyon: Burdy 1986 and other papers in the same volume. Arles: Haberey 1972, 157.
41. Hauck and Novak 1988.
42. Grenier 1958, part 2. For recent discussion see *Les Amphithéâtres de la Gaule* (*DossHA* 116, 1987); Niffeler 1988, 124–77, 213–40; Golvin 1988, 226–36. Paris: Forni in *Lutèce ...* 1984, 167–71; P.-M. Duval 1961, 180–93.
43. Ward-Perkins 1981, 230–3; Rivet 1988; Goudineau 1980, 294–5.
44. Arles and Nîmes: Lugli 1965; Espérandieu 1967; see also note 43 above. Avenches: Ward-Perkins 1981, 232; Bögli 1984, 12–15. See Golvin 1988 for general discussion of amphitheatres.
45. Humphrey 1986, 388–431.
46. Goudineau 1980, 296–304. Vaison: Goudineau and De Kisch 1984; Goudineau 1979; Rivet 1988, 286ff.
47. Amiens: Bayard and Massy 1983. Corseul: Langouet 1988, ch. 5.
48. Goudineau and De Kisch 1984; Ward-Perkins 1981, 238.
49. Wall-paintings: Barbet 1987. Mosaics: *Recueil général des Mosaïques de la Gaule* (Gallia Supp. 10), esp. II, 1 (Lyon) and III, 2 (Vienne); Stern 1969; Lancha 1977. Autun: Blanchard-Lemée *et al.* 1986. Poitiers statue: Audouin 1902. Vaison silver bust: Sautel 1953.
50. Glanum: see note 8. Wood and mud walling techniques: Lasfargues 1985. Lyon: Desbat 1984; Desbat in Walker 1981a, 55–81. Other similar discoveries are known from Bordeaux (Barraud 1984a), Rouen (Halbout *et al.* 1982) and Besançon (Passard and Urlacher 1983). For a southern example of an Augustan house with wooden walls and mosaic floors from Narbonne see Solier *et al.* 1979, 50 and 53.
51. Cologne: Fremersdorf 1956. Vienne: Pelletier *et al.* 1981. Aix-en-Provence: Boiron *et al.* 1986. Narbonne: Sabrié *et al.* 1987. St Romain-en-Gal: Laroche and Savay-Guerraz 1984.
52. See chapter 4, note 2.
53. Espérandieu *et al.* 1907–81; *CIL* XII and XIII; also the various supplementary publications listed in Bérard *et al.* 1986. For tombs in Gaul: Hatt 1986. For cremation cemeteries see the papers in *Nécropoles à Incineration du Haut-Empire* (Lyon 1987).
54. Drinkwater in King and Henig 1981, 215–33; see also Gabelmann 1987. Monument of the Julii: Rolland 1969; Picard 1981; Gros 1986. Tomb of Poblicius: Precht 1979.
55. Goudineau 1980, 387–90.
56. Wightman 1985, 32–3. It should be noted that this figure

applies to the conquest period and may well have been higher later.

57. Loustaud 1981, 28; see also the same author's *Limoges gallo-romain* (Limoges 1980).
58. Goudineau 1980, 390.
59. The so-called *terror Gallicus*, see Drinkwater 1983, 7.

4 Rural Life

1. Kolling 1972.
2. Mangin 1985. See also Bekker-Nielsen 1984; Wightman in *Le Vicus gallo-romain* 1976, 59–64. Pottery production: see chapter 5. Ardres: Wightman 1985, 94. Tournai: Amand 1984.
3. Wederath: Haffner 1970. Mâlain: Roussel 1979. Pommeroeul: De Boe in Taylor and Cleere 1978, 22–30; De Boe and Hubert 1977.
4. Vici in southern Gaul: Février in *Le Vicus gallo-romain* 1976, 309–21; Fiches 1986 (for excavations in Ambrussum); Bessac *et al.* 1987 (for Beaucaire). Lausanne: Kaenel 1977, and the excavation reports *Lousonna* 1–6 (1969–86) in the series *Cahiers d'Arch. Romande*. Martigny: Wiblé 1981. Verdes: Provost 1988, 105–10; Jalmain 1977.
5. Le Gall 1980; Bénard and Mangin in *Les Débuts de l'Urbanisation* 1985, 103–15.
6. Ribemont: Cadoux 1984a. Vendeuvre: Nicolini in *Le Vicus gallo-romain* 1976, 256–71. Other rural sanctuaries: Horne and King 1988; Ollivier and Fritsch 1982 (for Vieux-Poitiers); Wood 1988 (for recent work at Pouzay, Indre-et-Loire).
7. Picard 1970; 1983; Picard in *Le Vicus gallo-romain* 1976, 47–9.
8. Walthew 1982.
9. Grand: Frézouls 1982. Aix-les-Bains: Prieur in *Le Vicus gallo-romain* 1976, 157–66.
10. Villas and the countryside: Ferdière 1988; Percival 1976, 67–87; Harmand 1970. Regional surveys: Leday 1980; Coulon and Holmgren 1982; Holmgren and Leday 1981; *La Villa romaine* ... 1982, especially the contributions by Délétang, Galliou, Lambert and Rioufreyt, and Monguilan; Agache 1978; 1975; 1970; Agache and Bréart 1975.
11. Agache 1978, ch. 6. Warfusée: *ibid.* fig. 24.
12. Lack of *gallo-romaine précoce*: Ferdière 1988, I, 66–8. L'Etoile: Agache 1978, 169. Beaurieux: Haselgrove and Lowther 1987.
13. Montmaurin: Fouet 1969. Chiragan: Joulin 1901. Embellishment of Aquitaine villas: Braemer 1982; *Recueil général des Mosaïques de la Gaule* (Gallia Supp. 10), volumes for Aquitaine.
14. Anthée: Wankenne 1972. Echternach: Metzler *et al.* 1981. Otrang: Cüppers 1975. Oberentfelden: Drack 1975, 50. Seeb: Drack 1975, 51. Levet: Leday in *Le Vicus gallo-romain* 1976, 237–54; Holmgren and Leday 1981.
15. See Wightman 1978a, Agache and Smith in *La Villa romaine* ... 1982, 3–10, 321–36 and Harmand 1988 for discussions of villas and social structure, each presenting variations on the same basic theme. Daubigny 1979, 176, Belova 1987, Ferdière 1988, I, 109–14 and MacMullen 1987, 369–70 discuss the extent of slavery in rural Gaul. Demarez 1987 looks at the agricultural buildings in villas, focusing on the problem of analysing the functions of some of the subsidiary buildings – whether they were for people, animals, crops or equipment.
16. Lutz 1971/2.
17. Galliou 1983, ch. 6. La Roche Maurice: Sanquer and Galliou 1972a. Vieux-Rouen: Agache 1973.
18. Wightman 1970, 139–50.
19. Smith 1978a.
20. Ferdière 1988, I, 184–5. Rivet 1988 has references to villa sites in the province.
21. Harmand 1970. Wasserwald: Lutz 1970; Pétry in *La Villa romaine* ... 1982, 211–27.
22. Montagnieu: Chastel *et al.* 1988. Picardy: Agache 1978. Rijswijk: Bloemers 1978. For examples of native settlements in western Gaul see Ferdière 1988, I, 190–1.
23. White 1970 is a useful reference for the classical authorities.
24. Ferdière 1988, I, 122–4.
25. Ferdière 1988, I, 133–55; Clavel-Lévêque 1983; Chouquer *et al.* 1987. Orange: Piganiol 1962; Chouquer in Clavel-Lévêque 1983, 275–95.

26. Optical filtration: Favory 1980. Béziers: Clavel-Lévêque 1983, 207–58.
27. Ferdière 1988, II, 60ff.; Marinval 1988; Bakels 1984.
28. White 1969; Groupe d'Etudes Arch. Champagne Ardenne 1982.
29. Roos 1986.
30. Ferdière 1988, II, 85–106. Vegetational history: Guilaine 1976, 35–103 for the south of France and other areas. Moselle viticulture: Cüppers 1970 and in *2000 Jahre Weinkulter an Mosel–Saar–Ruwer* (Trier 1987), 9–40.
31. Olive presses: Brun 1986. Allas-les-Mines: Maurin 1964. Donzère: Dechandol *et al.* 1983. Amphora production: Laubenheimer 1985. Large barrels: Molin 1984.
32. Chevallier and Harmand in *Le Bois et la Forêt* ... 1985, 112–20, 140–60.
33. Pollen analysis: Munaut 1988. Vegetational history in other regions: Guilaine 1976, 35–103; Bats and Bui-Thi-Mai 1984. Silviculture and wood products: Meiggs 1982, ch. 12; articles by Ternes, Audin, Bedon and Lagrange in in *Le Bois et la Forêt* ... 1985.
34. Strabo 4, 4, 3.
35. King in Blagg and King 1984, 187–217. See also Luff 1982; Poulain-Josien and Poulain 1973.
36. Méniel 1987; Poulain-Josien 1964; Poulain in Guilaine 1976, 104–15.
37. Goudineau 1988.
38. Drinkwater 1982. Igel column: Zahn 1982; Drinkwater in King and Henig 1981, 215–33. Gynaecia: Wild 1976.
39. Epona: Oaks in Henig and King 1986, 77–83. Horses: Méniel 1987, 32–46.
40. Méniel 1987.
41. Ferdière 1988, II, 163–81; Méniel 1987, 89–99. Montmaurin: Poulain-Josien in Fouet 1969. German forts: Piehler 1976, 103ff.; Luff 1982; King in Blagg and King 1984, 187–217. Bears: Binsfeld 1975.
42. Notre-Dame-d'Amour: Ferdière 1988, II, 187; G 22 (1964), 588–90. Brittany: Sanquer and Galliou 1972b.
43. Gouletquer 1970; Thoen 1975.
44. Ferdière 1988, I, 71–86 is the source for most of the calculations in this section. Ausonius, *Idyllia* 12, 2.
45. Ferdière 1988, I, 82–4.
46. Corseul: Langouet 1988, 113–17. Béziers: Clavel 1970, 301.
47. Ferdière 1988, I, 86.
48. *Ibid.*
49. Beloch 1889. Drinkwater 1983, 169–70 discusses Beloch's and Jullian's population estimates. Wightman 1985, 32–3 estimates the late Iron Age population of Gallia Belgica to be 1–1½ million.
50. City population figures based on Goudineau 1980, 386–90. Army figures from Birley in King and Henig 1981, 39–53.
51. See Percival 1988, 8–12.

5 Markets and Merchandise

1. Nash 1987; Allen 1980.
2. Allen 1976; Haselgrove 1984; Nash 1987, ch. 3; Buchsenschutz and Ralston 1987 discuss coin usage. See also Nash and Scheers in Cunliffe 1981, 10–17, 18–23. Athenaeus 4, 37.
3. Allen 1976, 202.
4. Scheers 1987. See also Reece in Blagg and King 1984, 143–60.
5. Nash 1987, ch. 2; 1978c.
6. Nash 1978c; see also Reece 1973. Military supply and the economy: Middleton 1979.
7. Hopkins 1980; Drinkwater 1983, 128–9.
8. Reece 1973. See also Reece 1987 for general background.
9. Reece 1973; Hodder and Reece 1976; 1980; C. E. King in King and Henig 1981, 89–126.
10. Military supply routes: Middleton 1979; 1980; 1983. Economic axis: Goudineau 1980, 386–9. Lyon as trading centre: A. Audin 1979; Drinkwater 1975; 1983, 197.
11. *CIL* XIII, 1945.
12. Use of river transport: Strabo 4, 1, 2; Bonnard 1913; Kneissl 1981. Chalon and transhipment: Bonnamour 1975. Trade to

free Germany: chapter 7, note 25. For examples of river-boats see Weerd 1988 (Zwammerdam), and De Boe in Taylor and Cleere 1978, 22–30 (Pommeroeul).

13. Middleton 1980.
14. Strabo 4, 1, 14; Roman 1983; Galliou 1986; Cunliffe 1988, 81–6. Bordeaux inscription: *CIL* XIII, 634; Chastagnol 1981, 66. Guernsey wreck: *Observer* 7/4/1985, 4. See also note 22 for Ploumanac'h wreck.
15. Parker 1984.
16. Charlin *et al.* 1978.
17. Long 1987; F. Benoit 1961.
18. E. L. Will 1979, fig. 2; see also Tchernia 1983.
19. Tchernia *et al.* 1978. See Formenti *et al.* 1978 for an amphora from the wreck still containing wine. Tchernia 1969 discusses the similar later first-century BC Planier amphora wreck.
20. Colls *et al.* 1977. See Remesal Rodriguez 1986 for olive oil trade from Spain to Germany.
21. Corsi-Sciallano and Liou 1985. Hesnard *et al.* 1988 show that dolia 'tankers' were also used for shipping wine from Italy to Gaul and Spain at a slightly earlier date.
22. See note 14 for Guernsey. For a wreck with Brigantian lead ingots off Ploumanac'h (Côtes-du-Nord): L'Hour in *Les Mines et la Métallurgie . . . 1987*, 137–48.
23. Dangréaux and Desbat 1988. Domitian: Suetonius, *Domitian* 7,2.
24. Laubenheimer 1985.
25. Davies 1935, 76–93, 165–81 remains the best survey, but is out of date in its details. See also the conference proceedings *Mines et Fonderies . . . 1982*, *Les Mines et la Métallurgie . . . 1987*, Braemer 1986. Tin: Penhallurick 1986, 85ff. Coal: Bouthier 1977.
26. Tamain and Ratz in *Mines et Fonderies . . . 1982*, 33–78; Tamain in Braemer 1986, 119–31.
27. Desbordes and Lacotte in *Les Mines et la Métallurgie . . . 1987*, 291–6.
28. Dubois and Guilbaut in *Mines et Fonderies . . . 1982*, 95–123, and in Braemer 1986, 91–116; Guilbaut 1981. Massiac: Tixier 1978, but there is some dispute in *Mines et Fonderies . . . 1982*, 121 on the dating of the shafts.
29. Dubois and Guilbaut in *Mines et Fonderies . . . 1982*, 95–123; Laubenheimer-Leenhardt 1973.
30. Lead-sealings: Barruol and Gourdiole in *Mines et Fonderies . . . 1982*, 79–93. Ingots: Laubenheimer-Leenhardt 1973; L'Hour in *Les Mines et la Métallurgie . . . 1987*, 137–48.
31. Boucher 1976.
32. Montagne Noire: Cambon *et al.* in Braemer 1986, 77–89; Domergue *et al.* in *Mines et Fonderies . . . 1982*, 215–36; Rebiscoul in *Les Mines et la Métallurgie . . . 1987*, 59–71. Area surveys of iron workings can be found in *Mines et Fonderies . . . 1982* and in *Les Mines et la Métallurgie . . . 1987*.
33. Domergue *et al.* 1977; *ibid.* in *Mines et Fonderies . . . 1982*, 215–36.
34. Mangin 1981; *ibid.* in *Mines et Fonderies . . . 1982*, 237–58; Mangin and Thouvenin 1976. For iron-working at Bliesbruck *vicus* (Moselle) see Forrières *et al.* 1987.
35. Procurator *CIL* XIII, 1797. Weapons manufacture: Scott 1985; S. James 1988.
36. Namnetes: Galliou in *Mines et Fonderies . . . 1982*, 21–32. Entre-Sambre-et-Meuse: Wightman 1985, 139.
37. Minot: Peyre in *Mines et Fonderies . . . 1982*, 157–77.
38. Bedon 1984, fig. 14; Braemer 1986, 287–328. The former is the main survey of the Gallo-Roman stone industry.
39. Niedermendig and Volvic: Röder 1953. La Turbie: Bedon 1984, fig. 46–7. Nîmes area: Bessac 1986. Lyon area: A. Audin and Burnand 1977.
40. Seyssel: Dufournet 1976; Bedon 1984, 142, fig. 20. Drachenfels: Röder 1974; Horn 1987, 523–7. Strasbourg wreck: Forrer 1911; Bedon 1984, 138. St Tropez: Bedon 1984, 139–40; chapter 6, note 41.
41. Bedon 1984, 92, fig. 43.
42. Röder 1957/9.
43. Norroy: Bedon 1984, 118. St Boil: Monthel and Pinette 1977; Bedon 1984, 120–2.
44. Braemer 1986, 287–328. Reuse of stone: Blagg 1983.
45. Treteau: Corrocher 1987. Iversheim: Sölter 1970.
46. Le Ny 1988; Hofmann 1975. Fifth-century BC kiln: Ugolini and Olive 1988.
47. Laubenheimer 1978.
48. Samian ware: Bémont and Jacob 1986; Garbsch 1982. Studies of coarse wares: Tuffreau-Libre 1988; Menez 1985; Paunier 1981; Aquitaine pottery: Santrot 1979. Kilns: Duhamel 1973; 1975; 1979. Pottery in Gaul is generally surveyed in *Les Potiers Gaulois* (*DossHA* 6, 1974) and *Céramique en Gaule Romaine* (*DossHA* 9, 1975). See also *Céramiques Hellenistiques et Romaines* I–II (Paris 1980/7), esp. II, 203ff.
49. King 1983 briefly surveys the place of samian ware in Roman art and economy. Peacock 1982, ch. 7 is the best analysis of the development of the manufacturing processes in the industry.
50. Picon *et al.* 1975; Lasfargues 1973.
51. La Graufesenque and south Gaul: Bémont and Jacob 1986, 31–120; Vernhet and Balsan 1975. Recent excavations at La Graufesenque are summarised in the information sections of *Gallia*. Lezoux and early Central Gaul: Bémont and Jacob 1986, 137–44; Vertet 1967.
52. Graffiti: Marichal 1988. Kiln excavation: Vernhet 1981.
53. Distribution: Vernhet in Bémont and Jacob 1986, 39–41; Marsh 1981. Pompeii: Atkinson 1914.
54. Bémont and Jacob 1986, 43–5, 121–71; Marsh 1981.
55. Lezoux: Vertet *et al.* 1980. Les Martres-de-Veyre: Terrisse 1968. Boucheporn: Lutz 1977. East Gaul: Bémont and Jacob 1986, 173–263; Garbsch 1982.
56. Stanfield and Simpson 1958; Vertet 1979. Distribution: Marsh 1981; King 1985, ch. 7; Raepsaet 1987.
57. Rheinzabern: Bernhard 1981; Reutti 1983. Trier: Huld-Zetsche 1971; 1972.
58. King 1985.
59. Favory 1974; Goudineau 1974; Delplace 1978; King 1985, ch. 6.

6   Romano-Celtic and Other Religions

1. 3, 399–426; Loeb translation, with some phrases omitted.
2. E.g. Pliny, *Nat. Hist.* 16, 95, 249–51; Livy 5, 48; 23, 24; Justinus 24, 6, 4; Strabo 4, 4, 5; Dio Cassius 62, 7.
3. Tacitus, *Ann.* 11, 23–5; see Drinkwater 1983, 7.
4. Bessac and Bouloumié 1985. Glanum: Rolland 1968; *G 27* (1969), 443–6. Roquepertuse: de Gérin-Ricard 1927. Entremont: Lantier 1943; F. Benoit 1981.
5. As quoted in Strabo 4, 4, 5. See also Livy 10, 26.
6. Chabot 1983.
7. Rolland 1958, 88.
8. Lewis 1966, 4.
9. See Goudineau 1980, 76, 182 for discussion.
10. Rolland 1958, 79ff. See also Lavagne 1970.
11. Gournay: Brunaux *et al.* 1985. Ribemont: Cadoux 1984b.
12. Cadoux 1984b, 76–8.
13. Commenta Bernensia in Lucan, *Pharsalia* 1, 445.
14. Caesar, *BG* 6, 17; Diodorus Siculus 5, 32.
15. Piggott 1974, 108–11. See also Clavel-Lévêque 1985 for the survival of the Druids after their 'suppression'.
16. Cadoux 1984a, 1984b.
17. Horne and King 1980.
18. Autun: P.-M. Duval and Quoniam 1963. Fréteval: *G 24* (1966), 254–6. Pesch: Lehner 1919. Avallon: Horne and King 1980, 381–2. See also Horne in Henig and King 1986, 15–24.
19. Horne and King 1980, 446, 490–1. See also Koethe 1933.
20. Figurines: Rouvier-Jeanlin 1972. Miniature swords: Béal and Feugère 1987. Miniature wheels: Green 1984. Stone age axe hoard from Essarts temple (Seine-Maritime): De Vesly 1909, 84–92.
21. See for instance Fauduet in Henig and King 1986, 25–8 (Argenton-sur-Creuse); Le Gall and Sénéchal 1974 (Alesia). Other sites are given in Horne and King 1980.
22. Stone sculpture is catalogued in Espérandieu *et al.* 1907–81, together with a complementary volume on Germany, 1931. For German sculpture see also the *Corpus Signorum Imperii Romani* volumes for Germania Inferior and Superior. For bronzes see Boucher 1976. Inscriptions are mainly assembled

in the *Corpus Inscriptionum Latinarum* XII and XIII, but for more recent finds see Bérard *et al.* 1986 for bibliography.

23. Caesar, *BG* 6, 17, Tacitus, *Germ.* 43.
24. Planson and Lagrange 1975; Planson and Pommeret 1985. P. Berger 1984 and Planson and Lagrange interpret the central figure as a hermaphrodite Cybele. See Bober 1951 for discussion of Cernunnos, and Espérandieu (note 22 above) III, no. 2131 for a similar sculpture.
25. Bauchhenss and Noelke 1981; Green in Henig and King 1986, 65–75; Lambrechts 1942.
26. E.g. Tremblois: Paris 1960, Trier: Gose 1972. For further discussion see King forthcoming.
27. For southern Gaulish temples see in particular Py 1978, 88–90 (Nages); Vidal 1973 (Vielle-Toulouse); and Horne and King 1980, 379 (Aumes). Temples near the Rhône–Rhine axis include Tremblois and Trier (see note 26). For Elst see Bogaers 1955.
28. Buche 1903; P.-M. Duval and Pinault 1986, esp. 35–7.
29. Lambrechts 1942, maps at end of volume. See also Oaks in Henig and King 1986, 77–83; Fellendorf-Börner 1986 for Epona, and *Deae Nehalenniae* 1971 for Nehalennia.
30. Grenier 1960, 608–39. Grenier also discusses other healing sanctuaries in Gaul.
31. Voinot 1984. See also Thevenot 1950 and Rémy 1984. For medicine in Gaul see Pelletier 1985.
32. Montbellet: Feugère *et al.* 1985. Montiers-sur-Saulx: Espérandieu *et al.* 1907–81, VI, 4665.
33. Sources de la Seine wooden statues: Deyts 1983; 1988. Chamalières: Romeuf 1986. Sequana statuette: Blanchet 1934.
34. *Pan. Lat.* 6, 21, 3–4 and Galletier 1950. See also Billoret 1980 for the site in general and Cüppers *et al.* 1982 for Aachen.
35. Cassius Dio 77, 15, 5 and Weber 1981.
36. Picard 1970; 1983; Braemer 1973. See chapter 4, note 7. See Horne and King 1980 for references to the sites mentioned.
37. Argenton: Picard 1969; Dumazy 1989. Trier: Gose 1972. See also Bouley 1983 and *Les Théâtres de la Gaule romaine* (*DossHA* 134, 1989). Some rural theatres are Roman in design, e.g. Les Bouchauds: Maurin 1981.
38. Bouray: Lantier 1934. Sources de la Seine: see note 33. See also Mitard 1982 for the most interesting Genainville bronze bust of late second-century date.
39. Guyonvarc'h and Le Roux-Guyonvarc'h 1986, 442ff. For changes in Romano-Celtic cults during the early Empire see Carré 1978, 124–5 for south Gaul and Wightman 1985, 186; 1986, 549 for Gallia Belgica. Language change: Schmidt 1983; Whatmough 1970.
40. Amy and Gros 1979.
41. Gayraud 1981, 258–72; Solier 1986, 41–6; Ward-Perkins 1981, 227.
42. *CIL* XII, 4333. See also *ibid.* 6038 for laws regulating the priesthood.
43. Nîmes: Amy and Gros 1979, 194. Vienne: Formigé 1924.
44. *CIL* XIII, 3149. *Ibid.* 3148–52 are very similar. See Rouanet-Liesenfelt 1980, 20–2, 187–99 (Chastagnol) for discussion.
45. Fishwick 1972; 1978; 1987, II, 317ff.
46. Augst: Laur-Belart 1978, 79–85. Antigny: Richard 1988. Masamas: De Lavergne *et al.* 1982.
47. Lar figurines: Boucher 1976. Rezé: Boon 1983, 40–3. Argenton: Coulon 1986.
48. Barruol 1985.
49. Turcan 1972; 1986; Schwertheim 1974; 1986. See Vermaseren 1981 for general consideration of the eastern cults.
50. *CIL* XIII, 1751; also 1752–6. For the temple site: A. Audin 1985; also discussion in Turcan 1972, 80–98.
51. Vienne: Pelletier 1980. Neuss: Schwertheim 1974, 9–10.
52. Heddernheim: Schwertheim 1974, 67–9. Bourg-Saint-Andéol: Turcan 1972, 7–10. Saarbrücken: Schindler 1964. For a Mithraeum in a Romano-Celtic temple area at Les Bolards: Planson *et al.* 1973. See generally Walters 1974.
53. Speidel 1978; Merlat 1951.
54. Nîmes temple: *CIL* XII, 3058b. Sarapis: Kater-Sibbes 1973. Sabazios: Vermaseren 1983. Judaism: Blumenkranz 1969.

7   The Frontier Land

1. Smith 1978a; 1978b.
2. Mayen: Oelmann 1928. Kaalheide-Krichelberg: Ferdière 1988, I, 62. Köln-Mungersdorf: Fremersdorf 1933. Otrang: Cüppers 1975.
3. Smith 1978a, fig. 60.
4. Rüger 1968; Bechert 1982.
5. Bauchhensss and Neumann 1987; Leunissen 1986.
6. Osterburken: Schallmayer 1982. Romano-Celtic temples in Germany: Follman-Schulz 1986.
7. Von Petrikovits 1980, 50ff.; Vanvinckenroye 1975, 14; Gechter forthcoming.
8. Hind 1984. Cf. Tacitus, *Germ.* 29. For a Gallic-type villa in the region at Fischbach: Kuntze and Wagner 1988. For a hall-type villa at Lauffen: Spitzing 1988.
9. Brandt and Slofstra 1983, especially the article by Bloemers.
10. Willems 1981/4; *ibid.* in Brandt and Slofstra 1983, 105–28; Van Es 1982. See also Sanden 1987.
11. Rüger 1968.
12. Bloemers 1978.
13. Groenman-van Waateringe in Hanson and Keppie 1980, 1037–44.
14. Groenman-van Waateringe 1980; 1983.
15. Holwerda 1923; Bogaers 1972; Van Es 1972.
16. Bloemers forthcoming. Nijmegen: Bogaers *et al.* 1980.
17. Xanten early levels: Heimberg 1987. Tongeren early levels: Vanderhoeven *et al.* 1987.
18. La Baume 1973.
19. La Baume *et al.* 1980; Doppelfeld 1975; Hellenkemper 1975 are the best recent surveys of Roman Cologne. An English account is given in La Baume 1967. Praetorium: Precht 1973. Town houses: Fremersdorf 1956. Pottery-kilns: Schauerte 1987. Glass production: Fremersdorf 1966. Trade: see chapter 5 and the papers in Taylor and Cleere 1978. Villas: Gaitsch 1986; Knorzer 1984.
20. Esser 1972; Decker and Selzer 1976; Selzer 1988. Late Roman boats: Rupprecht 1984; Höckmann 1988. For Mainz's role as a trading centre: Kuhoff 1984.
21. Hinz 1975; 1976; Bridger and Siegmund 1987, 112–18. Late fort: Rüger 1979.
22. Sommer 1988, 465–83, 500–28; Schönberger 1951.
23. See chapter 6, notes 52 and 53. Epigraphic evidence for origins of *vicani*: Sommer 1988, 610.
24. Baatz and Herrmann 1982, 275–92; Sommer 1988, 627ff.; cf. *Germ* 39, 164–6.
25. Hedeager 1978; 1987; Hansen 1987; Künzl 1988.
26. Wijster: Van Es 1967. See also Bennekom for an exceptional site that peaks in the fifth century: Van Es *et al.* 1985. Trade across frontier: Bloemers in Brandt and Slofstra 1983, 159–209. Site statistics: Kunow 1987; 1988; forthcoming; see also Gechter and Kunow 1986; Gechter forthcoming.
27. Fulford 1985; Whittaker 1983. Randsborg 1981 discusses trade and raid ideas.
28. C. M. Wells 1972, 241–3.
29. Rüger 1968.
30. Gechter 1979; Schönberger 1969; 1985. Nijmegen: Bogaers *et al.* 1980. Neuss: Rüger in Chantraine *et al.* 1984, 9–48, and other articles in the same volume.
31. Tacitus, *Ann.* 3, 40–46. Wightman 1985, 64. See chapter 2, note 49.
32. W. Will 1987. Cf. Luttwak 1976, ch. 1. Velsen: J.-M. Morel 1986.
33. Glasbergen and Groenman-van Waateringe 1974; Groenman-van Waateringe and van Beek 1988.
34. Baatz 1975; Hind 1984.
35. Von Petrikovits 1980, 65–7.
36. Brunt 1959; *CAH* X, 810–11; Drinkwater 1983, 40–3.
37. Tacitus, *Histories*, is by far the most important source for these events. See also Chilver 1957; Campbell 1984, 365–74; Brunt 1960.
38. *Hist.* 3, 1–35.
39. Urban 1985; Von Petrikovits 1980, 70ff.
40. Drinkwater 1983, 46. See also Drinkwater 1978.
41. Bogaers *et al.* 1980.

42. Schönberger 1969; 1985. See also Luttwak 1976, ch. 2.
43. Baatz 1975.
44. Strobel 1987.
45. Frontinus, *Strat.* 1, 3, 10; Baatz 1974; 1975. For one of the rearward forts at Wiesbaden: Schoppa 1974.
46. Von Petrikovits 1980, 80.
47. Strobel 1987 gives the date for creation of the provinces as AD 84. Wightman 1977c is the best discussion of the problem of the boundary in Germania Superior. Rüger 1968 discusses the boundary in Germania Inferior.
48. Baatz 1975. Zugmantel and the Saalburg: Baatz and Herrmann 1982, 469–74, 501–4.
49. Schallmayer 1984. For Köngen fort to the south of the Odenwald frontier: Unz 1982. For Rottweil: Rüsch 1981; Klee *et al.* 1988 and earlier volumes in the same series.
50. Baatz 1974; 1975; Filtzinger *et al.* 1986.
51. Beck and Planck 1980.
52. Schönberger 1969; Birley 1971; Böhme 1975.
53. Dietz 1986. Holzhausen: Pferdehirt 1976, 17–32. Dalkingen: Beck and Planck 1980.
54. Von Petrikovits 1980, 168–70; Filtzinger *et al.* 1986.
55. Von Petrikovits 1980, 170–1.
56. Schönberger 1969, 176–7; Hind 1984; Eadie in Hanson and Keppie 1980, 1045–50.
57. Pirling 1986, 32–5.

8   Breakdown and Revival

1. Drinkwater 1983, 80. Both Strasbourg and Poitiers have been suggested as sites affected by Maternus, neither on very certain grounds.
2. Birley 1988, ch. 12.
3. Lyon: Desbat in Walker 1981, 105–17. Samian: King 1985, *contra* Stanfield and Simpson 1958, xli.
4. Walker in King and Henig 1981, 317–42; Desbat and Vallat in Walker 1981, 105–17, 239–50; Drinkwater 1975, 136. For the late Roman town: Reynaud *et al.* 1977.
5. See chapter 5, note 9.
6. Lyon: Turcan in Walker 1981, 83–103. Mainz: Behrens 1921.
7. Blagg in King and Henig 1981, 167–88. See also Horne in *ibid*, 21–6 on temples in the third century.
8. *Decem Pagi*: Hind 1984. Tarraco: Keay 1988, 177. Sense of crisis: Alföldy 1974.
9. Reece in King and Henig 1981, 79–88. Koethe 1942 is the main source for maps of hoards of the period.
10. Baratte 1984; Henig in King and Henig 1981, 127–43; Baratte and Painter 1989. Rethel and neighbouring hoards: Baratte *et al.* 1988. Berthouville: Babelon 1916.
11. Wightman in King and Henig 1981, 235–43; 1985, 195–7.
12. Drinkwater 1987 is the main discussion of the Gallic Empire. See also Wightman 1985, ch. 8; Eadie in Hanson and Keppie 1980, 1045–50.
13. Johnson 1983, ch. 4 and 10, App. 3; Mertens in Hanson and Keppie 1980, 423–70; Gilles 1985; Brulet 1978a. Furfooz: Brulet 1978b. Wittnauer Horn: Bersu 1945; L. Berger 1976.
14. Johnson 1983 is the main source of reference.
15. Le Mans: Biarne and Guilleux 1980. Tours: Wood 1983. Orléans: Petit 1983; *Rev. Arch. Loiret* 9 (1983), 61. Poitiers: Le Masne de Chermont 1987. See also Saintes: Maurin 1978, 332–41.
16. Johnson 1983, ch. 5, App. 1. Paris: Périn in *Lutèce* ... 1984, 362–72.
17. This is Reece's (1980) hypothesis for Roman Britain. Poitiers: Le Masne de Chermont 1987.
18. Reuse of masonry: Blagg 1983. Arlon: Mertens 1973. Pottery and samian ware: King 1983; 1985, ch. 7. Metal ware: Baratte 1984. The Kaiseraugst Treasure is a good example of late Roman metalwork style: Cahn and Kaufmann-Heinimann 1984.
19. MacMullen 1965.
20. MacMullen 1963.
21. Von Petrikovits 1971. Gallic coast: Johnson 1976, ch. 5; Galliou in Hanson and Keppie 1980, 397–422. Defence in depth: Luttwak 1976, ch. 3.
22. Froitzheim: Barfield *et al.* 1968. Moers: Krause 1974.
23. Von Petrikovits 1971; Johnson 1983, ch. 2 and 6. Liberchies: Mertens and Brulet 1974; Mertens in Hanson and Keppie 1980, 423–70.
24. Jones 1964, ch. 17.
25. Thompson 1952; Czuth 1965; Ferdière 1988, II, 209–12, who refers to *Praefecti latrocinio arcendo* in various towns of northern and eastern Gaul. Jublains: Rebuffat 1985. Larçay: Wood 1986.
26. Carausius in Gaul: Casey 1977. Boulogne: Seillier 1984. Beaurains hoard and medallion: Bastien and Metzger 1977.
27. Nesselhauf 1938; Rivet 1976 for maps of the late Roman provincial boundaries.
28. Wightman 1970 is the main source on Trier in English. See also Rheinisches Landesmuseum Trier 1984b; Heinen 1985.
29. Wightman 1970, 103–9. Rheinisches Landesmuseum Trier 1984b, 139–57.
30. Wightman 1970, 98–102, 113–15. Krencker and Krüger 1929.
31. Arles: Rivet 1988, 190–6. St Pierre-aux-Nonnains: Delestre 1988.
32. Wightman 1970, 162–72. Konz: Neyses 1987. Pfalzel: Gauthier 1980, 332 n. 339 for bibliography.
33. Wightman 1970, 62–7.
34. *Pan. Lat.* for AD 312, 310, 298, 297. See Buckley in King and Henig 1981, 287–315 for Autun at this time.
35. Vienne: Pelletier 1967. Arles: see note 31; F. Benoit 1954.
36. Amiens: Bayard and Massy 1983, 244. Orléans and Poitiers: see note 15. Arras: Jacques *et al.* 1986. Paris: see note 16.
37. Ausonius, *Idyllia*; Salvian, *De Gub. Dei*. Villas: Percival 1976, 70–2; Ferdière 1988, II, 214. See also Stevens 1933; Sid. App., *Litt.* 2, for fifth-century villas.
38. Northern Gaul: Wightman 1978b; Van Ossel 1987; Agache 1978, 380–2. Climatic change, coastal flooding and environmental factors: Thoen and Porter in King and Henig 1981, 245–57, 353–62; Groenman-van Waateringe 1980. Burgundy: Berry 1987. Dambron: Ferdière *et al.* 1979–81.
39. Février 1978; Raynaud in Landes 1988, 125–9. Lunel-Viel: Raynaud 1984b. Burgundy: Berry 1987. Lombren: Charmasson 1970. Grotte de l'Hortus: Démians-d'Archimbaud 1972. For similar suggestions of sites under modern villages in Picardy: Agache 1978, 436–51.
40. Salvian, *De Gub. Dei*. Mienne-Marboué: Blanchard-Lemée 1981. Marais-de-Famechon: Vermeersch 1981.
41. Von Petrikovits 1980, 178–83. Köln-Deutz: Horn 1987, 513–16.
42. Amm. Marc. 16, 10, 20–16, 12, 68. Von Petrikovits 1980, 190–5.
43. Von Petrikovits 1971, 184–5. Alzey: Oldenstein 1986. Germanic settlements: Van Es in Bohner 1976, 114–44. See Bennekom: Van Es *et al.* 1985.
44. Von Petrikovits 1971, 185–7; Hoffmann 1974. Rhine-Iller-Danube *limes*: Garbsch 1970; 1988.

9   Churches and the Church

1. Eusebius of Caesaria, *Hist. Eccl.* 5, 1, 3–63. See also the articles by Thomas, Grant, Barnes, Frend and Pietri in Rougé and Turcan 1978; Saumagne and Meslin 1979; A. Audin 1977. For Vienne at this time see Pelletier 1977.
2. A. Audin and Le Glay 1970.
3. A. Audin and Burnand 1959; A. Audin 1979, 139; articles by Thomas, Cracco-Ruggini and Rougé in Rougé and Turcan 1978; Frend 1980, ch. 13.
4. The Danubian market for samian ware shipped through Lyon was apparently lost at this time; see King 1985.
5. Irenaeus, *Adv. Haereses*; H. Chadwick 1967, 63.
6. The excavations of the cathedral have not yet been published in full, but see Kempf 1964 and in W. Krämer 1958, 368–79. More recent summaries are in *Der Trierer Dom*, Neuss, 1980 (Rheinisches Ver. für Denkmalpflege u. Landschaftsschutz J. 1978/9); Rheinisches Landesmuseum Trier 1984b, 161–3; Gauthier and Picard 1986, I, 21–5; Wightman 1970, 109–13, 116–7; Krautheimer 1975, 49–51, 89–90. Pre-cathedral frescos: Simon 1986.
7. Hubert 1963.

8. Bonnet 1987, 333.
9. *Apol. ad Constantium* 14–15.
10. Gauthier and Picard 1986, I, 24–5.
11. Krautheimer 1975, 89–90.
12. For Christianity in the Trier region see Wightman 1970, 227–37; Heinen 1985, 327–45; Binsfeld in Rheinisches Landesmuseum Trier 1984b; Gauthier 1980, ch. 4 and 7.
13. St Gereon: Krautheimer 1975, 90–1. St Mathias: Cüppers 1969; Rheinisches Landesmuseum Trier 1984b, 203–10; Gose 1958, 1–48; K. Krämer 1974; Gauthier and Picard 1986, I, 27–8.
14. Wightman 1970, 237–40; Rheinisches Landesmuseum Trier 1984b, 202–3; Moreau 1960.
15. Sid. Apoll., *Epist.* 2,10. See Stevens 1933. For the excavations see Reynaud 1986; *ibid.* in Rougé and Turcan 1978; Gauthier and Picard 1986, IV, 22–8.
16. Bonnet 1986; 1987; Gauthier and Picard 1986, III, 1986, 44–7.
17. David-Roy 1979. For Fréjus, Aix and Riez see Gauthier and Picard 1986, II. Fréjus: Février 1981. Aix: Guild *et al.* 1983. Poitiers: Eygun 1964; Heitz 1977, 12–15.
18. Blanc 1980, 49ff. The date of the mosaic is put as fifth century by the excavator, but other commentators have placed it rather later; see Février in Gauthier and Picard 1986, III, 72. Traces of finely worked mosaics have been found at Aix (Guild *et al.* 1983), and Marseille (Barral ı Altet and Drocourt 1974).
19. Gauthier and Picard 1986, II, 86–8.
20. Doppelfeld 1967, 113–14.
21. R. P. C. Hanson 1985, ch. 15 and 17; Van Dam 1985. Germanus: Thompson 1984.
22. Gauthier and Picard 1986, IV, 37–45.
23. Van Dam 1985; Brown 1981.
24. *Epist.* 5, 17, 3–4.
25. The published reports do not give precise dating; see Reynaud 1973, 352–4; Gauthier and Picard 1986, IV, 27–8.
26. See Y. Duval and Picard 1986, especially the articles by Reynaud and Jannet-Vallat on Lyon and Vienne, Bonnet on Switzerland and Fixot on Provence. Also Brown 1981.
27. St Seurin: Duru 1972; Etienne 1962, 271–6. Aquitaine sarcophagi: Sivan 1986.
28. Xanten: Borger 1961, 404–7; Bridger and Siegmund 1987. Cologne: Fremersdorf in W. Krämer 1958, 329–39.
29. Doppelfeld 1967, 112–14.
30. F. Benoit 1966; Demians d'Archimbaud 1971; 1974; Gauthier and Picard 1986, III, 129–30. For Marseille sarcophagi see F. Benoit 1954.
31. Cassian: O. Chadwick 1968; Frend 1984, 719–21. Marseille monastery: Gauthier and Picard 1986, III, 131. For Gallic monasticism generally see Prinz 1965; E. James 1981; Leinhard 1977.
32. Pricoco 1978; Fletcher 1980.
33. Martin: Stancliffe 1983; Leinhard 1977, 94ff.; Van Dam 1985, ch 6. Ligugé: Coquet 1977; Heitz 1977, 21–2; G 25 (1967), 260–2.
34. Life at the monastery is described in Sulpicius Severus, *Vita Martini* 10, 5–8; Stancliffe 1983, 85. For the church of St Martin at Tours: Pietri 1983; Gauthier and Picard 1987, V, 19–39.
35. Horne and King 1980, 433–4; Beck *et al.* 1988; Bulliot and Thiollier 1892, 385–90. See also Stancliffe 1979 for countryside churches associated with Martin.
36. Wightman 1985, 299; Pietri 1986.
37. St Julien: Colardelle 1977. Sézegnin: Privati 1986a. For early Christianity in Switzerland and southern Germany see Müller 1986.

10   From Gaul to France

1. Pilet 1980; Pilet and Alduc-Le Bagousse 1987.
2. Vron: Seiller 1976; *ibid.* in *La Picardie ...* 1986, 55–8. Krefeld: Pirling 1986. Sézegnin: Privati 1986a. Cemeteries in the Low Countries: Bloemers in Brandt and Slofstra 1983, 193–8. On problems of ethnic distinction see the conference proceedings, *Le Phénomène des Grandes 'Invasions'* (Valbonne 1983), and E.

James 1988, who also discusses the general background to the cemetery evidence.
3. Pilet and Alduc-Le Bagousse 1987.
4. Brebières: Demolon 1973; E. James 1988, 212–14. Juvincourt-et-Damary: Bayard in *La Picardie ...* 1986, 204–11. St Martin-de-Mondeville: Lorren 1985. Sézegnin: Privati 1986b.
5. Redknap 1987.
6. See chapter 7, note 27. Also Demougeot 1979, vol. 1.
7. Demougeot 1979 is the best discussion of the movement and history of the barbarians.
8. Von Petrikovits 1980, 212, 266ff. Jones 1964 is the best general account of the period.
9. Rheinisches Landesmuseum Trier 1984b, 38–42. See also Matthews 1975.
10. *Laeti*: MacMullen 1963. Archaeological evidence: Böhme 1974; *ibid.* in Böhner 1976, 71–87; E. James 1988, 44–51.
11. La Baume *et al.* 1980.
12. Von Petrikovits 1980, 274–6.
13. Cleary 1989, ch. 3.
14. E. James 1988, 51ff. Pfalzel: chapter 8, note 32. Trier in the fifth century: chapter 9, note 12.
15. Visigoths: E. James 1977, ch. 1; Thompson 1982, ch. 2–3; Teillet 1984; Barral ı Altet 1986; Landes 1988. Marduel: Raynaud 1984a. Marseille: Cavaillès-Llopis 1986. Port-Vendres I and other late Roman wrecks: Liou 1974; Negrel 1973.
16. Thompson 1982, ch. 2.
17. Bordeaux: Barraud 1984b. Rural sites: E. James 1977; Landes 1988; Bassier *et al.* 1981; Balmelle and Dousseau 1982. See also Ellis 1988 on late Roman houses in Gaul. Salvian: *De. Gub.* 7, 8.
18. Burgundian archaeology: Martin in Bohner 1976, 201–7. Geneva: Bonnet 1974. Alamanni: Christlein 1979. Cultural frontier: Braudel 1988, 85–103.
19. Thompson 1948, ch. 6.
20. E. James 1988, 67–71. Brittany and Breton cemeteries: Giot 1983; Giot and Monnier 1977.
21. Visigothic expansion: Thompson 1982, ch. 3. Sidonius Apollinaris: Stevens 1933.
22. E. Will 1966; Bayard in *La Picardie ...* 1986, 26–35; E. James 1988, 67–71; Werner 1988. Childeric's tomb: Kazanski and Périn 1988, and contribution by Brulet *et al.* in the same volume; E. James 1988, 58–64; *Childéric-Clovis: Rois des Francs*, exhib. cat. (Tournai 1988).
23. E. James 1988; Périn and Feffer 1987; Geary 1988 are the best recent discussions of the Franks. The later history of the Franks is given in E. James 1982.

Select bibliography

Abbreviations

AB	Archaeologia Belgica
AJA	American Journal of Archaeology
ANRW	Aufstieg und Niedergang der Römischen Welt
Aquit	Aquitania
Arch	Archéologia
BJ	Bonner Jahrbücher
BRGK	Bericht der Römisch-Germanischen Kommission
Brit	Britannia
BROB	Berichten van de Rijksdienst voor het Oudheidkundig Bodemonderzoek
BSNAF	Bulletin de la Société Nationale des Antiquaires de France
CAH	Cambridge Ancient History
CIL	Corpus Inscriptionum Latinarum
CNSS	Congrès National des Sociétés Saventes
CRAI	Comptes Rendus de l'Académie des Inscriptions et Belles-Lettres
DAM	Documents d'Archéologie Méridionale
DHA	Dialogues d'Histoire Ancienne
DossHA	Dossiers Histoire et Archéologie
FBW	Fundberichte aus Baden-Württemberg
G	Gallia
Germ	Germania
HelvArch	Helvetia Archaeologia
JRGZM	Jahrbuch des Römisch-Germanischen Zentralmuseum Mainz
JRS	Journal of Roman Studies
JSGU	Jahrbuch der Schweizerischen Gesellschaft für Urgeschichte
KJ	Kölner Jahrbuch
MEFRA	Mélanges de l'Ecole Française de Rome, Antiquité
MonPiot	Fondation Eugène Piot, Monuments et Mémoires
OJA	Oxford Journal of Archaeology
RA	Revue Archéologique
RAECE	Revue Archéologique de l'Est et du Centre-Est
RAN	Revue Archéologique de Narbonnaise
RAP	Revue Archéologique de Picardie
REA	Revue des Etudes Anciennes
REL	Revue des Etudes Latines
RevNord	Revue du Nord
RSL	Rivista di Studi Liguri
TZ	Trierer Zeitschrift

References to classical authors are abbreviated in general conformity with those in the larger Latin and Greek dictionaries that cite quotations. Full expansions of the titles can be found there.

AGACHE, R. 1970. *Détection aérienne de Vestiges protohistoriques, gallo-romains et médiévaux dans le Bassin de la Somme et ses Abords* (Amiens).

AGACHE, R. 1973. 'Découverte d'une très grande villa gallo-romaine en Normandie', *Arch* 65, 66–7.

AGACHE, R. 1975. 'La campagne à l'époque romaine dans les grandes plaines du Nord de la France d'après les photographies aériennes', *ANRW* II, 4, 658–713.

AGACHE, R. 1978. *La Somme pré-romaine et romaine* (Amiens).

AGACHE, R. AND BRÉART, B. 1975. *Atlas d'Archéologie aérienne de la Picardie I* (Amiens).

ALFÖLDY, G. 1974. 'The crisis of the third century as seen by contemporaries', *Greek, Roman and Byzantine Studies* 15, 89–111.

ALLAG, C. 1985. 'Le décor des cryptoportiques en Gaule', *RevNord* 67, 9–20.

ALLEN, D. F. 1976. 'Wealth, money and coinage in a Celtic society', in J. V. Megaw (ed.), *To Illustrate the Monuments* (London), 199–208.

ALLEN, D. F. 1980. *The Coins of the Ancient Celts* (Edinburgh).

AMAND, M. 1984. 'L'industrie, la taille et le commerce de la pierre dans le bassin du Tournaisis à l'époque romaine', *RevNord* 66, 209–19.

AMBARD, R. 1985. *Aix Romaine* (Aix).

AMY, R. AND GROS, P. 1979. *La Maison carrée de Nîmes* (Paris).

AMY, R. et al. 1962. *L'Arc d'Orange* (Paris).

ANDERSON, J. C. 1987. 'The date of the arch at Orange', *BJ* 187, 159–92.

ARCELIN, P. AND CAYOT, A. 1984. 'Réflexions sur l'abandon de l'agglomération hellénistique de Saint-Blaise', *RAN* 17, 53–70.

ARCELIN, P. et al. 1982. 'Le village protohistorique du Mont-Garou (Sanary, Var)', *DAM* 5, 53–137.

ARNAL, J., MAJUREL, R. AND PRADES, H. 1974. *Le Port de Lattara, Lattes, Hérault* (Bordighera/Montpellier).

ATKINSON, D. 1914. 'A hoard of samian ware from Pompeii', *JRS* 4, 27–64.

AUDIN, A. 1977. 'Les jeux de 177 à Lyon et le martyre des chrétiens', *Arch* 111, 18–27.

AUDIN, A. 1979. *Lyon: miroir de Rome dans les Gaules* (Paris).

AUDIN, A. 1985. 'Dossier des fouilles du sanctuaire lyonnais de Cybèle et de ses abords', *G* 43, 81–126.

AUDIN, A. AND BURNAND, Y. 1959. 'Chronologie des épitaphes romaines à Lyon', *REA* 61, 320–52.

AUDIN, A. AND BURNAND, Y. 1977. 'Le marché lyonnais de la pierre sous le Haut-Empire romain', *Actes 98e CNSS, St Etienne, 1973*, 143–56.

AUDIN, A. AND LE GLAY, M. 1970. 'L'amphithéâtre des Trois Gaules, première campagne', *G* 28, 67–89.

AUDIN, P. 1985. 'L'équipement des villes entre Gironde et Loire d'Auguste à Claude', in *Les Débuts de l'Urbanisation …*, 61–82.

AUDOUIN, E. 1902. 'La Minerve de Poitiers', *MonPiot* 9, 43–71.

BAATZ, D. 1974. 'Zur Grenzpolitik Hadrians in Obergermanien', in E. Birley et al. (eds), *Roman Frontier Studies 1969* (Cardiff), 112–24.

BAATZ, D. 1975. *Der Römische Limes* (2nd edition, Berlin).

BAATZ, D. AND HERRMANN, F.-R. 1982. (eds) *Die Römer in Hessen* (Stuttgart).

BABELON, E. 1916. *Le Trésor de Berthouville* (Paris).

BAKELS, C. C. 1984. 'Carbonised seeds from northern France', *Analecta Praehistorica Leidensia* 17, 1–27.

BALMELLE, C. AND DOUSSEAU, S. 1982. 'La mosaïque à l'Océan trouvée à Maubourguet (Hautes-Pyrénées)', *G* 40, 149–70.

BARATTE, F. 1984. *Römisches Silbergeschirr in den gallischen und germanischen Provinzen* (Aalen).

BARATTE, F. AND PAINTER, K. (eds) 1989. *Trésors d'Orfèvrerie gallo-romains* exhib. cat. (Paris).

BARATTE, F. et al. 1988. *Orfèvrerie gallo-romaine: le Trésor de Rethel* (Paris).

BARBET, A. 1987. 'La diffusion des Ier, IIe et IIIe styles pompéiens en Gaule', *Cahiers d'Archéologie Romande* 43 (Aventicum V), 7–27.

BARFIELD, L. et al. 1968. 'Ein Burgus in Froitzheim, Kreis Düren', *Rheinische Ausgrabungen* 3, 9–119.

BARRAL i ALTET, X. 1986. 'Le royaume visigothique de Gaule', *DossHA* 108, 12–17.

BARRAL I ALTET, X. AND DROCOURT, D. 1974. 'Le baptistère paléochrétien de Marseille', *Arch* 73, 6–19.

BARRAUD, D. 1984A. 'Porte-Dijeaux: Bordeaux à l'époque gauloise', *Arch* 192, 71–3.

BARRAUD, D. 1984B. 'L'ilot Saint-Christoly, arrière port de Burdigala', *Arch* 192, 61–5.

BARRUOL, G. 1969. *Les Peuples préromains du Sud-Est de la Gaule: étude de géographie historique* (Paris).

BARRUOL, G. 1985. 'Miroirs votifs découverts en Provence et dédiés à Sélène et à Aphroditè, *RAN* 18, 343–73.

BARRUOL, G. AND PY, M. 1978. 'Recherches récentes sur la ville antique d'Espeyran à Saint-Gilles-du-Gard', *RAN* 11, 19–100.

BARRUOL, G. *et al.* 1979. *Au Temps des Gaulois en Gaule méridionale* (Dijon).

BASSIER, C. *et al.* 1981. 'La grande mosaïque de Migennes (Yonne)', *G* 39, 123–48.

BASTIEN, P. AND METZGER, C. 1977. *Le Trésor de Beaurains (dit d'Arras)* (Arras).

BATS, M. 1982. 'Commerce et politique massaliètes aux IVe et IIIe siècles av. J.-C.', *La Parola del Passato* 37, 256–68.

BATS, M. AND BUI-THI-MAI 1984. 'Une étude pollinique aux origines de Beneharnum gallo-romaine (Lescar, Pyrénées-Atlantiques)', *Aquit* 2, 269–75.

BATS, M. AND TRÉZINY, H. (eds) 1986. *Etudes massaliètes I: le territoire de Marseille grecque* (Aix-en-Provence).

BAUCHHENSS, G. AND NEUMANN, G. (eds) 1987. *Matronen und verwandte Gottheiten* (Cologne).

BAUCHHENSS, G. AND NOELKE, P. 1981. *Die Jupitersäulen in den germanischen Provinzen* (Cologne/Bonn).

BAYARD, D. AND MASSY, J.-L. 1983. *Amiens romain: Samarobriva Ambianorum* (Heilly).

BÉAL, J.-C. AND FEUGÈRE, M. 1987. 'Epées miniatures à fourreau en os, d'époque romaine', *Germ* 65, 89–105.

BECHERT, T. 1982. *Römisches Germanien zwischen Rhein und Maas: die Provinz Germania Inferior* (Zürich).

BECK, F. *et al.* 1988. 'Mont-Beuvray: fouilles de la Chapelle (1984–1985)', *RAECE* 39, 107–27.

BECK, W. AND PLANCK, D. 1980. *Der Limes in Südwestdeutschland* (Stuttgart).

BEDON, R. 1984. *Les Carrières et les Carriers de la Gaule romaine* (Paris).

BEDON, R. *et al.* 1988. *Architecture et Urbanisme en Gaule romaine* (Paris).

BEHRENS, G. 1921. 'Eine römische Falschmünzerwerkstätte in Mainz-Kastel', *Mainzer Zeitschrift* 15/16, 25–31.

BEKKER-NIELSEN, T. 1984. *Bydannelse i det romerske Gallien* (Aarhus).

BELLET, M.-E. 1976. 'Les huileries gallo-romaines de Provence', *Arch* 92, 53–9.

BELOCH, J. 1889. 'Die Bevölkerung Galliens zur Zeit Caesars', *Rheinisches Museum für Philologie* 54, 414–45.

BELORA, N. 1987. 'Die Sklaverei im römischen Gallien', in E. Staerman *et al.*, *Die Sklaverei in den westlichen Provinzen des römischen Reiches im 1.–3. Jahrhundert* (Stuttgart), 103–46.

BÉMONT, C. AND JACOB, J.-P. 1986. *La Terre sigillée gallo-romaine* (Paris).

BÉNARD, J. 1987. 'César devant Alésia: les témoins sont dans le sol', *Revue Historique des Armées* 167, 29–43.

BENOIT, F. 1954. *Sarcophages paléochrétiens d'Arles et de Marseille* (Paris).

BENOIT, F. 1961. *L'Epave du Grand Congloué à Marseille* (Paris).

BENOIT, F. 1966. 'Le *martyrium* rupestre de l'abbaye Saint-Victor', *CRAI* (1966), 110–26.

BENOIT, F. 1968. 'Résultats historiques des fouilles d'Entremont (1946–1967)', *G* 26, 1–31.

BENOIT, F. 1969. *Art et Dieux de la Gaule* (Paris).

BENOIT, F. 1981. *Entremont: capitale celto-ligure des Salyens de Provence* (Gap).

BENOIT, J. 1985. 'L'étude des cadastres antiques: à propos d'Olbia de Provence', *DAM* 8, 25–48.

BÉRARD, F. *et al.* 1986. *Guide de l'Epigraphiste: bibliographie choisie des épigraphies antiques et médiévales* (Paris).

BERGER, L. 1976. 'Zur Datierung und Bedeutung der spätrömischen Befestigungsanlagen auf dem Wittnauer Horn', *JSGU* 59, 206–7.

BERGER, P. 1984. 'La Cybèle bisexuée des Bolards (Nuits-Saint-Georges, Côte-d'Or)', *RAECE* 35, 277–85.

BERNHARD, D. 1980. 'Zur Diskussion um die Chronologie Rheinzaberner Relieftöpfer', *Germ* 59, 79–93.

BERRY, W. E. 1987. 'Southern Burgundy in late Antiquity and the Middle Ages', in C. Crumley and W. Marquardt (eds), *Regional Dynamics: Burgundian landscapes in historical perspective* (San Diego), 447–607.

BERSU, G. 1945. *Das Wittnauer Horn* (Basel).

BERTIN, D. AND GUILLAUMET, J.-P. 1987. *Bibracte (Saône-et-Loire): une ville gauloise sur le Mont Beuvray* (Paris).

BESSAC. J.-C. 1980. 'Le rempart hellénistique de Saint-Blaise (Saint-Mitre-les-Remparts, BdR): techniques de construction', *DAM* 3, 137–57.

BESSAC, J.-C. 1986. 'La prospection archéologique des carrières de pierre à taille: approche méthodologique', *Aquit* 4, 151–71.

BESSAC, J.-C. AND BOULOUMIÉ, B. 1985. 'Les stèles de Glanum et de Saint-Blaise et les sanctuaires préromaines du Midi de la Gaule', *RAN* 18, 127–87.

BESSAC, J.-C. *et al.* 1987. *Ugernum: Beaucaire et le Beaucairois à l'époque romaine 1–2* (Caveirac).

BIARNE, J. AND GUILLEUX, J. 1980. 'Le Mans, la plus belle enceinte gallo-romaine du Bas-Empire en Gaule', *Arch* 145, 6–19.

BIEL, J. 1985. *Der Keltenfürst von Hochdorf* (Stuttgart).

BILLORET, R. 1980. *The Ancient Town of Grand, Vosges* (Colmar).

BINSFELD, W. 1975. 'Eifelbären und römische Kunst', *Kurtrierisches Jahrbuch* 15, 155–9.

BIRLEY, A. R. 1971. 'Roman frontier policy under Marcus Aurelius', in S. Applebaum (ed.), *Seventh Congress of Roman Frontier Studies* (Tel Aviv), 7–13.

BIRLEY, A. R. 1988. *The African Emperor, Septimius Severus* (London).

BLAGG, T. F. 1983. 'The reuse of monumental masonry in late Roman defensive walls', in J. Maloney and B. Hobley (eds), *Roman Urban Defences in the West* (London), 130–5.

BLAGG, T. F. AND KING, A. C. (eds) 1984. *Military and Civilian in Roman Britain: cultural relationships in a frontier province* (Oxford).

BLANC, A. 1980. *La Cité de Valence à la Fin de l'Antiquité* (Paris).

BLANCHARD-LEMÉE, M. 1981. 'La villa à mosaïques de Mienne-Marboué (Eure-et-Loir)', *G* 39, 63–83.

BLANCHARD-LEMÉE, M. *et al.* 1986. 'Deux maisons à pavements d'*Augustodunum*, Autun (Saône-et-Loire)', *G* 44, 121–49.

BLANCHET, A. 1934. 'Statuettes de bronze trouvées près des Sources de la Seine', *MonPiot* 34, 59–74.

BLOEMERS, J. H. 1978. *Rijswijk (Z. H.), 'De Bult': eine Siedlung der Cananefaten* (Amersfoort).

BLOEMERS, J. H. forthcoming. 'Lower Germany: *plura consilia quam vi*', in T. Blagg and M. Millett (eds), *The Early Roman Empire in the West* (Oxford).

BLUMENKRANZ, B. 1969. 'Les premières implantations de juifs en France: du Ier au début du Ve siècle', *CRAI* (1969), 162–74.

BOARDMAN, J. 1980. *The Greeks Overseas. Their Early Colonies and Trade* (2nd edition, London).

BOBER, P. F. 1951. 'Cernunnos: the origin and transformation of a Celtic divinity', *AJA* 55, 13–51.

BÖCKING, W. 1974. *Die Römer am Niederrhein und in Norddeutschland* (Frankfurt).

BOGAERS, J. 1955. *De Gallo-Romeinse Tempels te Elst in de Over-Betuwe* (s'Gravenhage).

BOGAERS, J. 1972. 'Civitas und Civitas-Hauptorte in der nördlichen Germania Inferior', *BJ* 172, 310–33.

BOGAERS, J. *et al.* 1980. *Noviomagus: auf den Spuren der Römer in Nijmegen* (Nijmegen).

BÖGLI, H. 1984. *Aventicum: la ville romaine et le musée* (Lausanne).

BÖHME, H. W. 1974. *Germanische Grabfunde des 4. bis 5. Jahrhunderts* (Munich).

BÖHME, H. W. 1975. 'Archäologische Zeugnisse zur Geschichte der Markomannenkriege (166–180 n. Chr.)', *JRGZM* 22, 153–217.

BOHNER, K. (ed.) 1976. *Les Relations entre l'Empire romain tardif, l'Empire franc et ses voisins* (Nice).

BOIRON, R. *et al.* 1986. *Les Fouilles de l'Aire du Chapitre* (Aix-en-Provence).

BOISSINOT, P. 1984. 'Les constructions en terre du IIe s. av. J.-C. sur l'oppidum du Baou-Roux (Bouc-Bel-Air, BdR)', *DAM* 7, 79–96.

BONNAMOUR, L. 1975. 'Le port gauloise et gallo-romaine de Chalon: état de la recherche', *Mémoires de la Société d'Histoire et d'Archéologie de Chalon-sur-Saône* 45, 61–73.

BONNARD, L. 1913. *La Navigation intérieure de la Gaule à l'Epoque gallo-romaine* (Paris).

BONNET, C. 1974. 'Genève, capitale burgonde', *Arch* 66, 12–17.

BONNET, C. 1986. *Genève aux premiers Temps chrétiens* (Geneva).

BONNET, C. 1987. 'The archaeological site of the cathedral of Saint Peter (Saint-Pierre), Geneva', *World Archaeology* 18, 330–40.

BOON, G. C. 1983. 'Some Romano-British domestic shrines and their inhabitants', in B. Hartley and J. Wacher (eds), *Rome and her Northern Provinces* (Gloucester), 33–55.

BORGER, H. 1961. 'Die Ausgrabungen unter der Stiftskirche des hl. Viktor zu Xanten in den Jahren 1945–1960', *BJ* 161, 396–448.

BOST, J.-P. 1986. '"P. Crassum … in Aquitaniam profisci iubet": les chemins de Crassus en 56 avant Jésus-Christ', *REA* 88, 21–40.

BOUCHER, S. 1973. 'Trajets terrestres du commerce étrusques aux Ve et IVe siècles avant J.-C.', *RA* (1973), 1, 79–96.

BOUCHER, S. 1976. *Recherches sur les Bronzes figurés de Gaule pré-romaine et romaine* (Rome).

BOULEY, E. 1983. 'Les théâtres cultuels de Belgique et des Germanies', *Latomus* 42, 546–71.

BOULOUMIÉ, B. 1973. 'Les oenochoés en bronze du type Schnabelkanne en France et en Belgique', *G* 31, 1–35.

BOULOUMIÉ, B. (ed.) 1979. *Le bucchero nero étrusque et sa diffusion en Gaule méridionale* (Brussels).

BOULOUMIÉ, B. 1982. 'Saint-Blaise et Marseille au VIe s. av. J.-C. L'hypothèse étrusque', *Latomus* 41, 74–91.

BOULOUMIÉ, B. 1984. *Un Oppidum gaulois à Saint-Blaise en Provence* (Dijon).

BOULOUMIÉ, B. *et al.* 1981. 'Le rempart hellénistique de Saint-Blaise II. Sondage stratigraphique de la campagne 1981', *Acta Antiqua* 29, 227–66.

BOUTHIER, A. 1977. 'L'exploitation et l'utilisation de la houille en Gaule romaine: une preuve apportée par une fouille de sauvetage à Cosne-sur-Loire (Nièvre)', *Actes 98e CNSS, St Etienne*, 1971, 143–56.

BRAEMER, F. 1973. 'Recherches sur l'implantation des sanctuaires dans la Gaule romaine', in *Pour une Géographie sacrée de l'Occident romaine* conf. proc. (Tours), 144–55.

BRAEMER, F. 1982. 'L'ornementation des établissements ruraux de l'Aquitaine méridionale pendant le Haut-Empire et la Basse Antiquité', *Actes 104e CNSS, Bordeaux, 1979*, 103–46.

BRAEMER, F. (ed.) 1986. *Les Ressources minérales et l'Histoire de leur Exploitation* (Paris).

BRANDT, R. AND SLOFSTRA, J. (eds) 1983. *Roman and Native in the Low Countries* (Oxford).

BRAUDEL, F. 1988. *The Identity of France, volume 1: history and environment* (London).

BRIDGER, C. AND SIEGMUND, F. 1987. 'Die Xantener Stiftsimmunität', *Rheinische Ausgrabungen* 27, 63–133.

BROGAN, O. AND DESFORGES, E. 1940. 'Gergovia', *Archaeological Journal* 97, 1–36.

BROWN, P. 1981. *The Cult of the Saints* (London).

BRULET, R. 1978a. 'Fortifications et défense du territoire au Bas-Empire en Gaule septentrionale', *Travaux militaires en Gaule romaine et dans les Provinces du Nord-Ouest* conf. proc. (Paris), 3–20.

BRULET, R. 1978b. *La Fortification du Hauterecenne à Furfooz* (Louvain-La-Neuve).

BRUN, J.-P. 1986. *L'Oleiculture antique en Provence: les huileries du département du Var* (Paris).

BRUNAUX, J.-L. *et al.* 1985. *Gournay I* (Amiens).

BRUNT, P. 1959. 'The revolt of Vindex and the fall of Nero', *Latomus* 18, 531–59.

BRUNT, P. 1960. 'Tacitus on the Batavian revolt', *Latomus* 19, 494–517.

BUCHE, J. 1903. 'Le Mars de Coligny', *MonPiot* 10, 61–90.

BUCHSENSCHUTZ, O. 1977. 'Recherches sur l'Age du Fer en Berry: l'exemple du Canton de Levroux (Indre)', *Marburger Studien zur Vor- und Frühgeschichte* 1, 87–105.

BUCHSENSCHUTZ, O. (ed.) 1981. *Les Structures d'Habitat à l'Age du Fer en Europe tempérée* (Paris).

BUCHSENSCHUTZ, O. 1982. 'Le village gaulois des Arènes à Levroux', *Arch* 167, 44–7.

BUCHSENSCHUTZ, O. 1984. *Structures d'Habitat et Fortifications de l'Age du Fer en France septentrionale* (Paris).

BUCHSENSCHUTZ, O. AND RALSTON, I. B. 1987. 'Réflexions sur l'économie de la Gaule d'après César et les données archéologiques', in *Mélanges offerts au Docteur J.-B. Colbert-de-Beaulieu* (Paris), 163–73.

BULLIOT, J.-G. AND THIOLLIER, F. 1892. *La Mission et le Culte de Saint-Martin … dans le Pays éduen* (Autun).

BURDY, J. 1986. 'Les aqueducs de Lugdunum', *L'Araire* 66, 5–75.

CADOUX, J.-L. 1984a. 'Le sanctuaire gallo-romain de Ribemont-sur-Ancre (Somme): état de recherches en 1983', *RevNord* 66, 125–45.

CADOUX, J.-L. 1984b. 'L'ossuaire gaulois de Ribemont-sur-Ancre (Somme). Premières observations, premières questions', *G* 42, 53–78.

CAHEN-DELHAYE, A. *et al.* (eds) 1984. *Les Celtes en Belgique et dans le Nord de la France* (Lille).

CAHN, H. AND KAUFMANN-HEINIMANN, A. (eds) 1984. *Der spätrömische Silberschatz von Kaiseraugst* (Derendingen).

CAMPBELL, J. B. 1984. *The Emperor and the Roman Army 31 BC–AD 235* (Oxford).

CARRÉ, R. 1978. 'Les cultes voconces', *DHA* 4, 119–33.

CASEY, P. J. 1977. 'Carausius and Allectus – rulers in Gaul?', *Brit* 8, 283–301.

CAVAILLÈS-LLOPIS, M.-T. 1986. 'Céramiques de l'antiquité tardive à Marseille', *DAM* 9, 167–95.

CHABOT, L. 1983. 'L'*oppidum* de la Cloche aux Pennes-Mirabeau (Bouches-du-Rhône)', *RAN* 16, 39–80.

CHADWICK, H. 1967. *The Early Church* (Harmondsworth).

CHADWICK, O. 1968. *John Cassian* (Cambridge).

CHANTRAINE, H. *et al.* 1984. *Das römische Neuss* (Stuttgart).

CHARLIN, G. *et al.* 1978. 'L'épave antique de la Baie de Cavalière (Le Lavandou, Var)', *Archéonautica* 2, 9–93.

CHARMASSON, J. 1968. 'Grecs et Celtes dans la basse vallée du Rhône', *RSL* 34, 107–26.

CHARMASSON, J. 1970. 'Un oppidum du Bas-Empire, Lombren à Venejean (Gard)', *Arch* 36, 54–61, 88.

CHARMASSON, J. 1971. 'Quelques aspects de la civilisation gallo-grecque de la basse vallée du Rhône', *Arch* 42, 30–7; 43, 44–51.

CHASTAGNOL, A. 1981. 'Une firme de commerce maritime entre l'Ile de Bretagne et le continent gaulois à l'époque des Sévères', *Zeitschrift für Papyrologie und Epigraphik* 43, 63–6.

CHASTEL, J. *et al.* 1988. 'L'habitat gallo-romain du Pré de la Cour à Montagnieu (Ain)', *RAECE* 39, 135–40.

CHAUSSERIE-LAPRÉE, J. et al. 1988. *Le Village gauloise de Martigues* (Dijon).

CHILVER, G. E. 1957. 'The army in politics, AD 68–70', *JRS* 47, 29–35.

CHOUQUER, G. et al. 1987. *Structures agraires en Italie centro-méridionale* (Paris).

CHRIST, K. 1974. 'Caesar und Ariovist', *Chiron* 4, 251–92.

CHRISTLEIN, R. 1979. *Die Alamannen* (2nd edition, Stuttgart).

CHRISTOL, M. AND GOUDINEAU, C. 1988. 'Nîmes et les Volques Arécomiques au Ier siècle avant J.-C.', *G* 45, 87–103.

CLAVEL, M. 1970. *Béziers et son Territoire dans l'Antiquité* (Paris).

CLAVEL-LÉVÊQUE, M. 1977. *Marseille grecque: la dynamique d'un impérialisme marchand* (Marseille).

CLAVEL-LÉVÊQUE, M. (ed.) 1983. *Cadastres et Espace rural* (Paris).

CLAVEL-LÉVÊQUE, M. 1985. 'Mais ou sont les druides d'antan …? Tradition religieuse et identité culturelle en Gaule', *DHA* 11, 557–604.

CLEARY, A. 1989. *The Ending of Roman Britain* (London).

CLERC, M. 1927–9. *Massalia: histoire de Marseille dans l'antiquité, des origines à la fin de l'Empire romaine de l'Ouest*, 2 vols (Marseille).

COLARDELLE, R. AND M. 1977. 'Une basilique funéraire à Saint-Julien en Genevois', *Arch* 111, 64–71.

COLBERT DE BEAULIEU, J.-B. AND RICHARD, J.-C. 1969. 'La numismatique de la Gaule et la numismatique de Narbonnaise', *RSL* 35, 90–100.

COLLIS, J. 1984a. *The European Iron Age* (London).

COLLIS, J. 1984b. *Oppida: earliest towns north of the Alps* (Sheffield).

COLLIS, J. et al. (eds) 1982. *Le Deuxième Age du Fer en Auvergne et en Forez* (Sheffield).

COLLS, D. et al. 1977. 'L'épave Port-Vendres II et le commerce de la Bétique à l'époque de Claude', *Archéonautica* 1.

CONNOLLY, P. 1981. *Greece and Rome at War* (London).

COQUET, Dom 1977. 'A Ligugé, un ensemble exceptionnel d'art chrétien primitif', *Arch* 113, 23–30.

CORROCHER, J. 1987. 'Découverte d'un four à chaux gallo-romain', *Arch* 220, 8.

CORSI-SCIALLANO, M. AND LIOU, B. 1985. 'Les épaves de Tarraconnaise à chargement d'amphores Dressel 2–4', *Archéonautica* 5.

COULON, G. 1986. 'Découverte d'un autel domestique gallo-romaine', *Arch* 218, 6–8.

COULON, G. AND HOLMGREN, J. 1982. 'L'habitat rural gallo-romain en Bas-Berry', *Arch* 167, 48–50, 73–7.

COUPRY, J. 1968. 'Olbia de Ligurie', *RSL* 34, 237–46.

COUPRY, J. 1986. 'Les fortifications d'Olbia de Ligurie: prospections, questions', in P. Leriche and H. Tréziny (eds), *La Fortification dans l'Histoire du Monde grec* (Paris), 389–99.

COUPRY, J. AND GIFFAULT, M. 1982. 'La clientèle d'un sanctuaire d'Aristée aux Iles d'Hyères (Ier siècle avant J.-C.)', *La Parola del Passato* 37, 360–70.

CUNLIFFE, B. W. (ed.) 1981. *Coinage and Society in Britain and Gaul* (London).

CUNLIFFE, B. W. 1988. *Greeks, Romans and Barbarians: spheres of interaction* (London).

CÜPPERS, H. 1969. 'Der bemalte Reliefsarkophag aus der Gruft unter der Quirinuskapelle auf dem Friedhof von St Matthias', *TZ* 32, 269–93.

CÜPPERS, H. 1970. 'Wein und Weinbau zur Römerzeit im Rheinland', *Gymasium Beiheft* 7, 138–45.

CÜPPERS, H. 1975. *Römische Villa Otrang* (Mainz).

CÜPPERS, H. AND BIÉVELET, H. 1965. 'Die römischen Fora in Bavai und Trier', *TZ* 28, 53–67.

CÜPPERS, H. et al. 1982. *Aquae Granni: Beiträge zur Archäologie von Aachen* (Cologne/Bonn).

CZUTH, B. 1965. *Die Quellen der Geschichte der Bagauden* (Szeged).

DANGRÉAUX, B. AND DESBAT, A. 1988. 'Les amphores du dépotoir flavien du Bas- de-Loyasse à Lyon', *G* 45, 115–53.

DAUBIGNY, A. 1979. 'Reconnaissance des formes de la dépendance gauloise', *DHA* 5, 145–89.

DAUBIGNY, A. AND GUILLAUMET, J.-P. 1985. 'L'entrave de Glanon (Côte-d'Or): les Eduens et l'esclavage', in *Les Ages du Fer dans la Vallée de la Saône*, conf. proc. (Paris), 171–7.

DAVID-ROY, M. 1979. 'Les baptistères de la Gaule', *Arch* 135, 51–9.

DAVIES, O. 1935. *Roman Mines in Europe* (Oxford).

Deae Nehalenniae 1971, exhib. cat. (Middelburg/Leiden).

DE BOE, G. AND HUBERT, F. 1977. 'Une installation portuaire d'époque romaine à Pommeroeul', *AB* 192.

DEBORD, J. 1982. 'Premier bilan de huit années de fouilles à Villeneuve-Saint-Germain (Aisne)', *RAP* (1982), 213–64.

DEBORD, J. 1984. 'Les origines gauloises de Soissons: oscillation d'un site urbain', *RAP* (1984), 3/4, 27–40.

DECHANDOL, H. et al. 1983. 'Le grand domaine viticole du Molard', *DossHA* 78, 56–7.

DECKER, K.-V. AND SELZER, W. 1976. 'Mogontiacum: Mainz von der Zeit des Augustus bis zum Ende der römischen Herrschaft', *ANRW* II, 5.1, 457–559.

DEDET, B. 1987. *Habitat et Vie quotidienne en Languedoc au Milieu de l'Age du Fer: l'unité domestique no. 1 de Gailhan, Gard* (Paris).

DE LAET, S. J. 1966. 'Claude et la romanisation de la Gaule septentrionale', in R. Chevallier (ed.), *Mélanges d'Archéologie et d'Histoire offerts à André Piganiol* (Paris), 951–61.

DE LAVERGNE, E. et al. 1982. 'Résultats de 17 années de fouilles à Masamas (Saint-Léomer)', *Bulletin de la Société des Antiquaires de l'Ouest* ser. 4, 16, 469–78.

DELESTRE, X. 1988. *Saint-Pierre-aux-Nonnains* (Paris).

DELMAIRE, R. 1976. *Etude archéologique de la Partie orientale de la Cité des Morins (Civitas Morinorum)* (Arras).

DELPLACE, C. 1978. 'Les potiers dans la société et l'économie de l'Italie et de la Gaule au Ier siècle av. et au Ier siècle ap. J.-C.', *Ktema* 3, 55–76.

DEMAREZ, J.-D. 1987. 'Les bâtiments à fonction économique dans les fundi de la provincia Belgica', *Amphora* 50, 1–36.

DEMIANS D'ARCHIMBAUD, G. 1971. 'Les fouilles de Saint-Victor de Marseille', *CRAI* (1971), 87–117.

DEMIANS D'ARCHIMBAUD, G. 1972. 'Le matériel paléochrétienne de la Grotte de l'Hortus', in H. de Lumley (ed.), *La Grotte de l'Hortus (Valflaunès, Hérault)* (Marseille), 635–57.

DEMIANS D'ARCHIMBAUD, G. 1974. 'Saint-Victor de Marseille: fouilles récentes et nouvelles interprétations architecturales', *CRAI* (1974), 313–45.

DEMOLON, P. 1973. 'Le village mérovingien de Brebières', *Arch* 65, 39–46.

DEMOUGEOT, E. 1979. *La Formation de l'Europe et les Invasions barbares* 2 vols (Paris).

DESBAT, A. 1984. *Les Fouilles de la Rue des Farges à Lyon, 1974–1980* (Lyon).

DE VESLY, L. 1909. *Les Fana ou petits Temples gallo-romaines de la Région normande* (Rouen).

DEYTS, S. 1983. *Les Bois sculptés des Sources de la Seine* (Paris).

DEYTS, S. 1988. 'Les ex-voto de guérison en Gaule', *DossHA* 123, 82–7.

DIETZ, K. 1986. 'Zum Feldzug Caracallas gegen die Germanen', *Studien zu den Militärgrenzen Roms III* (Stuttgart), 135–8.

DOMERGUE, C. et al. 1977. 'L'activité de la fonderie gallo-romaine des Martys (Aude)', *Actes 98e CNSS, St Etienne, 1973*, 115–42.

DOPPELFELD, O. (ed.) 1967. *Römer am Rhein* exhib. cat. (Cologne).

DOPPELFELD, O. 1975. 'Das römische Köln, I: Ubier-Oppidum und Colonia Agrippinensium', *ANRW* II, 4, 783–824.

DOREAU, J. et al. 1985. 'Contribution à l'étude du forum de Vésone (Périgeux, Dordogne)', *Aquit* 3, 91–104.

DRACK, W. (ed.) 1975. *Ur- und Frühgeschichtliche Archäologie der Schweiz V: die römische Epoche* (Basel).

DRACK, W. AND FELLMAN, R. (eds) 1988. *Die Römer in der Schweiz* (Stuttgart).

DRINKWATER, J. F. 1975. 'Lyon: "natural capital" of Gaul?', *Brit* 6, 133–40.

DRINKWATER, J. F. 1978. 'The rise and fall of the Gallic Iulii', *Latomus* 37, 817–50.

DRINKWATER, J. F. 1982. 'The wool textile industry of Gallia Belgica and the Secundinii of Igel', *Textile History* 13, 111–28.

DRINKWATER, J. F. 1983. *Roman Gaul* (Beckenham).

DRINKWATER, J. F. 1985. 'Urbanisation in the Three Gauls: some observations', in F. Grew and B. Hobley (eds), *Roman Urban Topography in Britain and the Western Empire* (London), 49–55.

DRINKWATER, J. F. 1987. *The Gallic Empire: separatism and continuity in the north-western provinces of the Roman Empire, AD 260–274* (Stuttgart).

DUBY, G. (ed.) 1980. *Histoire de la France urbaine. 1. La Ville antique* (Paris).

DUFOURNET, P. 1976. 'Pierre blanche et carrières antiques de Seyssel', *Actes 96e CNSS, Toulouse, 1971*, 245–72.

DUHAMEL, P. 1973. 'Les fours céramiques gallo-romaines', *Recherches d'Archéologie Celtique et Gallo-Romaine* 5, 141–54.

DUHAMEL, P. 1975. 'Les ateliers céramiques de la Gaule romaine', *DossHA* 9, 12–20.

DUHAMEL, P. 1979. 'Morphologie et évolution des fours céramiques en Europe occidentale', *Acta Praehistorica et Archaeologica* 9/10, 49–76.

DUMASY, F. 1989. 'Argentomagus', *DossHA* 134, 64–8.

DUNCAN-JONES, R. P. 1985. 'Who paid for public buildings in Roman cities?', in F. Grew and B. Hobley (eds), *Roman Urban Topography in Britain and the Western Empire* (London), 28–33.

DURU, R. 1972. 'Aux origines chrétiennes de Bordeaux: les fouilles de Saint-Seurin', *Arch* 47, 18–24.

DUVAL, P.-M. 1961. *Paris Antique, des Origines au Troisième Siècle* (Paris).

DUVAL, P.-M. 1968. 'Le milliaire de Domitius et l'organisation de la Narbonnaise', *RAN* 1, 3–6.

DUVAL, P.-M. AND PINAULT, G. 1986. *Recueil des Inscriptions Gauloises (RIG) III, Les Calendriers* (Paris).

DUVAL, P.-M. AND QUONIAM, P. 1963. 'Relevés inédits des monuments antiques d'Autun', *G* 21, 155–89.

DUVAL, Y. AND PICARD, J.-C. (eds) 1986. *L'Inhumation Privilégiée du IVe au VIIIe Siècle en Occident* (Paris).

DYSON, S. L. 1971. 'Native revolts in the Roman Empire', *Historia* 20, 239–74.

DYSON, S. L. 1975. 'Native revolt patterns in the Roman Empire', *ANRW* II, 3, 138–75.

DYSON, S. L. 1985. *The Creation of the Roman Frontier* (Princeton).

EBEL, C. 1976. *Transalpine Gaul: the emergence of a Roman province* (Leiden).

ELLIS, S. P. 1988. 'The end of the Roman house', *AJA* 92, 565–76.

ESPÉRANDIEU, E. 1967. *L'Amphithéâtre de Nîmes* (2nd edition, Paris).

ESPÉRANDIEU, E. et al. 1907–81. *Recueil général des Bas-reliefs, Statues et Bustes de la Gaule romaine* (Paris).

ESSER, K. H. 1972. 'Mogontiacum', *BJ* 172, 212–27.

ETIENNE, R. 1962. *Bordeaux Antique* (Bordeaux).

EUZENNAT, M. 1981. 'Ancient Marseille in the light of recent excavations', *AJA* 84, 133–40.

EYGUN, F. 1964. 'Le baptistère Saint-Jean de Poitiers', *G* 22, 137–72.

FAVORY, F. 1974. 'Le monde des potiers gallo-romains', *DossHA* 6, 90–102.

FAVORY, F. 1980. 'Détection des cadastres antiques par filtrage optique: Gaule et Campanie', *MEFRA* 92, 347–86.

FELLENDORF-BÖRNER, G. 1986. 'Die bildlichen Darstellungen der Epona auf den Denkmälern Baden-Württembergs', *FBW* 10, 77–141.

FERDIÈRE, A. 1988. *Les Campagnes en Gaule romaine* 2 vols (Paris).

FERDIÈRE, A. et al. 1979–81. 'Fouille de sauvetage du site gallo-romain de la "Fosse-Dieppe" à Dambron (E.-et-L.)', *Revue Archéologique du Loiret* 5, 31–48; 6, 29–83; 7, 51–96.

FEUGÈRE, M. et al. 1985. 'Les aiguilles à cataracte de Montbellet (Saône-et-Loire): contribution à l'étude de l'ophtalmologie antique et islamique', *JRGZM* 32, 436–508.

FÉVRIER, P.-A. 1973. 'The origin and growth of the cities of southern Gaul to the third century AD: an assessment of the most recent archaeological discoveries', *JRS* 63, 1–28.

FÉVRIER, P.-A. 1975. 'L'habitat dans la Gaule méridionale (IIe–Ier siècle avant notre ère)', *Cahiers Ligures de Préhistoire et d'Archéologie* 24, 7–25.

FÉVRIER, P.-A. 1977. *Fréjus (Forum Julii) et la basse vallée d'Argens* (2nd edition, Cuneo).

FÉVRIER, P.-A. 1978. 'Problèmes de l'habitat du Midi méditerranéen à la fin de l'Antiquité et dans le Haut-Moyen Age', *JRGZM* 25, 208–47.

FÉVRIER, P.-A. 1980. 'Vetera et nova: le poids du passé, les germes de l'avenir, IIIe–VIe siècle', and other sections in Duby 1980, 101–23, 393–493.

FÉVRIER, P.-A. 1981. *Le Groupe épiscopal de Fréjus* (Paris).

FÉVRIER, P.-A. 1983. 'Le souvenir de la petite patrie et l'histoire', in *La Patrie gauloise d'Agrippa au VIe siècle*, conf. proc. (Lyon), 19–25.

FICHES, J.-L. 1986. *Les Maisons gallo-romaines d'Ambrussum (Villetelle-Hérault): la fouille du secteur IV 1976–1980* (Paris).

FILTZINGER, P. et al. 1986. *Die Römer in Baden-Württemberg* (3rd edition, Stuttgart).

FISHWICK, D. 1972. 'The temple of the Three Gauls', *JRS* 62, 46–52.

FISHWICK, D. 1978. 'The development of provincial ruler worship in the western Roman Empire', *ANRW* II, 16, 2, 1201–53.

FISHWICK, D. 1987. *The Imperial Cult in the Latin West* 2 vols (Leiden).

FITZPATRICK, A. 1985. 'The distribution of Dressel 1 amphorae in North-West Europe', *OJA* 4, 305–40.

FLETCHER, LORD 1980. 'The monastery at Lérins', *Journal of the British Archaeological Association* 133, 17–29.

FOLLMANN-SCHULZ, A.-B. 1986. 'Die römischen Tempelanlagen in der Provinz Germania Inferior', *ANRW* II, 18, 1, 672–793.

FORMENTI, F. et al. 1978. 'Une amphore "Lamboglia 2" contenant du vin dans l'épave de la Madrague de Giens', *Archéonautica* 2, 95–100.

FORMIGÉ, J. 1924. (Note on Vienne temple inscription), *CRAI* (1924), 275–9.

FORMIGÉ, J. 1949. *La Trophée des Alpes (La Turbie)* (Paris).

FORRER, R. 1911. 'Ein versunkener spätantike Mühlsteintransport in Wanzenau bei Strassburg', *Cahiers d'Archéologie et d'Histoire d'Alsace* 1911, 131–43.

FORRIÈRES, C. et al. 1987. *Etude de la Métallurgie du Fer du Vicus gallo-romain de Bliesbruck (Moselle)* (Paris).

FOUET, G. 1969. *La Villa gallo-romaine de Montmaurin* (Paris).

FREMERSDORF, F. 1933. *Der römische Gutshof Köln-Mungersdorf* (Berlin).

FREMERSDORF, F. 1956. *Das römische Haus mit dem Dionysos-Mosaik vor dem Südportal des Kölner Domes* (Berlin).

FREMERSDORF, F. 1966. 'Die Anfänge der römischen Glashütten Kölns', *KJ* 9, 24ff.

FREND, W. H. 1980. *Town and Country in the Early Christian Centuries* (London).

FREND, W. H. 1984. *The Rise of Christianity* (London).

FRERE, S. S. 1979. 'Town planning in the western provinces', in *Festschrift zum 75jährigen Bestehen der Römisch-Germanischen Kommission* (Mainz), 87–104.

FRÉZOULS, E. (ed.) 1982. *Les Villes antiques de la France. Belgique 1, Amiens, Beauvais, Grand, Metz* (Strasbourg).

FRÉZOULS, E. 1984. 'Evergétisme et construction romaine dans les Trois Gaules et les Germanies', *RevNord* 66, 27–54.

FULFORD, M. G. 1985. 'Roman material in barbarian society, *c.* 200 BC–*c.* AD 400', in T. Champion and J. Megaw (eds), *Settlement and Society: aspects of West European prehistory in the first millenium BC* (Leicester), 91–108.

FURGER-GUNTI, A. 1979. *Die Ausgrabungen im Basler Münster I: die spätkeltische und augusteische Zeit* (Solothurn).

GABBA, E. 1988. 'Significato storico della conquista Augustea delle Alpi', in M. Vacchina (ed.), *La Valle d'Aosta e l'Arco Alpino nella Politica del Mondo Antico* (Quart), 53–61.

GABELMANN, H. 1987. 'Römische Grabbauten der Nordprovinzen im 2. u. 3. Jh. n. Chr.', in H. von Hesberg and P. Zanker (eds), *Römische Gräberstrassen* (Munich), 291–308.

GAITSCH, W. 1986. 'Grundformen römischer Landsiedlungen im Westen der CCAA', *BJ* 186, 397–427.

GALLET DE SANTERRE, H. 1980. *Ensérune: les silos de la terrasse est* (Paris).

GALLETIER, E. 1950. 'La mort du Maximien d'après le panégyrique de 310 et la vision de Constantine au temple d'Apollon', *REA* 52, 288–99.

GALLIOU, P. 1983. *L'Armorique Romaine* (Braspars).

GALLIOU, P. 1986. 'Wine and the Atlantic trade in the later Iron Age', in P. Johnston (ed.), *The Archaeology of the Channel Islands* (Chichester).

GARBSCH, J. 1970. *Der spätrömische Donau–Iller–Rhein–Limes* (Stuttgart).

GARBSCH, J. 1982. *Terra Sigillata: ein Weltreich im Spiegel seines Luxusgeschirrs* (Munich).

GARBSCH, J. 1988. 'Übersicht über den spätrömischen Donau-Iller-Rhein-Limes', in J. Garbsch and P. Kos, *Das spätrömische Kastell Vemania bei Isny I* (Munich), 105–27.

GAUTHIER, N. 1980. *L'Evangelisation des Pays de la Moselle* (Paris).

GAUTHIER, N. AND PICARD, G.-C. (eds) 1986–7. *Topographie chrétienne des Cités de la Gaule, I: Trèves, II: Aix et Embrun, III: Vienne et Arles, IV: Lyon, V: Tours* (Paris).

GAYRAUD, M. 1981. *Narbonne antique des origines à la fin du IIIe siècle* (Paris).

GEARY, P. J. 1988. *Before France and Germany: the creation and transformation of the Merovingian world* (New York/Oxford).

GECHTER, M. 1979. 'Die Anfänge des Niedergermanischen Limes', *BJ* 179, 1–138.

GECHTER, M. forthcoming. 'Early Roman military installations and Ubian settlements in the Lower Rhine', in T. Blagg and M. Millett (eds), *The Early Roman Empire in the West* (Oxford).

GECHTER, M. AND KUNOW, J. 1986. 'Zur ländlichen Besiedlung des Rheinlandes in römischer Zeit', *BJ* 186, 377–96.

GELZER, M. 1968. *Caesar, Politician and Statesman* (Oxford).

GÉRIN-RICARD, H. DE 1927. *Le Sanctuaire préromaine de Roquepertuse* (Marseille).

GILLES, K.-J. 1985. *Spätrömische Höhensiedlungen in Eifel and Hunsrück* (Trier).

GIOT, P.-R. 1973. 'Les caractères originaux de l'Age du Fer en Armorique', *Etudes Celtiques* 13, 595–606.

GIOT, P.-R. 1983. 'La migration des Bretons: le problème de l'immigration des Bretons insulaires en Armorique', in L. Buchet (ed.), *Le Phenomène des Grandes ''Invasions'': realité ethnique ou échanges culturels* (Valbonne), 45–50.

GIOT, P.-R. AND MONNIER, J.-L. 1977. 'Le cimetière des anciens Bretons de Saint-Urnel ou Saint-Saturnin en Plomeur (Finistère)', *G* 35, 141–71.

GJØDESEN, M. 1963. 'Greek bronzes: a review article', *AJA* 67, 333–51.

GLASBERGEN, W. AND GROENMAN-VAN WAATERINGE, W. 1974. *The Pre-Flavian Garrisons of Valkenburg Z. H.* (Amsterdam).

GOGUEY, R. 1978. 'La forteresse de legionnaires de Mirebeau', in *Travaux militaires en Gaule romaine et dans les Provinces du Nord-Ouest*, conf. proc. (Paris), 329–33.

GOLVIN, J.-C. 1988. *L'Amphithéâtre romain* 2 vols (Paris).

GOSE, E. 1958. *Katalog der frühchristlichen Inschriften in Trier* (Berlin).

GOSE, E. 1972. *Der gallo-römische Tempelbezirk im Altbachtal zu Trier* (Mainz).

GOUDINEAU, C. 1974. 'La céramique dans l'économie de la Gaule', *DossHA* 6, 103–9.

GOUDINEAU, C. 1976. 'Une enceinte protohistorique: l'oppidum du Fort à Taradeau', in *UISPP Livret-Guide B3. Sites de l'Age du Fer et gallo-romains de la Région de Nice* (Nice), 7–39.

GOUDINEAU, C. 1979. *Les Fouilles de la Maison du Dauphin à Vaison-la-Romaine* (Paris).

GOUDINEAU, C. 1980. 'Les villes de la paix romaine' and other sections in Duby 1980, 42–69, 72–100, 141–93, 233–391.

GOUDINEAU, C. 1983. 'Marseilles, Rome and Gaul from the third to the first century BC', in P. Garnsey *et al.* (eds), *Trade in the Ancient Economy* (London), 76–86.

GOUDINEAU, C. 1984. 'Un contrepoids de pressoir à huile d'Entremont (Bouches- du-Rhône), *G* 42, 219–21.

GOUDINEAU, C. 1988. 'Le pastoralisme en Gaule', in C. Whittaker (ed.), *Pastoral Economies in Classical Antiquity* (Cambridge), 160–70.

GOUDINEAU, C. AND DE KISCH, Y. 1984. *Vaison-la-Romaine* (Vaison).

GOULETQUER, P. L. 1970. *Les Briguetages armoricains: technologie protohistorique du sel en Armorique* (Rennes).

GREEN, M. J. 1984. *The Wheel as a Cult Symbol in the Romano-Celtic World* (Brussels).

GREENHALGH, P. 1980. *Pompey, the Roman Alexander* (London).

GRENIER, A. 1958. *Manuel d'Archéologie gallo-romaine, III, L'Architecture* (Paris).

GRENIER, A. 1960. *Manuel d'Archéologie gallo-romaine, IV, Les Monuments des Eaux* (Paris).

GREWE, K. 1986. *Atlas der römischen Wasserleitungen nach Köln* (Bonn).

GROENMAN-VAN WAATERINGE, W. 1980. 'Die verhängnisvolle Auswirkung der römischen Herrschaft auf die Wirtschaft an den Grenzen des Reiches', *Offa* 37, 366–71.

GROENMAN-VAN WAATERINGE, W. 1983. 'The disastrous effect of the Roman occupation', in Brandt and Slofstra 1983, 147–57.

GROENMAN-VAN WAATERINGE, W. AND BEEK, B. L. VAN 1988. 'De Romeinse castella te Valkenburg ZH: seventiende opgravingscampagne 1980, werkput VI, L', in J. H. Bloemers (ed.), *Archeologie en Oecologie van Holland tussen Rijn en Vlie* (Assen/Maastricht), 1–120.

GROS, P. 1979. 'Pour une chronologie des arcs de triomphe de Gaule Narbonnaise', *G* 37, 55–83.

GROS, P. 1984. 'L'*Augusteum* de Nîmes', *RAN* 17, 123–34.

GROS, P. 1986. 'Le mausolée des Julii et le statut de Glanum', *RA* (1986), 65–80.

GROS, P. AND VARÈNE, P. 1984. 'Le forum et la basilique de Glanum: problèmes de chronologie et de restitution', *G* 42, 21–52.

GROUPE D'ETUDES ARCHÉOLOGIQUES CHAMPAGNE ARDENNE 1982. *La Moissonneuse gauloise (des Rèmes aux Trevires)* (Reims).

GUILAINE, J. (ed.) 1976. *La Préhistoire française II: les civilisations néolitiques et protohistoriques de la France* (Paris).

GUILBAUT, J. E. 1981. 'La mine de cuivre gallo-romaine du Goutil, à la Bastide-de-Sérou (Ariège)', *G* 39, 171–80.

GUILD, R. *et al.* 1983. 'Les origines du baptistère de la cathédrale Saint-Sauveur', *RAN* 16, 171–232.

GUYONVARC'H, C.-J. AND LE ROUX-GUYONVARC'H, F. 1986. 'Remarques sur la religion gallo-romaine: rupture et continuité', *ANRW* II, 18, 1, 423–55.

HABEREY, W. 1972. *Die römischen Wasserleitungen nach Köln* (2nd edition, Bonn).

HACHMANN, R. 1976. 'The problem of the Belgae seen from the Continent', *Bulletin of the Institute of Archaeology, University of London* 13, 117–37.

HACHMANN, R. *et al.* 1962. *Völker zwischen Germanen und Kelten* (Neumünster).

HAFFNER, A. 1970. 'Belginum, eine keltisch-römische Siedlung an der Ausoniusstrasse', *Kurtrierisches Jahrbuch* 10, 203–22.

HALBOUT, P. *et al.* 1982. *Rouen gallo-romain: fouilles et recherches archéologiques 1978–1982* (Rouen).

HANOUNE, R. AND MULLER, A. 1988. 'Recherches archéologiques à Bavai, I–II', *RevNord* 70, 39–56.

HANSEN, U. L. 1987. *Römischer Import im Norden* (Copenhagen).

HANSON, R. P. C. 1985. *Studies in Christian Antiquity* (Edinburgh).

HANSON, W. AND KEPPIE, L. (eds) 1980. *Roman Frontier Studies 1979* (Oxford).

HARMAND, J. 1967. *Une Campagne césarienne: Alésia* (Paris).

HARMAND, J. 1970. 'Ferme et village en Gaule romaine', *Arch* 33, 16–21; 35, 89.

HARMAND, J. 1984. *Vercingétorix* (Evreux).

HARMAND, J. 1988. 'La maison de ferme et le manoir en Gaule romaine', *Latomus* 47, 294–317.

HARRIS, W. V. 1985. *War and Imperialism in Republican Rome, 327–70 BC* (Oxford).

HASELGROVE, C. 1984. 'Warfare and its aftermath as reflected in the precious metal coinage of Belgic Gaul', *OJA* 3, 81–105.

HASELGROVE, C. 1987. 'Culture process on the periphery: Belgic Gaul and Rome during the late Republic and early Empire', in M. Rowlands *et al.* (eds), *Centre and Periphery in the Ancient World* (Cambridge), 104–24.

HASELGROVE, C. AND LOWTHER, P. 1987. *La Vallée de l'Aisne, France 1987. Fouilles et prospections de l'Université de Durham: rapport intérimaire no. 5* (Durham).

HASSALL, M. W. 1983. 'The origins and character of Roman urban defences in the west', in J. Maloney and B. Hobley (eds), *Roman Urban Defences in the West* (London), 1–3.

HATT, J.-J. 1986 *La Tombe gallo-romaine* (2nd edition, Paris).

HAUCK, G. F. 1988. *The Aqueduct of Nemausus* (Jefferson, N. Car.).

HAUCK, G. F. AND NOVAK, R. A. 1988. 'Water flow in the castellum at Nîmes', *AJA* 92, 393–407.

HEDEAGER, L. 1978. 'A quantitative analysis of Roman imports in Europe north of the Limes (O–400 AD), and the question of Roman-German exchange', in K. Kristiansen and C. Paludan-Müller (eds), *New Directions in Scandinavian Archaeology* (Copenhagen), 191–215.

HEDEAGER, L. 1987. 'Empire, frontier and the barbarian hinterland: Rome and northern Europe from AD 1–400', in M. Rowlands *et al.* (eds), *Centre and Periphery in the Ancient World* (Cambridge), 125–40.

HEIMBERG, U. 1987. 'Colonia Ulpia Traiana: die früheste Keramik aus der Forumsgrabung', *BJ* 187, 411–74.

HEINEN, H. 1985. *Trier und das Trevererland in römischer Zeit* (Trier).

HEITZ, C. 1977. 'Du IVe au Xe siècle: Poitiers, foyer d'art chrétien', *Arch* 113, 10–22.

HELLENKEMPER, H. 1975. 'Architektur als Beitrag zur Geschichte der Colonia Claudia Ara Agrippinensium', *ANRW* II, 4, 783–824.

HENIG, M. E. AND KING, A. C. (eds) 1986. *Pagan Gods and Shrines of the Roman Empire* (Oxford).

HESNARD, A. *et al.* 1988. 'L'épave romaine *Grand Ribaud D* (Hyères, Var)', *Archéonautica* 8.

HIND, J. G. 1984. 'Whatever happened to the *Agri Decumates*?', *Brit* 15, 187–92.

HINZ, H. 1975. 'Colonia Ulpia Traiana: die Entwicklung eines römischen Zentralortes am Niederrhein, I: Prinzipat', *ANRW* II, 4, 825–69.

HINZ, H. 1976. *Xanten zur Römerzeit* (Xanten).

HÖCKMANN, O. 1988. 'Late Roman river craft from Mainz, Germany', in O. L. Filgueiras (ed.), *Local Boats: 4th International Symposium on Boat and Ship Archaeology, Porto 1985* (Oxford), 23–34.

HODDER, I. AND REECE, R. 1976. 'A model for the distribution of coins in the western Roman Empire', *Journal of Archaeological Science* 4, 1–18.

HODDER, I. AND REECE, R. 1980. 'An analysis of the distribution of coins in the western Roman Empire', *Archaeo-Physika* 7, 179–92.

HODSON, F. R. AND ROWLETT, R. M. 1974. 'From 600 BC to the Roman conquest', in S. Piggott and G. Daniel (eds), *France before the Romans* (London), 157–91.

HOFFMANN, D. 1974. 'Die Neubesetzung des Grenzschutzes unter Valentinian I um 369', in E. Birley *et al.* (eds), *Roman Frontier Studies 1969* (Cardiff), 168–73.

HOFMANN, B. 1975. 'Les matériaux de construction antiques en terre cuite', *DossHA* 9, 111–20.

HOLLSTEIN, E. 1980. *Mitteleuropäische Eichendendrochronologie* (Mainz).

HOLMGREN, J. AND LEDAY, A. 1981. 'Esquisse d'une typologie des villas gallo-romaines du Berry d'après les prospections aériennes', *G* 39, 103–22.

HOLWERDA, J. 1923. *Arentsburg: een romeinsch militair vlootstation bij Voorburg* (Leiden).

HOPKINS, K. 1980. 'Taxes and trade in the Roman Empire', *JRS* 70, 101–25.

HORN, H. G. (ed.) 1987. *Die Römer in Nordrhein-Westfalen* (Stuttgart).

HORNE, P. D. AND KING, H. C. 1980. 'Romano-Celtic temples in Continental Europe: a gazetteer of those with known plans', in W. Rodwell (ed.), *Temples, Churches and Religion: recent research in Roman Britain* (Oxford), 369–555.

HUBERT, J. 1963. 'Les "cathédrales doubles" de la Gaule', *Genava* n.s. 11, 105–25.

HULD-ZETSCHE, I. 1971. 'Zum Forschungsstand über Trierer Reliefsigillaten', *TZ* 34, 233–45.

HULD-ZETSCHE, I. 1972. *Trierer Reliefsigillata Werkstatt I* (Bonn).

HUMPHREY, J. H. 1986. *Roman Circuses: arenas for chariot racing* (London).

JACQUES, A. *et al.* 1986. 'Les fouilles de la rue Baudimont à Arras en 1985', *RevNord* 68, 75–120.

JALMAIN, D. 1977. 'Beauce: reflexion sur la recherche archéologique et la sècheresse 1976', *DossHA* 22, 22–7.

JAMES, E. 1977. *The Merovingian Archaeology of South-West Gaul* (Oxford).

JAMES, E. 1981. 'Archaeology and the Merovingian monastery', in H. Clarke and M. Brennan (eds), *Columbanus and Merovingian Monasticism* (Oxford), 33–55.

JAMES, E. 1982. *The Origins of France; from Clovis to the Capetians, 500–1000* (Basingstoke).

JAMES, E. 1988. *The Franks* (Oxford).

JAMES, S. 1988. 'The *fabricae*: state arms factories of the Later Roman Empire', in J. Coulston (ed.), *Military Equipment and the Identity of Roman Soldiers* (Oxford), 257–331.

JANNORAY, J. 1955. *Ensérune: contribution à l'étude des civilisations préromaines de la Gaule méridionale* (Paris).

JOFFROY, R. 1960. 'Le bassin et le trépied de Sainte-Colombe (Côte-d'Or)', *MonPiot* 51, 1–23.

JOFFROY, R. 1979. *Vix et ses Trésors* (Paris).

JOHNSON, S. 1976. *The Roman Forts of the Saxon Shore* (London).

JOHNSON, S. 1983. *Late Roman Fortifications* (London).

JONES, A. H. M. 1964. *The Later Roman Empire, 284–602* (Oxford).

JOULIN, L. 1901. 'Les établissements gallo-romaines de la plaine de Martres-Tolosanes', *Mémoires de l'Académie des Inscriptions et Belle-Lettres* 11, 1, 219–516.

JULLIAN, C. 1908–26. *Histoire de la Gaule* 8 vols (Paris).

KAENEL, G. 1977. *Lousonna: la promenade archéologique de Vidy* (Lausanne).

KATER-SIBBES, G. J. 1973. *Preliminary Catalogue of Serapis Monuments* (Leiden).

KAZANSKI, M. AND PÉRIN, P. 1988. 'Le mobilier funéraire de la tombe de Childéric Ier: état de la question et perspectives', *RAP* (1988), 3/4, 13–38.

KEAY, S. 1988. *Roman Spain* (London).

KEMPF, T. 1964. 'Untersuchungen und Beobachtungen am Trierer Dom 1961–1963', *Germ* 42, 126–41.

KEPPIE, L. 1984. *The Making of the Roman Army from Republic to Empire* (London).

KIMMIG, W. 1983a. 'Die griechischen Kolonisation im westlichen Mittelmeergebiet und ihre Wirkung auf die Landschaften des westlichen Mitteleuropa', *JRGZM* 30, 3–78.

KIMMIG, W. 1983b. *Die Heuneburg an der oberen Donau* (2nd edition, Stuttgart).

KING, A. C. 1983. 'Pottery', in M. Henig (ed.), *A Handbook of Roman Art* (Oxford), ch. 8.

KING, A. C. 1985. *The Decline of Samian Ware Manufacture in the North-West Provinces of the Roman Empire* PhD dissertation (London).

KING, A. C. forthcoming. 'The emergence of Romano-Celtic religion', in T. Blagg and M. Millett (eds), *The Early Roman Empire in the West* (Oxford).

KING, A. C. AND HENIG, M. E. (eds) 1981. *The Roman West in the Third Century* (Oxford).

KLEE, M. *et al.* 1988. *Arae Flaviae IV* (Stuttgart).

KNEISSL, P. 1981. 'Die Utriclarii: ihr Rolle im gallo-römischen Transportwesen und Weinhandel', *BJ* 181, 169–204.

KNÖRZER, K. H. 1984. 'Veränderungen der Unkrautvegetation auf rheinischen Bauernhöfen seit der Römerzeit', *BJ* 184, 479–503.

KOETHE, H. 1933. 'Die keltische Rund- und Vielecktempel der Kaiserzeit', *BRGK* 23, 10–108.

KOETHE, H. 1942. 'Zur Geschichte Galliens im dritten Viertel des 3. Jahrhunderts', *BRGK* 32, 199–224.

KOLLING, A. 1972. 'Schwarzenacker an der Blies', *BJ* 172, 238–58.

KRAFT, K. 1957. 'Die Rolle der Colonia Julia Equestris und die römische Auxiliar-Rekrutierung', *JRGZM* 4, 81–107.

KRÄMER, K. 1974. *Die frühchristlichen Grabinschriften Triers* (Mainz).

KRÄMER, W. (ed.) 1958. *Neue Ausgrabungen in Deutschland* (Berlin).

KRAUSE, G. 1974. 'Ein spätrömischer Burgus von Moers-Asberg am Niederrhein', *Quellenschriften zur Westdeutschen Vor- und Frühgeschichte* 9, 115–64.

KRAUTHEIMER, R. 1975. *Early Christian and Byzantine Architecture* (Harmondsworth).

KRENCKER, D. AND KRÜGER, E. 1929. *Die Trierer Kaiserthermen* (Augsburg).

KÜHLBORN, J.-S. 1981. 'Die neuen Ausgrabungen in der Nordwestecke des römischen Legionslagers Oberaden', *Germ* 60, 501–12.

KUHOFF, W. 1984. 'Der Handel im römischen Süddeutschland', *Münstersche Beiträge zur Antiken Handelsgeschichte* 3, 1, 77–107.

KUNOW, J. 1987. 'Das Limesvorland der südlichen Germania Inferior', *BJ* 187, 63–77.

KUNOW, J. 1988. 'Zentrale Orte in der Germania Inferior', *Archäologisches Korrespondenz-Blatt* 18, 55–67.

KUNOW, J. forthcoming. 'Relations between Roman occupation and *Limesvorland* in the province of Germania Inferior', in T. Blagg and M. Millett (eds), *The Early Roman Empire in the West* (Oxford).

KUNTZE, C. AND WAGNER, H.-O. 1988. 'Neue Ausgrabungen im römischen Gutshof von Fischbach, Gde. Niedereschach, Schwarzwald-Baar-Kreis', *Fundberichte aus Baden-Württemberg* 13, 351–93.

KÜNZL, E. 1988. 'Romanisierung am Rhein – Germanische Fürstengräber als Dokument des römischen Einflusses nach der gescheiterten Expansionspolitik', in *Kaiser Augustus und die verlorene Republik*, exhib. cat. (Berlin), 546–605.

LA BAUME, P. 1967. *Colonia Agrippinensis: a brief survey of Cologne in Roman times* (Cologne).

LA BAUME, P. 1973. 'Oppidum Ubiorum und Zweilegionenlager in Köln', *Gymnasium* 80, 333–47.

LA BAUME, P. *et al.* 1980. 'Colonia Claudia Ara Agrippinensium (CCAA)', *Führer zu vor- und frühgeschichtliche Denkmälern* 37/1, 38–182.

LABROUSSE, M. 1968. *Toulouse antique* (Paris).

LAMBRECHTS, P. 1942. *Contribution à l'Etude des Divinitès celtiques* (Bruges).

LANCHA, J. 1977. *Mosaïques géometriques: les ateliers de Vienne (Isère)* (Rome).

LANDES, C. (ed.) 1988. *Gaule mérovingienne et Monde méditerranéen/Les derniers Romains en Septimanie, IVe–VIIIe siècles* exhib. cat. (Lattes).

LANGOUET, L. 1988. *Les Coriosolites: un peuple armoricain* (St Malo).

LANTIER, R. 1934. 'Le dieu celtique de Bouray', *MonPiot* 34, 35–58.

LANTIER, R. 1943. 'Les nouvelles statues d'Antremont', *MonPiot* 40, 87–106.

La Picardie: berceau de la France 1986, exhib. cat. (Amiens).

LAROCHE, C. AND SAVAY-GUERRAZ, H. 1984. *Saint-Romain-en-Gal: un quartier de Vienne antique sur la rive droite du Rhône* (Paris).

LASFARGUES, J. 1973. 'Les ateliers de potiers lyonnais, étude topographique', *RAECE* 24, 525–37.

LASFARGUES, J. (ed.) 1985. *Architectures de Terre et de Bois* (Paris).

LATOUR, J. 1985. 'L'oppidum du Baou-des-Noirs à Vence (A-M)', *DAM* 8, 9–24.

LAUBENHEIMER, F. 1978. 'Atelier de potier gallo-romain de Sallèles-d'Aude (Narbonne): le chargement du four B5', *Acta Praehistorica et Archaeologica* 9/10, 115–24.

LAUBENHEIMER, F. 1985. *La Production des Amphores en Gaule Narbonnaise* (Paris).

LAUBENHEIMER-LEENHARDT, F. 1973. *Recherches sur les Lingots de Cuivre et de Plomb d'Epoque romaine dans les Régions de Languedoc-Rousillon et de Provence-Corse* (Paris).

LAUR-BELART, R. 1978. *Führer durch Augusta Raurica* (4th edition, Basel).

LAVAGNE, H. 1970. 'Recherches sur l'interprétation romaine dans les cultes de la Narbonnaise', *Annuaire de l'Ecole Pratique des Hautes Etudes, IVe Section* 102, 707–14.

La Villa Romaine dans les Provinces du Nord-Ouest 1982, conf. proc. (Paris).

Le Bois et la Forêt en Gaule et dans les Provinces voisines 1985, conf. proc. (Paris)

LEDAY, A. 1980. *La Campagne à l'époque romaine dans le Centre de la Gaule* (Oxford).

LE GALL, J. 1980. *Alésia: archéologie et histoire* (Poitiers).

LE GALL, J. AND SÉNÉCHAL, R. 1974. 'Dépôts d'offrandes auprès du principal temple d'Alésia', *CRAI* (1974), 207–15.

LEHNER, H. 1919. 'Der Tempelbezirk der Matronae Vacallinehae bei Pesch', *BJ* 125, 74–162.

LEINHARD, J. T. 1977. *Paulinus of Nola and Early Western Monasticism* (Cologne and Bonn).

LEJEUNE, M. 1985. *Recueil des Inscriptions Gauloises (RIG) I. Textes gallo-grecs* (Paris).

LE MASNE DE CHERMONT, N. 1987. 'Les fouilles de l'ancien évêché de Poitiers (Vienne)', *Aquit* 5, 149–75.

LE NY, F. 1988. *Les Fours de Tuiliers gallo-romains* (Paris).

Les Débuts de l'Urbanisation en Gaule et dans les Provinces voisines 1985, conf. proc. (Paris).

Les Mines et la Métallurgie en Gaule et dans les Provinces voisines 1987, conf. proc. (Paris).

LEUNISSON, P. 1986. 'Römische Götternamen und einheimische Religion der Provinz Germania Superior', *FBW* 10, 155–95.

Le Vicus gallo-romain 1976, conf. proc. (Paris).

LEWIS, M. J. 1966. *Temples in Roman Britain* (Cambridge).

LIESE, W. 1986. *Wo Arminius die Römer schlug* (Münster).

LIOU, B. 1974. 'L'épave romaine de l'Anse-Gerbal à Port-Vendres', *CRAI* (1974), 414–34.

LONG, L. 1987. 'Les épaves du Grand Congloué: étude du journal de fouille de Fernand Benoit', *Archéonautica* 7, 9–36.

LORREN, C. 1985. 'Le village de Saint-Martin-de-Mondeville de l'Antiquité au Haut-Moyen Age', in P. Périn and L.-C. Feffer (eds), *La Neustrie: les pays au nord de la Loire de Dagobert à Charles le Chauve (VIIe–IXe siècles)* (Créteil), 350–61.

Los Foros Romanos de los Provincias Occidentales 1987, conf. proc. (Madrid).

LOUSTAUD, J.-P. 1980. *Limoges gallo-romain* (Limoges).

LOUSTAUD, J.-P. 1981. 'Limoges gallo-romain', *Arch* 157, 24–9.

LUFF, R.-M. 1982. *A Zooarchaeological Study of the Roman North-Western Provinces* (Oxford).

LUGLI, G. 1965. 'La datazione degli anfiteatri di Arles e di Nîmes in Provenza', *Rivista dell'Istituto Nazionale d'Archeologia e di Storia dell'Arte* 13/14, 145–99.

Lutèce: Paris de César à Clovis 1984, exhib. cat. (Paris).

LUTTWAK, E. 1976. *The Grand Strategy of the Roman Empire, from the first century AD to the third* (Baltimore).

LUTZ, M. 1970. 'La civilisation dite des "sommets vosgiens"', *Arch* 37, 50–7.

LUTZ, M. 1971/2. 'Le domaine gallo-romain de Saint-Ulrich (Moselle)', *G* 29, 17–44; 30, 41–82.

LUTZ, M. 1977. *La Sigillée de Boucheporn (Moselle)* (Paris).

MACMULLEN, R. 1963. 'Barbarian enclaves in the northern Roman Empire', *L'Antiquité Classique* 32, 552–61.

MACMULLEN, R. 1965. 'The Celtic renaissance', *Historia* 14, 93–104.

MACMULLEN, R. 1987. 'Late Roman slavery', *Historia* 36, 359–82.

MAIER, U. 1978. *Caesars Feldzüge in Gallien (58–51 v. Chr.) in ihrem Zusammenhang mit der stadtrömischen Politik* (Bonn).

MANDY, B. 1983. 'Le quartier antique du Verbe Incarné', *DossHA* 78, 23–6.

MANGIN, M. 1981. *Un Quartier de Commerçants et d'Artisans d'Alésia* (Paris).

MANGIN, M. 1985. 'Artisanat et commerce dans les agglomérations secondaires du centre-est de la Gaule sous l'Empire', in P. Leveau (ed.), *L'Origine des Richesses dépensées dans la ville antique* (Aix-en-Provence), 113–31.

MANGIN, M. AND THOUVENIN, A. 1976. 'La destination réelle des installations de travail des bronziers d'Alésia: la cuisson des moules', *RAECE* 27, 505–21.

MARICHAL, R. 1988. *Les Graffites de la Graufesenque* (Paris).

MARINVAL, P. 1988. *L'Alimentation végétale en France du Mésolithique jusqu'à l'Age du Fer* (Paris).

MARSH, G. 1981. 'London's samian supply and its relationship to the development of the Gallic samian industry', in A. C. and A. S. Anderson (eds), *Roman Pottery Research in Britain and North-West Europe* (Oxford), 173–238.

MATTHEWS, J. 1975. *Western Aristocracies and the Imperial Court, AD 364–425* (Oxford).

MAURIN, L. 1964. 'Établissement vinicole à Allas-les-Mines (Dordogne)', *G* 22, 209–21.

MAURIN, L. 1978. *Saintes antique* (Saintes).

MAURIN, L. 1981. *Les Ruines gallo-romaines des Bouchauds à Saint-Cybardeaux (Charente)* (Bordeaux).

MAY, R. 1985. *Saint-Bertrand-de-Comminges: antique Lugdunum Convenarum. Le point sur les connaissances* (Toulouse).

MEGAW, J. V. AND MEGAW, R. 1988. *Celtic Art* (London).

MEIER, C. 1982. *Caesar* (Berlin).

MEIGGS, R. 1982. *Trees and Timber in the Ancient Mediterranean World* (Oxford).

MELVIN, M. 1980. *Expedition Alpine Elephant: a report on the 1979 Cambridge Hannibal expedition* (Cambridge).

MENEZ, Y. 1985. *Les Céramiques fumigées de l'Ouest de la Gaule* (Quimper).

MÉNIEL, P. 1987. *Chasse et Élevage chez les Gaulois* (Paris).

MERLAT, P. 1951. *Répertoire des Inscriptions et Monuments figurés du Culte de Jupiter Dolichenus* (Rennes).

MERLAT, P. 1982. *Les Vénètes d'Armorique* (Brest).

MERTENS, J. 1973. *Le Rempart romain d'Arlon* (Brussels).

MERTENS, J. 1983. 'Urban wall-circuits in Gallia Belgica in the Roman period', in J. Maloney and B. Hobley (eds), *Roman Urban Defences in the West* (London), 40–57.

MERTENS, J. AND BRULET, R. 1974. 'Le castellum du Bas-Empire romain de Brunehaut-Liberchies', *AB* 163.

METZLER, J. *et al.* 1981. *Ausgrabungen in Echternach* (Luxembourg).

MICHELOZZI, A. AND PY, M. 1980. 'L'habitat de plaine de la Chazette à Congénies, Gard (Ve s. av. J.-C.)', *DAM* 3, 125–35.

MIDDLETON, P. 1979. 'Army supply in Roman Gaul: an hypothesis for Roman Britain', in B. Burnham and H. Johnson (eds), *Invasion and Response: the case of Roman Britain* (Oxford), 81–97.

MIDDLETON, P. 1980. 'La Graufesenque: a question of marketing', *Athenaeum* 58, 186–91.

MIDDLETON, P. 1983. 'The Roman army and long-distance trade', in P. Garnsey and C. Whittaker (eds), *Trade and Famine in Classical Antiquity* (Cambridge), 75–83.

Mines et Fonderies antiques de la Gaule 1982, conf. proc. (Paris).

MITARD, P.-H. 1982. 'La tête en tôle de bronze de Genainville (Val-d'Oise)', *G* 40, 1–33.

MOLIN, M. 1984. 'Quelques considérations sur le chariot des vendanges de Langres (Haute-Marne)', *G* 42, 97–114.

MONTHEL, G. AND PINETTE, M. 1977. 'La carrière gallo-romaine de Saint-Boil', *RAECE* 28, 37–62.

MOREAU, J. 1960. *Das Trierer Kornmarktmosaik* (Cologne).

MOREL, J.-M. 1986. 'The early Roman defended harbours at Velsen, North-Holland', *Studien zu den Militärgrenzen Roms III* (Stuttgart), 200–12.

MOREL, J.-P. 1975. 'L'expansion phocéenne en Occident: dix années de recherche (1966–1975)', *Bulletin de Correspondance Hellenique* 99, 853–96.

MOREL, J.-P. 1982. 'Les Phocéens d'Occident: nouvelles données, nouvelles approches', *La Parola del Passato* 37, 479–500.

MOREL, J.-P. 1983. 'Greek colonisation in Italy and the West (problems of evidence and interpretation)', in T. Hackens *et al.* (eds), *Crossroads of the Mediterranean* (Providence, R.I./Louvain-la-Neuve), 123–61.

MÜLLER, W. 1986. 'Archäologische Zeugnisse frühen Christentums zwischen Taunus und Alpenkamm', *HelvArch* 65/66, 3–77.

MUNAUT, A.-V. 1988. 'La forêt gauloise dans le nord de la Gaule Belgique: enquête palynologique préliminaire', *RevNord* 70, 5–21.

MUSSO, J.-P. 1985. 'L'oppidum de Roquefavour à Ventabren (BdR)', *DAM* 8, 67–86.

NAPOLÉON III 1866. *Histoire de Jules César, II, Guerre des Gaules* (Paris).

NASH, D. 1978a. 'Territory and state formation in Central Gaul', in D. Green *et al.* (eds), *Social Organisation and Settlement* (Oxford), 455–75.

NASH, D. 1978b. *Settlement and Coinage in Central Gaul, c. 200–50 BC* (Oxford).

NASH, D. 1978c. 'Plus ça change . . .: currency in Central Gaul from Julius Caesar to Nero', in R. Carson and C. Kraay (eds), *Scripta Nummaria Romana: essays presented to Humphrey Sutherland* (London), 12–31.

NASH, D. 1985. 'Celtic territorial expansion and the Mediterranean world', in T. Champion and J. Megaw (eds), *Settlement and Society: aspects of West European prehistory in the first millenium BC* (Leicester), 45–67.

NASH, D. 1987. *Coinage in the Celtic World* (London).

NEGREL, J.-C. 1973. 'Une coque du Bas-Empire dans la rade de Marseille', *Arch* 55, 59–65.

NEISS, R. 1984. 'La structure urbaine de Reims antique et son évolution du Ier au IIIe siècle', *RAP* (1984), 3/4, 171–91.

NESSELHAUF, H. 1938. 'Die spätrömische Verwaltung der gallisch-germanischen Länder', *Abhandlungen der Preussischen Akademie fur Wissenschaften, Philosophisch-Historische Klasse* 1938/2.

NEYSES, A. 1987. *Die spätrömische Kaiservilla zu Konz* (Trier).

NICKELS, A. 1976. 'Les maisons à abside d'époque grecque archaïque de la Monédière, à Bessan (Hérault)', *G* 34, 95–128.

NICKELS, A. 1982. 'Agde grecque: les recherches récentes', *La Parola del Passato* 37, 269–80; also in *DAM* 4 (1981), 29–50.

NIFFELER, U. 1988. *Römisches Lenzburg: Vicus und Theater* (Brugg).

OELMANN, F. 1928. 'Ein gallorömischer Bauernhof bei Mayen', *BJ* 133, 51–140.

OLDENSTEIN, J. 1986. 'Neue Forschungen im spätrömischen Kastell von Alzey', *BRGK* 67, 289–356.

OLLIVIER, A. AND FRITSCH, R. 1982. 'Le vicus de Vieux-Poitiers', *Arch* 163, 52–61.

PARKER, A. J. 1984. 'Shipwrecks and ancient trade in the Mediterranean', *Archaeological Review from Cambridge* 3, 2, 99–113.

PARIS, R. 1960. 'Un temple celtique et gallo-romaine en Forêt de Châtillon-sur-Seine (Côte-d'Or)', *RAECE* 11, 164–75.

PASSARD, F. AND URLACHER, J.-P. 1983. 'Aux origines de Besançon gallo-romain', *Arch* 182, 32–6.

PAUNIER, D. 1981. *La Céramique gallo-romaine de Genève* (Geneva).

PEACOCK, D. P. 1982. *Pottery in the Roman World: an ethnographic approach* (London).

PELLETIER, A. 1967. 'Vienne et la réorganisation provinciale de la Gaule au Bas-Empire', *Latomus* 26, 491–8.

PELLETIER, A. 1977. 'Paganisme et christianisme à Vienne au 2e siècle', *Arch* 111, 28–35.

PELLETIER, A. 1980. *Le Sanctuaire métroaque de Vienne (France)* (Leiden).

PELLETIER, A. (ed.) 1985. *La Médecine en Gaule* (Paris).

PELLETIER, A. *et al.* 1981. 'Découvertes archéologiques récentes à Vienne (Isère)', *MonPiot* 64, 17–40.

PENHALLURICK, R. 1986. *Tin in Antiquity* (London).

PERCIVAL, J. 1976. *The Roman Villa* (London).

PERCIVAL, J. 1988. 'The villa economy: problems and perspectives', in K. Branigan and D. Miles (eds), *The Economies of Romano-British Villas* (Sheffield), 5–13.

PÉRIN, P. AND FEFFER, L.-C. 1987. *Les Francs* 2 vols (Paris).

PETIT, D. 1983. 'Saint-Pierre-Lentin, 1977–1978, rapport préliminaire', *Revue Archéologique du Loiret* 9, 10–37.

PEYRE, C. 1978. 'Le champ de bataille de l'Aisne (César, BG, II, 8–9)', *REL* 56, 175–215.

PFERDEHIRT, B. 1976. *Die Keramik des Kastells Holzhausen* (Berlin).

PICARD, G. C. 1967. *Hannibal* (Paris).

PICARD, G. C. 1969. 'Les théâtres ruraux sacrés en Gaule', *Arch* 28, 68–77.

PICARD, G. C. 1970. 'Les conciliabula en Gaule', *BSNAF* (1970), 66ff.

PICARD, G. C. 1981. 'La mythologie au service de la Romanisation dans les provinces occidentales de l'Empire romain', in L. Kahil and C. Augé (eds), *Mythologie gréco-romain, mythologies périphériques: études d'iconographie* (Paris), 41–52.

PICARD, G. C. 1983. 'Les centres civiques ruraux dans l'Italie et la Gaule romaine', in *Architecture et Société*, conf. proc. (Paris), 415–23.

PICON, M. *et al.* 1975. 'A Lyons branch of the pottery-making firm of Ateius', *Archaeometry* 17, 45–59.

PIEHLER, W. 1976. *Die Knochenfunde aus dem spätrömischen Kastell Vemania*, dissertation (Munich).

PIETRI, L. 1983. *La Ville de Tours du IVe au VIe siècle: naissance d'une cité chrétienne* (Rome).

PIETRI, L. 1986. 'La Christianisation de la Belgique Seconde (IVe–VIe siècle)', in *La Picardie ...*, 173–82.

PIGANIOL, A. 1962. *Les Documents cadastraux de la Colonie romaine d'Orange* (Paris).

PIGGOTT, S. 1974. *The Druids* (Harmondsworth).

PILET, C. 1980. *La Nécropole de Frénouville: étude d'une population de la fin du IIIe à la fin du VIIe siècle* 3 vols (Oxford).

PILET, C. AND ALDUC-LE BAGOUSSE, A. 1987. 'Les vivants et les morts en Gaule romaine', in F. Hinard (ed.), *La Mort, les Morts et l'Au-delà dans le Monde romain* (Caen), 13–31.

PIRLING, R. 1986. *Römer und Franken am Niederrhein* (Mainz).

PLANSON, E. AND LAGRANGE, A. 1975. 'Un nouveau document sur les syncrétismes dans les religions gallo-romaines: le groupe de divinités des Bolards', *RA* 2, 267–84.

PLANSON, E. AND POMMERET, C. 1985 *Les Bolards* (Paris).

PLANSON, E. *et al.* 1973. 'Le mithraeum des Bolards à Nuits-Saint-Georges', *Arch* 54, 54–63.

POTTER, T. W. 1987. *Roman Italy* (London).

POULAIN-JOSIEN, T. 1964. *Les Animaux domestiques et sauvages en France du Néolithique au Gallo-Romain* doctoral dissertation (Paris).

POULAIN-JOSIEN, T. AND POULAIN, P. 1973. 'La notion du région dans l'étude des vestiges alimentaires', in *L'Homme: hier et aujourd'hui* (Paris), 455–61.

PRECHT, G. 1973. *Baugeschichtliche Untersuchung zum römischen Praetorium in Köln* (Cologne/Bonn).

PRECHT, G. 1979. *Das Grabmal des L. Poblicius* (2nd edition, Cologne).

PRICOCO, S. 1978 *L'Isola dei Santi: il cenobio di Lerino e le origini del monachesimo gallico* (Rome).

PRIEUR, J. 1986. 'L'itinéraire transalpin d'Hannibal', in *Les Celtes et les Alpes* exhib. cat. (Chambéry), 11–12.

PRINZ, F. 1965. *Frühes Möncktum in Frankenreich* (Munich and Vienna).

PRIVATI, F. 1986a. *La Nécropole de Sézegnin (IVe–VIIIe siècle)* (Genève).

PRIVATI, B. 1986b. 'Sézegnin GE: une unité agricole du Haut Moyen Age', *Archäologie der Schweiz* 9, 9–19.

PROVOST, M. 1988. *Carte archéologique de la Gaule: le Loir-et-Cher*, 41 (Paris).

PY, M. 1969. 'Les influences méditerranéennes en Vaunage du VIIIe au Ier siècle avant J.-C.', *Bulletin de l'Ecole Antique de Nîmes* n.s., 3, 39–91.

PY, M. 1971. 'Les oppida de Vaunage: douze ans de recherche sur la protohistoire de la region nîmoise', *Arch* 43, 32–43.

PY, M. 1978. *L'Oppidum des Castels à Nages (Gard)* (Paris).

PY, M. 1981. *Recherches sur Nîmes préromaine* (Paris).

RAEPSAET, G. 1987. 'Aspects de l'organisation du commerce de la céramique sigillée dans le nord de la Gaule au IIe siècle de notre ère I: les données matérielles', *Münstersche Beiträge zur Antiken Handelsgeschichte* 6, 2, 1–29.

RAMBAUD, M. 1953. *L'Art de la Déformation historique dans les Commentaires de César* (Paris).

RAMBAUD, M. 1974. 'La bataille de Gergovie', *REL* 52, 35–41.

RANCOULE, G. 1980. *La Lagaste: agglomération gauloise du Bassin de l'Aude* (Carcassonne).

RANCOULE, G. 1984. 'Contribution à l'étude des céramiques modelées de l'Age du Fer dans le département de l'Aude', *DAM* 7, 7–26.

RANCOULE, G. 1985. 'Observations sur la diffusion des importations italiques dans L'Aude aux IIe et Ier siècles avant J.-C.', *RAN* 18, 263–75.

RANDSBORG, K. 1981. 'Les activités internationales des Vikings: raids ou commerce', *Annales (ESC)* 36, 862–8.

RAYNAUD, C. 1984a. 'Stratigraphie du Marduel (Saint-Bonnet-du-Gard)' II', *DAM* 7, 111–19.

RAYNAUD, C. 1984b. 'Le quartier sud de l'agglomération antique de Lunel-Viel (Hérault)', *DAM* 7, 121–47.

REBISCOUL, A. 1987. 'Recherche en vue de l'établissement d'une méthode de photo-interprétation appliquée à l'étude de vestiges miniers antiques dans la Montagne Noire', in *Les Mines et la Métallurgie ...*, 59–71.

REBUFFAT, R. 1985. 'Jublains: un complex fortifié dans l'ouest de la Gaule', *RA* (1985), 237–56.

REDDÉ, M. 1984. 'Fouilles à Arlaines (1977–1980)', *Cahiers du Groupe de Recherche sur l'Armée Romaine et Provinces* 3, 103–38.

REDKNAP, M. 1987. *Mayener Ware and Eifelkeramik: the Roman and Medieval pottery industries of the West German Eifel* PhD dissertation (London).

REECE, R. 1973. 'Roman coinage in the Western Empire', *Brit* 4, 227–52.

REECE, R. 1980. 'Town and country: the end of Roman Britain', *World Archaeology* 12, 77–92.

REECE, R. 1987. *Coinage in Roman Britain* (London).

REMESAL RODRIGUEZ, J. 1986. *La Annona Militaris y la Exportación de Aceite Bético a Germania* (Madrid).

RÉMY, B. 1984. 'Les inscriptions de médecins en Gaule', *G* 42, 115–52.

REUTTI, F. 1983. 'Tonverarbeitende Industrie im römischen Rheinzabern', *Germ* 61, 33–69.

REYNAUD, J.-F. 1973. 'Les fouilles de sauvetage de l'église St Just et du groupe épiscopal de Lyon', *CRAI* (1973), 346–64.

REYNAUD, J.-F. 1986. *Lyon aux premiers Temps chrétiens* (Paris).

REYNAUD, J.-F. *et al.* 1977. 'Lyon du IIIe siècle au Haut Moyen Age: les fouilles retrouvent l'enceinte fortifiée de la ville basse près de la Saône', *Arch* 112, 50–9.

RHEINISCHES LANDESMUSEUM TRIER 1984a. *Trier: Augustusstadt der Treverer*, exhib. cat. (Mainz).

RHEINISCHES LANDESMUSEUM TRIER 1984b. *Trier: Kaiserresidenz und Bischofssitz*, exhib. cat. (Mainz).

RICE-HOLMES, T. 1911. *Caesar's Conquest of Gaul* (2nd edition, Oxford).

RICHARD, C. 1988. 'Du fanum gaulois au temple classique au vicus du Gué de Sciaux', *Arch* 231, 48–53.

RIVET, A. L. F. 1971. 'Hill-forts in action', in M. Jesson and D. Hill (eds), *The Iron Age and its Hillforts* (Southampton), 189–201.

RIVET, A. L. F. 1976. 'The Notitia Galliarum: some questions', in R. Goodburn and P. Bartholemew (eds), *Aspects of the Notitia Dignitatum* (Oxford), 119–41.

RIVET, A. L. F. 1988. *Gallia Narbonensis: southern Gaul in Roman times* (London).

RÖDER, J. 1953. 'Zur Lavaindustrie von Mayen und Volvic (Auvergne)', *Germ* 31, 24–7.

RÖDER, J. 1957/9. 'Zur Steinbruchgeschichte des Pellenz- und Brohltaltuffs', *BJ* 157, 213–71; 159, 47–88.

RÖDER, J. 1974. 'Römische Steinbruchtätigkeit am Drachenfels', *BJ* 174, 509–44.

ROLLAND, H. 1958. *Fouilles de Glanum 1947–1956* (Paris).

ROLLAND, H. 1968. 'Nouvelles fouilles du sanctuaire des Glaniques', *RSL* 34, 7–34.

ROLLAND, H. 1969. *Le Mausolée de Glanum (Saint-Rémy-de-Provence)* (Paris).

ROLLAND, H. 1977. *L'Arc de Glanum* (Paris).

ROMAN, Y. 1983. *De Narbonne à Bordeaux: un axe économique au Ier siècle avant J.-C.* (Lyon)

ROMEUF, A.-M. 1986. 'Ex-voto en bois de Chamalières (Puy-de-Dôme) et des Sources de la Seine: essai de comparaison', *G* 44, 65–89.

ROOS, P. 1986. 'For the fiftieth anniversary of the excavation of the water-mill at Barbegal: a correction of a long-lived mistake', *RA* (1986), 327–33.

ROTH-CONGÈS, A. 1985. 'Glanum préromaine: recherche sur la métrologie et ses applications dans l'urbanisme et l'architecture', *RAN* 18, 189–220.

ROUANET-LIESENFELT, A.-M. 1980. *La Civilisation des Riedones* (Brest).

ROUGÉ, J. AND TURCAN, R. (eds) 1978. *Les Martyrs de Lyon (177)* (Paris).

ROUSSEL, L. (ed.) 1979. *Mâlain-Mediolanum 1968–1978: le mobilier* (Besançon).

ROUVIER-JEANLIN, M. 1972. *Les Figurines gallo-romaines en Terre-cuite au Musée des Antiquités nationales* (Paris).

ROWLETT, R. M. 1968. 'The Iron Age north of the Alps', *Science* 161, 123–34.

RÜGER, C. B. 1968. *Germania Inferior* (Cologne).

RÜGER, C. B. 1979. 'Die spätrömische Grossfestung in der Colonia Ulpia Traiana', *BJ* 179, 499–524.

RUPPRECHT, G. (ed.) 1984. *Die Mainzer Römerschiffe* (3rd edition, Mainz).

RÜSCH, A. 1981. *Das römische Rottweil* (Stuttgart).

SABRIÉ, M. *et al.* 1987. *La Maison à Portiques du Clos de la Lombarde à Narbonne, et sa Décoration murale* (Paris).

SALVIAT, F. AND BARRUOL, G. (eds) 1976. *Provence et Languedoc méditerranéen: sites protohistoriques et gallo-romains. UISPP Livret-Guide C3* (Nice).

SANDEN, W. VAN DER 1987. 'The Ussen project: large-scale settlement archaeology of the period 700 BC–AD 250, a preliminary report', *Analecta Praehistorica Leidensia* 20, 95–123.

SANQUER, R. AND GALLIOU, P. 1972a. 'Une maison de campagne gallo-romaine à la Roche-Maurice (Finistère)', *Annales de Bretagne* 79, 215–51.

SANQUER, R. AND GALLIOU, P. 1972b. 'Garum, sel et salaisons en Armorique gallo-romaine', *G* 30, 199–223.

SANTROT, H. AND J. 1979. *Céramiques communes gallo-romaines d'Aquitaine* (Paris).

SAUMAGNE, C. AND MESLIN, M. 1979. 'De la légalité du procès de Lyon de l'année 177' *ANRW* II, 23, 1, 316–39.

SAUTEL, J. 1953. 'Le buste en argent de Vaison', *MonPiot* 47, 149–52.

SCHALLMAYER, E. 1982. 'Ausgrabung eines Benefiziarier-Weihebezirkes und römischer Holzbauten in Osterburken, Neckar-Odenwald-Kreis', *Archäologische Ausgrabungen in Baden-Württemberg* (1982), 138–46.

SCHALLMAYER, E. 1984. *Der Odenwald Limes* (Stuttgart).

SCHAUERTE, G. 1987. 'Der römische Töpfereibezirk am Rudolfplatz in Köln', *KJ* 20, 23–82.

SCHEERS, S. 1987. 'La numismatique d'Alésia: quelques précisions', in *Mélanges offerts au Docteur J.-B. Colbert de Beaulieu* (Paris), 743–52.

SCHINDLER, R. 1964. *Die Mithrashöhle von Saarbrücken* (Saarbrücken).

SCHMIDT, K. H. 1983. 'Keltisch-lateinische Sprachkontakte im römischen Gallien der Kaiserzeit', *ANRW* II, 29, 2, 988–1018.

SCHÖN, F. 1986. *Der Beginn der römischen Herrschaft in Rätien* (Sigmaringen).

SCHÖNBERGER, H. 1951. 'Plan zu den Ausgrabungen am Kastell Zugmantel bis zum Jahre 1950', *Saalburg Jahrbuch* 10, 55–75.

SCHÖNBERGER, H. 1969. 'The Roman frontier in Germany: an archaeological survey', *JRS* 59, 144–97.

SCHÖNBERGER, H. 1985. 'Die römischen Truppenlager der frühen und mittleren Kaiserzeit zwischen Nordsee und Inn', *BRGK* 66, 321–497.

SCHOPPA, H. 1974. *Aquae Mattiacae* (Wiesbaden).

SCHWERTHEIM, E. 1974. *Die Denkmäler orientalischer Gottheiten im römischen Deutschland* (Leiden).

SCHWERTHEIM, E. 1986. 'Die orientalischen Religionen im römischen Deutschland: verbreitung und synkretistische Phänomene', *ANRW* II, 18, 1, 794–813.

SCOTT, I. R. 1985. 'First century military daggers and the manufacture and supply of weapons for the Roman army', in M. C. Bishop (ed.), *The Production and Distribution of Roman Military Equipment* (Oxford), 160–213.

SEILLIER, C. 1976. 'Une nécropole de l'époque des invasions à Vron (Somme)', *Arch* 90, 37–43.

SEILLIER, C. 1984. 'Les enceintes romaines de Boulogne-sur-Mer', *RevNord* 66, 169–80.

SELZER, W. 1988. *Römische Steindenkmäler: Mainz in römischer Zeit* (Mainz).

SIMON, E. 1986. *Die konstantinischen Deckengemälde in Trier* (Mainz).

SIREIX, M. AND C. 1984. 'Une ville-marché gauloise', *Arch* 197, 60–6.

SIVAN, H. S. 1986. 'Funerary monuments and funerary rites in Late Antique Aquitaine', *OJA* 5, 339–53.

SMITH, J. T. 1978a. 'Villas as a key to social structure', in M. Todd (ed.), *Studies in the Romano-British Villa* (Leicester), 149–85.

SMITH, J. T. 1978b. 'Halls or yards? A problem of villa interpretation', *Brit* 9, 351–8.

SOLIER, Y. 1968. 'Céramiques puniques et ibéro-puniques sur le littoral du Languedoc au VIe siècle au début du IIe siècle avant J.-C.', *RSL* 34, 127–50.

SOLIER, Y. 1986. *Narbonne: monuments et musées* (Paris).

SOLIER, Y. *et al.* 1979. 'Découvertes récentes à Narbonne', *Arch* 133, 50–9.

SÖLTER, W. 1970. *Römische Kalkbrenner im Rheinland* (Düsseldorf).

SOMMER, C. S. 1988. 'Kastellvicus und Kastell', *FBW* 13, 457–707.

SPEIDEL, M. P. 1978. *The Religion of Iuppiter Dolichenus in the Roman Army* (Leiden).

SPITZING, T. 1988. *Die römische Villa von Lauffen a. N. (Kr. Heilbronn)* (Stuttgart).

STANCLIFFE, C. E. 1979. 'From town to country: the Christianisation of the Touraine 370–600', *Studies in Church History* 16, 43–59.

STANCLIFFE, C. E. 1983. *St Martin and his Hagiographer* (Oxford).

STANFIELD, J. AND SIMPSON, G. 1958. *Central Gaulish Potters* (Oxford).

STERN, H. 1969. 'Deux mosaïques de Vienne (Isère)', *MonPiot* 56, 13–43.

STEVENS, C. E. 1933. *Sidonius Apollinaris and his Age* (Oxford).

STEVENS, C. E. 1952. 'The "Bellum Gallicum" as a work of propaganda', *Latomus* 11, 3–18, 165–79.

STROBEL, K. 1987. 'Der Chattenkrieg Domitians: historische und politische Aspekte', *Germ* 65, 423–52.

SZIDAT, J. 1970. *Caesars diplomatische Tätigkeit im gallischen Krieg* (Wiesbaden).

TASSAUX, D. AND F. 1983–4. 'Aulnay-de-Saintonge: un camp augusto-tibérien en Aquitaine', *Aquit* 1, 49–95; 2, 105–57.

TAYLOR, J. AND CLEERE, H. (eds) 1978. *Roman Shipping and Trade: Britain and the Rhine provinces* (London).

TCHERNIA, A. 1969. 'Les fouilles sous-marines de Planier (Bouches-du-Rhône)', *CRAI* (1969), 292–309.

TCHERNIA, A. 1983. 'Italian wine in Gaul at the end of the Republic', in P. Garnsey *et al.* (eds), *Trade in the Ancient Economy* (London), 87–104.

TCHERNIA, A. *et al.* 1978. *L'Epave romaine de la Madrague de Giens (Var)* (Paris).

TEILLET, S. 1984. *Des Goths à la Nation gothique: les origines de l'idée de nation en Occident du Ve au VIe siècle* (Paris).

TERNES, C.-M. 1978. 'Les origines de la ville de Trèves: le problème des relations entre les oppida préromaines et l'urbanisation', in *Travaux militaires en Gaule romaine et dans les Provinces du Nord-Ouest* conf. proc. (Paris), 261–77.

TERRISSE, J.-R. 1968. *Les Céramiques sigillées gallo-romaines des Martres-de-Veyre (Puy-de-Dôme)* (Paris).

THEVENOT, E. 1950. 'Médecine et religion aux temps gallo-romains: le traitement des affections de vue', *Latomus* 9, 415–26.

THEVENOT, E. 1960. *Les Eduens n'ont pas trahi* (Brussels).

THOEN, H. 1975. 'Iron Age and Roman salt-making sites on the Belgian coast', in K. de Brisay (ed.), *Salt: the study of an ancient industry* (Colchester), 56–60.

THOMPSON, E. A. 1948. *Attila and the Huns* (Oxford).

THOMPSON, E. A. 1952. 'Peasant revolts in late Roman Gaul and Spain', *Past and Present* 2, 11–23.

THOMPSON, E. A. 1965. *The Early Germans* (Oxford).

THOMPSON, E. A. 1982. *Romans and Barbarians: the decline of the western empire* (Madison, Wisc.).

THOMPSON, E. A. 1984. *Saint Germanus of Auxerre and the End of Roman Britain* (Woodbridge).

TIXIER, L. 1978. 'Une exploitation minière gallo-romaine à Massiac (Cantal)', *Arch* 117, 30–7.

TODD, M. 1985. 'Oppida and the Roman army: a review of recent evidence', *OJA* 4, 187–99.

TODD, M. 1987. *The Northern Barbarians: 100 BC – AD 300* (2nd edition, London).

TRÉZINY, H. 1986. 'Les techniques grecques de fortification et leur diffusion à la périphérie du monde grec d'Occident', in P. and H. Tréziny (eds), *La Fortification dans l'Histoire du Monde grec* (Paris), 185–200.

TUFFREAU-LIBRE, M. 1988. 'Les facies régionaux de la céramique gallo-romaine du Nord de la France et du bassin parisien', *Helinium* 28, 81–112.

TURCAN, R. 1972. *Les Religions de l'Asie dans la Vallée du Rhône* (Leiden).

TURCAN, R. 1986. 'Les religions orientales en Gaule Narbonnaise', *ANRW* II, 18, 1, 456–518.

UGOLINI, D. AND OLIVE, C. 1988. 'Un four de potier du Ve. s. av. J.-C. à Béziers, Place de la Madeleine', *G* 45, 13–28.

UNZ, C. 1982. *Grinario: das römische Kastell und Dorf in Köngen* (Stuttgart).

URBAN, R. 1985. *Der Bataveraufstand und die Erhebung des Julius Civilis* (Trier).

VAGINAY, M. AND GUICHARD V. 1988. *L'Habitat gaulois de Feurs (Loire): fouilles récentes (1978–1981)* (Paris).

VAGINAY, M. AND VALETTE, P. 1983. 'Dégagement du forum augustéen', *DossHA* 78, 41–2.

VAN DAM, R. 1985. *Leadership and Community in Late Antique Gaul* (Berkeley).

VANDERHOEVEN, A. *et al.* 1987. 'Het oudheidkundig bodemonderzoek aan de Kielenstraat te Tongeren', *AB* III, 127–38.

VAN ES, W. A. 1967. 'Wijster: a native village beyond the Imperial frontier, 150–425 AD', *Palaeohistoria* 11.

VAN ES, W. A. 1972. *Die Romeinen in Nederland* (2nd edition, Bussum).

VAN ES, W. A. 1982. 'Ländliche Siedlungen der Kaiserzeit in den Niederlanden', *Offa* 39, 139–54.

VAN ES, W. A. *et al.* 1985. 'Eine Siedlung der römischen Kaiserzeit in Bennekom, Provinz Gelderland', *BROB* 35, 533–652.

VAN OSSEL, P. 1987. 'Les établissements ruraux au Bas-Empire dans le Nord de la Gaule', *AB* III, 185–96.

VANVINCKENROYE, W. 1975. *Tongeren Romeinse Stad* (Tongeren).

VARÈNE, P. 1987. 'La Tour Magne et l'Augusteum de Nîmes', *RA* (1987), 1, 91–6.

VERMASEREN, M. J. (ed.) 1981. *Die orientalischen Religionen im Römerreich* (Leiden).

VERMASEREN, M. J. 1983 *Corpus Cultus Iovis Sabazii (CCIS), I, The Hands* (Leiden).

VERMEERSCH, D. 1981. 'Le site archéologique du Marais de Famechon (Somme): bilan provisoire', *Cahiers Archéologiques de Picardie* 1981, 8.

VERNHET, A. 1981. 'Un four de la Graufesenque (Aveyron): la cuisson des vases sigillées', *G* 39, 25–43.

VERNHET, A. AND BALSAN, L. 1975. 'La Graufesenque', *DossHA* 9, 21–34.

VERTET, H. 1967. 'Céramique sigillée tibérienne à Lezoux', *RA* (1967), 255–86.

VERTET, H. 1979. 'Les fours de potiers gallo-romaines du Centre de la Gaule', *Acta Praehistorica et Archaeologica* 9/10, 145–57.

VERTET, H. *et al.* 1980. *Recherches sur les Ateliers de Potiers gallo-romaines de la Gaule centrale* (Le Blanc Mesnil).

VEYNE, P. 1976. *Le Pain et le Cirque: sociologie historique d'un pluralisme politique* (Paris).

VIDAL, M. 1973. 'Vestiges d'un édifice du Ier siècle av. J.-C. à Vieille-Toulouse', *Pallas* 20, 105–13.

VILLARD, F. 1960. *La Céramique grecque de Marseille (VIe–IVe siècle). Essai d'Histoire economique* (Paris).

VOINOT, J. 1984. *Inventaire des Cachets d'Oculistes gallo-romaines* (Annonay).

VON PETRIKOVITS, H. 1971. 'Fortifications in the north-western Roman Empire from the third to the fifth centuries AD', *JRS* 61, 178–218.

VON PETRIKOVITS, H. 1980. *Rheinische Geschichte, I, i, Altertum* (2nd edition, Düsseldorf).

VON SCHNURBEIN, S. 1981. 'Zur Geschichte der römischen Militärlager an der Lippe', *BRGK* 62, 5–101.

WALKER, S. 1981. *Récentes Recherches en Archéologie gallo-romaine et paléochrétienne sur Lyon et sa Région* (Oxford).

WALSER, G. 1956. *Caesar und die Germanen* (Wiesbaden).

WALSER, G. 1984. *Summus Poeninus: Beiträge zur Geschichte des Grossen St. Bernhard-Passes in römischer Zeit* (Wiebaden).

WALTERS, V. J. 1974. *The Cult of Mithras in the Roman Provinces of Gaul* (Leiden).

WALTHEW, C. V. 1982. 'Early Roman town development in Gallia Belgica: a review of some problems', *OJA* 1, 225–36.

WANKENNE, A. 1972. *La Belgique à l'Epoque romaine: sites urbains, villageois, religieux et militaires* (Brussels).

WARD-PERKINS, J. B. 1970. 'From Republic to Empire: reflections on the early provincial architecture of the Roman West', *JRS* 60, 1–19.

WARD-PERKINS, J. B. 1981. *Roman Imperial Architecture* (Harmondsworth).

WEATHERHILL, C. 1985. 'The ships of the Veneti: a fresh look at the Iron Age tin ships', *Cornish Archaeology* 24, 163–9.

WEBER, G. 1981. 'Neue Ausgrabungen am "Apollo-Grannus-Heiligtum" in Faimingen: Zwischenbericht', *BRGK* 62, 103–217.

WEERD, M. DE 1988. 'A landlubber's view of shipbuilding procedure in the Celtic barges of Zwammerdam, the Netherlands', in O. L. Filgueiras (ed.), *Local Boats: 4th International Symposium on Boat and Ship Archaeology, Porto 1985* (Oxford), 35–51.

WELLS, C. M. 1972. *The German Policy of Augustus: an examination of the archaeological evidence* (Oxford).

WELLS, P. S. 1981. *Culture Contact and Culture Change* (Cambridge).

WERNER, K.-F. 1988. 'De Childéric à Clovis: antécedents et conséquences de la bataille de Soissons en 486', *RAP* (1988), 3/4, 3–7.

WHATMOUGH, J. 1970. *The Dialects of Ancient Gaul* (Cambridge, Mass.).

WHEELER, R. E. M. AND RICHARDSON, K. M. 1957. *Hill-Forts of Northern France* (London).

WHITE, K. D. 1969. 'The economics of the Gallo-Roman harvesting machines', in J. Bibauw (ed.) *Hommages à Marcel Renard II* (Brussels), 804–9.

WHITE, K. D. 1970. *Roman Farming* (London).

WHITTAKER, C. R. 1983. 'Trade and frontiers of the Roman Empire', in P. Garnsey and C. Whittaker (eds), *Trade and Famine in Classical Antiquity* (Cambridge), 110–27.

WIBLÉ, F. 1981. *Forum Claudii Vallensium: la ville romaine de Martigny* (Martigny).

WIGHTMAN, E. M. 1970. *Roman Trier and the Treveri* (London).

WIGHTMAN, E. M. 1974. 'La Gaule chevelue entre César et Auguste', in D. Pippidi (ed.), *Actes du IXe Congrès international d'Etudes sur les Frontières romaines* (Bucharest), 473–83.

WIGHTMAN, E. M. 1977a. 'Military arrangements, native settlements and related developments in early Roman Gaul', *Helinium* 17, 105–21.

WIGHTMAN, E. M. 1977b. 'Soldier and civilian in early Roman Gaul', in J. Fitz (ed.), *Limes: Akten des XI internationalen Limeskongresses* (Budapest), 75–86.

WIGHTMAN, E. M. 1977c. 'The Lingones: Lugdunensis, Belgica or Germania Superior?', in *Studien zu den Militärgrenzen Roms* II (Cologne/Bonn), 207–17.

WIGHTMAN, E. M. 1978a. 'Peasants and potentates: an investigation of social structure and land tenure in Roman Gaul', *American Journal of Ancient History* 3, 97–128.

WIGHTMAN, E. M. 1978b. 'North-eastern Gaul in late Antiquity: the testimony of settlement patterns in an age of transition', *BROB* 28, 241–50.

WIGHTMAN, E. M. 1985. *Gallia Belgica* (London).

WIGHTMAN, E. M. 1986. 'Pagan cults in the province of Belgica', *ANRW* II, 18, 1, 542–89.

WILD, J. P. 1976. 'The gynaecia', in R. Goodburn and P. Bartholemew (eds), *Aspects of the Notitia Dignitatum* (Oxford), 51–8.

WILL, E. 1962. 'Recherches sur le développement urbain sous l'Empire romain dans le Nord de la France', *G* 20, 79–101.

WILL, E. 1966. 'Remarques sur la fin de la domination romaine dans le nord de la Gaule', *RevNord* 48, 517–34.

WILL, E. L. 1979. 'The Sestius amphoras: a reappraisal', *Journal of Field Archaeology* 6, 339–50.

WILL, W. 1987. 'Römische "Klientel-Randstaaten" am Rhein?', *BJ* 187, 1–61.

WILLEMS, W. J. 1981/4. 'Romans and Batavians: a regional study in the Dutch Eastern River Area', *BROB* 31, 7–217; 34, 39–331.

WIMMEL, W. 1974. *Die technische Seite von Caesars Unternehmen gegen Avaricum (BG 7, 13ff.)* (Mainz).

WOLFF, H. 1976. 'Kriterien für lateinische und römische Städte in Gallien und Germanien und die "Verfassung" der gallischen Stammesgemeinden', *BJ* 176, 45–121.

WOOD, J. 1983. 'Le castrum de Tours: étude architecturale du rempart du Bas-Empire', *Recherches sur Tours* 2, 11–60.

WOOD, J. 1986. 'Etudes archéologiques à Larçay, 1985, rapport préliminaire', *Bulletin de la Société Archéologique de Touraine* 41, 323–40.

WOOD, J. 1988. *Pouzay: archaeological excavations at the Roman site at Soulangé ('Les Cholettes'), 1987 preliminary report* (Lancaster).

WUILLEUMIER, P. 1963. *Inscriptions latines des Trois Gaules (France)* (Paris).

ZAHN, E. 1982. *Die Igeler Säule in Igel bei Trier* (5th edition, Cologne).

Photographic acknowledgements

The author and publishers gratefully acknowledge the following for providing the illustrations:

R. Agache pp. 29, 53, 73; R. Boissinot p. 24; C. Bonnet pp. 9, 195; British Museum: back cover, half-title page, pp. 35, 122, 129, 151, 162, 165, 175; J.-L. Cadoux p. 137; P. D. Horne pp. 140, 150; Institut d'Archéologie Méditerranéenne p. 118; Institute of Archaeology, London, Roman Department p. 59; Christian Labeaune p. 14; F. Laubenheimer p. 126; Mann Verlag, Berlin p. 168; Musée d'Art et d'Histoire, Geneva p. 206; Musées des Antiquités Nationales, St Germain-en-Laye p. 98; T. W. Potter: front cover, pp. 101, 181; Rheinisches Landesmuseum Trier pp. 113, 144; Rijksmuseum van Oudheten, Leiden p. 155; G. Soffe p. 57; J. J. Wilkes p. 100; R. J. A. Wilson pp. 79, 86; Jason Wood pp. 19, 21, 71, 82, 83, 177, 184, 208

The line drawings (except on p 168) are by Stephen Crummy; all other material is the copyright of the author

Index

Figures in italic refer to pages
with illustrations